Motivation and Self-Regulation Across the Life Span

In the last two decades, an approach to the study of motivation has emerged that focuses on specific cognitive and affective mediators of behavior, in contrast to more general traits or motives. The "social-cognitive" approach grants goal-oriented motivation its own role in shaping cognition, emotion, and behavior, rather than reducing goal-directed behavior to cold-blooded information processing or to an enactment of a personality type or trait.

This book adds to this process-oriented approach a developmental perspective. Critical elements of motivational systems can be specified and their interrelations understood by charting the origins and the developmental course of motivational processes. Moreover, a process-oriented approach helps to identify critical transitions and effective developmental interventions. The chapters in this book cover various age groups throughout the life span and stem from four traditions in motivational psychology: achievement motivation, action theory, the psychology of causal attribution and perceived control, and the psychology of personal causation and intrinsic motivation.

Jutta Heckhausen is senior research scientist at the Center for Lifespan Psychology at the Max Planck Institute for Human Development in Berlin. In 1995–6 she was a Fellow at the Center for Advanced Study in the Behavioral Sciences at Stanford University. She publishes on development and motivation throughout the life span and is the author of *Developmental Regulation in Adulthood: Age-Normative and Sociostructural Constraints as Adaptive Challenges.*

Carol S. Dweck is a professor of psychology at Columbia University. She has published widely in the fields of motivation, development, personality, and social psychology, and her previous books include *Personal Politics,* co-written with Ellen Langer, and *Self-Theories and Motivation: Effects on Achievement and Social Processes.*

Motivation and Self-Regulation Across the Life Span

Edited by

Jutta Heckhausen and Carol S. Dweck

CAMBRIDGE
UNIVERSITY PRESS

PUBLISHED BY THE PRESS SYNDICATE OF THE UNIVERSITY OF CAMBRIDGE
The Pitt Building, Trumpington Street, Cambridge CB2 1RP, United Kingdom

CAMBRIDGE UNIVERSITY PRESS
The Edinburgh Building, Cambridge CB2 2RU, UK   http://www.cup.cam.ac.uk
40 West 20th Street, New York, NY 10011-4211, USA   http://www.cup.org
10 Stamford Road, Oakleigh, Melbourne 3166, Australia

First published 1998

Printed in the United States of America

Typeset in Times Roman 10.5/13, in QuarkXPress™ [AG]

*A catalog record for this book is available from
the British Library.*

Library of Congress Cataloging-in-Publication Data
Motivation and self-regulation across the life span / edited by Jutta
Heckhausen, Carol S. Dweck
p.   cm.
"Based on a conference entitled Life-Span Perspectives on
Motivation and Control . . . July 1995 at the Max Planck Institute
for Human Development and Education in Berlin" – Pref.
ISBN 0-521-59176-7 (hardcover)
1. Motivation (Psychology).   2. Self-control.   I. Heckhausen,
Jutta (date).   II. Dweck, Carol S. (date).
BF501.M887   1998   97-32110
153.8 – dc21   CIP

ISBN 0 521 59176 7 hardback

Contents

Preface and Acknowledgments

This book is based on a conference entitled "Life-Span Perspectives on Motivation and Control," organized by Jutta Heckhausen and Carol Dweck and held in July 1995 at the Max Planck Institute for Human Development in Berlin.

We are grateful to a number of people and institutions for their contributions to the conference and to this volume. First, we thank Paul Baltes, director of the Center for Lifespan Psychology, and the Max Planck Institute for Human Development in Berlin for hosting and providing financial support for the conference. We also thank Ulrich Knappek for his excellent work on the administrative tasks involved in organizing the conference, and Kim Saccio-Kent for her most professional copyediting of the book manuscript. Moreover, we thank all the authors for submitting superb chapters, and for patiently and expertly responding to our editorial comments. Finally, the work on this edited volume profited much from a most conducive environment at the Center for Advanced Study in the Behavioral Sciences, Stanford, where Jutta Heckhausen spent the year 1995–6 as a fellow (MacArthur Foundation Grant #8900078).

Contributors

Jochen Brandstädter, *University of Trier*
Nancy Cantor, *Princeton University*
Laura A. Carstensen, *Stanford University*
Ulrich Dillmann, *University of Trier*
Carol S. Dweck, *Columbia University, New York*
Arno Fuhrmann, *University of Osnabruck*
Peter M. Gollwitzer, *University of Konstanz*
Sandra Graham, *University of California, Los Angeles*
Jutta Heckhausen, *Max Planck Institute for Human Development, Berlin*
E. Tory Higgins, *Columbia University, New York*
Oliver Kirchhof, *University of Konstanz*
Julius Kuhl, *University of Osnabruck*
Todd D. Little, *Max Planck Institute for Human Development, Berlin*
Susan Nolen-Hoeksema, *University of Michigan*
Eva Pomerantz, *New York University*
Richard M. Ryan, *University of Rochester*
Richard Schulz, *University of Pittsburgh*
Klaus Rothermund, *University of Trier*
Diane Ruble, *New York University*
Catherine A. Sanderson, *Princeton University*
Israela Silberman, *Columbia University, New York*
Ellen A. Skinner, *Portland State University*
John R. Weisz, *University of California at Los Angeles*

Introduction: A Developmental and Process-Oriented Approach to Motivation and Self-Regulation

Jutta Heckhausen and Carol S. Dweck

What Is the Approach Presented in This Volume?

In the past decade or two there has emerged an approach to the study of motivation that focuses on specific cognitive and affective mediators of behavior rather than more general traits or motives. This "social-cognitive" approach attempts to identify very specific psychological processes that, in interaction with situational cues, shape people's actions. This approach grants motivation its own role in shaping cognition, emotion, and behavior, rather than reducing goal-directed behavior to cold-blooded information processing or to mere enactment of a personality type. As we will see, viewing motivation in these terms allows for an understanding of how motivational processes guide and organize patterns of cognition, emotion, and behavior. Thus, this social-cognitive approach leads us to investigate the dynamic interplay of psychological processes as people pursue their goals.

Historical Roots and Emergence of Process-Oriented Approaches to Motivation

Psychologists, as well as laypeople, have always been intrigued by dynamic theories of motivation. A telling example is the sustained fascination with Freud's psychodynamic theory, although many would argue there is little empirical support for it. The process-oriented approach to motivation and self-regulation presented in this volume captures much of the richness of a dynamic approach and avoids many of the pitfalls of previous approaches.

Long before the current emphasis on social-cognitive mediators, scholars such as Kurt Lewin (1935, 1936) and Fritz Heider (1958a,b) developed rich models of motivated behavior, which integrated preference and affect as well as beliefs and inferences as determinants of individuals' judgments and behavior (see also Mischel, 1973).

Lewin's field theory of action (Lewin, 1935, 1936) explains behavior in

1

terms of internal and external forces in the action field, which provide directionality to the individual's activity. Lewin's model of person and environmental forces spawned the expectancy x value models that have been immensely influential in motivational psychology ever since (see, e.g., Atkinson, 1957; Eccles, 1985; Eccles & Wigfield, 1995). In his classic book *The Psychology of Interpersonal Relations,* Heider (1958a) detailed the factors that can influence our inferences (or attributions) about the causes of people's behavior, and showed how the manner in which one interprets others' behavior will guide our reactions to it.

These seminal contributions not only gave us a blueprint for studying social-cognitive processes, but provided a way to conceptualize the manner in which the combination of personal characteristics and environmental conditions may affect behavior. Many current lines of psychology research in the United States and Europe owe much to these pioneers of motivational psychology. Among those are achievement motivation research (Atkinson, 1964; H. Heckhausen, 1967; McClelland, 1953, 1976), action theory (H. Heckhausen, 1991; Kuhl, 1987), the psychology of causal attribution and perceived control (Bandura, 1977; Rotter, 1966; Watson, 1966; Weiner, 1972; Weiner & Kukla, 1970), and the psychology of personal causation and intrinsic motivation (Csikszentmihalyi, 1975; DeCharms, 1968; Deci, 1975; Deci & Ryan, 1985). In these different lines of scholarship, process-oriented approaches to motivation began to flourish.

Achievement motivation research integrated the psychology of individual motives and situational affordances into an expectancy x value model of goal setting in achievement behavior (Atkinson, 1964; H. Heckhausen, 1967). According to this theory, the motivational and emotional forces that direct achievement behavior are determined by the expectancy of success and failure and the value attached to positive and negative outcomes. Expectancy and value in turn are influenced not only by situational conditions (e.g., task difficulty, desirability of the goal) but also by the individual's preferences and risk perceptions.

Out of achievement motivation research grew a renewed interest in the "other side of motivation," namely, volition or action theory (H. Heckhausen, 1991; H. Heckhausen & Gollwitzer, 1987; H. Heckhausen & Kuhl, 1985; Kuhl, 1984, 1985; Kuhl & Beckmann, 1985). A unified theory of action integrates the motivational phenomena of both goal selection and goal setting, with volitional phenomena of goal pursuit in terms of action initiation and action control. This recent line of research has led to the identification and functional analyses of specific processes involved in action implementation, self-regulation (see Kuhl & Fuhrmann, Chapter 1, this volume), and compensatory goal pursuit via symbolic self-completion (see Gollwitzer & Kirchhoff (Chapter 15, this volume).

A related line of action-theoretical research focuses on the selection and pursuit of developmental goals throughout the human life span (Brandt-städter, 1998, Brandtstädter, Rothermund, & Dillmann, Chapter 14, this volume; J. Heckhausen, 1998, J. Heckhausen & Schulz, 1995, and Chapter 2, this volume). This approach integrates theoretical conceptions from motivation psychology with life-span developmental research, and investigates the "life course" of developmental goals across life-span transitions that involve improved or impoverished opportunities for goal attainment. Key questions in developmental action theory are: How do individuals adapt their developmental goals to the changing opportunities and constraints at different age levels? Which processes promote persistent pursuit or disengagement from developmental goals?

The emergence of this European approach coincides with a revival of interest in goal-directed behavior in the United States (Cantor & Kihlstrom, 1987; Cantor & Sanderson, Chapter 7, this volume; Dweck & Leggett, 1988; Emmons, 1986; Klinger, 1977; Little, 1989; Markus & Ruvolo, 1989; Pervin, 1983). Many now saw goals as being at the heart of motivation and as its defining feature. People's goals were what drove, guided, and organized their behavior, as well as their cognition and affect. Indeed, cognition, affect, and behavior could now be seen as a coherently related set of variables, a set of processes that interacted as people pursued valued ends.

The study of causal attributions for success and failure was another important paradigm (Kruglanski, 1975; Weiner, 1972). Weiner, who had been trained in the tradition of achievement motivation, proposed that motivational phenomena (persistence, for example) could be analyzed more precisely and fruitfully by examining people's causal attributions for their successes and failures, that is, their explanations for why they succeeded or failed. He and his colleagues (e.g., Weiner & Kukla, 1970) then showed how different attributions lead to different expectancies for future success and different levels of persistence. This research demonstrates how personal characteristics and environmental cues could both influence behavior, through common mechanisms. That is, not only do clear individual differences exist among people in their tendencies to make certain attributions, but also attributions can be situationally induced (see Dweck, 1975; Graham, Chapter 5, this volume).

A related research tradition stemmed from Rotter's (1966) seminal work on how people's motivation and behavior are influenced by their perceptions of control over their environment and over the outcomes that befall them. Researchers (Langer & Rodin, 1978; Watson, 1966; Weiss, 1970; Weisz & Stipek, 1982) took this concept of perceived control and demonstrated compellingly how it could be experimentally induced and what powerful effects it could have on the most important aspects of functioning (see also research on "self-efficacy," Bandura, 1977, 1982). Other researchers formulated a more differentiated model of control-related beliefs, using a more elaborate scheme to investigate age-related differences in control-related beliefs and their relation to intellectual and social outcomes (see Skinner, 1995; Skinner, Chapman, & Baltes, 1988; Little, Chapter 11, this volume). Integrating the ideas of attributional psychology, the study of perceived control, and Kelly's (1955) "psychology of personal constructs" with a developmental perspective, Dweck and her colleagues (Dweck, 1975, and Chapter 10, this volume; Dweck & Leggett, 1988) demonstrated how conceptions about intelligence and ability in general develop into persistent theories that either empower the individual or render him or her vulnerable to situational pressures.

Another research tradition focuses on self-determination and autonomy in goal selection and pursuit as a critical condition for motivation, success, and pleasure (DeCharms, 1968; Deci, 1975; Deci & Ryan, 1985; Ryan, Chapter 4, this volume). Social coercion and external control in general are detrimental to motivation, performance, and enjoyment of activities (see also Pomerantz & Ruble, Chapter 6, this volume). In addition, this approach views activity-irrelevant positive consequences of action (e.g., concrete rewards) as potentially detrimental to intrinsic motivation and thus performance (Deci, 1975; Deci & Ryan, 1985; Lepper, Greene, & Nisbett, 1973). A related line of research focuses on the experience of "flow" in self-determined and challenging activities, which leads to optimal performances and highly positive affect (Csikszentmihalyi, 1975; Csikszentmihalyi & Rathunde, 1993).

Merits of the Motivational Approach

A motivational theory emphasizing process and built around goals has many advantages. First, this approach allows us to understand the way in which cognitive and affective factors work together to produce motivational patterns. That is, viewing behavior as goal-directed leads us to think more about how cognition and affect come together in action. In this way, goal-focused approaches to human behavior are prototypical examples of integrated and process-oriented approaches that link motivation, affect, and cognition to their behavioral correlates and consequences.

Second, this approach encourages us to identify the specific variables (such as beliefs, values, and strategies) that are important in motivation and that play critical roles in people's pursuit of their goals. Models of perceived control, for example, show how control beliefs affect goal-directed behavior and its outcomes.

Third, process-oriented approaches illuminate the role of these factors in dysfunctional patterns of behavior. For example, much of the work in this volume clearly illustrates how certain self-theories, self-regulatory strategies, attributional biases, or goal selection biases can set up maladaptive behavior.

Fourth, this approach helps us to understand how motivational or self-regulatory variables can form the basis of rather stable individual differences but can also be dynamic and context-sensitive. Even in the presence of strong individual differences, motivational variables can show dynamic and context-sensitive variation.

A Life-Span Developmental Perspective on Mediating Processes

This book adds a developmental perspective to this process-oriented approach. As these chapters demonstrate, a process-oriented approach enriches any developmental analysis; however, a developmental perspective also greatly enriches any process-oriented approach to motivation.

A life-span developmental perspective (Baltes, 1987; Baltes, Lindenberger, & Staudinger, 1998) adds the insight that different processes follow different life-span trajectories. Indeed, by charting the origins and the developmental course of motivational processes, this approach helps us to identify the critical elements of motivational systems and to understand their interrelations. In addition, the life-span perspective highlights context-driven variations in psychological processes, such as those resulting from different historical periods, different cultures, and different periods of life. It brings with it the optimistic conception of great intraindividual plasticity in behavior and psychological functioning, while acknowledging the constraints that may accompany different developmental periods and different contexts in which development takes place. Moreover, the life-span perspective brings to the foreground the idea that stable individual differences can be highly sensitive to contextual variation. Several of the chapters in this volume show that as important motivational and self-regulatory processes develop with age, they can be transformed by the age-related issues and experiences the individual confronts.

Finally, the life-span perspective gives us unique insight into the development of adaptive and maladaptive motivational patterns. First, it allows us to study and conceptualize in precise terms how patterns that develop early in life provide important resources and constraints for development later on. Second, by highlighting the processes involved in adaptive motivational patterns at different points in development and by identifying the contexts that promote adaptive patterns at different points in development, this approach promises to generate interventions that are uniquely suited to a person's developmental phase and context.

This developmental perspective is represented in the present volume in several ways. Chapters 2, 3, 5, 6, 8, 10, and 12 describe research on the developmental origins and trajectories of specific motivational or self-regulatory processes, with some also addressing how dysfunctional patterns may persist over development periods (Dweck; Graham; Heckhausen & Schulz; Higgins & Loeb; Pomerantz & Ruble; Skinner; Weisz). Chapters 4, 5, 8, 9, 12, and 16 go a step further and consider potential intervention strategies to prevent the emergence of maladaptive patterns or to break their influence on subsequent development (Graham; Nolen-Hoeksema; Ryan; Schulz; Skinner; Weisz). In addition, many of the chapters describe research on the impact of variations in context, including variations owing to age-related developmental tasks (Chapters 2, 7, 10, 13, and 14, by Brandtstädter, Rothermund, & Dillmann; Cantor & Sanderson; Carstensen; Dweck; Heckhausen & Schulz, respectively), situational challenges to self-identity (Chapter 15, by Gollwitzer & Kirchhoff) or ethnic or cultural setting (Chapters 5 and 11, by Graham and Little, respectively).

In summary, a developmental perspective – and a life-span perspective in particular – gives us the means to address important and interesting questions in future research. This perspective leads us to investigate the potential for and limits of plasticity in the psychological processes involved in motivation and self-regulation. To what extent are maladaptive patterns relatively entrenched after childhood and adolescence, and to what extent can they be influenced by developmentally appropriate and context-appropriate interventions? It also leads us to examine the "age-relativity" of adaptive processes. What is adaptive at one segment of the life span may be maladaptive at another. In fact, the developmental literature provides excellent examples of how the full-blown expression of certain patterns (such as stranger anxiety and intense mother–child attachment) is entirely normal and perhaps even necessary at certain points in development, but clearly not at others. Yet, there may well be more general underlying processes that we can identify as adaptive or maladaptive across developmental periods. The challenge is both to pinpoint adaptive and maladaptive patterns at each point in the life span and to search for general "laws" of adaptive and maladaptive functioning. We hope this volume represents a step toward those goals.

References

Atkinson, J. W. (1957). Motivational determinants of risk-taking behavior. *Psychological Review, 64,* 359–372.

Atkinson, J. W. (1964). *An introduction to motivation.* Princeton, NJ: Van Nostrand.

Baltes, P. B. (1987). Theoretical propositions of life-span developmental psychology: On the dynamics between growth and decline. *Developmental Psychology, 23,* 611–626.

Baltes, P. B., Lindenberger, U., & Staudinger, U. M. (1998). Life-span theory in developmental psychology. In R. M. Lerner (Ed.), *Handbook of child psychology: Vol. 1. Theoretical models of human development* (5th ed., Editor-in-Chief W. Damon, pp. 1029–1143). New York: Wiley.

Bandura, A. (1977). Self-efficacy: Toward a unifying theory of behavioral change. *Psychological Review, 84,* 191–215.

 (1982). Self-efficacy mechanisms in human agency. *American Psychologist, 37,* 122–147.

Brandtstädter, J. (1998). Action perspectives on human development. In R. M. Lerner (Vol. Ed.), *Handbook of child psychology: Vol. 1. Theoretical models of human development* (5th ed., Editor-in-Chief W. Damon, pp. 807–863). New York: Wiley.

Brandtstädter, J., Rothermund, K., & Dillmann, U. (1998). Maintaining self-integrity and efficacy through adulthood and later life: The adaptive functions of assimilative persistence and accommodative flexibility. In J. Heckhausen & C. S. Dweck (Eds.), *Motivation and self-regulation across the life span.* New York: Cambridge University Press.

Cantor, N., & Kihlstrom, J. F. (1987). *Personality and social intelligence.* Englewood Cliffs, NJ: Prentice-Hall.

Cantor, N., & Sanderson, C. A. (1998). The functional regulation of adolescent dating relationships and sexual behavior: An interaction of goals, strategies, and situations. In J. Heckhausen & C. S. Dweck (Eds.), *Motivation and self-regulation across the life span.* New York: Cambridge University Press.

Carstensen, L. L. (1998). A life-span approach to social motivation. In J. Heckhausen & C. S. Dweck (Eds.), *Motivation and self-regulation across the life span.* New York: Cambridge University Press.

Csikszentmihalyi, M. (1975). *Beyond boredom and anxiety.* San Francisco: Jossey-Bass.

Csikszentmihalyi, M., & Rathunde, K. (1993). The measurement of flow in everyday life: Toward a theory of emergent motivation. In J. E. Jacobs (Ed.), *Nebraska symposium on motivation: Developmental perspectives on motivation. Current theory and research in motivation (Vol. 40)* (pp. 57–97). Lincoln: University of Nebraska Press.

DeCharms, R. (1968). *Personal causation.* New York: Academic Press.

Deci, E. L. (1975). *Intrinsic motivation.* New York: Plenum Press.

Deci, E. L., & Ryan, R. M. (1985). *Intrinsic motivation and self-determination in human behavior.* New York: Plenum Press.

Dweck, C. S. (1975). The role of expectations and attributions in the alleviation of learned helplessness. *Journal of Personality and Social Psychology, 36,* 451–462.

—— (1998). The development of early self-conceptions: Their relevance for motivational processes. In J. Heckhausen & C. S. Dweck (Eds.), *Motivation and self-regulation across the life span.* New York: Cambridge University Press.

Dweck, C. S., & Leggett, E. L. (1988). A social-cognitive approach to motivation and personality. *Psychological Review, 95,* 256–273.

Eccles, J. S. (1985). Sex differences in achievement patterns. In B. Sonderegger (Ed.), *Psychology and gender. Nebraska symposium on motivation, 1984* (pp. 97–132). Lincoln: University of Nebraska Press.

Eccles, J. S., & Wigfield, A. (1995). In the mind of the actor: The structure of adolescents' achievement task values and expectancy-related beliefs. *Personality and Social Psychology Bulletin, 21,* 215–225.

Emmons, R. A. (1986). Personal strivings: An approach to personality and subjective well-being. *Journal of Personality and Social Psychology, 51,* 1058–1068.

Gollwitzer, P. M., & Kirchhof, O. (1998). The willful pursuit of identity. In J. Heckhausen & C. S. Dweck (Eds.), *Motivation and self-regulation across the life span.* New York: Cambridge University Press.

Graham, S. (1998). Social motivation and perceived responsibility in others: Attributions and behavior of African American boys labeled as aggressive. In J. Heckhausen & C. S. Dweck (Eds.), *Motivation and self-regulation across the life span.* New York: Cambridge University Press.

Heckhausen, H. (1967). *The anatomy of achievement motivation.* New York: Academic Press.

—— (1991). *Motivation and action.* New York: Springer.

Heckhausen, H., & Gollwitzer, P. M. (1987). Thought contents and cognitive functioning in motivational vs. volitional states of mind. *Motivation & Emotion, 11,* 101–120.

Heckhausen, H., & Kuhl, J. (1985). From wishes to action: The dead ends and short cuts on the long way to action. In M. Frese & J. Sabini (Eds.), *Goal-directed behavior: Psychological theory and research on action* (pp. 134–160). Hillsdale, NJ: Erlbaum.

Heckhausen, J. (1998). *Developmental regulation in adulthood: Age-normative and sociostructural constraints as adaptive challenges.* New York: Cambridge University Press.

Heckhausen, J., & Schulz, R. (1995). A life-span theory of control. *Psychological Review*, 102, 284–304.

Heckhausen, J., & Schulz, R. (1998). Developmental regulation in adulthood: Selection and compensation via primary and secondary control. In J. Heckhausen & C. S. Dweck (Eds.), *Motivation and self-regulation across the life span*. New York: Cambridge University Press.

Heider, F. (1958a). *The psychology of interpersonal relations*. New York: Wiley.

(1958b). Social perception and phenomenal causality. In R. Tagiuri & L. Petrullo (Eds.), *Person perception and interpersonal behavior* (pp. 1–21). Stanford, CA: Stanford University Press.

Higgins, E. T., & Loeb, I. (1998). Development of regulatory focus: Promotion and prevention as ways of living. In J. Heckhausen & C. S. Dweck (Eds.), *Motivation and self-regulation across the life span*. New York: Cambridge University Press.

Kelly, G. A. (1955). *The psychology of personal constructs*. New York: Norton.

Klinger, E. (1977). *Meaning and void: Inner experience and the incentives in people's lives*. Minneapolis, MN: University of Minnesota Press.

Kruglanski, A. W. (1975). The endogenous-exogenous partition in attribution theory. *Psychological Review*, 82, 387–406.

Kuhl, J. (1984). Motivational aspects of achievement motivation and learned helplessness: Toward a comprehensive theory of action control. In B. A. Maher & W. B. Maher (Eds.), *Progress in experimental personality research* (Vol. 13, pp. 99–171). New York: Academic Press.

(1985). Volitional mediators of cognition-behavior consistency: Self-regulatory processes and action versus state orientation. In J. Kuhl & J. Beckmann (Eds.), *Action control: From cognition to behavior* (pp. 101–128). Berlin/Heidelberg/New York: Springer.

(1987). Action control: The maintenance of motivational states. In F. Halisch & J. Kuhl (Eds.), *Motivation, intention and volition* (pp. 279–291). Berlin: Springer.

Kuhl, J., & Beckmann, J. (Eds.). (1985). *Action control from cognition to behavior*. New York: Springer.

Kuhl, J., & Fuhrmann, A. (1998). Decomposing self-regulation and self-control: The Volitional Components Inventory. In J. Heckhausen & C. S. Dweck (Eds.), *Motivation and self-regulation across the life span*. New York: Cambridge University Press.

Langer, E. J., & Rodin, J. (1978). The effects of choice and enhanced personal responsibility for the aged: A field experiment in an institutional setting. *Journal of Personality and Social Psychology*, 34, 191–198.

Lepper, M. R., Greene, D., & Nisbett, R. E. (1973). Undermining children's intrinsic interest with extrinsic rewards: A test of the "overjustification" hypothesis. *Journal of Personality and Social Psychology*, 28, 129–137.

Lewin, K. (1935). *A dynamic theory of personality*. New York: McGraw-Hill.

(1936). *Principles of topological psychology*. New York: McGraw-Hill.

Little, B. R. (1989). Personal projects analysis: Trivial pursuits, magnificent obsessions, and the search for coherence. In D. M. Buss & N. Cantor (Eds.), *Personality psychology: Recent trends and emerging directions* (pp. 15–31). New York: Springer.

Little, T. D. (1998). Sociocultural influences on the development of children's action-control beliefs. In J. Heckhausen & C. S. Dweck (Eds.), *Motivation and self-regulation across the life span.* New York: Cambridge University Press.

Markus, H., & Ruvolo, A. (1989). Possible selves: Personalized representations of goals. In L. A. Pervin (Ed.), *Goal concepts in personality and social psychology.* Hillsdale, NJ: Erlbaum.

McClelland, D. C. (1953). *The achievement motive.* New York: Appleton-Century-Crofts.

   (1976). New introduction. In D. C. McClelland (Ed.), *The achieving society.* New York: Irvington.

Mischel, W. (1973). Toward a cognitive social learning reconceptualization of personality, *Psychological Review, 80,* 252–283.

Nolen-Hoeksema, S. (1998). Ruminative coping with depression. In J. Heckhausen & C. S. Dweck (Eds.), *Motivation and self-regulation across the life span.* New York: Cambridge University Press.

Pervin, L. A. (1983). The stasis and flow of behavior: Toward a theory of goals. In M. M. Page (Ed.), *Nebraska symposium on motivation* (pp. 1–53). Lincoln: University of Nebraska Press.

Pomerantz, E., & Ruble, D. (1998). A multidimensional perspective of social control: Implications for the development of sex differences in self-valuation and depression. In J. Heckhausen & C. S. Dweck (Eds.), *Motivation and self-regulation across the life span.* New York: Cambridge University Press.

Rotter, J. B. (1966). Generalized expectancies for internal versus external locus of control of reinforcement. *Psychological Monographs, 80* (609).

Ryan, R. M. (1998). Human psychological needs and the issues of volition, control, and outcome focus. In J. Heckhausen & C. S. Dweck (Eds.), *Motivation and self-regulation across the life span.* New York: Cambridge University Press.

Schulz, R. (1998). Commentary: Motivation through the life course. In J. Heckhausen & C. S. Dweck (Eds.), *Motivation and self-regulation across the life span.* New York: Cambridge University Press.

Skinner, E. A. (1995). *Perceived control, motivation, and coping.* Newbury Park, CA: Sage.

   (1998). Commentary: Strategies for studying social influences on motivation. In J. Heckhausen & C. S. Dweck (Eds.), *Motivation and self-regulation across the life span.* New York: Cambridge University Press.

Skinner, E. A., Chapman, M., & Baltes, P. B. (1988). Control, means-ends, and agency beliefs: A new conceptualization and its measurement during childhood. *Journal of Personality and Social Psychology, 54,* 117–133.

Watson, J. S. (1966). The development and generalization of "contingency awareness" in early infancy: Some hypotheses. *Merrill-Palmer Quarterly, 12,* 123–135.

Weiner, B. (1972). *Theories of motivation: From mechanism to cognition.* Chicago, IL: Markham.

Weiner, B., & Kukla, A. (1970). An attributional analysis of achievement motivation. *Journal of Personality and Social Psychology, 15,* 1–20.

Weiss, J. M. (1970). Some effects of predictable and unpredictable shock. *Psychosomatic Medicine, 32,* 397–409.

Weisz, J. R. (1998). Commentary: Self-regulation, motivation and developmental psychopathology. In J. Heckhausen & C. S. Dweck (Eds.), *Motivation and self-regulation across the life span.* New York: Cambridge University Press.

Weisz, J. R., & Stipek, D. J. (1982). Competence, contingency, and the development of perceived control. *Human Development, 25,* 250–281.

PART ONE

Regulation of Self, Action, and Development

1   Decomposing Self-Regulation and Self-Control: The Volitional Components Inventory

Julius Kuhl and Arno Fuhrmann

Abstract

In this chapter we introduce a new questionnaire based upon a theory of volition. This theory postulates two different modes of volition: self-control and self-regulation. Our approach to self-control and self-regulation decomposes global concepts of volition into many functional constituents. Some of these components are currently studied in isolated paradigms across various psychological disciplines. According to the central assumption underlying the new questionnaire, volitional processes have to be seen in conjunction with processes relating the "self" (the integrated and implicit representation of a person's experiences, beliefs, and needs) to individual goals and others' expectations.

A Theory of Volition

From a macroscopic perspective, the two most important tasks of volition are maintaining both one's goals and the integrity of one's "self." The mode of volition supporting the maintenance of an active goal is called *self-control* (Kuhl, 1992) or *action control* (Kuhl, 1984), whereas the mode supporting the task of maintaining one's actions in line with one's integrated self is called *self-regulation.* According to our theory, *central coordination* of processing across a variety of psychological subsystems (e.g., explicit and implicit cognition, emotion, motivation, arousal) is the defining characteristic common to either mode of volition. This interpretation of volition in terms of a central executive requires a *modular* conception of mind: Many cognitive, emotional, motivational, and temperamental (arousal) processes are active in parallel, and each of them can modulate a different behavioral tendency competing for access to an operating system that controls ongoing behavior.

When people are acting volitionally, as, for instance, when they are trying to stop smoking but are confronted with strong situational cues for

15

smoking (e.g., someone offering a cigarette, having feelings of boredom, experiencing frustration or high stress), they can accomplish both volitional tasks simultaneously (i.e., self-maintenance and goal maintenance) by actualizing the appropriate integrated representation of personal needs and beliefs supporting a healthy lifestyle (self-maintenance), thereby enhancing their ability to focus on the goal of not smoking and ignore competing motivations (goal maintenance). This concurrent operation of both maintenance systems (i.e., self-maintenance and goal maintenance) is of particular relevance in the early phase of establishing a goal that later might require volitional support. This is because the cooperative participation of either system strongly determines the type and the degree of *commitment,* and thus the amount of volitional efficiency in striving for the goal: The extent to which people who decide to quit smoking become committed to that goal and are able to stick to it depends on the extent to which they have become aware of and maintain integrated aspects of the self that support this goal and to which they make use of appropriate strategies that maintain that goal when confronted with competing motivations. When using the term *self-regulation* in a broader sense, we mean this concurrent satisfaction of a majority of short- and long-term personal needs representing an integrated self (self-maintenance) when pursuing a goal (goal maintenance).

A second way to accomplish both global volitional tasks (goal maintenance and self-maintenance) would be to alternate between them serially rather than activate them simultaneously in a balanced way. For instance, one could try to satisfy important needs representing vital aspects of one's self (self-maintenance) after a period of strict goal maintenance requiring temporal neglect even of important self-aspects. This goal maintenance at the expense of self-maintenance can be useful for at least two situations: pursuing important social goals that are not (yet) compatible with one's personal needs, or pursuing personal goals that are supported by the anticipation of future consequences of one's actions but are not (yet) supported by emotional and other aspects of the self and past experiences.

If, for instance, the goal to quit smoking has been established without participation of the self and has been adopted ("introjected") – for instance, through a doctor's advice or requests of significant others – without being integrated in a person's network of interrelated needs, the person might still be able to maintain this goal effectively, as long as it can help reach other long-term goals (i.e., saving money, getting respect from others, or reducing the risk of myocardial infarction). Self-control may require a temporary or permanent suppression of the integrated self in order to establish the restriction of attention that is sometimes needed to prevent a top-priority goal from being interfered with by competing preferences, needs, beliefs, or other self-aspects. This suppression of the self can best be achieved by activation of the *punishment system* and is characterized by negative emotionality. Thus, the goal-maintaining mode of self-control is seen as requiring a high amount of conscious effort. According to the most important aspect of self-control in this theory, this mode of volition is seen as a temporary means to accomplish the initiation or maintenance of goal-directed behavior that is not yet an integral part of the self. Thus it allows one to maintain limited volitional efficiency, but at considerably higher costs than does self-regulation.

The Development of Self-Control and Self-Regulation

In contrast to theories emphasizing the potentially maladaptive aspects of self-control (e.g., Deci & Ryan, 1991), our theory suggests adaptive aspects of moderate and temporary forms of self-control such as the pursuit of important, sometimes life-saving, goals (e.g., those imposed by caretakers) that are not (yet) supported by the self and the adoption of cultural values that are not (yet) compatible with the self. Although excessive self-control contains many risks to one's physical and subjective well-being – and adoption of important goals and social norms through the self-compatible mode is preferable wherever possible – we concede that there may be situations in which self-supported goal pursuit is not possible. In these instances the maintenance of self-incongruent goals may be the only way to pursue end-states important to the individual or to society. In some cases, one needs to be gently pushed into activities that one would not initiate spontaneously (i.e., on the basis of one's self) in order to make new experiences, part of which may later be integrated into one's self. Trying to reduce psychological development to the basically preferred, "healthy" mode of self-actualization can be compared to trying to keep a newborn healthy by keeping it away from all viruses and bacteria: The resulting organism would be an uncontaminated physical self that would be unable to live in a natural environment. In this respect, self-control may be considered the psychological cost that is necessary for people to develop their selves in order to deal effectively with their social and nonsocial environment.

Life-Span Development

A life-span view of development has been elaborated by Russian psychologists (Leontjev, 1977; Luria, 1973; Vygotski, 1978). According to their research, the early development of volitional competence is based upon the internalization of controlling behaviors of primary caretakers, especially by utilizing the self-controlling power of language. This developmental approach has been adopted and elaborated by Western psychologists (Block & Block, 1982; Diaz, Neal, & Amaya-Williams, 1990; Diener & Dweck, 1978; Meichenbaum, 1986; Mischel & Mischel, 1983). Its bias toward the self-control component can be remedied by combining it with an approach that emphasizes identification with rather than introjection of cultural values (Deci & Ryan, 1991; Ryan, 1995). A developmental approach including both forms of volition has been proposed by Kopp (1982). From a life-span perspective, the development of volition in adult and older age typically proceeds from stages in which self-control dominates to stages in which self-awareness and self-maintenance are strengthened until a higher form of *integration* of holistic self-awareness and analytical goal awareness can be accomplished (Jung, 1936/1990; Labouvie-Vief, Hakim-Larson, DeVoe, et al., 1989).

A Personality Framework for the Study of Volition

In order to understand how various modes of volition work, we need a functional analysis of major processing systems involved. According to personality-systems-interaction (PSI) theory, macrosystems related to different forms of volition are (1) analytical, "Thinking"; (2) holistic processing of information, "Feeling"; (3) elementary, "Sensation"; (4) "Intuitive Acting"; (5) positive emotionality; and (6) negative emotionality. The latter (i.e., macrosystems 5 and 6) can be understood in terms of the sensitivity and activational strength of motivational reward and punishment systems evoked under demanding or stressful conditions (see Kuhl, 1995, for a more comprehensive description of the underlying theoretical assumptions).

Different configurations of these subsystems are associated with each of the two main modes of volition, namely *goal maintenance* and *self-maintenance*. As mentioned, the term *volition* describes a central *coordination* of cognitive, motivational, emotional, and temperamental processes represented by the above listed macrosystems. It is proposed that specific constellations of macrosystems 5 and 6, namely the phasic or tonic activation of reward and punishment systems under stress, moderate the accessibility or effectiveness of various subcomponents located within macrosystems 1 to 4 (see Figure 1.1).

According to the first affect-cognition modulation hypothesis, a phasically or tonically heightened activity of the reward system (i.e., a positive

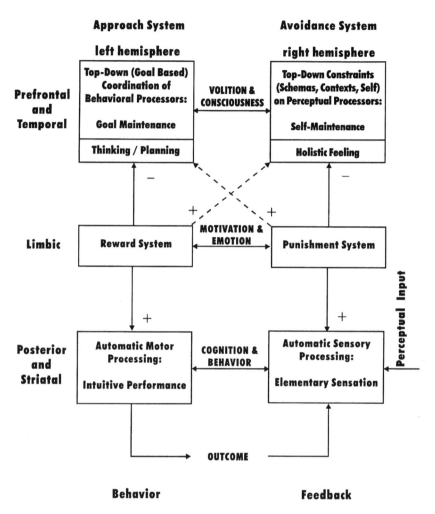

Figure 1.1. Personality-systems-interactions (PSI) theory: General framework for different configurations of six macrosystems of personality underlying various modes of volition.

mood or anticipation of positive consequences of an intended action) reduces the impact of analytically based, intentional information or serial information processing mediated by the macrosystem of sequentially organized (planned) "Thinking" on the activation of intended instrumental behavior. On the other hand, strong activation of the reward system facilitates "intuitive" (nonvolitional) behavioral control and access to and usage of information constituting a person's "self" (i.e., an integrated, holistic representation of interrelated needs and past experiences located within the functional domain of "Feeling"). Through this moderating influence, the reward system (Figure 1.1) contributes to maintaining important self-aspects throughout the course of action, given that at the same time the activational level of the punishment system (Figure 1.1) is moderate to low. Since space limitations prevent us from describing the functional characteristics of each of these systems, we refer the reader to additional sources (Epstein, 1994; Gray, 1987; Jung, 1936/1990; Kuhl, 1983b, 1994a, 1995; Paivio, 1983).

Activation of the reward system for long or at least intermediate periods of time is useful for another reason: Tonically maintained positive emotionality enables the organism to tolerate brief ("phasic") periods of negative emotionality that may be needed to trigger self-controlling functions such as planning or impulse control *without falling into a long-lasting activation of excessive negative emotionality.* A stable activation of positive emotionality can also be useful for maintaining an "action-oriented" system configuration under stress that is characterized by a dampening of the tonic level of negative emotionality and facilitation of "feeling" and self-maintenance produced by that dampening mechanism (see Figure 1.1): According to the second affect-cognition modulation hypothesis, an excessive and tonic arousal of the punishment system and the negative emotionality associated with it (1) dampens accessibility to the "feeling" system (Figure 1.1) and its integrated self-representations and (2) intensifies elementary sensory representations including a discrepancy- or mismatch-sensitive type of attention associated with it (Figure 1.1).

Therefore, when people respond to stress with a strong and enduring (tonic) arousal of the punishment system (Gray, 1987), they have difficulty accessing those parts of the "feeling" system that provide integrated self-representations of all needs – for example, preferences, beliefs, and attitudes – that are relevant in a given situation. As a result, subjective experience and overt behavior are governed by isolated sensations and self-components that are mediated by the sensory systems participating in the macronetwork called "sensation" (Figure 1.1). A chronic disposition toward a dominance of this mode of control can seriously impair the development of an integrated self. This part of PSI theory explains some of the devastating effects that exaggerated forms of punishment-biased socialization can have on self-development.

We can now specify some of the most significant antecedent conditions for the activation of the two major modes of volition: The optimal system configuration for entering the "self-regulation" mode or style of volition would thus be a moderate to high sensitivity/activity of the motivational reward system and an active dampening of the punishment system to moderate to low activity. An increased activation of the punishment system, on the other hand, hinders access to the implicit "knowledge base" of the self, and instead facilitates access and use of information within the Thinking domain (i.e., planned and serial processing of information and attentional focusing). Under stressful, punishment-prone conditions, this mechanism facilitates initiation and maintenance of goal-pursuing activities and other functions related to *self-control* – given that the reward system is not highly active at the same time, which would counteract this effect (see Figure 1.1). In other words, all situational conditions reducing positive affect (e.g., frustration, exposure to uncontrollable events) or enhancing negative affect (e.g., time pressure, excessive ego involvement emphasizing self-threatening implications of failure, unpredictability of aversive events) can be regarded as antecedents of goal-oriented behavior or of the inhibition of access to integrated self-representations, respectively.

Decomposing Volition in Subjective Experience

In neurophysiological research, subcomponents of volition have been isolated and related to different parts of the frontal neocortex (Fuster, 1989; Shallice, 1988; Stuss & Benson, 1984). Similarly, experimental psychologists have collected much evidence for the separability of various volitional functions, such as goal maintenance versus alternation (Allport, Styles, & Hsieh, 1994), planning (Shallice, 1988), impulse control (Mischel, 1974), and volitional inhibition (Kuhl & Beckmann, 1994a). The Volitional Competence Inventory (VCI) is based on an attempt to assess *subjective concomitants* of these and other volitional components supporting central coordination of goal maintenance and self-maintenance. Subjective experience of volitional activity should reflect not only global components of volition such as self-maintenance and goal maintenance, but also the operational availability of certain subcomponents such as initiating of goal behavior, controlling unwanted impulses and intrusive thoughts, restoring waning motivation for goal attainment, and so on. To the extent that a questionnaire provides valid and reliable access to such functional differentiations, it can serve as a highly valuable tool providing rough information on the functional components of volition.

The VCI aims at a fine-grained decomposition of the main components of volition, namely self-control and self-regulation, into theoretically separable specific volitional subcomponents serving the global purposes of goal maintenance and self-maintenance. The overall perspective is twofold. The first part of the VCI tries to capture signs of volitional competence under conditions that require the person to overcome what we call *difficulties of enactment* (Kuhl, 1983a, 1984). These particular difficulties are present when a self-related interest or goal cannot be pursued as long as the system remains in its current configuration: Strong habitual tendencies, competing motivations, paralyzing or agitating moods, or over- or underarousal may interfere with the performance of self-congruent and/or goal-directed action unless appropriate changes in relevant subsystems are centrally coordinated. In sum, various components of self-control and self-regulation form the first part of the VCI.

The second part of the VCI tries to capture symptoms of *reduced access* to volitional competencies under conditions of frustration or stress and the resulting decrease in the functional efficiency of specific volitional subcomponents in demanding situations. It is important to keep in mind that these "deficit" symptoms are supposed to show up under conditions of frustration and aversive forms of stress, which are referred to in the questionnaire via instructions pointing to respective situations (i.e., the frustrating experience of failure or sudden aversive changes of important goal-relevant aspects). Stressful conditions of this kind are not described in the "competence section" of the questionnaire. Instead, the general formulation "something (a goal) with difficult or unpleasant aspects" is used in that section to describe the common conditions that require volitional competence. Items assessing various components of volitional competence (subcomponents of self-maintenance and goal maintenance) refer to some sort of difficulty of enactment (e.g., a source of temptation), whereas items assessing subcomponents of reduced accessibility of those volitional competencies (i.e., items assessing volitional inhibition or "state orientation") allude to frustrating or aversive experiences.

Detailed Overview of the Internal Structure of the Instrument

The list of scales is subdivided into the two sections described in terms of components of volitional competence and components of volitional inhibition (Tables 1.1 and 1.2).

The first section consists of scales designed to assess volitional components that support self-maintenance and goal maintenance. We can interpret these functions in terms of various aspects of *volitional competence*. Scales 1 to 11 assess such components of *volitional competence* (Table 1.1).

Table 1.1. *Overview of the theoretically distinguishable main dimensions within the "competence" part of the VCI (scales 1 to 12) and possible further differentiations within single dimensions (including sample items)*

Volitional Competencies	F1	F2	F3	Cronbach's Alpha (no. of items)
Self-regulation/self-maintenance				
1. *Attention control*[a]				
1.1 Conscious/explicitly[b] "Trying consciously to keep my attention stable"		.71[c]	.42	.81 (08)
1.2 Unconscious/implicitly[b] "Being absorbed in the matter without losing sight of the goal"		.58	.46	.77 (08)
2. Motivation control "Considering positive incentives concerning the matter"		.70[c]	.41	.90 (16)
3. Emotion control "Cheering myself up to make things work"		.70[c]		.86 (16)
4. *Arousal control*				
4.1 Adaptive activating "Being fit if matters get serious"		.71[c]		.80 (08)
4.2 Adaptive calming "Being able to calm down if this will help"		.67[c]		.86 (08)
5. Self-determination "Feeling at one with my decision"	−.37	.62[c]	.38	.88 (16)
6. Decision control "Having no difficulties with spontaneous decisions"	−.61[c]	.47	.39	.92 (20)
Self-control/goal pursuit				
7. Intention control/monitoring "Often rehearsing my decision"	.59	.32		.79 (08)
8. Planning "Thinking out details of the matter"		.40	.51	.95 (16)
9. Initiating "Simply getting started"		.40	.57	.87 (08)
10. Impulse control "Feeling defenseless in view of a temptation" (inverted)		.31	.74[c]	.81 (16)
11. Failure control "Immediately learning from my mistakes"		.41	.36	.83 (16)
Self-reflection				
12. Volitional self-confidence				
12.1 Volitional self-efficacy beliefs "Being certain not to become weak"	−.62	.52	.39	.89 (08)
12.2 Volitional optimism "Being optimistic"	−.51	.65[c]		.88 (08)

Notes: Titles of dimensions shown in italics mark scales that combine those differentiating aspects. Together with Table 1.2 the structure of the joint factor-loadings matrix of all VCI scales and the scales of the ACS-90 is clarified by displaying each scale's loading (> 0.30) onto three factors. Varimax rotation following principal-components analyses was used ($n = 136$) (see also Table 1.2 for further details).
[a]Macrocomponents.
[b]Microcomponents.
[c]A significant part (> 0.50) of this scale's communality (h^2) is explained by the factor (Fürntratt, 1969).

Table 1.2. *Overview of the theoretically distinguishable main dimensions within the "volitional inhibition" part of the VCI (scales 13 to 18) and possible further differentiations (including respective sample items) within single dimensions*

Loss of Access to Volitional Functions under Stress[d]	F1	F2	F3	Cronbach's Alpha (no. of items)
Frustration-contingent inhibition of behavior/passive goal fixation				
AOD enactment (vs. hesitation)	−.33	.31	.57	−.70 (12)
13. Energy deficit[a]	.43		−.68[c]	.90 (08)
"Feeling dull."				
14. *Implicit rejection*				
14.1 Intrusions[b]	.42		−.66[c]	.92 (08)
"All of a sudden thinking of totally other things."				
14.2 Neglection[b]	.32		−.79[c]	.89 (08)
"Postponing the matter."				
15. *Alienation*				
15.1 Informed introjection	.59		−.43	.91 (16)
"Feeling obliged to meet the expectations of others."				
15.2 External control			−.74[c]	.84 (16)
"Getting going only if someone threatens to become angry."				
Punishment-contingent inhibition of "feeling" and "self"				
AOF disengagement (vs. preoccupation)	−.55	.39		−.78 (12)
16. *Emotional perseverance*				
16.1 Ruminative thinking	.71[c]	−.39		.78 (08)
"Constantly asking myself how I could have done better."				
16.2 Emotional perseverance/Behavioral inhibition	.80[c]		−.31	.95 (16)
"Losing my drive after a failure."				
17. *Rigidity*				
17.1 Behavioral shift costs	.71[c]			.71 (08)
"Finding it difficult to abandon an old habit."				
17.2 Cognitive/perceptual rigidity	.60[c]	−.39		.78 (08)
"Finding it difficult to adjust to a sudden change of the rules."				
18. *Overcontrol*				
18.1 Pressure	.71[c]	.31		.72 (08)
"Imposing diiscipline on myself."				
18.2 Negative anticipations	.77[c]			.85 (08)
"Imagining how awful another failure will be."				

Notes: Titles of dimensions shown in italics mark scales that combine those differentiating aspects. In conjunction with Table 1.1 the structure of the joint factor-loadings matrix of all VCI scales and two scales of the ACS-90 (AOD, AOF) is clarified by displaying each scale's loading (> 0.30) onto three extended factors. Scales 19 to 21 (reactance, effort avoidance, and spontaneity) subsumed under the label "spontaneous control" are not listed here. These scales and the AOP scale (volatility) of the ACS-90 formed specific factors (F4 and F5) and were excluded before Varimax rotation of a three-factor-solution (F1, F2, F3).
[a]Macrocomponents.

Scale 12 (Table 1.1) refers to *self-reflections* about volitional competence and efficiency and may have an intermediate status: Conscious judgments about one's volitional efficiency can be affected both by one's actual competences and by the accessibility of these competences under stressful or frustrating conditions.

The second section of the VCI includes scales that assess various forms of *volitional inhibition* invoked under frustrating or stressful (aversive) conditions. Scales 13 to 18 assess such components of *volitional inhibition* (Table 1.2).

Finally, the VCI contains scales that address the *spontaneous* mode, mentioned earlier, in which volitional control is reduced to a minimum (i.e., scales 19 to 21, not listed in Table 1.1 or 1.2). We expect this mode of low rather than inhibited volitional control to show up when people rely on established behavioral routines and inclinations that do not require much central coordination. Within this mode, individual subsystems cooperate autonomously, a configuration of the system we call *self-organization* because individual processes organize "themselves" without central guidance. Self-organization is characterized by neglecting long-lasting goal-striving and self-integration. Theoretically, individuals in this mode are not expected to show symptoms of reduced volitional efficiency (because of their tendency to avoid engagement in volitionally based goal maintenance) but are considered to be at risk for experiencing a form of self-disintegration caused by a fragmentation of the self into temporarily pursued needs and behaviors that are not integrated into high-inferential representations of feelings and self-aspects.

Despite the expected interrelationships among the various components of volitional competence described in Table 1.1, each component can have idiosyncratic determinants that can lead to dissociation among the volitional components. For this reason, we considered it worthwhile to construct a separate scale for each volitional component.

Basic Functions within the Self-Regulatory Mode of Volition

The components of volitional competence are subdivided into components of self-regulation and components of self-control. The first six scales (Table

Notes to Table 1.2 (*cont.*)
[b]Microcomponents.
[c]A significant part (> 0.50) of this scale's communality (h^2) is explained by the factor (Fürntratt, 1969).
[d]This reduced efficiency in the use of volitional competencies is caused by *inhibition of self-aspects* (need, preference, and belief systems, etc.) or *inhibition of behavioral facilitation of self-based goals*.

1.1), which relate to central control of attention and subcognitive states (emotion, motivation, arousal), are seen as supported by the "feeling" and "self-maintenance" systems because these right-hemispheric systems are much more closely involved in the control of emotional functions than left-hemispheric analytical and goal-maintenance systems (Kolb & Wishaw, 1990). Evidence for this claim stems from, for example, the finding that projecting an emotional movie into the right hemisphere has considerably stronger effects on physiological concomitants of emotional arousal (e.g., blood pressure, heart rate) than projection into the left hemisphere (Wittling, 1990). Scales 1 to 6 assess functions that depend on elaborated knowledge about a variety of measures one can take to maintain a "self-generated" intention, to motivate oneself, and so on. This knowledge may or may not be consciously accessible and verbally expressed.

Subjects who operate in the self-regulatory mode while trying to pursue a desired goal are expected to need less time to arrive at particular decisions related to the goal and to employ volitional mechanisms and strategies in a phasic, context-sensitive way: They moderately use conscious monitoring of their intentions; they plan specific actions and initiate the planned behavior at the right times and in suitable situations. They are implicitly able to control their attention and inhibit disturbing impulses in order to stay with a difficult task (cf. scales 1 to 11 in Table 1.1). In addition, the self-regulatory mode of volitional control is characterized by a flexible style of handling goals that have difficult or unpleasant aspects.

Flexibility, efficient decision making, and other features of the self-regulation mode are attributed to the functional characteristics of the implicit memory system activated in this mode. This system – which can be related to the right prefrontal cortex – provides extended networks of remote semantic meanings, alternative options for action, compatibilities with self-aspects, and potential consequences associated with an intended action (Beeman, Friedman, Grafman, et al., 1994; Knight & Grabowecky, 1995; Nakagawa, 1991).

Overall, these subjects show high proficiency in making intuitive use of metamotivational mechanisms to control their own motivational and emotional states, either to maintain a goal in the face of waning motivating incentives or to cope with failure or other aversive consequences in the context of goal-directed actions. When asked to reflect upon their volitional competence, these subjects are expected to rate themselves higher in volitional self-efficacy and in feelings of self-determination than subjects not using this mode of volition.

Basic Functions within the Self-Control Mode of Volition

The competence-related part of the VCI (Table 1.1) also includes scales having a strong self-control component (e.g., intention control, planning, impulse control). These functions are components of volitional competence, too, as long as they are under the guidance of self-maintenance functions (i.e., as long as they do not produce conflicts with self-related concerns). This is the case, for instance, when temporary suppression of an impulse or repeated rehearsal of an uncompleted intention is supported by active self-representations rather than being in conflict with them. On the other hand, each of the mechanisms and strategies described can also be activated in a volitional mode in which self-control based on negative emotionality dominates the system and suppresses self-maintenance functions, that is, when the cooperative antagonism between self-control and self-regulation turns into an opposing one. An example is the case when somebody chronically pursues a goal that violates a central need or other self-components (e.g., a young woman enrolls in medical school to please her parents despite having quite different personal preferences). This case, which we refer to under the label "overcontrol," can be identified when high scores on competence-related scales (especially self-control scales) are associated with high scores on scales of volitional inhibition (Table 1.2). Overcontrol should be associated with volitional inhibition because the latter always requires a persistent activation of negative emotionality resulting in impaired access to self-representations (Figure 1.1).[1]

Volitional Self-Reflection

One scale specifically assesses the amount of self-confidence that a person experiences in volition-demanding situations. Volitional self-confidence (scale 12) can be based on *beliefs about volition-centered control* and *self-efficacy beliefs* or upon a more generalized form of optimism toward successful volitional action. This latter form of self-confidence implies a positive and open attitude toward perceived or anticipated difficulties in trying to reach difficult or discomforting goals. Volition-centered self-efficacy beliefs differ from Bandura's (1982) concept of self-efficacy beliefs: The former specifically focus on beliefs about one's own efficacy in the use of volitional competencies, the latter focus on self-efficacy beliefs that only implicitly address volitional competencies (among other abilities).

Volitional efficacy beliefs can be important because they may have an effect over and above the effects of the specific volitional functions under-lying them. For example, an overestimation of their objective abilities in planning, initiating, and maintaining an activity can put people in many sit-uations in which they can develop these functions (e.g., self-fulfilling prophecies). Of course, neither global self-confidence ratings nor ratings of specific volitional functions can ultimately replace objective measures of those volitional functions (Kuhl, 1983a).

Inhibition of Volitional Competences Under Stressful or Demanding Conditions: State-Orientation

According to the affect-cognition modulation hypotheses, it is possible to access holistically stored right-hemispheric information ("feeling") that supports the self-maintaining mode of volition when the activation of the reward system (or positive mood) is moderate or high and the activation of the punishment system is low; overall volitional efficiency should be high under this condition. On the other hand, frequent activation of the punish-ment system and low activation of the reward system should facilitate over-all goal maintenance but ultimately lead to symptoms of volitional inhi-bition. Although this implication of the theory may seem somewhat paradoxical at first glance, it directly follows from its assumptions: Perma-nently reduced access to "vital" aspects of the self (for instance, to the abil-ity to form complex decisions satisfying multiple constraints derived from interrelated needs, preferences, norms, mood states, and other concerns re-quiring participation of the "feeling" system) leaves the individual in a state of nonintegrated, alienated goal-striving. Goals are maintained, but they lack the necessary guidance and facilitation by the integrated self.

The scales of the second part of the VCI describe subjective experi-ences related to reduced utilization of volitional functions under stress or frustration. The primary task of coping with aversive or frustrating situa-tions differs from the central task supported by the components of voli-tional competence described until now. The system has to choose among three alternatives: (1) a self-assertive mode of coping, or *action orienta-tion;* (2) a self-suppressive, but active and stimulus-sensitive mode, or *failure-related state orientation;* and (3) a self-inhibiting and passive mode of coping, or *prospective state orientation.* These three coping modes are highly elaborated human analogs of styles described in the animal litera-ture: (1) fight–flight, (2) active avoidance, and (3) passive avoidance (e.g., Gray, 1987). According to PSI theory, the latter two modes of coping are associated with inhibition of two different sets of volitional functions. In contrast to Gray's theory, the PSI theory holds that passive avoidance is not reduced to "behavioral inhibition" (Gray, 1987): The hesitating form of state orientation, which we consider the human analog to passive avoidance, leaves various pathways to behavioral facilitation intact; well-practiced routines or habits can be performed if the appropriate releasing cues are present; externally controlled behavior is possible (e.g., following instructions); and the *inhibition affects the pathway from the volitional system,* specifically from representations of plans, intentions, or goal structures, *to the operating system* controlling behavioral enactment.

An example of this important implication of the theory is the fact that individuals often perform habitual behaviors elicited by relevant cues or requests by others (i.e., well-practiced routines like brushing one's teeth or closing a door) irrespective of whether those individuals like them or whether they "really" want to perform them. This is tantamount to saying that low positive affect associated with low incentive values of available objects or low involvement of self-interests does not necessarily result in passivity. Whenever cues or social requests eliciting an available well-practiced routine are encountered, behavioral facilitation can occur via a route that is independent of incentive- and self-based facilitation of behavior.[2] An empirical confirmation of this assumption was found in a study in which children scoring high on the hesitation scale of state orientation performed even more of the actions they intended to perform in the afternoon, provided these intended actions related to daily routines or things typically requested by adults. In contrast, intentions related to attractive and self-chosen afternoon activities were enacted more often by action-oriented children (Kuhl, 1982).

The VCI contains scales assessing the following behavioral and cognitive concomitants and consequences of volitional inhibition: (1) the just-mentioned inhibition of the pathway from plans to the behavioral facilitation system ("energy deficit"); (2) a heightened proneness to external control (especially to being controlled by others), which results from the weakening of pathways from self and goal representations to the behavioral facilitation system; (3) a tendency to introject self-alien goals and wishes prematurely with or without being aware of their self-incompatibility (informed versus misinformed introjection), which occurs as a result of reduced accessibility of self-representations; (4) a tendency to engage in negative motivation control in terms of anticipating negative consequences of not acting or not reaching the goal (anxiety-based self-motivation); (5) an increased incidence of intrusive thoughts; and (6) procrastination in goal-related activities.

Action orientation, however, is described in terms of *volitional facilitation,* that is, an increased activation of various volitional functions such as self-representations, motivation control, arousal control, decision control, goal maintenance, and so forth. The action-oriented mode of coping is expected when an organism responds to stress with increased activation of the reward system and/or dampening of the punishment system. In contrast, the various aspects of volitional inhibition mentioned are expected when the activity of the reward system is tonically reduced in response to stress or frustration, often in conjunction with a tonically moderate or high activity of the punishment system (see Figure 1.1).

According to the two major configurations of the six macrosystems (listed in Figure 1.1) defined by reduced reward activity or heightened punishment activity, respectively, the scales can be subdivided into two groups (see Table 1.2 for sample items). First are scales assessing consequences of *frustration-contingent* inhibition of enacting volitionally intended behavior, that is, *hesitation* or *passive goal awareness* as seen with energy-deficit, intrusions, procrastination, and externally controlled goal maintenance. Frustration is seen as relating to the reward system more directly than to the punishment system because not reaching a self-chosen or desired goal or failing to satisfy one's needs is expected to affect the former system in particular. Second are scales assessing consequences of *punishment-contingent* inhibition of "feeling" and "self-representations" (i.e., preoccupation and alienation, self-infiltration, rigidity, and overcontrol).

Scales Assessing Symptoms of Spontaneous Control

Under this section we group an additional set of items that are not mentioned in Tables 1.1 or 1.2. These items are directed at behavioral and cognitive symptoms of *reactance* (scale 19) to others' requests or wishes (e.g., "Defending myself against expectations from others") and items concerned with a general *effort-avoidance* (scale 20) tendency (e.g., "Preferring to do things that can easily be handled"). Both aspects reflect modes of acting that do without goal-maintaining volitional support, resulting from a more or less conscious refusal to engage in either the self-controlled or self-regulated mode of volition. Although reactance behavior itself may be mediated volitionally, it may render volitionally supported *self-chosen* action goals difficult to install and maintain: For example, the rebellious child may invest so much energy in resisting external control that she or he fails to perceive or do what she or he really wants to do. The decreased availability of functional volitional resources is also illustrated by a high degree of *spontane-*

ity (scale 21) in action. Subjects in this nonvolitional mode prefer to act spontaneously without careful planning, and they tend to improvise when facing difficulties (e.g., "Following spontaneous ideas").

Empirical Findings

Factor-Analytic Confirmation of Volitional Competence and
Reward- versus Punishment-Based Forms of Volitional Inhibition

The theoretically expected relationships between phenotypically divergent behavioral symptoms were surprisingly well confirmed by our factor-analytic findings (see columns F1, F2, and F3 in Tables 1.1 and 1.2): An initial principal-components analysis revealed five factors. Factor 4 was a specific factor related to the "spontaneous control" scales (scales 19 to 21) of the VCI. Factor 5 explained only specific variance related to the third action control scale (ACS) performance-related action orientation (AOP) assessing volatility versus persistence (Kuhl, 1994b). When we computed an additional analysis extracting the first three factors, only Varimax rotation resulted in a highly interpretable factorial pattern confirming central theoretical assumptions: The first factor (F1) showed significant loadings of those scales aiming at punishment-contingent inhibition of feeling and self (Table 1.2). As expected, we found a clear, though not substantial, overlap according to the criterion introduced by Fürntratt (1969), with the "preoccupation" scale of state orientation failure-related action orientation (AOF) and with "overcontrol" (scale 18). Factor 2 (F2) is characterized by volitional competencies, with components relating to self-regulation having the highest loadings followed by self-control components (Table 1.1). Finally a factor (F3) emerged that could best be described as expressing behavioral facilitation and internal control (scales 13–15 and 8–10). This factor showed the expected overlap with the enactment versus hesitation scale of decision-related action orientation (AOD) of the ACS (Table 1.2).

The fact that, as reflected by the self-regulation and the self-control scales, the two central components of volitional competence (self-maintenance and goal maintenance) load on one common factor (F2) is consistent with our theoretical assumption that there is one mode of volitional functioning characterized by a balanced *cooperation* of these more or less opposing types of central control (referred to as "self-regulation" in Table 1.1). The finding that nearly all the scales reflecting access to self-maintenance functions (scales 1 to 6) have higher loadings on this factor than the scales primarily addressing goal-maintenance functions might even be an indication of the theoretical expectation that a balanced cooperation of goal maintenance and self-maintenance can best be achieved when the latter function plays the leading role, that is, when the goals supported by goal-maintenance mechanisms are generated within the self-system (i.e., satisfy multiple constraints defined by interrelated needs, preferences, beliefs, norms, and other self-concerns).

Interestingly, nine out of eleven components of volitional competence (i.e., attention control, motivation control, decision control, self-determination, planning, initiating, and impulse control) had positive loadings on both the competence factor (F2) and the behavioral facilitation factor (F3). This finding can be interpreted in terms of two distinct aspects of *volition* captured by F2 and F3: While F2 describes the use of basic volitional strategies and mechanisms when *difficulties of enactment* are encountered (i.e., in situations that involve no frustration but that require centrally mediated adjustment of participating subsystems), F3 may reflect facilitated versus inhibited use of self-regulatory and self-control mechanisms and strategies when exposed to *frustration* (e.g., repeated failure). Specifically, F3 may assess whether the various components of volitional competence remain accessible when repeated attempts to attain a goal fail or whether experiences of frustration quickly drain the positive energy supposedly underlying this factor. The observable orthogonality of F3 with F1 underlines the factorial separability of the two modes of coping with threat (F1) versus frustration (F3), respectively. We expected the separability of these two modes of coping, on the basis of facilitation versus inhibition of reward (F1) and punishment systems (F3), respectively.

To the extent that perseverance of negative emotions (ruminative thinking and resulting behavioral inhibition) indicate an increased punishment sensitivity, the high loading of rigidity (scale 17) and (excessive) self-control (overcontrol, scale 18) on a common factor with scales of emotional perseveration (i.e., F1) is consistent with our hypothesis that negative emotionality reduces access to holistic "Feeling" (Figure 1.1). This effect is expected to result in rumination, alienation, and rigidity, because access to this system is needed to inhibit unwanted intrusions and to access alternative options for action. The fact that scales assessing external control (scale 15.2) and, to a lesser extent, informed introjection (scale 15.1) have high loadings on a different factor (F3) is consistent with the assumption that self-report measures of introjection assess informed more than misinformed introjection. According to the theory (see Figure 1.1) the former should load on a factor associated with low behavioral facilitation (energy deficit), which is the case (see F3 in Tables 1.1 and 1.2): Introjected and other directed goals can control behavior when the pathway from volitional systems to their output systems is inhibited.

Another important finding can be seen in the fact that each of the symptoms loading on the negative emotionality factor (F1 in Table 1.2) has also been experimentally demonstrated in subjects scoring high on the *preoccupation* factor of state orientation (SOF), which is characterized by uncontrollable ruminations about *aversive* events (Kuhl & Beckmann, 1994a). These experimental data confirm the assumption that elevated activity of the punishment system causes the inhibition of feeling and self-maintenance functions in these subjects (see Figure 1.1).

Empirical Findings Concerning the Validity of the Volitional Components Inventory

Validity of Scales Related to Resistance to Temptation. One traditional measure of strength of will is resistance to temptation – which depends, among other things, upon self-regulatory strategies of attention control (Patterson & Mischel, 1976). In addition, impulse control should be a basic prerequisite for the ability to maintain a goal despite tempting competing motivations. We examined the validity of VCI scales relevant to resistance to temptation (especially impulse control and attention control) by using a nonreactive measure of resistance to temptation. Theoretically, attention control must be distinguished from other forms of attentional selectivity that can work without volitional intervention (i.e., by attentional networks that do not involve the frontal volitional system). Neurophysiologically speaking, many forms of perceptual selectivity are supported by parietal and even subcortical systems (Posner & Rothbart, 1992). In contrast, we theorize that motivational temptations typically seem to invoke the type of *difficulty of enactment* that requires volitional (i.e., "prefrontal") intervention.

In one study we tried to differentiate experimentally between a perceptual and a motivational form of distraction (Kuhl & Kraska, 1992). We had two groups of subjects work on a visual search task located on one side of a computer screen. While they were trying to complete the task quickly, with as few errors as possible, in order to receive achievement-contingent payment, we repeatedly distracted them with an animated display on the other side of the screen. The study was run using a modified version of the self-regulation test for children (SRTC) test program for measuring children's self-regulation capabilities (Kuhl & Kraska, 1992). In the temptation condition, it was explained to the subjects ($N = 16$) that the simple black and white symbols moving along a vertical bar were "monkeys" performing a tree-climbing contest. Subjects were further told that whenever the black monkey reached the top of the tree before the white one, it would add some extra points to the subject's account. On the other hand, if the white monkey were first, it would steal some points from the subject's account (which was also visible in that area of the screen).

A second group of subjects ($N = 16$) were assigned to the nonmotivational distraction condition: These subjects were not informed of the significance of the distractors. Postsession interviews revealed that throughout the experiment, these subjects had no idea of the meaning of those moving symbols. Any interference of this condition with subjects' performance on the visual search task is thus attributable to physical properties of the stimuli (e.g., sudden onset, their size and movement), which presumably are predominantly controlled by nonvolitional mechanisms of selective attention. In contrast, performance decreases in the temptation group are more likely to be attributable to incentive aspects of the stimuli and the resulting attempts of subjects to cope volitionally with this situation.

The results of this experiment were clear: Subjects who were informed of the meaning of the distracting stimuli showed a significant increase in reaction times during temptation episodes when the visual search task was made difficult, that is, when an additional load was placed on the volitional system (alternating target search). Subjects who were not informed of stimulus meaning did not show a decrease in performance even in a condition in which volitional resources were invoked to cope with alternating targets for visual search (cf. Allport, Styles, & Hsieh, 1994). If our theoretical assumption is correct that motivationally loaded distraction requires the use of volitional strategies such as impulse control and attention control, then high scorers on these VCI scales would be likely to show less performance interference during temptation episodes than subjects who see themselves as having difficulties using these competences in everyday situations. This was exactly what we found when correlating subjects' VCI scale values with an index of performance deficits during distraction (Table 1.3). The analysis clearly showed that motivationally distracted subjects who had small drops in performance at the visual search task compared to the no-distraction baseline had relatively high values on the impulse control, initiating, and attention control VCI scales. In addition, these subjects showed a higher degree of positive volitional self-reflection in terms of feelings of self-determination, thus indicating with some probability a disposition toward the self-regulation mode of volition.

Validity of Scales Related to Alienation. Various indicators of manifest and latent alienation are reliably associated with individual differences in

Table 1.3. *Correlations between VCI (1 to 20) and ACS-90 (AOF, AOD, AOP) scale values and experimentally induced distraction costs (Reaction-time differences between a perceptual or a motivational distraction condition and a baseline without distraction)*

		Type of Distraction:	
	VCI scales[a]	Perceptual	Motivational
1	Attention control	n.s.	$-.53^{b}$
2	(Motivation control)	—	—
3	(Emotion control)	—	—
4.1	Arousal control/activating	n.s.	n.s.
5	Self-determination	n.s.	$-.53^{b}$
6	(Decision control)	—	—
7	(Intention control)	—	—
8	Planning	n.s.	n.s.
9	Initiating	n.s.	$-.56^{b}$
10	Impulse control	n.s.	$-.54^{b}$
11	(Failure control)	—	—
12	Volitional self-confidence	n.s.	n.s.
AOD	Enactment (vs. hesitation)	n.s.	n.s.
13	Energy deficit	n.s.	n.s.
14.1	Implicit rejection/intrusions	n.s.	n.s.
15.1	Alienation/informed introjection	n.s.	n.s.
15.2	Alienation/external control	n.s.	n.s.
AOF	Disengaggement (vs. preoccupation)	n.s.	n.s.
16	Emotional perseverance	n.s.	n.s.
17.1	Rigidity/behavioral shift costs	n.s.	n.s.
17.2	Rigidity/cognitive/perceptual rigidity	n.s.	n.s.
18	Overcontrol	n.s.	n.s.
19	Effort avoidance/reactance	n.s.	n.s.
20	(Spontaneity)	—	—
APO	Volatility (vs. persistence)	n.s.	n.s.

Note: While the perceptual condition models everyday distraction, the motivational condition simulates a temptation situation.
[a]An early version of the instrument was used. Scales set in parenthesis were not part of this version.
[b]$p < 0.05$.

action versus state orientation (Kuhl & Beckmann, 1994b). A study by Guevara (1994) used a newly designed experimental technique to induce and assess a phasic form of alienation in terms of brief inhibition of access to high-inferential representations of emotional preferences (i.e., integrated self-representations supported by the holistic "feeling" system). Guevara developed a task that required subjects to categorize a number of randomly generated pairs of black and white graphic designs according to their emotional preference for one of the two designs displayed on a computer screen.

Subjects were instructed to think of the patterns as representing wallpaper patterns from which they would have to choose for their own homes. Under the alienation treatment, emotionally tinted (positive or negative) standard words were displayed directly above each of the two patterns in a pair. Presumably, words rendered the subjects' access to holistic representations difficult because words tend to activate analytical processing more than holistic processing.

When the emotional words were "incongruently" matched with the side (left versus right) of the subjects' (formerly) preferred pattern – a positive word above a rejected pattern or a negative word above a preferred pattern – state-oriented subjects displayed a higher tendency to react in accordance with the newly introduced emotionality of the words even though they were not explicitly said to be of relevance to the task; subjects were instructed simply to repeat their initially given emotional preferences on the pattern-categorizing task. Thus the level of inconsistency with the subjects' former self-generated preference for one of the two patterns can serve as a nonreactive measure of alienation; reliable access to (holistic) representations of emotional preferences should result in an increased reliability of repeated judgments.

The results were consistent with theoretical expectations. The results derived from both dividing the sample in terciles according to this alienation index (i.e., retest reliability scores of repeated preference judgments) and inspecting VCI scale scores for the two extreme groups with regard to this objectively constructed measure of alienation (see Table 1.4) clearly support the validity of the VCI scales in addressing symptoms of alienation: Scores for informed introjection and external control of action were elevated in the high-alienation group (i.e., the group with low consistency of preference judgments). In addition, subjects with high alienation scores are marked by higher scores on the energy deficit and emotional perseverance scales and have a significantly lower score on self-determination. These findings are consistent with our theory (Figure 1.1) that alienation results from low behavioral facilitation and low positive affect as indexed by a high score on energy deficit and/or high tonic punishment sensitivity as indexed by emotional perseverance.[3]

In another study, the VCI was administered to three clinical groups that included patients with alcohol addiction, anxiety disorders, or overeating disorders, and a control group that consisted of university students (Table 1.5).[4] Subjects in the alcohol addiction group showed no marked differences with the control group, but exhibited a slight overall trend toward heightened self-regulatory competence scores and lowered scores for scales

Table 1.4. *VCI (1 to 20) and ACS-90 (AOF, AOD, AOP) scale values for two extreme-groups (n = 12) of subjects (students)*

	VCI scales[a]	High alienation from emotional preferences	Low alienation from emotional preferences
1	Attention control	3.4	3.5
2	(Motivation control)	—	—
3	(Emotion control)	—	—
4.1	Arousal control/activating	3.6[d]	3.2
5	Self-determination	3.1	3.6[c]
6	(Decision control)	—	—
7	(Intention control)	—	—
8	Planning	3.2	3.5
9	Initiating	3.1	3.3
10	Impulse control	2.7	2.6
11	(Failure control)	—	—
12	Volitional self-confidence	3.6	3.8
AOD[b]	Enactment (vs. hesitation)	4.9	7.2[c]
13	Energy deficit	2.6[d]	2.0
14.1	Implicit rejection/intrusions	2.7[c]	2.2
15.1	Alienation/informed introjection	2.6[d]	2.0
15.2	Alienation/external control	2.7[d]	2.2
AOF[b]	Disengagement (vs. preoccupation)	3.9	7.1[e]
16	Emotional perseverance	2.6[d]	2.1
17.1	Rigidity/behavioral shift costs	2.8	2.7
17.2	Rigidity/cognitive/perceptual rigidity	3.3	3.4
18	Overcontrol	3.1[d]	2.5
19	Effort avoidance/reactance	2.7	2.5
20	(Spontaneity)	—	—
AOP	Volatility (vs. persistence)	8.0	10.5[e]

Note: Scales set in parentheses were not part of this earlier version of the instrument. Subjects showed either (1) low temporal stability of their emotional preference reactions after an experimental alienation treatment (incidental pairing of affectively categorized graphical patterns with emotionally incongruent words) or (2) high temporal stability of their emotional preference reactions after the alienation treatment.
[a]Range of scale means: 1–5.
[b]Range of scale sums: 0–12.
[c]$p < 0.10$.
[d]$p < 0.05$.
[e]$p < 0.01$.
Source: Guevara (1994).

measuring volitional inhibition. This trend is quite consistent with our application of the second affect modulation hypothesis to the psychological effects of alcohol consumption: To the extent that alcohol reduces negative emotionality (Gray, 1987), it should facilitate the accessibility of holistic feeling and self-maintenance functions. This interpretation appears paradoxical in light of the loss of volitional control that is associated with any

Table 1.5. *VCI scale means for three clinical samples and one sample of control subjects (students) (Control: n = 21; 15 women; age 19–35; median of age = 26)*

VCI Scales		Control	Alcohol (1)	Anxiety (2)	Eating (3)
1	Attention control	3.1	3.3a	2.6b	2.8
2	Motivation control	3.2	3.3a	2.5b*	2.5b*
3	Emotion control	3.0	3.1a	2.4b*	2.2b*
4	Arousal control	3.0	3.2a	2.1b*	2.3b*
5	Self-determination	3.1	3.3a	2.4b	2.4b*
6	Decision control	3.1	3.2a	2.4b	2.6b
7	Intention control	3.3	3.2a	2.5b*	2.5b*
8	Planning	3.4	3.6	3.4	3.1
9	Initiating	2.7	3.2a	2.2b	1.9b
10	Impulse control	2.8	3.2a	2.8	2.5b
11	Failure control	3.4	3.2	3.0	2.9
12	Volitional self-confidence	3.5	3.3	2.5	2.4
13	Energy deficit	2.7	2.5b	2.8b	3.6a*
14	Implicit rejection	2.9	2.5b	2.8	3.1a
15.1	Alienation/informed introjection	3.0	2.8b	3.5a	3.8a*
15.2	Alienation/external control	2.7	2.2	2.6	2.6
16.1	Emotional perseverance/ruminative thinking	2.8	3.1	3.5	3.6*
16.2	Emotional perseverance/blocking of action	2.6	2.7	3.3	3.4*
17	Rigidity	2.7	2.8	3.3	3.4*
18	Overcontrol	3.0	3.0	3.5	3.5
19	Effort avoidance/reactance	2.9	3.0b	3.5	3.6a*
20	Spontaneity	3.1	3.3a	2.7b	2.6b*

Notes: The three clinical groups covered the following disorders: Alcohol addiction (alcohol: n = 25; 7 women; age 32–58; median of age = 40), anxiety disorders (Anxiety: n = 20; 13 women; age 17–66; median of age = 39.5), and eating disorders (Eating: n = 19; 14 women, age 24–45; median of age = 29). The scale values shown are based upon a short form of the instrument (split half), which showed satisfactory reliabilities of the scales (Cronbach's alpha > 0.70). The table indicates significant differences between the groups analyzed through one-way-ANOVAS and post hoc comparisons of pairs (Scheffé tests).
(1) Patients of the Landeskrankenhaus Osnabrück: (a) patients showed no signs of additional substance abuse, (b) patients were not under the acute influence of medication, and (c) organic diseases of the brain were ruled out at the time of study.
(2) Patients of the Christoph-Dornier Center for Clinical Psychology, Münster. Diagnoses in the sample: social phobias, panic disorders (with and without agoraphobia), specific phobias, and generalized anxiety disorders. The conductors of the study had no access to individual diagnoses.
(3) Patients of the Paracelsus-Wittekindsklinik, Bad Essen, and members of Overeaters Anonymous, Osnabrück. Diagnoses: bulimia (n = 12) and adipositas (n = 7).
*Significant differences of means between clinical group and control group.
a,b Significant differences of means between the clinical groups marked with different indexes.

kind of addiction. Possibly, the latter volitional impairments are confined to the control of the addiction, at least in an early or less severe stage of alcoholism. An alternative interpretation would be that alcoholics *overestimate* their volitional competence as a result of excessive self-maintenance. Since the latter effect is also consistent with the theoretically expected reduction of negative emotionality resulting from alcohol consumption, we cannot discriminate between these two interpretations on the basis of the present data.

The anxiety and eating disorders groups showed some interesting differences in comparison with normal subjects. Both of these clinical groups had significantly reduced values of the basic volitional mechanism of arousal control and reduced strategic competences of intention control, motivation control, and emotion control. Subjects with eating disorders also showed a significantly lower score in feelings of self-determination and higher scores than control subjects on the emotional perseverance, energy deficit, rigidity, and informed introjection scales as one aspect of alienation (see Table 1.5). Identification of specific deficits associated with an individual disorder can be useful in guiding therapy. The decomposition of volitional competence provided by the VCI can be useful for deciding which specific steps should be taken at which stages during therapy to optimize overall effectiveness. This approach is compatible with modern behavioral approaches to the therapy of volitional deficits that can be used for strengthening both self-controlling and self-regulatory functions (Kanfer & Schefft, 1988).

In light of the many similarities of patients with anxiety and eating disorders with regard to volitional deficits, the only significant difference between the two groups deserves special attention: Energy deficit scores were significantly higher in the eating disorder group than in the anxiety group of patients. This result is in accordance with findings suggesting that anxiety is associated with agitated emotionality and behavior whereas eating disorders may be associated with dejected emotionality and low sensitivity for reward (Higgins, 1987). It should be noted, however, that anxiety cannot be equated with punishment sensitivity and its link with inhibition of feeling and self-maintenance (i.e., failure-related state orientation). According to several factor-analytic and experimental studies, anxiety and state orientation can dissociate: Individuals can feel afraid without losing access to their feelings and self-representations and without having ruminative thoughts, and they can show the latter signs of state orientation without feeling afraid (Kuhl & Beckmann, 1994a).

VCI-Correlates of the Big Five Personality Dimensions

In a study conducted by Holling, Wübbelmann, and Geldschläger (1994), the VCI was used in conjunction with the Neuroticism-Extraversion-Openness Five-Factor-Inventory (NEO-FFI), the German adaptation of Costa and McCrae's Five-Factor Inventory (Borkenau & Ostendorf, 1991) and a measure

Table 1.6. *Correlations between VCI scale values and the scales of the NEO-FFI[a] and the IST-70 IQ.*

	VCI scales	NEU	EXT	OPE	AGR	CON	IQ
1	Attention control	$-.39^d$	$.49^d$	.15	.20	$.38^d$	$-.04$
2	Motivation control	$-.27^d$	$.51^d$	$.33^d$	.18	$.35^d$	$-.26^c$
3	Emotion control	$-.17$	$.43^d$	$.38^d$	.10	$.36^d$	$-.20$
4	[Arousal control]	$-.35^d$	$.45^d$	$.28^c$	.23	.12	$-.22$
5	Self-determination	$-.68^d$	$.50^d$	$.24^c$	.05	$.27^c$	.04
6	Decision control	$-.52^d$	$.36^d$	.00	$-.08$	.23	$-.04$
7	[Intention control]	$-.13$	$.36^d$	.08	$.25^c$	.18	$-.13$
8	Planning	$-.18$	$-.38^d$	.14	.13	$.45^d$	$-.07$
9	[Initiating]	$-.40^d$	$.46^d$	.17	.09	.18	$-.15$
10	Impulse control	$-.33^d$	.07	.00	.11	$.26^c$	.06
11	[Failure control]	$-.40^d$	$.43^d$	.13	$.29^c$	$.49^d$	$-.10$
12	Volitional self-confidence	$-.63^d$	$.72^d$	$.36^d$	.12	$.32^d$	$-.14$
13	Energy deficit	$.52^d$	$-.40^d$	$-.01$	$-.03$	$-.22$	.05
14	Implicit rejection	$.51^d$	$-.31^d$	$-.09$	$-.10$	$-.35^d$	.05
15.1	Alienation/informed introjection	$.43^d$	$-.02$	.00	.16	.04	.12
15.2	Alienation/external control	.20	.01	.10	$-.07$	$-.30^d$	$-.01$
16.1	Emotional perseverance/ ruminative thinking	$.74^d$	$-.45^d$	$-.23$	$-.12$	$-.28^c$	.05
16.2	Emotional perseverance/ blocking of action	$.70^d$	$-.45^d$	$-.21$	$-.09$	$-.36^d$	.07
17	Rigidity	$.45^d$	$-.46^d$	$-.21$	$-.08$	$-.27^c$	$-.10$
18	[Overcontrol]	$.52^d$	$-.17$	$-.13$	$-.10$	$-.20$	$-.07$
19	[Efffort avoidance/ reactance]	$.49^d$	$-.52^d$	$-.20$	$-.09$	$-.13$	$-.09$
20	[Spontaneity]	$.32^d$	.00	.07	.02	$-.21$	$-.14$

Notes: The sample ($n = 76$) consists off 29 men and 47 women between ages 20 and 27 (mean age = 23.2) from diverse, nonacademical professions. The VCI was used in an abbreviation form split half). For a few scales, satisfactory reliabilities were not achieved in this sample (Cronbach's alpha > 0.50 and < 0.70). These scales are shown in brackets. NEU = neuroticism; EXT = extraversion; OPE = openness to experience; AGR = agreeableness; CON = conscientiousness.
[a]Borkenau & Ostendorf (1991).
[b]Amthauer (1973).
[c]$p < 0.05$.
[d]$p < 0.01$.

for general intelligence, the IST-70 (Amthauer, 1973). According to our affect modulation hypothesis to the extent that extraversion and neuroticism are associated with sensitivity to reward and punishment, respectively, we expected some overlap with VCI scales, which are also related to reward and punishment. Consistent with these expectations, the correlational analysis revealed an overlap of nearly all VCI scales with neuroticism and extraversion as measured by the NEO-FFI (Table 1.6). Scales that indicate an impaired accessibility of volitional competences available show a positive relationship with neuroticism and a negative correlation with extraversion. This is especially salient for the two scales measuring aspects of emotional perseverance after failure. The content of these scales certainly bears a close relationship to emotional lability, which is one aspect of the NEO-FFI neuroticism scale. The three VCI scales showing the highest correlation with extraversion were volitional self-confidence, feelings of self-determination, and motivation control. The two former scales also show a significant negative relationship with neuroticism.

How can we interpret this pattern of results from a theoretical point of view? The broad and generally moderate overlap of the scales with neuroticism and extraversion does not necessarily mean that we are measuring these same constructs under different labels. The pattern of correlations is not consistent with such an interpretation because several VCI scales have significant correlations across three or four "big five" dimensions. The pattern of correlations is more consistent with the assumption that neuroticism, introversion, and volitional inhibition share negative emotionality as a common characteristic. We have already outlined our understanding of the role negative emotionality plays in the context of an interaction of the macrosystems of personality (including the two basic motivational systems of punishment and reward).

Specifically, the factors of extraversion and neuroticism may be more saturated with individual differences in sensitivity to reward and punishment, respectively, than with the impact of either motivational system on volitional functions. This interpretation is based on the assumption that the links between motivational systems and cognitive as well as volitional functions depend on more factors than activational strength of reward and punishment systems alone. For example, the inhibitory effect of negative emotionality might be more pronounced in some individuals (e.g., in state-oriented ones) than in others. According to our theory, state orientation is based on an acquired disposition to inhibit volitional functions under stress or frustration.

This assumption was corroborated by results from a study comparing identical and fraternal twins: Whereas earlier findings showing higher concordance regarding extraversion and neuroticism in identical twins as compared to fraternal twins were replicated, no indication of a genetic component was found with regard to state orientation (Kästele, 1988). These results are in accordance with the theoretical claim that whereas the sensitivity to reward and punishment might have a genetic component, the links between volitional inhibition and reduced reward sensitivity or heightened punishment sensitivity, respectively, may be based on early learning. Results confirming this expected relationship between socialization and state-oriented patterns of coping are available (Kästele, 1988; Keller & Gauda, 1987). To the extent that volitional inhibition is based on an originally adaptive strategy of reducing volitional control in an unpredictable environment, its dependence on early learning is theoretically plausible.

We also explain the correlations of volitional functions across several "big five" dimensions as an indication that volitional functions can be facilitated through several alternative "sources of energy" stemming from orthogonal sources. For example, attention control can be facilitated (1) through the system that dampens perseveration of negative emotionality (i.e., the reverse of neuroticism), or (2) through the system that mediates positive incentive motivation and facilitation of incentive-seeking instrumental behavior (e.g., extraversion), or (3) through the system that mediates performance of elaborated behavioral routines and habits (e.g., conscientiousness), and so on.[5]

Concluding Remarks

The empirical correlates of the various components of volition and volitional inhibition provide surprisingly consistent support for the validity of the VCI scales and the theoretical assumptions they are based upon. Nonetheless, attempts to explore the various functional components that may be reflected in self-report measures of personality should not be carried too far. To the extent that psychologists do not want to replace the psychology of personality by a psychology of subjective theories of personality as assessed by questionnaires, they should take the initiative in the search for better ways of isolating functional components of personality than can ever be achieved by self-report measures. Because psychologists can specify those functional components much better now than was possible in the past (Figure 1.1), such a new start is very promising: Today they can develop objective methods providing less confounded measures of specific system components (e.g., reward sensitivity, inhibition of self-representations, attention control, etc.) than can be achieved by self-report instruments. Our own standardized instruments for obtaining nonreactive measures of volitional components point in that direction (Kuhl & Kraska, 1992), as do a variety of nonreactive measures reported in the recent literature, for example, measures of reward and punishment sensitivity (Derryberry & Reed, 1994), reward and punishment effects on cognitive functioning (Isen, 1987), and nonreactive measures of volitional functions such as delayed response and response alternation tasks (e.g., Allport, Styles, & Hsieh, 1994; Fuster, 1989). Obviously, it would be impossible to evaluate by objective methods as many functional components as assessed by the VCI (which has up to thirty components) within a reasonable amount of time. Therefore, the VCI may be considered a useful screening instrument for discovering those components that may be related to other variables of interest. The validity of relationships suggested by correlations between individual VCI scales and other variables can then be tested by employing objective methods, as illustrated by our study on resistance to temptation.

In conclusion, we emphasize the finding that there is virtually no evidence for a substantial relationship between VCI scales and general intelligence (see Table 1.6) – with the exception of a low correlation with motivation control. This result strongly confirms one of our central assumptions regarding volitional competence and volitional efficiency: Volitional functions cannot be equated with general intelligence. Learning difficulties, behavioral deficits, and emotional problems associated with self-regulatory impairments are independent of intellectual deficits. A child may fail at school despite having sufficient motivation and intellectual abilities if he or she has not developed appropriate volitional mechanisms and strategies, or if available volitional competence cannot be accessed under conditions of stress or frustration. A depressed person's problems may be caused not primarily by invalid negative controllability beliefs but by *actual* deficits in volitional functioning that may be caused by abnormal levels of positive and/or negative emotionality. A husband or wife having substantial conflicts with her or his spouse because daily he or she is not performing everyday chores may not really be lazy, poorly motivated, or even guided by unfavorable gender stereotypes.

Each of the problems mentioned may be based on impairments of metacognitive abilities related to the tasks we have attributed to the volitional system in our theory: the central coordination of the many states and operations across various subsystems may thus be impaired. The difference between this theoretical alternative and competing interpretations is not trivial: Whenever a volitional impairment is identified as the primary cause, different steps are indicated than when primary deficits in terms of (invalid) controllability beliefs, lack of interest, or impaired intellectual abilities are the root of the problem. To the extent that impaired volitional functioning is involved, changing cognitive beliefs and emotional encouragement alone may not be sufficient. That is, blaming the spouse for being prejudiced or uninterested may be inappropriate, just as it is not very helpful to blame a disabled person for not being motivated or for having insufficient self-confidence to get out of a wheelchair and walk.

The time when people responded in such inappropriate ways to mentally or physically disabled individuals is only in the recent past, if indeed it is in the past. There is no mental domain where the distinction between the controllable and the uncontrollable is as difficult to define as in the domain of volitional abilities: The ability to meet goals such as finishing daily chores or maintaining a diet may be controllable for one person and uncontrollable for another, depending on the availability and accessibility of volitional competences such as attention control, motivation control, initiative, and so on. To the extent that individuals learn to understand the functional characteristics of this most complex of all mental functions, their way of treating people who have mild or severe forms of volitional impairments will change dramatically.

Moreover, psychologists will be in a better position to appreciate the adaptive aspects of what might appear to be a maladaptive deficit. Note that the volitional impairments associated with state orientation occur under conditions of frustration or stress only. In friendly and safe environments, state-oriented subjects are expected to perform at least as well as action-oriented ones – or even better. The fact that researchers know much more about the deficits associated with state orientation under stressful conditions than about its benefits under friendly conditions reflects a societal bias: They seem to be more interested in how people perform under stress than how they function in friendly, warm, and accepting environments. Recent results show that indexes of volitional inhibition can be reversed when individuals move from stressful to relaxed conditions. In one study, state-oriented subjects had *superior* performance in a self-paced complex learning task (comprehension of an unfamiliar study text) when they could work without time pressure under relaxed instruction (Menec, 1995). We found analogous results in our EEG lab: Positive slow potential shifts over prefrontal electrodes, usually associated with volitional inhibition and impaired performance when state-oriented subjects are exposed to some sort of stress (Haschke & Kuhl, 1994; Rosahl, Tennigkeit, Kuhl, & Haschke, 1993), turned into *negative* slow potential shifts when "friendly" conditions were signaled by brief exposures to positive words such as "success" and "friend" (Kuhl, Schapkin, & Gusew, 1994).

Undoubtedly, reduced accessibility of volitional functions as it occurs under stressful conditions can have detrimental effects, especially when it contributes to depression, obsessive-compulsive disorder, and the like (Hartung & Schulte, 1994; Hautzinger, 1994; Kuhl & Helle, 1986). However, mild forms of volitional inhibition might have some adaptive aspects. From the biased perspective of an industrial society that focuses almost exclusively on those rational and self-regulatory functions that may have developed for predictable environments during evolution, people may have an incomplete view of the adaptive sides of volitional inhibition under stress. In light of the many unpredictable risks that seem to threaten the human species and the planet in general today, people might even learn to have a greater appreciation for the positive sides of a state of mind that is sensitive to the *unpredictable* risks in this world than for a state of mind more suited to the action-oriented coping style.

Notes

1. This case should be distinguished from "informed introjection," which would apply when the medical student knows about the incompatibility between her parents' expectations and her own preferences and has decided to comply. In this case, the behavior can be supported by at least parts of integrated self-representations.
2. Neurophysiologically, incentive-independent behavioral facilitation of habitual or introjected routines might be attributable to the nigrostriatal dopamine system of the brain. Requests imposed by others may directly activate this system (provided the behavioral routines conforming with a request are available) *without* additional facilitation through incentive-based (e.g., amygdala) or self-based (e.g., prefrontal cortex) systems.
3. The relationship between emotional perseverance and informed introjection suggests that the latter scale may partially reflect punishment-based *misinformed* introjection as well. This conclusion is further confirmed by the moderate loading of informed introjection on the punishment-related factor (Table 1.2) in addition to its loading on the reward-related factor.
4. We thank Katy Knopf and Ricarda Schmidt for running this experiment.
5. On a neurophysiological level, these three behavioral facilitation systems may be supported by three different dopaminergic systems, respectively: the mesocortical, the mesolimbic, and the nigrostriatal.

References

Allport, D. A., Styles, E. A., & Hsieh, S. (1994). Shifting intentional set: Exploring the dynamic control of tasks. In C. Umilta & M. Moscovitch (Eds.), *Attention and performance XV: Conscious and unconscious information processing.* Cambridge, MA: MIT Press.

Amthauer, R. (1973). *Intelligenz-Struktur-Test 70* [Intelligence-Structure Test, IST 70]. Göttingen: Hogrefe.

Bandura, A. (1982). Self-efficacy mechanism in human agency. *American Psychologist, 37,* 122–147.

Beeman, M., Friedman, R. B., Grafman, J., Perez, E., Diamond, S., Lindsay, M. B.

(1994). Summation priming and coarse semantic coding in the right hemisphere. *Journal of Cognitive Neuroscience, 6,* 26–45.

Block, J. H., & Block, J. (1982). The role of ego-control and ego-resiliency in the organization of behavior. In W. A. Collins (Ed.), *Development of cognition, affect, and social relations: The Minnesota Symposium on Child Psychology* (pp. 39–101). Hillsdale, NJ: Erlbaum.

Borkenau, P., & Ostendorf, F. (1991). Ein Fragebogen zur Erfassung fünf robuster Persönlichkeitsfaktoren [A questionnaire for the measurement of five robust personality factors]. *Diagnostica, 37,* 29–41.

Deci, E. L., & Ryan, R. M. (1991). A motivational approach to self: Integration in personality. In E. Dienstbier (Ed.), *Nebraska Symposium on Motivation* (pp. 237–288). Lincoln, NE: University of Nebraska Press.

Derryberry, D., & Reed, M. A. (1994). Temperament and attention: Orienting toward and away from positive and negative signals. *Journal of Personality and Social Psychology, 66,* 1128–1139.

Diaz, R. M., Neal, C. J., & Amaya-Williams, M. (1990). The social origins of self-regulation. In L. Moll (Ed.), *Vygotsky and education.* Cambridge, MA: Harvard University Press.

Diener, C. J., & Dweck, C. S. (1978). An analysis of learned helplessness: Continuous changes in performance, strategy, and achievement cognitions following failure. *Journal of Personality and Social Psychology, 36,* 451–462.

Epstein, S. (1994). Integration of the cognitive and the psychodynamic unconscious. *American Psychologist, 49,* 709–724.

Fürntratt, E. (1969). Zur Bestimmung der Anzahl interpretierbarer gemeinsamer Faktoren in Faktorenanalysen psychologischer Daten [Determining the numer of interpretable common factors in factor analysis of psychological data]. *Diagnostica, 15,* 62–75.

Fuster, J. M. (1989). *The prefrontal cortex.* 2d ed. New York: Raven Press.

Gray, J. A. (1987). *The psychology of fear and stress.* 2d ed. Cambridge, UK: Cambridge University Press.

Guevara, M. L. (1994). *Alienation und Selbstkontrolle: Das Ignorieren eigener Gefühle.* [Alienation and self-control: Ignoring one's preferences]. Bern: Lang.

Hartung, J., & Schulte, D. (1994). Action and state orientation during therapy of phobic disorders. In J. Kuhl & J. Beckmann (Eds.), *Volition and personality: Action versus state orientation.* Göttingen/Seattle, WA: Hogrefe.

Haschke, R., & Kuhl, J. (1994). Action control and slow potential shifts. *Proceedings of the 41st International Congress of Aviation and Space Medicine.* Bologna: Monduzzi.

Hautzinger, M. (1994). Action control in the context of psychopathological disorders. In J. Kuhl & J. Beckmann (Eds.), *Volition and personality: Action versus state orientation* (pp. 209–215). Seattle, WA: Hogrefe.

Higgins, E. T. (1987). Self-discrepancy: A theory relating self and affect. *Psychological Review, 94,* 319–340.

Holling, H., Wübbelmann, K., & Geldschläger, H. (1994). *4. Zwischenbericht des BMFT-Projektes Begabtenförderung und berufliche Bildung: Die Auswahl der Stipendiaten in der Förderpraxis des Programms und Weiterentwicklung der Kriterien und Instrumente zum Erkennen besonderer beruflicher Leistungsfähigkeit und Begabung in der Berufs/Förderpraxis* [4th intermediate report on the BMFT project on funding highly gifted students in occupational training areas]. Münster: Universität Münster.

Isen, A. M. (1987). Positive affect, cognitive processes, and social behavior. In L. Berkowitz (Ed.), *Advances in experimental social psychology,* Vol. 20 (pp. 203–253). New York: Academic Press.

Jung, C. G. (1936/1990). *Typologie.* München: dtv.

Kästele, G. (1988). Anlage- und umweltbedingte Determinanten der Handlungs- und Lageorientierung nach Mißerfolg im Vergleich zu anderen Persönlichkeitseigenschaften [Genetic and environmental determinants of action- and state-orientation after failure in comparison with other personality characteristics]. Unpublished dissertation. University of Osnabrück, Germany.

Kanfer, F. H., & Schefft, B. K. (1988). *Guiding the process of therapeutic change.* Champaign, IL: Research Press.

Keller, H., & Gauda, G. (1987). Eye contact in the first months of life and its developmental consequences. In H. Rau & H. C. Steinhauser (Eds.), *Psychobiology and early development* (pp. 129–143). Amsterdam: Elsevier.

Knight, R. T., & Grabowecky, M. (1995). Escape from linear time: Prefrontal cortex and conscious experience. In M. S. Gazzaniga (Ed.), *The cognitive neurosciences.* Cambridge, MA: MIT Press.

Kolb, B., & Wishaw, I. Q. (1990). *Fundamentals of human neuropsychology.* New York: Freeman.

Kopp, C. B. (1982). Antecedents of self-regulation: A developmental perspective. *Developmental Psychology, 18,* 199–214.

Kuhl, J. (1982). Handlungskontrolle als metakognitver Vermittler zwischen Intention und Handeln: Freizeitaktivitäten bei Hauptschülern [Action control as a metacognitive mediator between intention and action]. *Zeitschrift für Entwicklungspsychologie und Pädagogische Psychologie, 14,* 141–148.

Kuhl, J. (1983a). *Motivation, Konflikt und Handlungskontrolle* [Motivation, conflict and action control]. Heidelberg/New York: Springer.

Kuhl, J. (1983b). Emotion, Kognition und Motivation: II. Die funktionale Bedeutung der Emotionen für das problemlösende Denken und für das konkrete Handeln [Emotion, cognition and motivation II: The functional status of emotions for problem-solving and concrete action]. *Sprache & Kognition, 4,* 228–253.

Kuhl, J. (1984). Volitional aspects of achievement motivation and learned helplessness: Toward a comprehensive theory of action-control. In B. A. Maher (Ed.), *Progress in Experimental Personality Research,* Vol. 13 (pp. 99–171). New York: Academic Press.

Kuhl, J. (1992). A theory of self-regulation: Action versus state orientation, self-discrimination, and some applications. *Applied Psychology: An International Review, 41,* 95–173.

Kuhl, J. (1994a). Motivation and volition. In G. d'Ydewalle, P. Bertelson, & P. Eelen (Eds.), *Current advances in psychological science: An international perspective.* Hillsdale, NJ: Erlbaum.

Kuhl, J. (1994b). Action versus state orientation: Psychometric properties of the Action-Control-Scale (ACS-90). In J. Kuhl & J. Beckmann (Eds.), *Action control: From cognition to behavior.* Göttingen/Toronto: Hogrefe.

Kuhl, J. (1995). Motivation und Persönlichkeit: Koalitionen neuropsychischer Systeme [Motivation and personality: Architectures of mind and body]. Manuscript. University of Osnabrück, Germany.

Kuhl, J., & Beckmann, J. (1994a). *Volition and personality: Action versus state orientation.* Göttingen/Seattle, WA: Hogrefe.

Kuhl, J., & Beckmann, J. (1994b). Alienation: Ignoring one's preferences. In J. Kuhl & J. Beckmann (Eds.), *Volition and personality: Action versus state orientation.* Göttingen/Seattle, WA: Hogrefe.

Kuhl, J., & Helle, P. (1986). Motivational and volitional determinants of depression: The degenerated-intention hypothesis. *Journal of Abnormal Psychology, 95,* 247–251.

Kuhl, J., & Kraska, K. (1992). *Der Selbstregulations- und Konzentrationstest für Kinder (SRKT-K)* [The self-regulation test for children (SRTC)]. Göttingen/Seattle, WA: Hogrefe.

Kuhl, J. Schapkin, S., & Gusew, A. (1994). *A theory of volitional inhibition and an empirical test: Individual differences in the topography of ERP patterns for action- versus state-oriented processing of emotional words.* Research Report No. 99. University of Osnabrück, Germany.

Labouvie-Vief, G., Hakim-Larson, J., DeVoe, M., & Schoeberlein, S. (1989). Emotions and self-regulation: A life span view. *Human Development, 32,* 279–299.

Leontjev, A. N. (1977). Tätigkeit, Bewußtsein, Persönlichkeit [Activity, consciousness, personality]. Stuttgart: Klett.

Luria, A. R. (1973). *The working brain.* London: Penguin.

Meichenbaum, D. (1986). Metacognitive methods of instruction: Current status and future prospects. *Special Services in the Schools, 3,* 23–32.

Menec, V. H. (1995). *Volition and motivation: The effect of distracting learning conditions on students differing in action control and perceived control.* Dissertation. University of Manitoba.

Mischel, H. N., & Mischel, W. (1983). The development of children's knowledge of self-control strategies. *Child Development, 54,* 603–619.

Mischel, W. (1974). Processes in delay of gratification. In L. Berkowitz (Ed.), *Advances in experimental social psychology,* Vol. 7 (pp. 249–292). New York: Academic Press.

Nakagawa, A. (1991). Role of anterior and posterior attention networks in hemisphere asymmetries during lexical decisions. *Journal of Cognitive Neuroscience, 3,* 313–321.

Paivio, A. (1983). The empirical case for dual coding. In H. Yuille (Ed.), *Imagery, memory, and cognition* (pp. 397–432). Hillsdale, NJ: Erlbaum.

Patterson, C., & Mischel, W. (1976). Effects of temptation-inhibiting and task-facilitating plans on self-control. *Journal of Personality and Social Psychology, 33,* 209–217.

Posner, M. I., & Rothbart, M. K. (1992). Attentional mechanisms and conscious experience. In A. D. Milner & M. D. Rugg (Eds.), *The neuropsychology of consciousness* (pp. 91–111). New York: Academic Press.

Rosahl, S. K., Tennigkeit, M., Kuhl, J., & Haschke, R. (1993). Handlungskontrolle und langsame Hirnpotentiale: Untersuchungen zum Einfluß subjektiv kritischer Wörter (Erste Ergebnisse) [Action-control and slow brain potentials: Investigations on the influence of subjectively critical words (first results)]. *Zeitschrift für Medizinische Psychologie, 2,* 1–8.

Ryan, R. M. (1995). Psychological needs and the facilitation of integrative processes. *Journal of Personality, 63,* 397–427.

Shallice, T. (1988). *From neuropsychology to mental structure.* Cambridge: Cambridge University Press.

Stuss, D. T., & Benson, D. F. (1984). Neuropsychological studies of the frontal lobes. *Psychological Bulletin, 95,* 3–28.

Vygotski, L. S. (1978). *Mind in society: The development of higher psychological processes.* Cambridge, MA: Harvard University Press.

Wittling, W. (1990). Psychophysiological correlates of human brain asymmetry: Blood pressure changes during lateralized presentation of an emotionally laden film. *Neuropsychologia, 28,* 457–470.

2 Developmental Regulation in Adulthood: Selection and Compensation via Primary and Secondary Control

Jutta Heckhausen and Richard Schulz

Abstract

A life-span theory of control (J. Heckhausen & Schulz, 1995) is presented along with a set of empirical findings on the theory's implications for developmental regulation. Human behavior in general and human development in particular have to fulfill two fundamental requirements. Investment of behavioral resources (time, effort, skill, motivation) has to be selective, and inevitable failure experiences need to be compensated to protect motivational resources for action. The life-span theory of control distinguishes between primary control and secondary control. Primary control is directed at the external world and refers to attempts to change the environment in line with the individual's goals. Secondary control addresses internal processes and serves to minimize losses in, to maintain, and to expand existing levels of primary control. Both primary and secondary control processes serve to achieve selectivity in resource investment and the compensation of failure. Thus, four strategies of developmental regulation can be identified: selective primary control, compensatory primary control, selective secondary control, and compensatory secondary control. These four strategies are regulated by a higher-order process that aims at optimizing primary control across the life span. At different points in the life span, developmental regulation has to be adapted to shifting levels of primary control potential across age-related changes. Moreover, different socioeconomic life ecologies provide structures of opportunities and constraints, which the individual has to take into account for successful regulation of development.

This chapter presents findings from four studies that demonstrate the scope and limits of developmental regulation in adults at different ages and in contrasting socioeconomic life ecologies. Moreover, empirical support for the feasibility and usefulness of identifying four strategies of developmental regulation and a regulatory process of developmental optimization is discussed.

Introduction

This chapter first presents a life-span theory of control that Richard Schulz and I have developed over the past few years (J. Heckhausen & Schulz, 1993, 1995; Schulz & J. Heckhausen, 1996; Schulz, J. Heckhausen, & Locher, 1991). This theory will then be extended and specified with regard to phenomena involved in individuals' attempts to regulate their own development, thus outlining a life-span model of successful aging (Schulz & J. Heckhausen, 1995). Finally, the life-span theory of control will be applied to findings from various studies of developmental regulation (J. Heckhausen, 1998).

The Life-Span Theory of Control

The life-span theory of control conceives of the individual as the agent in development (Brandtstädter, 1984; Ryan, 1993) and focuses on the individual's ability to control his or her environment. It may be argued that striving for control, "competence" (White, 1959), or "mastery" (Harter, 1974) is not the only fundamental striving or need motivating human behavior. A group of scholars at the University of Rochester (Connell & Wellborn, 1991; Deci, Connell, & Ryan, 1985; Deci & Ryan, 1985; Ryan, 1995, Chapter 4, this volume; Ryan, Deci, & Grolnick, 1995), for instance, have proposed a triad of fundamental human needs: autonomy, competence, and (social) relatedness. The present approach addresses control striving as one of probably very few fundamental motivating systems for human behavior.

Basic Requirements of Human Functioning: Selectivity and Failure Compensation

The life-span theory starts from the assumption that in order to be effective, any human behavior needs to fulfill two basic requirements: the management of selectivity and the compensation of failure experiences (J. Heckhausen & Schulz, 1993, 1995). Both these requirements result from the extensive variability and flexibility of human behavior.

Because of the great flexibility and therefore immense scope of human behavior, the individual needs to select out specific behavioral options and protect this selection against competing action tendencies. This requires a powerful system of motivational and volitional regulation, which guides the *choice* of action goals and also safeguards and enhances focused commitment to a chosen action goal. These two aspects of selectivity – choice and focus – correspond to the distinction between motivation and volition in motivational psychology, proposed and elaborated by Julius Kuhl, Heinz Heckhausen, and Peter Gollwitzer (Gollwitzer, 1990, 1993; H. Heckhausen, 1991; H. Heckhausen & Gollwitzer, 1987; H. Heckhausen & Kuhl, 1985; Kuhl, 1984, 1994; Kuhl & Fuhrmann, Chapter 1, this volume). In the context of life-span development, the selectivity requirement becomes even more essential and amplified in its implications. This is due to three major characteristics of life-span change. First, ontogenetic change enhances the degree of potential variability. Second, life time is a scare resource, which constrains sequential investment in diverse domains of functioning. And third, life-course choices lead to sequentially amplified dynamics of gains and losses, which move nonchosen developmental tracks increasingly out of reach while the individual accumulates investments in a selected developmental track.

Developmental goals are the life-span equivalent to action goals studied in motivational psychology (for related concepts, see Brandtstädter, 1989; Brunstein, 1993; Cantor, Norem, Niedenthal, et al., 1987; Cantor & Sanderson, Chapter 7, this volume; Csikszentmihalyi, 1985; Emmons, 1986; Gollwitzer, 1987; Gollwitzer & Kirchhoff, Chapter 15, this volume; Klinger, 1975; Nurmi, 1991). Developmental goals, such as striving to become a successful scientist, usually span several years, if not decades, of the life span. And because life time itself is a scarce resource for any given individual, it has to be most carefully invested and protected against waste. In the case of the scientist, high investments are worthwhile only if the individual values intellectual challenge and autonomy much higher than monetary rewards. The choice and pursuit of developmental goals have to be guided by certain principles of developmental optimization, which will be explained further below. Also, the focused investment of resources into a given developmental goal needs to be enhanced and monitored in terms of potential waste or even destruction of resources. In our example, the young scientist has to scrutinize his or her career prospects in view of the larger picture of opportunities for an academic career and decide whether high selective investments stand a reasonable chance of paying off, whether alternative career tracks are feasible and as desirable from a personal intellectual perspective, and also whether pursuing an academic career harms the potential for pursuing an alternative profession. Again, this task requires a higher-order process of developmental optimization. However, before we consider criteria and strategies of developmental optimization, we discuss the second requirement of human functioning.

Human functioning and its development rely on experiences of failure.

Precisely because human behavior is flexible, failure is a likely event throughout processes of skill acquisition and problem solving. Moreover, failure is the prominent source of feedback for adjusting action means and improving performance. However, experiences of failure entail two types of costs: the negative affect that accompanies frustrations of goal intentions, and the detrimental impact of failure experiences on perceptions of the self. These two types of costs are intertwined in that conceptions of the self provide a powerful buffer against frustration. Anticipatory self-reinforcement enables the individual to maintain persistence in spite of failure (see also: Bandura, 1982; Mischel, Shoda, & Rodriguez, 1989). It relies on the ability to self-reflect, and thus relate action outcomes back to characteristics of the self, such as strength, ability, and skills. However, this powerful resource is also a major peril, because repeated experiences of failure may in fact deflate a positive self-image and lead to perceptions of low personal control, pessimism, embarrassment, and even helplessness. These are, of course, major threats to the individual's motivational resources for future action. Therefore, the individual needs to protect his or her perceived self by compensatory means. Again the context of the life span enhances the implications of failure experiences. Developmental goals typically span extensive periods of life time and therefore present ample opportunity for frustration. They also carry extensive risks in case of wrong decisions, because life time has been invested irretrievably. Moreover, toward the end of the life span, processes of aging confront the individual with experiences of loss and decline (e.g., P. B. Baltes, 1987; M. M. Baltes & P. B. Baltes, 1986; Schulz & J. Heckhausen, 1996). All these negative experiences have to be compensated for in order to maintain the individual's capacity to actively influence her or his environment.

Primary and Secondary Control

In our life-span theory of control, Richard Schulz and I apply the distinction between primary and secondary control, introduced by Rothbaum, Weisz, and Snyder (1982), to life-span development (J. Heckhausen & Schulz, 1995). Primary control refers to behaviors directed at the external world and involves attempts to change the world to fit the needs and desires of the individual. Secondary control is targeted at internal processes and serves to focus and protect motivational resources needed for primary control.

The life-span theory of control conceives of primary control as the driving force in the control system. Primary control holds functional primacy. Because primary control is directed outward, it enables individuals to shape

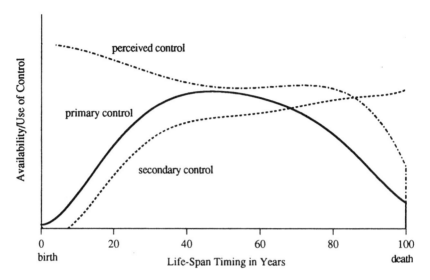

Figure 2.1. Hypothetical life-span trajectories of primary control, secondary control, and perceived control. (*Source:* Adapted with permission from Schulz & Heckhausen, 1996.)

their environment to fit their particular needs and developmental potential. Without engaging the external world, individuals cannot realize their developmental potential. This does not mean that secondary control is inferior or dysfunctional in any way. In contrast, secondary control is used to promote both the *current* and the *long-term* potentials of primary control. It is employed in view of the necessities of maintaining the primary control potential.

Across the life span, the availability of primary control undergoes major changes. Figure 2.1 illustrates hypothetical trajectories for the use of primary and secondary control strategies, and of perceived control. Primary control increases rapidly during childhood, plateaus in midlife, and declines in old age. The use of secondary control strategies depends on their developmental availability and their functional necessity. Children between the ages of 3 and 4 develop the ability to perceive failure as indicating a lack of competence, and thus experience failure-related threats to self-esteem (Geppert & H. Heckhausen, 1990; H. Heckhausen, 1980). Most likely such threats trigger the need for compensatory mechanisms. Moreover, during midchildhood the cognitive capacities of children increase dramatically, enabling them, for instance, to use complex schemes of causal attribution (H. Heckhausen, 1987). Accordingly, it is in middle childhood and throughout adolescence that secondary control strategies have been shown to flourish (Band & Weisz, 1990; see reviews in Compas, 1987; Compas, Banez, Malcarne, et al., 1991; J. Heckhausen & Schulz, 1995). The strategies used by children and adolescents include the change of aspiration levels, denial of failure or loss, egotistic attributions, and reinterpretations of action goals.

Primary and secondary control capacities develop further in early adulthood up into early midlife, when most people reach their occupational career goals and have established a family. During late midlife and in old age, primary control becomes increasingly constrained as social roles become restricted and biological declines take their toll. Moreover, during later adulthood the restricted future time extension of expected remaining life time increasingly constitutes a foreseeable ending to development (see for an analogous concept of "social endings," see Carstensen, 1993, Chapter 13, this volume), and thus renders futile time-intensive investments in long-term goals. Secondary control–type behavior therefore becomes more and more needed in later adulthood, and is used increasingly (e.g., on "accommodative processes," see Brandtstädter & Greve, 1994; Brandtstädter & Renner, 1992; Brandtstädter & Rothermund, 1994; Brandtstädter, Rothermund, & Schmitz, Chapter 14, this volume; on "emotion-focused coping," see Folkman, Lazarus, Pimley, et al., 1987; on "secondary control," see J. Heckhausen, 1997; J. Heckhausen & Krueger, 1993; Peng & Lachman, 1993; and on reinterpretations in terms of "brain over brawn," see Schulz & Decker, 1985).

Optimization in Primary and Secondary Control: A Model of Successful Development

Having identified the two basic requirements of human functioning, selectivity and failure compensation, and two fundamental types of control, primary and secondary, we can integrate these two dimensions into a joint model of developmental regulation (J. Heckhausen & Schulz, 1993). The four control strategies involved in the Optimization in Primary and Secondary Control (OPS) model are illustrated in Table 2.1. With regard to the major role of selectivity and failure compensation, our model converges with the Baltes and Baltes model of selective optimization with compensation (M. M. Baltes, 1987; P. B. Baltes, 1987; P. B. Baltes & M. M. Baltes, 1990; Marsiske, Lang, P. B. Baltes, et al., 1995). However, we integrate the concepts of selectivity and compensation with the life-span theory of primary and secondary control, and we conceptualize optimization as a higher-

Table 2.1. *Two-dimensional model of primary/secondary control and selection/compensation*

	Selective	Compensatory
Primary control	Investment of internal resources: effort, time, abilities, activity-inherent skills	Use of external resources: Technical aids, other people's assistance, activity-external skills
Secondary control	Metavolition: Enhancement of goal commitment, remaining focused in order to avoid distractions	Buffering negative effects of failure: Goal change, strategic social comparison, or strategic causal attribution

Source: Adapted with permission from J. Heckhausen & Schulz (1993).

order regulatory process (J. Heckhausen & Schulz, 1993; Schulz & J. Heckhausen, 1996).

The four types of control strategies are composed of two conceptually orthogonal dimensions: primary and secondary control on the one hand, and selection and compensation on the other. The integration of these two fundamental dimensions comprises a set of four strategies in developmental regulation: selective primary and compensatory primary control, and selective secondary and compensatory secondary control.

Selective primary control refers to the focused investment of resources such as effort, time, abilities, and skills into the pursuit of a chosen goal. Selective primary control may also include the development of skills by processes of acquisition and practice. Thus, selective primary control is action that directly aims at attaining goals.

Compensatory primary control is necessary when the given internal resources of individuals – for instance, young children or frail older people – prove insufficient to attain the chosen goal. Compensatory primary control typically involves other people's help or assistance, the utilization of technical aids such as glasses or a wheelchair, or the employment of activity-external skills. The latter type of compensations involves new or unusual action means to substitute lost or otherwise unavailable skills inherent to the activity. An example for this type of compensatory primary control is lip-reading, which enables hearing-impaired individuals to understand speech (Thompson, 1995).

Selective secondary control serves to enhance the *selectivity* of resource investment in *ongoing* pursuits of primary control goals. In motivational psychology terms, these selective secondary control strategies can be likened to volitional strategies (Kuhl, 1994). They keep the actors' attention, effort, and skill activation focused on the current action goal and prevent distractions by alternative action paths or goals.

Compensatory secondary control buffers the potential negative effects of failure on the motivational resources of the individual, and thus promotes the *long-term* potential for primary control. Experiences of failure can undermine an individual's perceived control, self-efficacy, and even self-esteem and therefore may endanger his or her future willingness to pursue challenging goals of primary control. Secondary control–type strategies such as disengagement from unobtainable goals (e.g., Brandtstädter & Rothermund, 1994; Brandtstädter, Rothermund, & Schmitz, Chapter 14, this volume; Klinger, 1977), downward social comparisons (e.g., J. Heckhausen & Krueger, 1993; Taylor & Lobel, 1989; Wills, 1981), and egotistic causal attributions (H. Heckhausen, 1987; Snyder, Stephan, & Rosenfield, 1978) are important instruments to buffer such negative consequences of inevitable failure experiences throughout the life span.

The employment of each of these strategies and combinations thereof have to be orchestrated in accordance with the structure of opportunities and constraints encountered in a given developmental ecology (J. Heckhausen, 1997, 1998). None of these four strategies is functional in and of itself. Indeed, a strategy might become dysfunctional under unfavorable situational conditions. Selective primary control, for instance, can become very ineffective and even harmful for future primary control when invested in the wrong goal. Wrong goals are those that are either unattainable or involve excessive costs, or that would endanger future goal engagements. Selective secondary control may narrow the perspective on a chosen action path to the extent that it prevents the individual from noticing the emergence of excessive costs of the chosen path and from realizing attractive alternatives. Again, such risks are enhanced in the context of life-span development, because costs and benefits of competing goal alternatives are likely to change over time. Compensatory primary and secondary control may become dysfunctional when the individual prematurely seeks assistance or gives up the goal altogether, although the goal could have been attained on the bases of internal resources.

Thus, the regulation of the four strategies requires a higher-order process, which we refer to as optimization (J. Heckhausen & Schulz, 1993). Optimization is also required for the maintenance of a balance between the four types of strategies in order to promote long-term outcomes. What are the desirable long-term outcomes of developmental regulation? What is the criterion of adaptive functioning across the life span?

Characteristics of Successful Development

Based on our basic position that primary control holds functional primacy, we (Schulz & J. Heckhausen, 1996) have defined the criterion of successful developmental optimization as follows: Human functioning is adaptive if, and insofar as, it promotes and maintains the potential for primary control across the life span (Schulz & J. Heckhausen, 1996). It is important to stress the life-span encompassing nature of this criterion, because short- and long-term primary control may be incompatible in certain cases (J. Heckhausen, 1998). The time and effort required in childhood and adolescence to become a world-class athlete, for instance, may seriously restrain education and occupational training and thereby damage the individual's long-term primary control potential. Moreover, we take a relativist stance with regard to the life-span timing of control striving (see also Schulz & Hanusa, 1980; Suls & Mullen, 1982). What is functional control striving at a certain point in the life span may be dysfunctional at another. It is the totality of realized primary control across domains of functioning and across the life span that composes a successful life. How does the individual regulate control striving across the life span in order to satisfy this general and ambitious criterion? We propose three general principles of optimization in developmental regulation: maintenance of diversity of functioning, adaptive selection of goals, and management of trade-offs between domains and life-span phases (Heckhausen, 1998; Schulz & J. Heckhausen, 1996).

First, control resources have to be invested selectively. While selectivity in general is a basic requirement of human functioning, *selection of appropriate goals* in particular is the key to optimization in developmental regulation. Appropriate goals are those that make the best use of developmental ecologies and have a long-range potential extending beyond the opportunities and constraints currently present. For the typical life course, such goals correspond to age-normative developmental tasks (see also Cantor, Norem, Niedenthal, et al., 1987; Cantor & Sanderson, Chapter 7, this volume). At higher ages, when the resources for primary control decrease, the selection of fewer goals becomes more important (P. B. Baltes & M. M. Baltes, 1990; Marsiske, Lang, P. B. Baltes, et al., 1995). Moreover, in old age the individual should focus his or her resources on fending off developmental losses in crucial domains of functioning, such as health.

Second, developmental regulation across the life span involves the *management of positive and negative trade-offs* across domains and life-span phases. Investments in one domain restrain simultaneous investments in other domains. This may have positive or negative implications for the non-chosen domain. In the case of superathletes, the select investment required for developing the athletic ability (Ericsson, 1990; Schulz & Curnow, 1988) usually prevents a broad education and therefore endangers the individual's functioning after the athletic career is over. In contrast, developing general purpose abilities, such as intellectual skills, typically has positive transfer to various domains of functioning. For instance, for a long time in Europe, learning Latin was supposed to have this general purpose advantage over modern languages, because of its strictly logical structure. Now in a much internationalized society, the instrumental value of modern languages may have weakened the plausibility of this reasoning. In general, we can assume that narrow, intense, and early life investment patterns involve higher risks for negative trade-offs to other domains and later phases of the life span.

Third, it is essential that the individual maintains some *diversity* (or variability) in primary control potential. Diversity is important in ontogenetic development for reasons similar to those applied to evolution (Scarr, 1993). Diversity avoids the vulnerability of overly narrow specialization, and, most important, diversity provides the "raw material" for selection to work on. Without variability, there is no opportunity for adaptive choice. The principle of diversity has important implications in childrearing, for example. Socialization agents and institutions are well advised to expose young children to a wide range of activities (as in fact they do), so as to avoid foreclosure and allow the development of general purpose abilities as well as the challenge of genetic potential. In general, diversity is particularly important early in life.

Empirical Illustrations

After presenting the conceptual framework of the life-span theory of control and its specification in a model of successful life-span development, we now report a few empirical illustrations of adaptive control strategies in developmental regulation (J. Heckhausen, 1997, 1998). These are empirical illustrations because these findings come from research that was conducted concurrently with the development of our theory. Therefore, the studies were not planned as empirical tests of the theory, and can at most be examined in terms of their consistency or inconsistency with the theory's assumptions. We are really at the beginning of a research program, and the empirical findings may help to illustrate the research potential of our model of developmental regulation.

Developmental Regulation at Different Ages in Adulthood

A study on East and West Berliners' developmental regulation (J. Heck-hausen, 1997) investigated the ways in which adults at different ages and in different parts of the city coped with their respective developmental challenges. The general assumption was that the specific structure of opportunities and constraints in a given developmental ecology shapes and scaffolds the individual's attempts at regulating his or her own development. Both aging-related challenges and challenges resulting from the sociohistorical transformation in East Germany were investigated. However, we focus here on the age-related differences only.

The majority of changes associated with aging imply a decline in functioning. This is based on the nature of biological changes in old age and the restriction of social roles after retirement. In general, developmental regulation of older adults can be expected to reflect increased selection of age-specific goals, including a focus on the avoidance of developmental losses, and especially an enhanced tendency to use secondary control strategies to compensate for the negative effects of losses on motivational resources. More specifically, the following pattern of findings for older as compared to younger adults was expected. *Selective primary control* strategies should be reflected in the selection of age-appropriate goals and the accompanying disengagement from unobtainable goals. Moreover, selective primary control of aging-related challenges would be indicated by a greater number of goals representing the avoidance of losses relative to goals representing the striving for gains. *Compensatory secondary control* would be expressed in high flexibility of goal adjustment (Brandtstädter & Renner, 1990), satisfaction with one's current life situation, and the identification with younger age groups.

In addition, we expected the patterns of control strategies in East Berliners as compared to West Berliners to be much more oriented toward primary control of work- and welfare-related goals, refraining from secondary control strategies. Thus, the specific challenges and threats associated with German reunification were expected to prompt the East Berliners to strive particularly hard to take their fate into their own hands. These expectations were confirmed by our findings (J. Heckhausen, 1994).

A total of 510 East and West Berlin young, middle-aged, and older adults took part in our questionnaire sessions in 1991. The sample was equally divided by age, sex, place of origin, and socioeconomic status. The questionnaire booklet given to the subjects contained questions about developmental goals, self-esteem, life satisfaction, subjective age identification, and tenaciousness in goal pursuit and flexibility of goal adjustment measured by the Brandtstädter and Renner (1990) scales. The latter scales were developed in the context of Brandtstädter's conception of assimilative versus accommodative coping, but appeared useful as indicators of one aspect of primary and secondary control striving, namely the engagement with versus disengagement from goals.

We consider a select set of findings that illustrates the employment of various control strategies in older as compared to younger adults. First of all, it is important to note that older adults expressed reduced perceptions of personal control over goal attainment, and reduced expected probabilities of goal attainment. Thus, the study's participants construed the developmental challenge raised by old age as one characterized by low control potential. Based on this finding, the question can be raised whether indicators of developmental regulation *also* reflect a developmental ecology characterized by reduced control.

The subjects' nominations of developmental goals reflect the focus of selective primary control. Goal assessment followed an open-ended response format. The goals were then categorized into domains: work, family, community issues, personal health, personal financial welfare, and free time.

Figure 2.2 shows the age trajectories of nominations for each of these six goal categories. Regarding the goal categories with increasing age trajectories (upper panel), we found a steady increase throughout adulthood only for the health-related goals, while goals relating to free time increased between midlife and old age, and community-related goals became more salient between young adulthood and midlife. These trajectories reflect a selective focus of primary control striving on age-appropriate goals, that is, goals associated with age-graded developmental tasks. Goals related to free time can be expected to become more important after retirement, community engagement may be associated with greater social influence in midlife, and health concerns probably reflect the increasing medical vulnerability throughout midlife and old age.

The lower panel of Figure 2.2 indicates that goals relating to the family (e.g., having a child, ensuring the well-being of a family member), financial welfare, and work decreased across adulthood, with work-related goals showing a drop toward old age, and family and finances already losing salience between young adulthood and middle age. These trajectories reflect disengagements from obsolete goals in the respective age groups.

Age-adapted selective primary control in older adults also is expected to show in younger adults a higher proportion of goals directed at avoiding losses; Figure 2.3 supports this expectation: Older adults expressed more

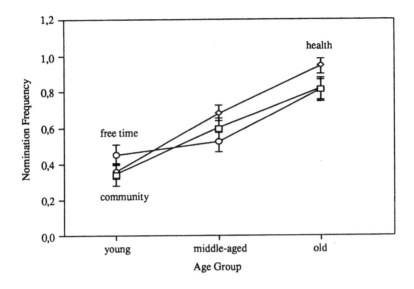

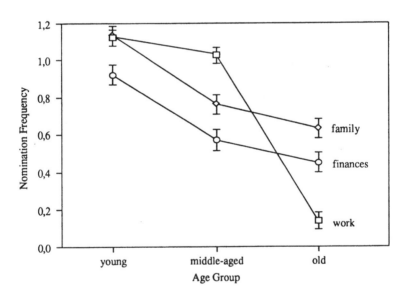

Figure 2.2. (A) Developmental goals with increasing age trajectories. (B) Developmental goals with decreasing age trajectories. (*Source:* Adapted with permission from J. Heckhausen, 1997.)

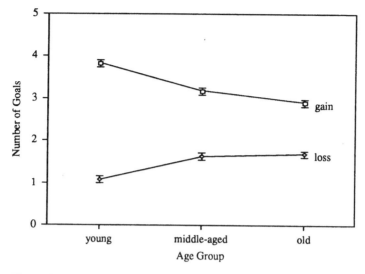

Figure 2.3. Gain- and loss-related developmental goals in young, middle-aged, and old adults. (*Source:* Adapted with permission from J. Heckhausen, 1997.)

loss-oriented and fewer gain-oriented goals than younger adults. In the context of Higgins and Loeb's (Chapter 3, this volume) theory of "outcome focus," one might say that across adulthood there is a shift from a positive-outcome focus, in terms of the striving for developmental growth in young adults, to a negative-outcome focus, in terms of the avoidance of developmental decline in older adults.

With regard to compensatory secondary control strategies, we had predicted that older adults would experience a greater need to use these to buffer the negative effects of inevitable aging-related losses on their motivational resources. Three indicators of compensatory secondary control were investigated: the satisfaction with one's current life, the flexibility of goal adjustment, and the tendency to identify with younger age groups. While no age group differences were found for past or future life satisfaction, older adults did express a greater satisfaction with present life than young and middle-aged adults. Thus, older adults can be assumed to have felt less need to change important aspects of their present life.

What about the flexibility in adjusting goals? Figure 2.4 displays the flexibility of goal adjustment, and tenaciousness of goal pursuit, across the three age groups. This figure indicates that flexibility of goal adjustment increased steadily across the three age groups. Thus, with increasing age the

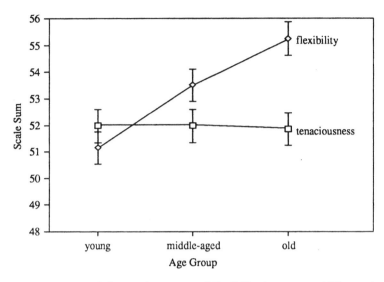

Figure 2.4. Tenaciousness and flexibility in young, middle-aged, and old adults. (*Source:* Adapted with permission from J. Heckhausen, 1997.)

subjects were more likely to refrain from striving for goals that were difficult or impossible to obtain and switched to other more accessible goals. It is interesting that tenaciousness remained stable across adulthood: This supports the assumption that the need for primary control is constantly high across the life span.

Finally, regarding subjective age identification, the pattern of findings also indicates increased employment of compensatory secondary control. Figure 2.5 displays subjective age conceptions as younger, same age, or older than one's actual age for various indicators of subjective age, such as the age one feels, the age one looks, the age friends or strangers ascribe to oneself, and so on. This figure shows that with increasing age people identified more with people of younger ages than with those of their own chronological age. Identifying with a younger age group can be interpreted as a compensatory secondary control strategy, because it means that one reinterprets one's own age as younger than it actually is and thereby protects oneself from the negative implications of an old-age stereotype.

Based on the findings from this study, we conclude that older individuals use more compensatory secondary control strategies and focus their primary control striving on age-appropriate goals and on preventing developmental losses.

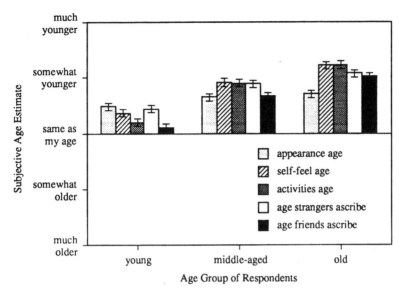

Figure 2.5. Subjective age identification in young, middle-aged, and old adults. (*Source:* Adapted with permission from J. Heckhausen, 1997.)

Developmental Expectations for the Self and "Most Other People" at Different Age Levels

Another set of relevant findings comes from our work on conceptions about self and other (J. Heckhausen & Krueger, 1993; Krueger & J. Heckhausen, 1993), and social comparison processes (J. Heckhausen, 1998; J. Heckhausen & Wrosch, 1996). In the conceptual framework of the life-span theory of control, upward social comparisons with superior targets can be viewed as conducive to the development of primary control. Upward social comparisons help to set goals and provide models for primary control striving. Downward social comparisons, by contrast, should serve compensatory secondary control purposes of self-enhancement and self-protection. The individual can feel elevated by comparing with others who are perceived as inferior in some way. Downward social comparisons should be most prevalent among those who feel threatened by loss. Lateral comparisons with others who share one's undesirable characteristics can also buffer the negative effect of losses on self-esteem (Wills, 1981).

In an earlier study (J. Heckhausen & Krueger, 1993), perceived trajectories of developmental growth and decline that were ascribed to the self were

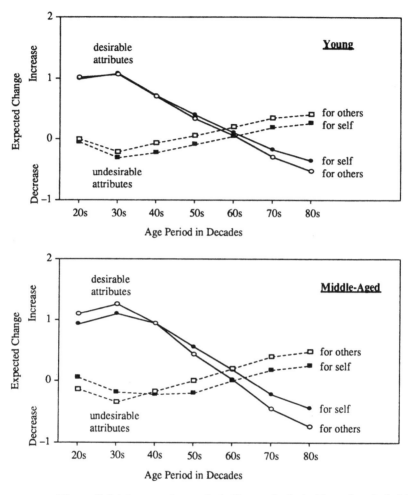

Figure 2.6 *(above and opposite).* Change in desirable and undesirable attributes expected for the self and most other people, separately for (A) young, (B) middle-aged, and (C) old adults. *(Source:* Adapted with permission from J. Heckhausen & Krueger, 1993.)

compared to those attributed to "most other people." Figure 2.6A–C displays the perceived age trajectories for desirable and undesirable psychological attributes, separately for the self and the generalized other. Figure 2.6A presents young adult conceptions about development; panel B presents middle-aged adult conceptions; and panel C presents older adult conceptions.

Young adults saw little difference between developmental expectations

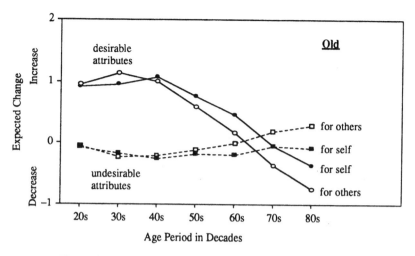

Figure 2.6. (*cont.*)

for themselves and for most other people; however, middle-aged adults and particularly older adults expressed characteristic differences. Specifically with regard to older target ages, the older adults indicated more optimistic expectations for the self than for most others. They expected less and later decreases in desirable attributes for the self compared to most others. Accordingly, for the undesirable attributes they expected earlier and stronger increases for most other people compared to themselves. This self-enhancing pattern is most pronounced for the old participants in the study. The older adults, who are presumably most immediately threatened by old-age losses, viewed themselves in later years as clearly less stricken by developmental losses than most other people. This self/other differential conception about psychological development can be interpreted as a compensatory secondary control strategy to buffer the negative effects of old age decline on self-esteem and motivational resources in general.

Social Comparisons in Adults at Different Ages

In a more recent study, we investigated processes of everyday social comparisons more directly (J. Heckhausen, 1998; J. Heckhausen & Wrosch, 1996; Wrosch & Heckhausen, 1996). We asked young, middle-aged, and older adults to report instances of social comparisons on a daily basis by means of a diary method. Subjects also rated each self-reported social comparison on a number of dimensions, such as the degree to which the target person was superior or inferior and younger or older, and how the subject had felt before and after the comparison.

This data set provided a rich source of interesting findings, out of which only the age effects can be considered here. Based on the life-span theory of control, we predicted that younger adults would use more upward comparisons than older adults, because their scope for improvement in primary control is larger. In contrast, older adults were expected to use relatively more downward comparisons, because they are likely to experience a greater need for compensatory secondary control. Our findings indicated partial support for these predictions. Older adults reported fewer upward comparisons ($M = 39.94\%$) than did young adults ($M = 46.55\%$), and more lateral comparisons ($M = 19.37\%$) than did young ($M = 8.99\%$) and middle-aged ($M = 13.54\%$) adults. No age differences were found for downward comparisons. This pattern of findings may indicate that the older adults were oriented less to improvements in functioning, and more concerned about maintaining given levels of functioning. Moreover, lateral comparisons can serve self-protective functions when they are directed at target persons who perform at a relatively low level, similar to one's own functioning. At the same time, these older adults apparently did not perceive a greater need to use more powerful compensatory strategies, such as downward comparisons, to buffer negative effects of inevitable losses on motivational resources.

Additional evidence comes from the findings pertaining to the age of the comparison target. The young adults in our study compared themselves more frequently ($M = 47.63\%$) with older adults than did the middle-aged ($M = 23.34\%$) and older ($M = 15.87\%$) adults. This makes sense, because middle-aged adults might provide upward comparisons for young adults, for instance, with regard to occupational achievements. Comparisons with younger target persons, on the other hand, were more frequent among old adults ($M = 54.19\%$) than among middle-aged ($M = 39.22\%$) and young ($M = 14.86\%$) adults. For older adults, comparing with a younger target may instantiate an upward comparison, and therefore may reflect the striving to maintain and defend previous levels of functioning against negative effects of aging.

Measurement of Strategies for Developmental Regulation: The OPS Scales

Finally, we report a few basic findings obtained by the development of a measurement instrument for our life-span model of developmental regula-

Table 2.2. *OPS scales for model of optimization in primary and secondary control (total of 46 items, with 2 items per subscale)*

I. Optimization
 1. Selection-choice I: Change goals to fit developmental tasks
 2. Selection-choice II: Invest in long-term potential goals
 3. Positive trade-off: Invest in general purpose abilities
 4. Negative trade-off: Avoid long-range costs in too costly goals
 5. Diversity I: Maintain multiple goal domains
 6. Diversity II: Avoid narrow dead-end paths
II. Selective primary control
 1. Invest effort
 2. Invest time
 3. Develop (learn, practice) relevant skills and abilities
 4. Fight difficulties
III. Compensatory primary control
 1. Other people's help
 2. Other people's advice
 3. Activity-external skills, new and unusual means
 4. Activity-external skills, take a detour
IV. Selective secondary control
 1. Enhancement of goal value
 2. Devaluation of other goals
 3. Enhanced perception of control for chosen goal
 4. Anticipated positive consequences of goal attainment for self-esteem
V. Compensatory secondary control
 1. Goal disengagement (incl. sour grapes)
 2. Self-protective attribution
 3. Social comparison
 4. Intraindividual comparison (temporal and interdomain)

Source: Adapted with permission from Heckhausen, Schulz, & Wrosch (1998).

tion. As we have described in this chapter, our Model of Optimization in Primary and Secondary Control OPS involves four strategies of developmental regulation and a higher-order process of optimization. We have designed a five-scale instrument with multiple subscales in each of the OPS components, as shown in Table 2.2 (J. Heckhausen, Schulz, & Wrosch, 1997).

As Table 2.2 shows, the subscales of the OPS scales reflect the three components of developmental optimization: selection, management of trade-offs (compensation), and diversity. Each of the four strategies of developmental regulation (selective primary, compensatory primary, selective secondary, and compensatory secondary control) is composed of subscales reflecting specific strategies that can be assumed to be functionally conducive to the respective regulatory goal.

A total of 262 young, middle-aged, and older adults took part in the study. The sample was equally divided by age, gender, East and West Berlin origin, and educational attainment. Subjects were requested to complete the

OPS scales (J. Heckhausen, Schulz, & Wrosch, 1998), along with some other questionnaires that were included to determine the relationships with other concepts, such as self-esteem, tenaciousness and flexibility, subjective well-being, and beliefs about control.

We focus here on differences between age groups in strategy endorsement, and on the relationships with indicators of well-being. The scales showed very satisfactory internal consistencies, ranging between 0.79 and 0.91 (Cronbach's alpha).

Selective primary control strategies were valued most by adults at all ages ($M = 4.14$, on a scale from 1 to 5), and compensatory secondary control received the lowest ratings ($M = 3.24$). This finding is consistent with our notion that primary control holds functional primacy. In addition, compensatory secondary control may be construed as the last resort, to be avoided if possible. Regarding the differences between age groups, all types of strategies received increasingly higher ratings with subjects' age (young adults: $M = 3.5$; middle-aged adults: $M = 3.7$; older adults: $M = 3.8$), except for compensatory primary control, which remained stable across age groups. Therefore, overall, with increasing age adults appear to know about, appreciate, and maybe rely more on strategies of developmental regulation.

Among all strategies of developmental regulation, optimization strategies are particularly important, because they regulate the employment of the other strategies. The three strategies most preferred are "Selection-choice II: invest in long-term potential goals"; ($M = 4.0$), "Positive trade-off: invest in general purpose abilities"; ($M = 4.0$), and "Diversity I: Maintain multiple goal domains" ($M = 4.1$). The age comparisons show the steepest age increase for the strategy "Selection-choice I: change of goals to fit developmental tasks" (young adults: $M = 2.7$; middle-aged adults: $M = 3.0$; older adults: $M = 3.8$).

Overall, this pattern of findings suggests that adults at all ages – and older adults in particular select goals for their primary control striving – that make use of age-specific opportunities. Adults at all ages also employ selective secondary control strategies to enhance their volitional commitment to these chosen goals. When failing to attain the chosen goals, older adults are more able to disengage and make themselves feel adequate in spite of failure than are younger adults. Older adults may thus be particularly well equipped to manage the greater challenges to developmental regulation experienced in old age.

Of course, the question arises: Do these strategies make any difference in determining outcomes of development? An investigation of the relationship between strategy endorsement and self-esteem measured by the Rosenberg scale suggests that these strategies of developmental regulation may indeed be beneficial. Correlations between the five subscales of the OPS questionnaire and self-esteem were all highly significant and ranged between 0.25 and 0.33, with compensatory primary control yielding a somewhat lower correlation ($r = 0.17$; $p < 0.01$). Regression analyses revealed that ratings of the five strategies of developmental regulation accounted for a third of the variance in self-esteem ratings. The relationship between ratings of developmental regulation and self-esteem can be viewed as substantial, especially when considering the fact that the strategies and outcomes do not involve semantic overlap.

Conclusion and Perspectives

Overall, these preliminary findings suggest that the OPS scales provide a useful instrument for measuring strategies of developmental regulation, which exhibits meaningful relationships to developmental outcomes and differentiates between age groups. In future research, the OPS scales should be applied to processes of developmental regulation in response to specific challenges that are extended over time and can be studied longitudinally. Such empirical inquiries could reveal sequential patterns of using specific regulatory strategies, so that the validity of the assumptions of the life-span model of developmental regulation can be more directly assessed. Moreover, such longitudinal studies would permit the investigation of differential adaptiveness of certain strategies in specific developmental ecologies. Other promising lines of future research are described below.

We need to know more about the use and effectiveness of specific control strategies across the life span and in different developmental ecologies. Such research should employ longitudinal assessment to investigate the sequencing of strategy use and how the strategies fit with regulatory challenges such as losses and major life transitions. The model of developmental regulation can, for instance, be applied to processes of disability (Schulz, Heckhausen, & O'Brien, 1994). Another fruitful class of phenomena involves shifts from urgent primary control to goal disengagement and secondary control in transitions before and after passing developmental deadlines (J. Heckhausen & Fleeson, 1993).

John Weisz (Band & Weisz, 1988, 1990), Bruce Compas (Compas, 1987; Compas, Banez, Malcarne, et al., 1991) and others have taken the lead in investigating the developmental origin and acquisition of secondary control strategies in childhood. However, we still know little about the first occurrence of secondary control in early childhood, the role of socialization agents in this process, and the emergence and consequences of interindividual differences.

Another area of study should identify functional limits of the control system. This can be done by investigating extreme circumstances where primary as well as secondary control may be insufficient to compensate for failures or losses experienced by the individual (Schulz, Heckhausen, & O'Brien, 1994). Such situations may involve threats to the individual's physical functioning, as in illness and disability, or be brought about by extremely unfavorable environmental conditions as in socioeconomic collapses, catastrophes, and wars.

Finally, on a metatheoretical level it may be argued that regulatory functions are not performed solely by the individual actor. Instead, biological, cultural, sociostructural, and individual factors work together jointly to construct the regulatory requirements. Cultures may differ in the way this "task-sharing" between individual agent, societal institutions, and biological determinants is organized. Contrasts between specifically selected cultures may reveal, for instance, whether social systems allow or avoid regulatory overlap between these three factors, and how given social communities walk the tightrope between over- and underregulation.

References

Baltes, M. M. (1987). Erfolgreiches Altern als Ausdruck von Verhaltenskompetenz und Umweltqualität [Successful aging as a product of behavioral competence and quality of environment]. In C. Niemitz (Ed.), *Der Mensch im Zusammenspiel von Anlage und Umwelt* (pp. 353–376). Frankfurt: Suhrkamp.

Baltes, M. M., & Baltes, P. B. (Eds.). (1986). *The psychology of control and aging.* Hillsdale, NJ: Erlbaum.

Baltes, P. B. (1987). Theoretical propositions of life-span developmental psychology: On the dynamics between growth and decline. *Developmental Psychology, 23,* 611–626.

Baltes, P. B., & Baltes, M. M. (1990). Psychological perspectives on successful aging: The model of selective optimization with compensation. In P. B. Baltes & M. M. Baltes (Eds.), *Successful aging: Perspectives from the behavioral sciences* (pp. 1–34). New York: Cambridge University Press.

Band, E. B., & Weisz, J. R. (1988). How to feel better when it feels bad: Children's perspectives on coping with everyday stress. *Developmental Psychology, 24,* 247–253.

(1990). Developmental differences in primary and secondary control coping and adjustment to juvenile diabetes. *Journal of Clinical Child Psychology, 19,* 150–158.

Bandura, A. (1982). Self-efficacy mechanisms in human agency. *American Psychologist, 37,* 122–147.

Brandtstädter, J. (1984). Personal and social control over development: Some implications of an action perspective in life-span developmental psychology. In P. B. Baltes & O. G. Brim, Jr. (Eds.), *Life-span development and behavior* (Vol. 6, pp. 1–32). New York: Academic Press.

(1989). Personal self-regulation of development: Cross-sequential analyses of development-related control beliefs and emotions. *Developmental Psychology, 25,* 96–108.

Brandtstädter, J., & Greve, W. (1994). The aging self: Stabilizing and protective processes. *Developmental Review, 14,* 52–80.

Brandtstädter, J., & Renner, G. (1990). Tenacious goal pursuit and flexible goal adjustment: Explication and age-related analysis of assimilative and accommodative strategies of coping. *Psychology and Aging, 5,* 58–67.

(1992). Coping with discrepancies between aspirations and achievements in adult development: A dual-process model. In L. Montada, S.-H. Filipp, & R. M. Lerner (Eds.), *Life crises and experiences of loss in adulthood* (pp. 301–319). Hillsdale, NJ: Erlbaum.

Brandtstädter, J., & Rothermund, K. (1994). Self-percepts of control in middle and later adulthood: Buffering losses by rescaling goals. *Psychology and Aging, 9,* 265–273.

Brandtstädter, J., Rothermund, K., & Schmitz, U. (1998). Maintaining self-integrity and efficacy through adulthood and later life: The adaptive functions of assimilative persistence and accommodative flexibility. In J. Heckhausen & C. S. Dweck (Eds.), *Motivation and self-regulation across the life span.* New York: Cambridge University Press.

Brunstein, J. C. (1993). Personal goals and subjective well-being: A longitudinal study. *Journal of Personality and Social Psychology, 65,* 1061–1070.

Cantor, N., Norem, J. K., Niedenthal, P. M., Langston, C. A., & Brower, A. M. (1987). Life tasks, self-concept ideals, and cognitive strategies in a life transition. *Journal of Personality and Social Psychology, 53,* 1178–1191.

Cantor, N., & Sanderson, C. A. (1998). The functional regulation of adolescent dating relationships and sexual behavior: An interaction of goals, strategies, and situations. In J. Heckhausen & C. S. Dweck (Eds.), *Motivation and self-regulation across the life span.* New York: Cambridge University Press.

Carstensen, L. L. (1993). Motivation for social contact across the life span: A theory of socioemotional selectivity. In J. Jacobs (Ed.), *Nebraska symposium on motivation* (Vol. 40, pp. 205–254). Lincoln: University of Nebraska Press.

(1998). A life-span approach to social motivation. In J. Heckhausen & C. S. Dweck (Eds.), *Motivation and self-regulation across the life span.* New York: Cambridge University Press.

Compas, B. E. (1987). Coping with stress during childhood and adolescence. *Psychological Bulletin, 101,* 393–403.

Compas, B. E., Banez, G. A., Malcarne, V., & Worsham, N. (1991). *Perceived control, coping with stress, and depressive symptoms in school-age children.* Burlington: University of Vermont.

Connell, J. P., & Wellborn, J. G. (1991). Competence, autonomy, and relatedness: A motivational analysis of self-system processes. In M. Gunnar & A. Sroufe (Eds.), *Minnesota Symposium on Child Psychology* (pp. 43–77). Chicago: University of Chicago Press.

Csikszentmihalyi, M. (1985). Emergent motivation and the evolution of the self. In M. Maehr (Ed.), *Advances in motivation and achievement* (pp. 93–119). Greenwich, CT: JAI.

Deci, E. L., Connell, J. P., & Ryan, R. M. (1985). A motivational analysis of self-determination and self-regulation in the classroom. In C. Ames & R. Ames (Eds.), *Research on motivation in education: Vol. 2. The classroom milieu* (pp. 13–52). San Diego, CA: Academic Press.

Deci, E. L., & Ryan, R. M. (1985). *Intrinsic motivation and self-determination in human behavior.* New York: Plenum Press.

Emmons, R. A. (1986). Personal strivings: An approach to personality and subjective wellbeing. *Journal of Personality and Social Psychology, 51,* 1058–1068.

Ericsson, K. A. (1990). Peak performance and age: An examination of peak performance in sports. In P. B. Baltes & M. M. Baltes (Eds.), *Successful aging: Perspectives from the behavioral sciences* (pp. 164–196). New York: Cambridge University Press.

Folkman, S., Lazarus, R. S., Pimley, S., & Novacek, J. (1987). Age differences in stress and coping processes. *Psychology and Aging, 2,* 171–184.

Geppert, U., & Heckhausen, H. (1990). Ontogenese der Emotion [Ontogenesis of emotion]. In K. R. Scherer (Ed.), *Enzyklopädie der Psychologie, Vol. C/IV/3, Psychologie der Emotionen* (pp. 115–213). Göttingen: Hogrefe.

Gollwitzer, P. M. (1987). Suchen, Finden und Festigen der eigenen Identität: Unstillbare Zielintentionen [Searching, finding, and consolidating of one's own identity: Unsaturatable goal intentions]. In H. Heckhausen, P. M. Gollwitzer, & F. E. Weinert (Eds.), *Jenseits des Rubikon: Der Wille in den Humanwissenschaften* (pp. 176–189). Berlin: Springer.

(1990). Action phases and mind-sets. In E. T. Higgins & R. M. Sorrentino (Eds.), *Handbook of motivation and cognition: Foundations of social behavior* (Vol. 2, pp. 53–92). New York: Guilford Press.

(1993). Goal achievement: The role of intentions. *European Review of Social Psychology, 4,* 141–185.

Gollwitzer, P. & Kirchhof, O. (1998). The willful pursuit of identity. In J. Heckhausen & C. S. Dweck (Eds.), *Motivation and self-regulation across the life span.* New York: Cambridge University Press.

Harter, S. (1974). Pleasure derived from cognitive challenge and mastery. *Child Development, 45,* 661–669.

Heckhausen, H. (1980). *Motivation und Handeln* [Motivation and action]. Berlin: Springer.

(1987). Causal attribution patterns for achievement outcomes: Individual differences, possible types, and their origins. In F. E. Weinert & R. H. Kluwe (Eds.), *Metacognition, motivation, and understanding* (pp. 143–184). Hillsdale, NJ: Erlbaum.

(1991). *Motivation and action.* New York: Springer.

Heckhausen, H., & Gollwitzer, P. M. (1987). Thought contents and cognitive functioning in motivational and volitional states of mind. *Motivation and Emotion, 11,* 101–120.

Heckhausen, H., & Kuhl, J. (1985). From wishes to action: The dead ends and short cuts on the long way to action. In M. Frese & J. Sabini (Eds.), *Goal-directed behavior: The concept of action in psychology* (pp. 134–159). Hillsdale, NJ: Erlbaum.

Heckhausen, J. (1994). Entwicklungsziele und Kontrollüberzeugungen Ost- und Westberliner Erwachsener [Developmental goals and control beliefs in East and West Berlin adults]. In G. Trommsdorff (Ed.), *Psychologische Aspekte des sozio-politischen Wandels in Ostdeutschland* (pp. 124–133). Berlin: DeGruyter.

(1997). Developmental regulation across adulthood: Primary and secondary control of age-related challenges. *Developmental Psychology, 33,* 176–187.

(1998). *Developmental regulation in adulthood.* New York: Cambridge University Press.

Heckhausen, J., & Fleeson, W. (1993). *Primary and secondary control shifts in developmental regulation around age deadline for developmental tasks. Actional and postactional functioning with impending versus passed action opportunities.* Unpublished research proposal, Max Planck Institute for Human Development and Education, Berlin, Germany.

Heckhausen, J., & Krueger, J. (1993). Developmental expectations for the self and most other people: Age grading in three functions of social comparison. *Developmental Psychology, 29,* 539–548.

Heckhausen, J., & Schulz, R. (1993). Optimisation by selection and compensation: Balancing primary and secondary control in life-span development. *International Journal of Behavioral Development, 16,* 287–303.

(1995). A life-span theory of control. *Psychological Review, 102,* 284–304.

Heckhausen, J., & Schulz, R., & Wrosch, C. (1998). *Developmental regulation in adulthood: Optimization in primary and secondary control.* Unpublished manuscript. Max Planck Institute for Human Development and Education, Berlin, Germany.

Heckhausen, J., & Wrosch, C. (1995). *Social comparison as a strategy of developmental regulation in adulthood.* Manuscript in preparation, Max Planck Institute for Human Development and Education, Berlin, Germany.

Higgins, T., & Loeb, I. (1998). Development of regulatory focus: Promotion and prevention as ways of living. In J. Heckhausen & C. S. Dweck (Eds.), *Motivation and self-regulation across the life span.* New York: Cambridge University Press.

Klinger, E. (1975). Consequences of commitment and disengagement from incentives. *Psychological Review, 82,* 1–25.

——— (1977). *Meaning and void: Inner experience and the incentives in people's lives.* Minneapolis: University of Minnesota Press.

Krueger, J., & Heckhausen, J. (1993). Personality development across the adult life span: Subjective conceptions versus cross-sectional contrasts. *Journal of Gerontology: Psychological Sciences, 48,* 100–108.

Kuhl, J. (1984). Motivational aspects of achievement motivation and learned helplessness: Toward a comprehensive theory of action control. In B. A. Maher & W. B. Maher (Eds.), *Progress in experimental personality research* (Vol. 13, pp. 99–171). New York: Academic Press.

——— (1994). Motivation and volition. In G. d'Ydevalle, P. Bertelson, & P. Eelen (Eds.), *Current advances in psychological science: An international perspective.* Hillsdale, NJ: Erlbaum.

Kuhl, J. & Fuhrmann, A. (1998). Decomposing self-regulation and self-control: The Volitional Components Inventory. In J. Heckhausen & C. S. Dweck (Eds.), *Motivation and self-regulation across the life span.* New York: Cambridge University Press.

Marsiske, M., Lang, F. R., Baltes, P. B., & Baltes, M. M. (1995). Selective optimization with compensation: Life-span perspectives on successful human development. In R. A. Dixon & L. Bäckman (Eds.), *Compensating for psychological deficits and decline: Managing losses and promoting gains* (pp. 35–79). Hillsdale, NJ: Erlbaum.

Mischel, W., Shoda, Y., & Rodriguez, M. L. (1989). Delay of gratification in children. *Science, 244,* 933–938.

Nurmi, J.-E. (1991). How do adolescents see their future? A review of the development of future orientation and planning. *Developmental Review, 11,* 1–59.

Peng, Y., & Lachman, M. E. (1993). *Primary and secondary control: Age and cultural differences.* Paper presented at the 101st annual convention of the American Psychological Association, Toronto, Canada.

Rothbaum, F., Weisz, J. R., & Snyder, S. S. (1982). Changing the world and changing the self: A two-process model of perceived control. *Journal of Personality and Social Psychology, 42,* 5–37.

Ryan, R. M. (1993). Agency and organization: Intrinsic motivation, autonomy, and the self in psychological development. In J. E. Jacobs (Ed.), *Nebraska Symposium on Motivation* (Vol. 40, pp. 1–56). Lincoln: University of Nebraska Press.

——— (1995). Psychological needs and the facilitation of integrative processes. *Journal of Personality, 63,* 397–427.

——— (1998). Human psychological needs and the issues of volition, control, and outcome focus. In J. Heckhausen & C. S. Dweck (Eds.), *Motivation and self-regulation across the life span.* New York: Cambridge University Press.

Ryan, R. M., Deci, E. L., & Grolnick, W. S. (1995). Autonomy, relatedness, and the self: Their relation to development and psychopathology. In D. Cicchetti & D. J. Cohen (Eds.), *Developmental psychology: Vol. 1. Theory and methods* (pp. 618–655). New York: Wiley.

Scarr, S. (1993). Biological and cultural diversity: The legacy of Darwin for development. *Child Development, 64,* 1333–1353.

Schulz, R., & Curnow, C. (1988). Peak performance and age among superathletes: Track and field, swimming, baseball, tennis, and golf. *Journal of Gerontology: Psychological Sciences, 43,* 113–120.

Schulz, R., & Decker, S. (1985). Long-term adjustment to physical disability: The role of social support, perceived control, and self-blame. *Journal of Personality and Social Psychology, 48,* 1162–1172.

Schulz, R., & Hanusa, B. H. (1980). Experimental social gerontology: A social psychological perspective. *Journal of Social Issues, 36,* 30–46.

Schulz, R., & Heckhausen, J. (1996). A life-span model of successful aging. *American Psychologist, 51,* 702–714.

Schulz, R., Heckhausen, J., & Locher, J. (1991). Adult development, control, and adaptive functioning. *Journal of Social Issues, 47,* 177–196.

Schulz, R., Heckhausen, J., & O'Brien, A. T. (1994). Control and the disablement process in the elderly. *Journal of Social Behavior and Personality, 9,* 139–152.

Snyder, M. L., Stephan, W. G., & Rosenfield, D. (1978). Attributional egotism. In J. H. Harvey, W. Ickes, & R. F. Kidd (Eds.), *New directions in attribution research* (Vol. 2, pp. 91–117). Hillsdale, NJ: Erlbaum.

Suls, J., & Mullen, B. (1982). From the cradle to the grave: Comparison and self-evaluation across the life span. In J. Suls (Ed.), *Psychological perspectives on the self* (Vol. 1, pp. 233–300). New York: Academic Press.

Taylor, S. E., & Lobel, M. (1989). Social comparison activity under threat: Downward evaluation and upward contacts. *Psychological Review, 96,* 569–575.

Thompson, L. A. (1995). Encoding and memory for visible speech and gestures: A comparison between young and older adults. *Psychology and Aging, 10,* 215–228.

White, R. W. (1959). Motivation reconsidered: The concept of competence. *Psychological Review, 66,* 297–333.

Wills, T. A. (1981). Downward comparison principles in social psychology. *Psychological Bulletin, 90,* 245–271.

Wrosch, C., & Heckhausen, J. (1996). Adaptivität sozialer Vergleiche: Entwicklungsregulation durch primäre und sekundäre Kontrolle [Adaptiveness of social comparisons: Developmental regulation via primary and secondary control]. *Zeitschrift für Entwicklungspsychologie und Pädagogische Psychologie, 28,* 126–147.

3   Development of Regulatory Focus: Promotion and Prevention as Ways of Living

E. Tory Higgins and Israela Silberman

Abstract

All children need both nurturance and security in order to survive. Still, parents' social regulatory style can emphasize either nurturance or security, by either bolstering or safeguarding in order to meet desired end-states, or by either withdrawing love or criticizing when desired end-states are not met. These different social regulatory styles communicate distinct viewpoints about the world. Nurturant social regulation engenders a promotion focus, in which self-regulation is concerned with maximizing the presence of positive outcomes and minimizing the absence of positive outcomes. Security social regulation engenders a prevention focus, in which self-regulation is concerned with maximizing the absence of negative outcomes and minimizing the presence of negative outcomes. These distinct self-regulatory systems produce different emotional vulnerabilities (e.g., depression versus anxiety) and different strategic inclinations (approaching goal-congruent actions versus avoiding goal-discrepant actions). The results of studies with both children and adults are presented that support each of these propositions.

Introduction

The different ways that significant others respond to an individual communicate information about the nature of the world and the individual's place in it. An individual's interactions with significant others send messages about his or her person–environment fit. In this chapter, we propose a basic distinction between nurturance-oriented parenting, which instills a promotion focus in children, and security-oriented parenting, which instills a prevention focus. We consider both the socialization determinants and the motivational consequences of acquiring regulatory focus. The "take away" message of this chapter is that learning about *one's relation to the world* – that it involves nurturance with a promotion focus on accomplishment or that it

78

involves security with a prevention focus on safety – can have a major impact on one's ways of living.

Models of socialization begin with the question, "How do the significant others in a person's life influence the values and beliefs the person acquires, and how do these values and beliefs in turn affect the person's responses to the world?" How does social regulation affect self-regulation? Historically, this question has been central to the social science of psychology, as evident in the work of Freud, Lewin, Murray, Vygotsky, Mead, and other founders of personality and social psychology.

First, we consider the traditional approach to understanding how social regulation affects self-regulation. It is recognized that the human child cannot survive without caretakers providing food, protection, shelter, and so on. As Bowlby (1969; 1973) points out, self-regulatory mechanisms arise from the child's dependence on others for survival. To survive, children require caretakers who are responsive to both their nurturance needs and their security needs. Because of children's dependence, socialization agents have a pervasive influence on the beliefs and values that children acquire. Children are motivated to adjust to the standards of their significant others, to behave as their significant others want and expect them to behave.

In the traditional approach, the acquisition of beliefs and values from interactions with significant others is linked to self-regulatory mechanisms that influence responses to the world. Both beliefs and values establish expectancies, and these expectancies in turn create a preparedness to respond to objects relevant to them. In this way, belief-relevant and value-relevant knowledge becomes highly accessible, which increases the likelihood that knowledge-related stimuli will be noticed, responded to, and remembered (see, e.g., Jones & Gerard, 1967).

This traditional approach to understanding how social regulation affects self-regulation and responses to the world has yielded significant advances in personality and social psychology, as evident in historical contributions to person perception (i.e., Bruner, 1957; Kelly, 1955), and in more recent work on chronic accessibility effects (for reviews, see Fazio, 1986; Higgins, 1996). There is a limitation, however, with this traditional approach. The beliefs and values that are internalized and become chronically accessible are conceptualized as specific, relatively distinct mental elements, such as the personal constructs of Kelly (1955), the accessible categories of Bruner (1957), and the "attitude object evaluation" units of Fazio (1986). In addition, expectancies themselves are typically conceptualized as specific, relatively distinct mental elements (see Olson, Roese, & Zanna, 1996). Given that beliefs and values, as well as the expectancies they establish, are distinctive and specific, how does socialization produce general ways of responding to the world? How can we account for the fact that society's codes and values become part of the very fabric of an individual's personality during the process of socialization?

An alternative approach, which we take in this chapter (see also Higgins, 1997), is to distinguish between different styles of socialization in terms of their regulatory focus, and then relate different types of regulatory focus to distinct worldviews that children can acquire. We begin with a general review of self-regulatory development that describes how children at different developmental levels represent the interpersonal significance of their behavior and appearance; that is, how children learn about their own person–environment fit. This section sets the stage for considering how different styles of caretaker–child interaction might shape the strength and quality of children's regulatory focus in life. The final section describes how regulatory focus, in turn, can create ways of living in the world.

Learning about One's Person–Environment Fit

Children need to obtain both nurturance and security to survive. To do so, they must establish and maintain relationships with caretakers who fulfill these needs (see Bowlby, 1969, 1973). In order to establish and maintain such relationships, children must learn how their behaviors and appearance influence caretakers' responses to them. Children must learn to regulate their behaviors and appearance in line with these relationship contingencies to increase the likelihood that caretakers will provide them the nurturance and security they need (cf. Bowlby, 1969; Cooley, 1902/1962; Mead, 1934; Sullivan, 1953).

Children must also learn about their own strengths and weaknesses. They must learn, for example, that certain activities are beyond their capabilities and that it is dangerous to attempt such activities. When there are alternative means to the same goal, it is adaptive for children to know which of the means best suits their capabilities. It is also adaptive for children to learn which of their attributes, including their physical and emotional states, facilitates or impedes the attainment of their goals. More generally, it is adaptive for children to acquire competence self-knowledge to be used in self-regulation.

We have proposed elsewhere (Higgins, 1997) that children acquire a self-knowledge that summarizes their personal relations to the world and the consequences of these relations, and that serves self-regulatory functions. This personal self-digest is a handy reference for children about their person–environment fit. It is distinguished from the classic notion of self-knowledge as self-description in terms of the kinds of information it contains. It answers the question, "What is my relation to the world?" rather than the question, "Who am I?" This section examines how shifts in children's mental representational capacity influences self-knowledge acquisition and extends previous chapters on self-regulatory development from the perspective of self-discrepancy theory (e.g., Higgins, 1989a, 1991; Moretti & Higgins, 1990).

Piagetian and neo-Piagetian models of cognitive development have described general changes in level of mental representation (e.g., Case, 1985; Damon & Hart, 1986; Fischer, 1980; Selman, 1980). Using Case's (1985) theory of intellectual change, we describe shifts in self-knowledge as a function of changes in level of mental representation (see also Higgins, 1989a, 1991).

Level 1: Early Sensorimotor Development

By the end of the first year, a child can represent the relation between two events, such as two successive responses his or her mother produces or the relation between a response that he or she produces and the mother's response to it (see Case, 1985). Children can produce and interpret communicative signals and anticipate the occurrence of some event, and thus are capable of the preliminary form of role-taking that Mead (1934) described – the ability to anticipate the responses of a significant other with whom one is interacting. They can represent the contingency, "When I produce X, this person responds Y," which is a preliminary step in acquiring interpersonal contingencies.

Level 2: Late Sensorimotor and Early Interrelational Development

Between 18 and 24 months of age, there is a dramatic shift in children's ability to represent events. This shift has been traditionally associated with the emergence of symbolic representation (e.g., Bruner, 1964; Case, 1985; Fischer, 1980; Piaget, 1951; Werner & Kaplan, 1963). Children can then represent the bidirectional relationship between themselves and another person as an interrelation between two distinct mental objects, self-as-object and other-as-object (see Harter, 1983; Lewis & Brooks-Gunn, 1979). They can represent the relation between two relations: the relation between a feature of themselves (e.g., their action, response, physical appearance) and a particular response by another person, and the relation between a particular response by another person and a particular state that they will experience. Children can represent, for example, the relation between their making a mess at mealtime and their mother's frowning, yelling, or leaving, and the relation between their mother's frowning, yelling, or leaving and their experiencing a negative state.

At level 2, then, a child is capable of a higher level of role-taking or perspective-taking, which is critical for symbolic interaction: the ability to anticipate the responses of others to his or her actions and the personal consequences of these social responses (see Stryker & Statham, 1985). A child's significant others link him or her to the larger society by providing the shared reality or social meaning of the child's features (i.e., societal responses to the child's features) as well as the importance of the child's features (i.e., the state produced in the child by these societal responses). In this way, children learn the *interpersonal significance* of their self-features.

Children can use the self-knowledge they acquire at level 2 in an instrumental, means–end fashion to regulate their actions, responses, or appearance. By representing the significance of their self-features and using this information to plan their actions, children at level 2 are better able to delay gratification, to control their momentary impulses, and to free themselves from the demands and forces of the immediate situation (see Miller & Green, 1985; Mischel & Moore, 1980; Mischel & Patterson, 1978).

Level 3: Late Interrelational and Early Dimensional Development

The dramatic shift in children's representational capacity that occurs between 4 and 6 years of age underlies the classic change from egocentric to nonegocentric thought (see Feffer, 1970; Flavell, Botkin, Fry, Wright, & Jarvis, 1968; Piaget, 1965; Selman & Byrne, 1974; Werner, 1957). Children in this age group can coordinate two separate systems of interrelations, such as coordinating observable responses with unobservable responses (see Case, 1985); this coordination underlies inferences about the thoughts, expectations, motives, and intentions of others (see Shantz, 1983).

At this point in their lives, children understand that other people have different attitudes about different types of responses; that they prefer some types of responses over others. They understand that performing the types of responses preferred by others is related to others' positive responses to them, and they are therefore motivated to learn the types of responses that are preferred by their significant others. In addition to learning about a significant other's preferences from his or her reactions to them personally, children learn by observing the significant other react to others (i.e., observational learning; see Bandura, 1977, 1986). For example, children can observe how their mother reacts to their siblings' responses and thereby infer which types of responses their mother prefers (see Bandura, 1986; Bandura & Walters, 1963).

The significant development at level 3 is that children now understand that the relation between their self-feature and another person's response to it is mediated by the other person's standpoint (or viewpoint) on this feature. They can now represent, for example, the fact that it is the discrepancy between their behavior and the behavior that their mother prefers that underlies the association between their behavior and their mother's response to it, which in turn produces a negative state in them. For this reason, children's self-features acquire a new kind of interpersonal significance, one tied to their representations of others' goals and standards for them. At level 3, children can use such guides (see Higgins, 1989a, 1991) as a basis for self-evaluation by assessing the amount of discrepancy between their current self-state and the end-state that others desire or demand of them (e.g., "How am I doing in relation to what Mother wants or demands of me?"). They can then respond to any perceived discrepancy by taking action to reduce it. They can also plan action by taking potential discrepancies into account, thereby using prospective self-evaluation in the service of self-regulation (see also Carver & Scheier, 1990).

Level 4: Late Dimensional and Early Vectorial Development

Between 9 and 11 years of age children become capable of coordinating values along two distinct dimensions (see Case, 1985; Fischer, 1980). When comparing their performance to that of another child, for example, children can now consider simultaneously the difference in actors' outcomes and the difference in actors' effort, thus making ability inferences possible (see Ruble, 1983). To be good at something now means to be better than others at something that is worthwhile, something that matters, as defined by a represented standard of value. Now the value of a target of comparison, such as performance on some task, depends on its relation to a represented goal or guide. Being "bad" or "good" at something thus acquires new significance.

At level 4, children's ability to interrelate distinct dimensions means that they can form cognitive structures relating their representation of their actual self to their representation of significant others' guides for them. Not only can they evaluate a particular action they just performed, by considering another person's likely response to that action, but they can also evaluate how the general traits they believe they possess relate to the general traits that significant others desire or expect them to possess. That is, they can now evaluate their success or failure at being the "type of person" that others desire or expect them to be. At level 4 there can also be a pattern of structural interconnections among actual self-attributes and a significant other's standpoint on those attributes that *as a whole* has psychological significance. This means that children at level 4 can evaluate themselves in more global, overall terms.

Level 5: Late Vectorial Development

Between 13 and 16 years of age children become capable of interrelating different perspectives on the same object, including conflicting perspectives on the self as object (Case, 1985; Fischer, 1980; Inhelder & Piaget, 1958; Selman & Byrne, 1974). For the first time, two distinct systems of guides – such as one system involving a peer standpoint and another system involving a parental standpoint – can themselves be interrelated. Most significant, adolescents are capable of constructing their *"own" standpoint,* distinct from the standpoint of "others," which can function as the integrated solution to the complex array of alternative self-guides.

The ability to interrelate different dimensional systems also means that competence and relationship self-knowledge can be integrated in the service of performance goals. For example, adolescents might know that different types of social situations make different kinds of social interactions more likely, and that a specific kind of social interaction produces a particular type of emotional state. As a separate kind of knowledge, adolescents might also know how their own emotional states influence their motivation and performance. By integrating both kinds of knowledge, adolescents can be highly strategic in their behaviors.

College students, for example, use social support in different ways to meet their academic goals (see Cantor, 1994). Some students turn to others to seek reassurance, while other students want to study with their "idols" to inspire self-improvement. Another group of students want others to listen to their worst-case analyses of why they might fail on an impending task. These latter, "defensive pessimists" might know, for instance, that when they feel calm and relaxed their motivation to prepare for exams is reduced. They need, then, to feel less calm and relaxed. They also know that some friends and some situations are more likely than others to support their worst-case analyses, and they know that such support disrupts their serenity. Demonstrating level 5 development, such students might then strategically select these particular friends and situations prior to exams in order to control their motivation and meet their academic goals.

In sum, as children's capacity to represent self-knowledge increases, they become increasingly able to regulate themselves in ways suitable to their personal characteristics and the particular environment in which they function. The social environment is especially important, and each mode of caretaker–child interaction provides a message to the child about the kind of world in which the child lives and to which he or she must adapt. As described next, different modes of caretaker–child interaction influence both the strength of self-knowledge and the regulatory focus that a child acquires.

The Message of Different Modes of Caretaker–Child Interaction

Previous models of caretaker–child interaction have classified different modes in terms of characteristics of the mother, such as whether the mother is warm or cold or whether she is permissive or authoritarian (for a review, see Maccoby & Martin, 1983). An alternative perspective is to consider what message about the world a child acquires from his or her interactions with significant others. One aspect of the message is whether or not it provides a cogent lesson about how to get along in the world. In learning terms, is the nature of the caretaker–child interactions such that strong self-regulatory knowledge can be acquired? Another aspect of the message is its statement about the kind of world in which the child lives. Does the individual need a promotion focus or a prevention focus to get along in the world?

Strength of Self-Regulatory Knowledge

Strong self-regulatory knowledge has three properties (see Higgins, 1989a, 1991): high *accessibility,* in which the self-regulatory knowledge units have high activation potential; high *commitment,* in which the procedural forces of the self-regulatory knowledge units are high in magnitude; and high *coherence,* in which the procedural forces of the self-regulatory knowledge units have a uniform direction. The socialization literature suggests that the following variables produce strong self-regulatory knowledge (e.g., Maccoby & Martin, 1983; Patterson, 1982; Radke-Yarrow, Zahn-Waxler, & Chapman, 1983; see Higgins, 1989a, 1991, for a review): *frequency* of exposure to interactions that instantiate some self-regulatory knowledge; *consistency* of instantiations; *clarity* of instantiations, including salience and comprehensibility; and *significance* of instantiations, including the significance to the child of the caretaker–child relationship.

There are general classifications of different modes of caretaker–child interaction that are likely to produce relatively strong self-regulatory knowledge or relatively weak self-regulatory knowledge (for a more complete discussion, see Higgins, 1989a, 1991). We hypothesize that *managing* modes (i.e., engineering and planning the child's environment to bring out desired attributes in the child) and *disciplinary* modes of caretaker–child interaction produce strong self-regulatory knowledge because the caretakers are responsive (i.e., they respond differentially to desired and undesired behaviors of the child) and sensitive (i.e., they closely monitor the attentional state of the child and adapt their demands to the child's state); caretaker responsivity and sensitivity increase both the frequency and the consistency of the interactions instantiating self-regulatory knowledge.

In contrast, we expect *rejecting* modes and *doting* modes to produce weaker self-regulatory knowledge. Children whose caretakers reject them (i.e., neglect or abuse them) are likely to acquire weaker self-regulatory knowledge because neglect implies low frequency of interactions, and instances of abuse are typically low in clarity. Children whose doting caretakers are either highly permissive (i.e., who take a tolerant, accepting attitude toward the child's impulses, make few demands, avoid enforcing rules or imposing restrictions) or overprotective (i.e., who supervise, restrict, and control every behavior of the child) are also likely to acquire weaker self-regulatory knowledge because these nondiscriminating responses to the child are low in clarity.

As one test of this hypothesized relation between modes of caretaker–child interaction and strength of self-regulatory knowledge, Newman, Higgins, and Vookles (1992) identified two groups of adolescents who, according to the logic of this analysis, should differ in the strength of their self-regulatory knowledge: first-borns and later-borns. First-borns are expected to acquire stronger self-regulatory knowledge because the frequency, consistency, clarity, and significance of their interactions with caretakers all tend to be greater than for later-borns (for a review, see Newman, Higgins, & Vookles, 1992). The "ideal" and "ought" guides represented in self-knowledge function both as goals to move toward and as standards for self-assessment (see Higgins, 1991). Children with stronger self-regulatory knowledge, therefore, are expected to have stronger procedural forces on them for both the locomotion and assessment. Therefore, on the one hand, these children generally are expected to have smaller discrepancies between

Table 3.1. *Classification
scheme of modes of
caretaker–child interaction*

Type of contingency knowledge
Desired state
Promotion focus
Prevention focus
Undesired state
Promotion focus
Prevention focus
Strong contingency
Managing modes
Bolstering
Prudent
Disciplining modes
Love withdrawal
Punitive/Critical
Weak contingency
Doting modes
Spoiling
Overprotective
Rejecting modes
Neglectful
Abusive

their actual self and their self-guides (as a result of working harder to move toward their significant others' goals for them); on the other hand, they are expected to suffer more from any discrepancy they do have (as a result of stronger feedback following assessed failure to meet their significant others' standards for them). Regarding discrepancies from significant other self-guides, Newman, Higgins, and Vookles (1992) found, consistent with these predictions, that first-borns did have smaller discrepancies than later-borns. Despite this, the discrepancies of first-borns predicted suffering to a greater extent than the discrepancies of later-borns.

Regulatory Focus of Self-Contingencies

Different modes of caretaker–child interaction not only produce self-knowledge varying in self-regulatory strength, but also produce self-knowledge varying in regulatory reference (i.e., a desired state as the reference point versus an undesired state as the reference point) and in regulatory focus (i.e., a focus on promotion versus a focus on prevention). As shown in Table 3.1, caretaker–child interactions can be classified in terms of whether the interaction communicates that the state of the child is desired by the caretaker or is undesired by the caretaker, and whether the interaction has a promotion focus or prevention focus. For the purpose of this chapter, the modes of caretaker–child interaction that produce strong self-regulatory knowledge are most relevant.

When caretaker–child interactions have a desired state as the reference point, the interactions can have either a promotion focus or a prevention focus. When these interactions have a promotion focus, such as caretakers hugging and kissing the child when he or she behaves in a desired manner, encouraging the child to overcome difficulties, or setting up opportunities for the child to engage in rewarding activities, this is the *bolstering* mode. The caretaker's message to the child in the bolstering mode is that what matters is accomplishing goals or fulfilling aspirations: "This is what I would ideally like you to do." When caretaker–child interactions have a desired state as the reference point and a prevention focus – for example, "child-proofing" the house, training the child to be alert to potential dangers, or teaching the child to "mind your manners" – this is the *prudent* mode. The caretaker's message to the child in the prudent mode is that what matters is attaining safety or meeting obligations: "This is what I believe you ought to do.'"

When caretakers have an undesired state as the reference point, the interactions again can have either a promotion focus or a prevention focus. When they have a promotion focus – for example, ending a meal when the child throws some food, taking away a toy when the child refuses to share it, stopping a story when the child is not paying attention – it is the *love withdrawal* mode. The caretaker's message to the child in the love withdrawal mode is that what matters is attaining accomplishments or fulfilling aspirations, but it is communicated with reference to an undesired state of the child: "This is *not* what I would ideally like you to do." When caretaker–child interactions have an undesired state as the reference point and a prevention focus – for example, playing roughly with the child to get his or her attention, yelling at the child when he or she doesn't listen, criticizing the child when he or she makes a mistake – this is the *critical/punitive* mode. The caretaker's message to the child in the critical/punitive mode is that what matters is attaining safety or meeting obligations; but it is communicated with reference to an undesired state of the child: "This is *not* what I believe you ought to do."

According to this model, children socialized by some combination of bolstering and love withdrawal modes of caretaker–child interaction are likely to acquire a promotion focus in which survival in the world means accomplishing goals and fulfilling aspirations. In contrast, children socialized by some combination of prudent and critical/punitive modes of caretaker–child interaction are likely to acquire a prevention focus in which survival in the world means attaining safety and meeting obligations.

What, then, are the consequences of these different types of regulatory focus? This is a critical question that we have only begun to address. Research on the socialization aspect of the model in particular has only just begun. Some supportive findings have been obtained, however, in an unpublished study by Higgins, Loeb, and Ruble (1994). The participants in the study were volunteers – mothers and their children from schools in the Farmingdale school system in Long Island, New York. The children in the study were sixty-eight seventh graders (thirty-four males and thirty-four females), forty-seven eighth graders (twenty-seven males and twenty females), and twenty-one ninth graders (eight males and thirteen females).

Both the children and their parents were given Parent–Child Interaction questionnaires. The parents were asked two questions: "For each of the following behaviors of your child, *how would you usually respond to the behavior?*" [Parental Response]; and "For each of the following behaviors of your child, *how would the behavior usually make you feel?*" [Parental Emotion]. Each of these questions was on a separate page in the questionnaire and was followed by a set of positive behaviors (e.g., friendly, helpful, kind, creative) and negative behaviors (e.g., selfish, rude, messy, lazy) that were ordered randomly. For the same sets of positive and negative behaviors, the children were asked how their mother's response to them usually made them feel when they behaved that way.

Table 3.2 shows the method used for classifying the mothers' reported responses to their children's behaviors and the emotions they reported experiencing in these interactions with their children. Both parental responses and parental emotions were classified in terms of the same psychological situations (see Higgins, 1989a, 1991): the promotion-focus psychological situations of presence of positive outcomes and absence of positive outcomes; and the prevention-focus psychological situations of absence of negative outcomes and presence of negative outcomes.

Self-discrepancy theory hypothesizes that there are specific interrelations among regulatory focus, type of psychological situation, and type of emotion (see Higgins, 1989b, in press). These hypothesized interrelations are shown in Table 3.3. According to self-discrepancy theory, when regulatory promotion is working people feel cheerful, and when it is not working people feel dejected. The theory also predicts that when regulatory prevention is working people feel quiescent, and when it is not working people feel agitated.

Table 3.2. *Examples off classification of parental response styles and emotional responses*

I.	Parental response styles
	Promotion focus
	Presence of positive: Show affection (e.g., hug, kiss, laugh)
	Show appreciation (e.g., thank, reward)
	Absence of positive: Withdraw love and affection
	Withdraw trust; ignore
	Prevention focus
	Presence of negative: Scold or reproach; be stern or strict
	Physical aggression; nag or criticize
	Absence of negative Do nothing or just accept, not nag or bother
II.	Parental emotions
	Presence of positive: Happy, satisfied (cheerfulness)
	Absence of positive: Disappointed, discouraged (dejection)
	Presence of negative: Worried, nervous (agitation)
	Absence of negative: Relaxed, relieved (quiescence)

Table 3.3. *Types of psychological situations and emotions as a function of regulatory focus and overall valence of experience*

	Overall Valence of Experience	
	Positive (Self-Regulation Working)	Negative (Self-Regulation Not Working)
Regulatory focus		
Promotion	Presence of Positive Happy Satisfied	Absence of Positive Sad Discouraged
Prevention	Absence of Negative Calm Relaxed	Presence of Negative Tense Nervous

Given the hypothesized relations between regulatory focus and emotional experiences, one would expect that the mothers' regulatory focus when interacting with their children, as reflected in their responses to the children's behaviors, would be related to the types of emotions they usually experience during such interactions. As shown in Table 3.4, this prediction was confirmed. The more often that mothers had a promotion focus when responding to their children, the more often they experienced cheerfulness-related emotions for positive child behaviors and dejection-related emotions for negative behaviors. In comparison, the more often that mothers had a prevention focus, the more often they experienced quiescence-related emotions for positive child behaviors and agitation-related emo-

Table 3.4. *Partial and zero-order correlations between parental response styles and emotions*

I. *Children's Positive Behaviors*

	Parental Response Styles			
	Presence of Positive (Promotion Focus)		Absence of Negative (Prevention Focus)	
Parental Emotions				
Presence of Positive (Cheerfulness)	0.73***	[0.72***]	0.14*	[0.07]
Absence of Negative (Quiescence)	0.26***	[0.13]	0.22**	[0.19*]

II. *Children's Negative Behaviors*

	Parental Response Styles			
	Absence of Positive (Promotion Focus)		Presence of Negative (Prevention Focus)	
Parental Emotions				
Absence of Positive (Dejection)	0.41***	[0.44**]	0.05	[0.21*]
Presence of Negative (Agitation)	0.08	[0.22*]	0.51***	[0.54***]

Note: Zero-order correlations are given in the square brackets. *$p < 0.05$; **$p < 0.01$; ***$p < 0.001$; $N = 136$.

tions for negative child behaviors. All other relations were much weaker or nonsignificant.

This study also permitted a comparison of reported mother emotions during the caretaker–child interactions and reported child emotions during the same interactions. If the caretaker's regulatory focus influences the child's regulatory focus, then one would expect the children's emotions to correspond to the mothers' emotions. The mothers' and the children's independent reports of the emotions that they experienced during their interactions confirm that this was indeed the case. The more that the mothers experienced promotion-focus emotions in their interactions with their children (i.e., emotions along the cheerfulness–dejection dimension), the more their children also experienced promotion-focus emotions ($r = 0.28$, $p < 0.01$). The more the mothers experienced prevention-focus emotions (i.e., emotions along the quiescence–agitation dimension), the more their children also experienced prevention-focus emotions ($r = 0.45, p < 0.01$). In contrast, there was no significant relation between the extent to which mothers experienced promotion-focus emotions and the extent to which their children experienced prevention-focus emotions, or between the extent to which mothers experienced prevention-focus emotions and the extent to which their children experienced promotion-focus emotions.

In sum, some preliminary evidence indicates that the regulatory focus of caretakers as reflected in their responses to children's positive and negative behaviors is related to the specific kinds of emotions they experience from their caretaker–child interactions. Specifically, caretakers (in this case mothers) who responded to the child with a promotion focus were more likely to experience emotions along the cheerfulness–dejection dimension, whereas caretakers who responded with a prevention focus were more likely to experience emotions along the quiescence–agitation dimension. There is also some evidence that the emotional responses of the children correspond to the type of emotions that the caretaker experiences in the interaction. This is another way that children can learn about the specific emotional conse-quences of caretaker–child interactions. Such knowledge contributes to children's own chronic promotion or prevention focus, which can have con-sequences for them throughout their lives. The next section describes how chronic regulatory focus can influence people's emotions, cognitions, and strategic responses to the world.

The Impact of Regulatory Focus on Ways of Living

Children are motivated to learn what to do in order to obtain the nurturance and security they need from their caretakers. Between 4 and 6 years of age they become capable of representing the goals and standards that their care-takers hold for them and that determine how their caretakers respond to them. By 9 to 11 years of age they can represent what type of person their care-taker would ideally like them to be and what type of person their caretaker believes they ought to be. By these ages, then, children with strong self-knowledge are motivated to regulate themselves in relation to significant oth-ers' *ideal* self-guides for them (i.e., representations of hopes, wishes, and as-pirations for them) and/or *ought* self-guides for them (i.e., representations of beliefs about their duties, obligations, and responsibilities). Later, adoles-cents and adults are also capable of representing their own personal "ideals" and "oughts" for themselves, which then become self-regulatory guides.

According to our earlier analysis, chronic self-regulation in relation to an ideal self-guide would involve a promotion focus, whereas chronic self-regulation in relation to an ought self-guide would involve a prevention fo-cus. By comparing ideal self-regulation with ought self-regulation, there-fore, it is possible to examine the consequences of chronic differences in people's regulatory focus. Several studies testing self-discrepancy theory have provided exactly this kind of comparison (for reviews, see Higgins, 1987, 1989b, 1997). Rather than reviewing all the findings, we here provide some examples of the impact that chronic self-regulatory focus has on emotional, cognitive, and strategic responses to the world, that is, on ways of living.

Chronic Regulatory Focus and Emotional Responses

One way to examine the impact of chronic regulatory focus on emotional responses is to identify both individuals who are strongly motivated to meet their ideal self-guides (ideal-focus individuals) and individuals who are strongly motivated to meet their ought self-guides (ought-focus individuals) and to test how they respond emotionally simply to imagining successes or failures in life. This kind of comparison is provided in a study by Higgins, Bond, Klein, and Strauman (1986, study 1).

Undergraduates filled out the "Selves" questionnaire weeks before the experimental session. This questionnaire asks respondents to list up to eight or ten attributes for each of a number of different self-states. It is administered in two sections, the first involving the respondent's own standpoint and the second involving the standpoints of the respondent's significant others (e.g., mother, father). On the first page of the questionnaire the different types of selves are defined (e.g., the actual, ideal, and ought self-states). On each subsequent page there is an item about a different self-state, such as "Please list the attributes of the type of person *you* think you *actually* are" or "Please list the attributes of the type of person your *mother* thinks you *should or ought* to be." The respondents are also asked to rate for each listed attribute the extent to which the standpoint person (self or other) believed they actually possessed that attribute, ought to possess that attribute, wanted them ideally to possess that attribute, and so on.

The two-step procedure for calculating the magnitude of a self-discrepancy is as follows: for each self-discrepancy, the attributes in one self-state (e.g., actual/own) are compared to the attributes in the other self-state (e.g., ideal/mother) in order to determine which attributes are synonyms and which are antonyms. Attributes that are neither are coded as *non-matches*. Antonyms are coded as *antonymous mismatches*. Synonyms with basically the same extent ratings are coded as matches. Synonyms with very different extent ratings (e.g., actual, "slightly attractive" versus ideal, "extremely attractive") are coded as *synonymous mismatches*. The magnitude of a self-discrepancy is the total number of mismatches minus the total number of matches. The undergraduates were divided into two groups on the basis of their questionnaire responses: a group with relatively high discrepancy between their actual and ideal selves but relatively low discrepancy between their actual and ought selves (the predominant ideal discrepancy or ideal-focus group), and a group with relatively high discrepancy between their actual and ought selves but relatively low discrepancy between their actual and ideal selves (the predominant ought discrepancy or ought-focus group).

When the undergraduates attended the experimental session weeks later, they were asked to imagine either a positive event in which performance matches a common standard (e.g., receiving an A grade in a course) or a negative event in which performances fails to match a common standard (e.g., receiving a D grade in a course that is necessary for obtaining an important job). The subjects filled out mood measures and performed a simple writing-speed task both at the beginning and at the end of the session.

We expected little difference between the ideal-focus and ought-focus groups when they imagined a positive event happening to them because both groups are dealing with chronic self-discrepancies and therefore would be more sensitive to problematic than nonproblematic events (see Brendl & Higgins, 1995). However, given that both groups possess self-discrepancies, they would be expected to have strong emotional responses to imagining a negative event. For negative events, then, the effect of regulatory focus on emotional responses should be more evident. What difference in emotional responses might be expected?

As shown in Table 3.3, self-discrepancy theory predicts that when regulatory promotion is working people feel cheerful (e.g., happy and satisfied), and when it is not working people feel dejected (e.g., sad and disappointed). Thus, chronic discrepancies between one's perceived actual self and a significant other's, or one's own, hopes and wishes for oneself (i.e., actual/ideal discrepancies) are expected to produce dejection. The theory also predicts that when regulatory prevention is working people feel quiescent (e.g., calm and relaxed), and when it is not working people feel agitated (e.g., nervous and worried). Therefore, chronic discrepancies between one's perceived actual self and a significant other's, or one's own, beliefs about one's duty and obligations (i.e., actual/ought discrepancies), are expected to produce agitation.

Self-discrepancy theory predicts that when the undergraduates imagined a negative event happening to them (i.e., self-regulation not working), those with a strong actual/ideal discrepancy or promotion focus would experience an increase in dejection-related emotions, and that those with a strong actual/ought or prevention focus would experience an increase in agitation-related emotions. As shown in Table 3.5, this prediction was confirmed. For undergraduates imagining the negative event, there was a clear pattern of correlations between the magnitude of their particular type of self-discrepancy or regulatory focus, as measured weeks earlier, and the specific kind of

Table 3.5. *Partial correlations between types of self-discrepancies
and types of postmanipulation mood in the positive event and negative
event conditions*

| | Guided-imagery manipulation task | | | |
| | Positive event | | Negative event | |
Type of postmoood	Dejection emotions	Agitation emotions	Dejection emotions	Agitation emotions
Type of self-discrepancy				
Actual/ideal	0.17	0.13	0.39 ($p < 0.01$)	−0.33 ($p < 0.05$)
Actual/ought	0.05	0.26	−0.04	0.46 ($p < 0.01$)

Note: Partial correlations shown have premanipulation mood and the alternative type of self-discrepancy partialed out of each.

mood change they experienced during the experiment. It should also be noted that the same pattern of results was found for a writing-speed measure, with writing speed decreasing (i.e., motor retardation) as actual/ideal discrepancy increased, and writing speed increasing (i.e., motor agitation) as actual/ought discrepancy increased.

If an ideal self-discrepancy involves a chronic promotion focus that is not working and an ought self-discrepancy involves a chronic prevention focus that is not working, then priming or activating these self-discrepancies is expected to produce the associated type of emotional syndrome. Specifically, priming an ideal self-discrepancy is expected to produce a dejection or depression-like syndrome, whereas priming an ought self-discrepancy is expected to produce an agitation or anxiety-like syndrome. This would happen even when the priming event is a positive attribute selected from the participants' own desired self-guides. Strauman and Higgins (1987) tested this prediction.

Ideal-focus and ought-focus undergraduates were selected on the basis of their responses to the Selves Questionnaire obtained weeks earlier – subjects who were predominant ideal-discrepant and subjects who were predominant ought-discrepant. A covert, idiographic priming technique was used to activate self-attributes in a task supposedly investigating the "physiological effects of thinking about other people." The participants were given phrases of the form, "An X person _____ " (where X was a trait adjective such as "friendly" or "intelligent"), and were asked to complete each sentence as quickly as possible. For each sentence, a participant's total verbalization time and skin conductance amplitude were recorded. The participants also reported their mood on scales measuring dejection-related and agitation-related emotions both at the beginning and at the end of the session.

The participants were randomly assigned to the following three priming conditions: *nonmatching priming,* in which the trait adjectives were attributes in a subject's self-guide but the attributes did not appear in the subject's actual self; *mismatching priming,* in which the trait adjectives were attributes in a subject's self-guide and the subject's actual self was discrepant from the self-guide for those attributes; and *yoked (mismatching) priming,* in which the trait adjectives were attributes that did not appear in either a subject's self-guide or actual self but were the same attributes that were used for some other subject in the "mismatching" priming condition.

As predicted, in the mismatching priming condition *only* a dejection-related syndrome (i.e., increased dejected mood, lowered standardized skin conductance amplitude, decreased total verbalization time) was produced in the ideal-focus group, whereas an agitation-related syndrome (i.e., increased agitated mood, raised standardized skin conductance amplitude, increased total verbalization time) was produced in the ought-focus group. Moreover, there was a striking shift into and out of these distinct emotional syndromes as the participants received either mismatching priming or priming of attributes that were irrelevant to their self-system, respectively (see Strauman & Higgins, 1987).

It could also be expected that chronic regulatory focus interacts with social life events such that these events have different emotional consequences. For example, one might expect that the significant life transition of becoming a parent for the first time might have different emotional consequences for new parents with a promotion focus (i.e., predominant ideal-discrepant parents) than for new parents with a prevention focus (i.e., predominant ought-discrepant parents). How might this work?

From a life transition perspective (see Higgins, Loeb, & Ruble, 1995), how might the new duties and obligations associated with becoming a parent affect individuals oriented toward their own life aspirations (chronic promotion focus) as compared to individuals oriented toward other responsibilities demanded of them by a significant other, particularly their spouse (chronic prevention focus)? The social role of parent involves norms or social prescriptions to fulfill certain duties and responsibilities. Focusing on the duties and responsibilities of parenthood, therefore, could reduce the accessibility of other duties and responsibilities that are associated with a different role, such as the role of spouse (see Alexander & Higgins, 1993). Stated more simply, the more parental role responsibilities become the focus of attention, the less the responsibilities associated with alternative roles will receive attention. This is especially true for roles that involve different responsibilities in the same sphere of life, such as family obligations to a child as opposed to those to a spouse.

This logic leads to the prediction that for individuals who possess an actual/ought (spouse) discrepancy before becoming a parent, the shift from attending to spousal responsibilities to attending to parental responsibilities after becoming a parent is expected to *decrease* their distress from their actual/ought (spouse) discrepancy. Moreover, given that activation of actual/ought discrepancies produces agitation-related suffering, a decrease specifically in their agitation-related emotions would likely result.

How is the new role of parent predicted to affect parents possessing actual/ideal discrepancies? The ideal self-guide does not involve duties and responsibilities. Instead, it involves personal hopes and aspirations, such as personal career aspirations. The ideal self-guide involves a promotion focus rather than the prevention focus of duties and obligations. Thus, attention to the new role of parent will not reduce the accessibility of ideal discrepancies. Still, the resources allocated to the new role of parent necessarily diminish the resources needed to attain the parent's aspirations. The early postpartum period involves significant change in daily routines, performance of unfamiliar tasks, and increased fatigue, which interferes with regulatory promotion. Thus, for individuals who possess actual/ideal discrepancies prior to the birth of their child, the more attention they give to the parental role, the more likely they are to suffer from these discrepancies. Also, given that activation of actual/ideal discrepancies produces dejection-related suffering, an *increase* specifically in dejection-related emotions is likely to result. These predictions were tested by Alexander and Higgins (1993).

Married couples expecting their first child were recruited during the last trimester of the pregnancy and were given the Selves questionnaire to measure self-discrepancies before the birth of their child. The couples were also given a questionnaire on chronic emotional distress that measured how often they felt different kinds of emotional/motivational states during the prior week. Higher ratings indicated that the state was experienced more often. The measure included both dejection-related items (e.g., disappointed, dissatisfied, hopeless) and agitation-related items (e.g. fearful, threatened, agitated). On the average, the measure of ideal and ought self-discrepancies was taken over six months before the postmeasure of chronic emotional distress. To calculate partial correlation coefficients between target discrepancies and target moods, hierarchical multiple regressions were performed. To examine the unique effect of pre–actual/ideal discrepancy on postdejection, for example, the postdejection score was regressed on pre–actual/ideal discrepancy, with postagitation (the complementary postdistress), pre–actual/ought discrepancy (the complementary discrepancy), and predejection entered before the target. As predicted, a significant *negative* relation was found between pre–actual/ought discrepancies and postagitation, whereas a significant *positive* relation was found between pre–actual/ideal discrepancies and postdejection.

Median splits revealed more clearly the nature of these correlations. It was found that the decrease in agitation was greater for those high in ought discrepancy than for those low in ought discrepancy, and the increase in dejection scores was greater for subjects high in ideal discrepancies than for those low in ideal discrepancies. For mothers, the difference between the pre-ought discrepancy relation to postagitation and the pre-ideal discrepancy relation to postdejection was highly reliable ($p < 0.01$). The strength of the relation found for mothers between pre-ought discrepancy and decreased postagitation, measured over six months later, was quite remarkable: $pr(24) = -0.50, p < 0.01$!

This study can also account for why women tend to experience more negative *and* more positive emotional changes than men during the transition to parenthood (for a review, see Alexander & Higgins, 1993). Women tend to embrace the new role of parent more strongly than do men, and paying attention to the new role demands can either increase dejection or decrease agitation, depending on its impact on the accessibility of pretransition self-discrepancies. The results of this study also suggest that the increase in suffering is more likely to involve dejection-related emotions than agitation-related emotions. Perhaps this could explain why postpartum distress is typically reported in the literature as involving dejection or depression rather than agitation or anxiety (for a review, see Alexander & Higgins, 1993).

Chronic Regulatory Focus and Cognitive Responses

General worldviews are likely to influence how one responds to the world (e.g., Kelly, 1955). Events that are relevant to a person's regulatory focus are expected to be remembered better than events that are irrelevant. This should be true not only for events in which perceivers themselves are involved (i.e., autobiographical memory) but also for events in which others are involved (i.e., biographical memory). Chronic regulatory focus, then, is expected to influence memory for events even when those events do not produce strong emotional responses in the perceiver. Consistent with this reasoning, Higgins and Tykocinski (1992) predicted that when people read descriptions of events in another person's life, those events involving the presence or absence of positive outcomes where promotion is working or not working would be remembered better by ideal-focus persons (i.e., predominant ideal discrepant persons) than by ought-focus persons (i.e., predominant ought discrepant persons), whereas the reverse would be true for remembering events involving the absence or presence of negative outcomes where prevention is working or not working.

Undergraduates were selected who were either predominant ideal-discrepant or predominant ought-discrepant. At the experimental session a few weeks later, all the participants were given the same essay to read about several days in the life of a target person. Ten minutes after reading the essay (following a nonverbal filler task), they were asked to reproduce the essay word for word. In the essay, the presence and absence of positive and negative outcomes were represented by events that the target person experienced over several days, such as the following:

- The presence of positive outcomes: "I found a twenty dollar bill on the pavement of Canal Street near the paint store." [A common wish that actually happens]
- The absence of positive outcomes: "I've been wanting to see this movie at the Eighth Street theater for some time, so this evening I went there straight after school to find out that it's not showing anymore." [A hope that doesn't work out]
- The presence of negative outcomes: "I was stuck in the subway for 35 minutes with at least 15 sweating passengers breathing down my neck." [A painful condition that can't be prevented]
- The absence of negative outcomes: "This is usually my worst school day. Awful schedule, class after class with no break. But today is election day – no school!" [Escape from a painful condition]

Because activating self-discrepancies can produce emotions, and mood in turn can influence memory (see Gilligan & Bower, 1984; Isen, 1984), this study was designed to control for any possible effects of mood on memory. The essay used as input in this study was purposely constructed to minimize such activation by including events that are unrelated to personal traits. Rather, the events are clearly circumstantial factors such as finding money by chance or getting stuck in a crowded subway. We did not expect, therefore, that reading the story would activate participants' self-discrepancies and produce strong emotions. Indeed, as expected, the participants' moods changed very little during the experiment. Not only did we seek to minimize

Table 3.6. *Mean recall of events reflecting different types of psychological situations as a function of regulatory focus of event, overall valence of event, and subject's type of predominant self-discrepancy*

Regulatory focus of event				
Promotion focus				
Positive valence				
Negative valence				
Prevention focus				
Positive valence				
Negative valence				
	(Presence of positive)	(Absence of positive)	(Absence of negative)	(Presence of negative)
Type of discrepancy				
Predominant ideal	2.7	3.5	2.2	2.3
Predominant ought	2.3	2.8	2.4	2.6

changes in mood during the experiment, but we also measured mood both before and after participants read the essay in order to control statistically for mood by including it as a covariate in the analyses.

As shown in Table 3.6, the predicted interaction between participants' chronic regulatory focus and the regulatory focus reflected in the events was obtained. Predominant ideal-discrepant participants tended to remember target events representing the presence and absence of positive outcomes better than did predominant ought-discrepant participants, whereas predominant ought-discrepant participants tended to remember target events representing the absence and presence of negative outcomes better than did predominant ideal-discrepant participants. No other interactions were significant, and the obtained interaction between perceivers' chronic regulatory focus and the regulatory focus reflected in the events was independent of premood, postmood, and change in mood.

Our subsequent studies considered further cognitive consequences of regulatory focus, particularly the consequences of the motivational strategies associated with each regulatory focus. Self-regulatory systems can have either a desired end-state functioning as a positive reference point or an undesired end-state functioning as a negative reference point (see, e.g., Carver & Scheier, 1990; Markus & Nurius, 1986). The literature also distinguishes between different directions of motivated movement – between approaching a positive self-state and avoiding a negative self-state. Carver and Scheier (1990) propose that when the reference point of a self-regulatory system is positive, the system attempts to move the currently perceived actual self-state as close as possible to the reference point (a discrepancy-

Table 3.7. *Summary of regulatory forms as a function of valence of end-state as reference point and direction of means*

	Valence of end-state as reference point	
	Desired end-state (Discrepancy-reducing)	Undesired end-state (Discrepancy-amplifying)
Direction of means		
Approach	Approaching matches to desired end-states	Approaching mismatches to undesired end-states
Avoidance	Avoiding mismatches to desired end-states	Avoiding matches to undesired end-states

reducing, approach system); when it is negative, the system attempts to move the actual self-state as far away as possible from the reference point (a discrepancy-amplifying, avoidance system).

In a discrepancy-reducing system, there are two alternative means to reduce the discrepancy between the actual self and a positive reference point: approach self-states that match the desired end-state or avoid self-states that mismatch the desired end-state. For example, a person who wants to get a good grade on a quiz (a desired end-state) could either study hard at the library the day before the quiz (approaching a match to the desired end-state) or turn down an invitation to go out drinking with friends the night before the quiz (avoiding a mismatch to the desired end-state). In a discrepancy-amplifying system, there are also two alternative means to amplify the discrepancy between the actual self and a negative reference point: approach self-states that mismatch the undesired end-state or avoid self-states that match the undesired end-state. For example, a person who dislikes interpersonal conflict (an undesired end-state) could either arrange a meeting with his or her apartment-mates to work out a schedule for cleaning the apartment (approaching a mismatch to the undesired end-state) or leave the apartment when his or her two apartment-mates start to argue (avoiding a match to the undesired end-state).

We can identify four different forms of self-regulation by considering the alternative means for discrepancy reduction and discrepancy amplification. Table 3.7 summarizes how valence of end-state as reference point combines with direction of means to produce the four different regulatory forms.

We would expect a promotion focus to be associated with a predilection for self-regulatory forms involving approach, and a prevention focus to be associated with a predilection for self-regulatory forms involving avoidance. Self-regulation in relation to ideal self-guides, therefore, is expected to involve an inclination toward approach strategies, whereas self-regulation in relation to ought self-guides is expected to involve an inclination toward avoidance strategies. Moreover, this difference in strategic predilections should have cognitive consequences as well, including influencing how social events are remembered. A study by Higgins, Roney, Crowe, and Hymes (1994) tested this prediction.

The study used a manipulation of self-guide activation developed by Higgins, Bond, Klein, and Strauman (1986, Study 2). The undergraduate participants were asked either to report on how their hopes and goals had changed over their lifetime (activating ideal self-guides) or to report on how their sense of duty and obligation had changed (activating ought self-guides). To examine memory effects, a free-recall technique similar to that used by Higgins and Tykocinski (1992) was employed. Subjects read a story about four days in the life of a target student; each of the four regulatory forms in Table 3.5 was exemplified by four different episodes, such as the following:

- Approaching matches to a desired end-state: "Because I wanted to be at school for the beginning of my 8:30 psychology class, which is usually excellent, I woke up early this morning."
- Avoiding mismatches to a desired end-state: "I wanted to take a class in photography at the community center, so I didn't register for a class in Spanish that was scheduled at the same time."
- Approaching mismatches to an undesired end-state: "I dislike eating in crowded places, so at noon I picked up a sandwich from a local deli and ate outside."
- Avoiding matches to an undesired end-state: "I didn't want to feel tired during my very long morning of classes, so I skipped the most strenuous part of my morning workout."

We predicted that activating an ideal or ought guide would induce its regulatory focus, which would make perceivers more sensitive to, and thus more likely to recall, those episodes in the story that exemplified the regulatory form corresponding to the regulatory focus. In particular, activating an ideal self-guide was expected to induce a promotion focus and increase the likelihood of remembering episodes where the target approached matches to attain a desired end-state, whereas activating an ought self-guide was expected to induce a prevention focus and increase the likelihood of remembering episodes when the target avoided mismatches to attain a desired end-state. As shown in Table 3.8, this prediction was confirmed.

Table 3.8. *Mean number of episodes recalled as a function of type of self-guide activated, valence of stated end-state, and direction of stated means*

	Valence of stated end-state			
	Desired end-state		Undesired end-state	
Direction of stated means	Approach matches	Avoid mismatches	Approach mismatches	Avoid matches
Type of activation				
Ideal guide	1.75	1.37	1.50	1.39
Ought guide	1.19	1.96	1.38	1.75

Chronic Regulatory Focus and Strategic Responses

The study by Higgins and colleagues (1994), described above, suggests that regulatory promotion in relation to ideal self-guides involves strategic responses to the world that are different from those used for regulatory prevention in relation to ought self-guides. If this is true, this difference in strategic responses should influence not only sensitivity to events in the world but also tactical decisions about how to deal with the world. Specifically, we would expect that chronic promotion-focus individuals would attempt to meet their goals with approach tactics, whereas chronic prevention-focus individuals would attempt to meet their goals with avoidance tactics. This possibility was examined in a second study conducted by Higgins and colleagues (1994).

This second study consisted of three phases. The first phase elicited undergraduates' spontaneous strategies for friendship as part of a battery of questions on a variety of issues. The participants were randomly assigned to answer one of two different questions about friendship. Half the participants received a question framed with a *promotion focus,* as follows: "Imagine that you are the kind of person who would like to be a good friend in your close relationships. What would your strategy be to meet this goal?" The other half received a question framed with a *prevention focus,* as follows: "Imagine that you are the kind of person who believes you should try not to be a poor friend in your close relationships. What would your strategy be to meet this goal?" Most subjects offered several strategies in response to the question they received.

A rough classification system was developed to group the strategies into different types. Six strategy types that most differentiated responses in the two framing conditions were selected: three that were used more in response to the promotion-focus framing and three that were used more in response to the prevention-focus framing. For each of these strategy types, one or more sentences that best captured the strategy were written, using the subjects' original words as much as possible. The strategies used more in response to the promotion-focus framing were: (1) "Be generous and willing to give of yourself"; (2) "Be supportive to your friends. Be emotionally supportive"; (3) "Be loving and attentive." The strategies used more in response to the prevention-focus framing were: (4) "Stay in touch. Don't lose contact with friends"; (5) "Try to make time for your friends and not neglect them"; (6) "Keep the secrets friends have told you and don't gossip about friends." Strategies 1 to 3 were selected as the approach strategies, and strategies 4 to 6 were selected as the avoidance strategies.

In phase 2 of the study, a new sample of undergraduates was randomly assigned to answer one of two different questions about friendship strategies, with half of the subjects answering each question. The question framed with a promotion focus was: "When you think about strategies for *being a good friend* in your close relationships, which *three* of the following would you choose?" The question framed with a prevention focus was: "When you think about strategies for *not being a poor friend* in your close relationship, which *three* of the following would you choose?" This study found that participants given the promotion-focus framing chose significantly more approach strategies than participants given the prevention-focus framing, whereas the reverse was true for choosing avoidance strategies. This phase of the study demonstrated a relation between momentary regulatory focus and choosing approach and avoidance strategies.

Phase 3 of the study tested whether chronic regulatory focus is related to strategic choices. Using another sample of undergraduates, predominant ideal-discrepant individuals and predominant ought-discrepant individuals were selected. In the experimental session, each participant was asked the *same, unframed* question about friendship, as follows: "When you think about strategies for *friendship,* which *three* of the following strategies would you choose?" This question was followed by the same six choices of strategies used in the phase 2 framing study. As predicted, predominant ideal-discrepant individuals chose significantly more approach strategies than did predominant ought-discrepant individuals, whereas the reverse was true for choosing avoidance strategies.

Among the avoidance strategies for friendship, ought-focus individuals chose "Stay in touch. Don't lose contact with friends" much more often than did ideal-focus individuals. This strategy was chosen by 46 percent of the predominant ought-discrepant individuals, compared to only 13 percent of the predominant ideal-discrepant individuals. The aim of this strategy is to avoid losing contact with friends. The tactical means for attaining this aim is to stay in touch. This avoidance strategy, then, involves *taking action.* It is not the case, therefore, that an avoidance strategy implies inhibition, suppression, or inaction. Indeed, as in the case of animals escaping electric shock, it can require vigorous action.

Regulatory Focus and Life-Span Development

This chapter has described how a person's interactions with significant others provide that person with messages about his or her person–environment fit. The message of particular interest here concerns learning about one's relation to the world. We proposed a basic distinction between nurturance-oriented parenting, which instills a promotion focus in children, and security-oriented parenting, which instills a prevention focus. We have described both the determinants of a strong regulatory focus and its emotional, cognitive, and motivational consequences, presenting research that suggests that a strong regulatory focus can have a major impact on people's ways of living.

We have assumed here that a strong regulatory focus, as a chronic personality variable, is generally stable over time. This does not imply, however, that emotional health necessarily remains stable over time. Life transitions, as well as more acute life events, can produce changes in emotional health even though the underlying self-regulatory system remains basically the same (see Higgins, 1991; Higgins, Loeb, and Ruble, 1995; see also Nolen-Hoeksema, Chapter 9, this volume). For example, the emotional and behavioral consequences of a strong regulatory focus can change during the life transition of adolescence (see Higgins, 1991).

We mentioned that the procedural forces of strong self-regulatory knowledge (i.e., the force for locomotion and the force for assessment) increase both the motivation to attain desired end-states and the emotional significance of attainment (see Higgins, 1991; Newman, Higgins, & Vookles, 1992). When high motivation is likely to yield a valued outcome, the locomotion force of strong self-regulatory knowledge is expected to increase the likelihood that desired end-states will be attained. For example, the presence of prosocial behaviors and the absence of antisocial behaviors are valued outcomes for most schoolchildren; high motivation is usually sufficient to control these behaviors. Therefore, strong self-regulatory knowledge concerning these behaviors is likely to yield these valued outcomes. In contrast, popularity and academic success are also valued outcomes for most school-children, however, high motivation is not sufficient to attain them. There-fore, the locomotion force of strong self-regulatory knowledge will not nec-essarily yield these valued outcomes. Moreover, if the valued popularity and academic success are not attained, the assessment force of strong self-regulatory knowledge will produce intense emotional discomfort. Strong self-regulatory knowledge, therefore, can have benefits or costs depending on whether increased motivation from strong self-regulatory knowledge is sufficient to attain valued end-states (see Higgins, 1991; see also Newman, Higgins, & Vookles, 1992).

Life transitions can influence the likelihood that motivation will be suf-ficient to attain valued end-states. In Western cultures at least, as children move through their various social-life phases (e.g., preschoolers, juveniles, preadolescents, adolescents), the self-attributes that they value shift (see Higgins & Eccles-Parsons, 1983; Higgins, Loeb, & Ruble, 1995). For ex-ample, from the juvenile period through to adolescence, there is a shift to new self-attributes associated with peer relationships, such as popularity and sexual attractiveness, that reflects in part the increasing importance of peers in their lives (see Floyd & South, 1972; Hartup, 1983; Simmons & Blyth, 1987; see also Gollwitzer & Kirchhof, Chapter 15, this volume, and Nolen-Hoeksema, Chapter 9, this volume). Moreover, many valued self-attributes are defined relative to others – such as "smart," meaning "My grades are higher than those of most other students" (see Dweck & Elliot, 1983; Ruble, 1983; Veroff, 1969) – in contrast to the more absolute mean-ings of "polite," "tidy," "nonaggressive," and so on.

When evaluation of success or failure is based on social comparison (e.g., being better than average), it is much more difficult for children to at-tain their valued end-states. Indeed, children's perceived self-competence begins to decrease between the early juvenile and preadolescent periods, and there is a further decline with entry into adolescence (see Aboud & Ru-ble, 1987; Harter, 1983; Rosenberg, 1979; Ruble & Frey, 1987; Simmons & Blyth, 1987). In these later periods, increased motivation from the loco-motion force of strong self-regulatory knowledge is often insufficient to at-tain valued end-states. But the assessment force of strong self-regulatory knowledge produces strong negative self-evaluation and intense emotional discomfort from any failure to attain these valued end-states. Thus, life tran-sitions can interact with stable strength of self-regulatory knowledge to pro-duce changes in emotional health (see Higgins, 1991). The results of the study by Alexander and Higgins (1993), described earlier, also demonstrate that life transitions, such as becoming a parent, can interact with stable regulatory focus to produce changes in emotional health.

The assumption that a strong regulatory focus, as a chronic personality variable, is relatively stable over time does not preclude the possibility that type and strength of regulatory focus might also vary during life-span development because of life transition effects. Indeed, such effects can be quite significant. For example, promotion focus might generally increase during adolescence when future life aspirations and current accomplishments become emphasized, whereas prevention focus might increase during the final phase of life. Moreover, life transition effects on type and strength of regulatory focus might also vary in different historical periods. During times of economic hardship, for example, adolescents might experience an increase in prevention focus because finding a secure career has become the major concern. Life transition effects might also vary for different individuals. Some retired individuals, for example, might experience an increase in promotion because generativity needs are emphasized (e.g., Erikson, 1963).

Life-span perspectives include multidirectionality and contextualism. Multidimensionality implies that there is considerable diversity in the patterns of stability and change across developmental periods; contextualism holds that the course of development is influenced by interactions among systems of developmental influences (see Baltes, 1987). A striking example of both multidirectionality and contextualism can be found in the developmental course of gender differences in vulnerability to different kinds of emotional and behavioral disorders (see also Nolen-Hoeksema, Chapter 9, this volume). As shown in Table 3.9, the pattern of gender differences in emotional and behavioral disorders changes between preadolescence and adolescence/early adulthood. What is also notable is that across these developmental periods, males are consistently more vulnerable to behavioral problems of undercontrol, and females are more vulnerable to emotional and behavioral problems of overcontrol.

This pattern of stability and change in emotional and behavioral gender differences can be interpreted in terms of an interaction between the life transition to adolescence described earlier and a general tendency for females to have stronger self-regulatory concern with others' ideals and oughts for them than do males (see Higgins, 1991). The central notion is that a stable tendency for males to be vulnerable to undercontrol and females to be vulnerable to overcontrol will produce stability in males' undercontrol behavioral problems across the adolescent life transition and

Table 3.9. *Strong gender differences in behavioral and emotional disorders during the preadolescent and adolescent/early adulthood developmental periods*

Developmental period	Type of disorder	Direction of difference
Preadolescence	Attention deficit disorder	M > F
	Conduct disorder	M > F
	Schizoid disorder	M > F
Adolescence/early adulthood	Impulse control disorders	M > F
	Antisocial personality disorder	M > F
	Substance abuse	M > F
	Major depressive disorder	F > M
	Panic disorder	F > M
	Histrionic personality disorder	F > M
	Eating disorders	F > M

change in females' overcontrol emotional and behavioral problems during this transition (see Higgins, 1991). Therefore, we propose a stable gender difference in self-regulation to account for both stability and change across developmental periods in behavioral and emotional gender differences.

Life-span perspectives also include the belief that development involves both gains and losses (see Baltes, 1987). Heckhausen, Dixon, and Baltes (1989) have found, moreover, that there is considerable consensus among young, middle-aged, and old adults concerning their beliefs about the gains and losses that occur over the adult life span. We can make additional distinctions from the perspective of regulatory focus. Adults also have beliefs about the nongains and the nonlosses that occur over the adult life span. That is, rather than positive growth during a developmental period (a gain), there can be a negative failure to grow (a nongain). In addition, rather than a negative decline during a developmental period (a loss), there can be a positive achievement of not declining (a nonloss).

Although people generally experience, and hold beliefs about, the pleasures and pains of life-span development, there can still be individual differences in whether a person is primarily concerned with the gains and nongains of life-span development (a promotion focus) or with the losses and nonlosses (a prevention focus). A regulatory-focus perspective suggests that such differences would influence how individuals respond emotionally to changes in life-span development, such as experiencing the gains and nongains of life changes as joys and sorrows as opposed to experiencing the losses and nonlosses as worries and reliefs, respectively. Thus, people's emotional lives could vary markedly throughout their development even when the positive and negative changes in their lives are quite similar. In addition, specific events clearly identified as gains, nongains, losses, or nonlosses can interact with individuals' chronic regulatory focus to influence emotional sensitivity (see Brendl & Higgins, 1995). Individuals with different types of regulatory focus could therefore be emotionally sensitive to different types of life-span changes. For example, promotion-focus individuals might be relatively more sensitive to positive and negative changes in their physical attractiveness (a more promotion-related concern), whereas prevention-focus individuals might be relatively more sensitive to positive and negative changes in their health (a more prevention-related concern).

Although this chapter has emphasized strength and type of regulatory focus as chronic personality variables, they can also be considered as life-span developmental variables. Because personality itself has developmental roots, fascinating questions emerge. How does early socialization interact with later life transitions to make promotion or prevention a predominant focus in a particular period, and how does such predominance shape people's life experiences during that period? More generally, what role does regulatory focus play in the interaction of social regulation and self-regulation in life-span development?

References

Aboud, F., & Ruble, D. N. (1987). Identity constancy in children: Developmental processes and implications. In T. M. Honess & K. M. Yardley (Eds.), *Self and identity: Individual change and development* (pp. 95–107). New York: Wiley.

Adler, A. (1954). *Understanding human nature.* New York: Fawcett.

Alexander, M. J., & Higgins, E. T. (1993). Emotional trade-offs of becoming a parent: How social roles influence self-discrepancy effects. *Journal of Personality and Social Psychology, 65,* 1259–1269.

Baltes, P. B. (1987). Theoretical propositions of life-span developmental psychology: On the dynamics between growth and decline. *Developmental Psychology, 23,* 611–626.

Bandura, A. (1977). *Social learning theory.* Englewood Cliffs, NJ: Prentice-Hall.
   (1986). *Social foundations of thought and action: A social cognitive theory.* Englewood Cliffs, NJ: Prentice-Hall.

Bandura, A. L., & Walters, R. H. (1963). Social learning and personality development. New York: Holt, Rinehart and Winston.

Bowlby, J. (1969). *Attachment and loss. Vol. 1: Attachment.* New York: Basic Books.
   (1973). *Attachment and loss. Vol. 2: Separation: Anxiety and anger.* New York: Basic Books.

Brendl, C. M., & Higgins, E. T. (1995). Sensitivity to varying gains and losses: The role of self-discrepancies and event framing. *Journal of Personality and Social Psychology, 69,* 1028–1051.

Bruner, J. S. (1957). On perceptual readiness. *Psychological Review, 64,* 123–152.

(1964). The course of cognitive growth. *American Psychologist, 19,* 1–15.

Cantor, N. (1994). Life task problem-solving: Situational affordances and personal needs. *Personality and Social Psychology Bulletin, 20,* 235–243.

Carver, C. S., & Scheier, M. F. (1990). Principles of self-regulation: Action and emotion. In E. T. Higgins and R. M. Sorrentino (Eds.), *Handbook of motivation and cognition: Foundations of social behavior* (Vol. 2). New York: Guilford Press.

Case, R. (1985). *Intellectual development: Birth to adulthood.* New York: Academic Press.

Cooley, C. H. (1902/1964). *Human nature and the social order.* New York: Schocken Books. (Original work published 1902.)

Damon, W., & Hart, D. (1986). Stability and change in children's self-understanding. *Social Cognition, 4,* 102–118.

Dweck, C. S., & Elliot, E. S. (1983). Achievement motivation. In P. H. Mussen (Ed.), *Handbook of child psychology. Vol. IV: Socialization, personality, and social development* (pp. 643–691). New York: Wiley.

Erikson, E. H. (1963). *Childhood and society* (Rev. ed.). New York: Norton.

Fazio, R. H. (1986). How do attitudes guide behavior? In R. M. Sorrentino and E. T. Higgins (Eds.), *Handbook of motivation and cognition: Foundations of social behavior* (pp. 204–243). New York: Guilford Press.

Feffer, M. (1970). Developmental analysis of interpersonal behavior. *Psychological Review, 77,* 197–214.

Fischer, K. W. (1980). A theory of cognitive development: The control and construction of hierarchies of skills. *Psychological Review, 87,* 477–531.

Fischer, K. W., & Watson, M. W. (1981). Explaining the Oedipus conflict. In K. W. Fischer (Ed.), *Cognitive development. New directions for child development, No. 12.* San Francisco: Jossey-Bass.

Flavell, J. H., Botkin, P. T., Fry, C. L., Wright, J. W., & Jarvis, P. E. (1968). *The development of role-taking and communication skills in children.* New York: Wiley.

Floyd, H. H., & South, D. R. (1972). Dilemma of youth: The choice of parents or peers as a frame of reference for behavior. *Journal of Marriage and the Family, 34,* 627–634.

Gilligan, S. G., & Bower, G. H. (1984). Cognitive consequences of emotional arousal. In C. E. Izard, J. Kagan, and R. B. Zajonc (Eds.), *Emotions, cognition, and behavior* (pp. 547–588). New York: Cambridge University Press.

Gollwitzer, P. & Kirchhoff, O. (1998). The willful pursuit of identity. In J. Heckhausen & C. S. Dweck (Eds.), *Motivation and self-regulation across the life span.* New York: Cambridge University Press.

Harter, S. (1983). Developmental perspectives on the self-system. In P. H. Mussen

(Ed.), *Handbook of child psychology. Vol. IV: Socialization, personality, and social development* (pp. 275–385). New York: Wiley.

Hartup, W. W. (1983). Peer relations. In P. H. Mussen (Ed.), *Handbook of child psychology. Vol. IV: Socialization, personality, and social development* (pp. 103–196). New York: Wiley.

Heckhausen, J., Dixon, R. A., & Baltes, P. B. (1989). Gains and losses in development throughout adulthood as perceived by different adult age groups. *Developmental Psychology, 25,* 109–121.

Higgins, E. T. (1987). Self-discrepancy: A theory relating self and affect. *Psychological Review, 94,* 319–340.

(1989a). Continuities and discontinuities in self-regulatory and self-evaluative processes: A developmental theory relating self and affect. *Journal of Personality, 57,* 407–444.

(1989b). Self-discrepancy theory: What patterns of self-beliefs cause people to suffer? In L. Berkowitz (Ed.), *Advances in experimental social psychology* (Vol. 22, pp. 93–136). New York: Academic Press.

(1991). Development of self-regulatory and self-evaluative processes: Costs, benefits, and tradeoffs. In M. R. Gunnar & L. A. Sroufe (Eds.), *Self processes and development: The Minnesota symposia on child psychology* (Vol. 23, pp. 125–165). Hillsdale, NJ: Erlbaum.

(1996). Knowledge activation: Accessibility, applicability, and salience. In E. T. Higgins & A. W. Kruglanski (Eds.), *Social psychology: Handbook of basic principles* (pp. 133–168). New York: Guilford.

(1997). The "self digest": Self-regulatory functions of self-knowledge. *Journal of Personality and Social Psychology.*

Higgins, E. T., Bond, R. N., Klein, R., & Strauman, T. (1986). Self-discrepancies and emotional vulnerability: How magnitude, accessibility, and type of discrepancy influence affect. *Journal of Personality and Social Psychology, 51,* 5–15.

Higgins, E. T., & Eccles-Parsons, J. (1983). Social cognition and the social life of the child: Stages as subcultures. In E. T. Higgins, D. N. Ruble, and W. W. Hartup (Eds.), *Social cognition and social development: A sociocultural perspective* (pp. 15–62). New York: Cambridge University Press.

Higgins, E. T., Loeb, I., & Ruble, D. N. (1994). *Socialization of emotions as a function of regulatory focus.* Unpublished manuscript, Columbia University, New York.

(1995). The four As of life transition effects: Attention, accessibility, adaptation, and adjustment. *Social Cognition, 13,* 215–242.

Higgins, E. T., Roney, C., Crowe, E., & Hymes, C. (1994). Ideal versus ought predilections for approach and avoidance: Distinct self-regulatory systems. *Journal of Personality and Social Psychology, 66,* 276–286.

Higgins, E. T., & Tykocinski, O. (1992). Self-discrepancies and biographical memory: Personality and cognition at the level of psychological situation. *Personality and Social Psychology Bulletin, 18,* 527–535.

Inhelder, B., & Piaget, J. (1958). *The growth of logical thinking from childhood to adolescence.* New York: Basic Books.

Isen, A. M. (1984). Toward understanding the role of affect in cognition. In R. S. Wyer & T. K. Srull (Eds.), *Handbook of Social Cognition* (Vol. 3, pp. 179–236). Hillsdale, NJ: Erlbaum.

Jones, E. E., & Gerard, H. B. (1967). *Foundations of social psychology.* New York: Wiley.

Kelly, G. A. (1955). *The psychology of personal constructs.* New York: Norton.

Lewis, M., & Brooks-Gunn, J. (1979). *Social cognition and the acquisition of self.* New York: Plenum Press.

Maccoby, E. E., & Martin, J. A. (1983). Socialization in the context of the family: Parent-child interaction. In P. H. Mussen (Ed.), *Handbook of child psychology. Vol. 4: Socialization, personality, and social development* (pp. 643–691). New York: Wiley.

Markus, H., & Nurius, P. (1986). Possible selves. *American Psychologist, 41,* 954–969.

McClelland, D. C. (1961). *The achieving society.* Princeton, NJ: Van Nostrand.

Mead, G. H. (1934). *Mind, self, and society.* Chicago: University of Chicago Press.

Miller, S. M., & Green, M. L. (1985). Coping with stress and frustration: Origins, nature, and development. In M. Lewis & C. Saarri (Eds.), *The socialization of emotions* (pp. 263–314). New York: Plenum Press.

Mischel, W., & Moore, B. (1980). The role of ideation in voluntary delay for symbolically presented rewards. *Cognitive Therapy and Research, 4,* 211–221.

Mischel, W., & Patterson, C. J. (1978). In W. A. Collins (Ed.), *Minnesota symposia on child psychology* (Vol. 11, p. 199–230). Hillsdale, NJ: Erlbaum.

Moretti, M. M., & Higgins, E. T. (1990). The development of self-system vulnerabilities: Social and cognitive factors in developmental psychopathology. In R. J. Sternberg and J. Kolligan, Jr. (Eds.), *Competence considered* (pp. 286–314). New Haven, CT: Yale University Press.

Newman, L. S., Higgins, E. T., & Vookles, J. (1992). Self-guide strength and emotional vulnerability: Birth order as a moderator of self-affect relations. *Personality and Social Psychology Bulletin, 18,* 402–411.

Nolen-Hoeksema, S. (1998). Ruminative coping with depression. In J. Heckhausen & C. S. Dweck (Eds.), *Motivation and self-regulation across the life span.* New York: Cambridge University Press.

Olson, J. M., Roese, N. J., & Zanna, M. P. (1996). Expectancies. In E. T. Higgins and A. W. Kruglanski (Eds.), *Social psychology: Handbook of basic principles* (pp. 211–238). New York: Guilford Press.

Patterson, G. R. (1982). *Coercive family process.* Eugene, OR: Castalia Press.

Piaget, J. (1951). *Play, dreams and imitation in childhood.* New York: Norton.
     (1965). *The moral judgment of the child.* New York: Free Press (Original trans. published 1932).

Radke-Yarrow, M., Zahn-Waxler, C., & Chapman, M. (1983). Children's prosocial dispositions and behavior. In P. H. Mussen (Ed.), *Handbook of child psychology. Vol. 4: Socialization, personality, and social development* (pp. 643–691). New York: Wiley.

Rosenberg, M. (1979). *Conceiving the self.* Malabar, FL: Robert E. Krieger.

Ruble, D. N. (1983). The development of social comparison processes and their role in achievement-related self-socialization. In E. T. Higgins, D. N. Ruble, & W. W. Hartup (Eds.), *Social cognition and social development: A sociocultural perspective* (pp. 134–157). New York: Cambridge University Press.

Ruble, D. N., & Frey, K. S. (1987). Social comparison and self-evaluation in the classroom: Developmental changes in knowledge and function. In J. C. Masters & W. P. Smith (Eds.), *Social comparison, social justice, and relative deprivation* (pp. 81–104). Hillsdale, NJ: Erlbaum.

Ruble, D. N., & Rholes, W. S. (1981). The development of children's perceptions and attributions about their social world. In J. D. Harvey, W. Ickes, & R. F. Kidd (Eds.), *New directions in attribution research* (Vol. 3, pp. 3–36). Hillsdale, NJ: Erlbaum.

Selman, R. L. (1980). *The growth of interpersonal understanding: Developmental and clinical analyses.* New York: Academic Press.

Selman, R. L., & Byrne, D. F. (1974). A structural-developmental analysis of levels of role-taking in middle childhood. *Child Development, 45,* 803–806.

Shantz, C. U. (1983). Social cognition. In P. H. Mussen (Series Ed.), J. H. Flavell, & E. M. Markman (Vol. Eds.), *Carmichael's manual of child psychology. Vol. 3: Cognitive development* (4th ed., pp. 495–555). New York: Wiley.

Simmons, R. G., & Blyth, D. A. (1987). *Moving into adolescence: The impact of pubertal change and school context.* New York: Aldine De Gruyter.

Strauman, T. J., & Higgins, E. T. (1987). Automatic activation of self-discrepancies and emotional syndromes: When cognitive structures influence affect. *Journal of Personality and Social Psychology, 53,* 1004–1014.

Stryker, S., & Statham, A. (1985). Symbolic interaction and role theory. In G. Lindzey and E. Aronson (Eds.), *Handbook of social psychology* (Vol. 1, pp. 311–378). New York: Random House.

Sullivan, H. S. (1953). *The collected works of Harry Stack Sullivan* (Vol. 1). H. S. Perry & M. L. Gawel (Eds.). New York: Norton.

Veroff, J. (1969). Social comparison and the development of achievement motivation. In C. P. Smith (Ed.), *Achievement-related motives in children* (pp. 46–101). New York: Russell Sage Foundation.

Werner, H. (1957). *Comparative psychology of mental development.* New York: International Universities Press.

Werner, H., & Kaplan, B. (1963). *Symbol formation.* New York: Wiley.

Wood, J. V. (1989). Theory and research concerning social comparisons of personal attributes. *Psychological Bulletin, 106,* 231–248.

4 Commentary: Human Psychological Needs and the Issues of Volition, Control, and Outcome Focus

Richard M. Ryan

Abstract

In this commentary, Chapters 1, 2, and 3 are each reviewed and discussed in terms of the extent to which they specify and meaningfully address the central motives operative in human psychological development. Drawing from work in self-determination theory (Deci & Ryan, 1991; Ryan, 1995), the author suggests that there are basic human psychological needs for autonomy, competence, and relatedness whose fulfillment is essential to personality growth and well-being, and for the integration of the individual into significant social relationships and cultural groups. The distinction between psychological needs and related concepts such as motives, desires, and personal goals is discussed. It is argued that, in broad terms, Kuhl and Fuhrmann primarily emphasize the issue of autonomy; Heckhausen and Schultz the issue of competence; and Higgins and Loeb the issue of relatedness. Each thus addresses a different fundamental need upon which both psychological development and well-being depend. All three chapters are further examined for comparisons, contrasts, and limitations with respect to each other and to the self-determination model of personality functioning. Furthermore, each is considered in terms of the degree to which it addresses social and cultural issues of import in human motivation and life-span development.

Introduction

If there is a cornerstone in the science of human behavior, it must be the field of motivation. Motivational theories ask a fundamental question, namely: What moves a person? Thus they are concerned with the prime

Preparation of this chapter was aided in part by a grant from the National Institute of Child Health and Human Development (HD19914) to the Human Motivation Program, Department of Psychology, University of Rochester.

114

forces at work in human nature and human culture. It is my difficult assignment to comment on three different chapters in this volume, each of which addresses questions of human motivation, yet each of which is organized by a somewhat different set of assumptions regarding the primary natural and cultural forces that move individuals to act. I focus on these differing assumptions in order to make explicit what, in my view, allows each of these theories to illuminate particular phenomena within the field of motivation, and at the same time leave other phenomena more or less in the dark.

My interest in the assumptions that underlie theoretical approaches to human motivation is neither disinterested nor neutral. My own commentary is itself shaped (i.e., biased) by our work within self-determination theory (Deci & Ryan, 1985, 1991; Ryan, 1995). In that work we have assumed that human *nature* plays a determinative role in personality development – particularly as nature has imbued every individual with fundamental *psychological needs* that energize developmental processes. Within self-determination theory, psychological needs are viewed as the essential elements that underlie personality growth and well-being. That is, human psychological needs specify the necessary nutriments for growth and integration in human personality. When needs are not fulfilled, either because of impoverished social circumstances or as a result of organismic frailties, ill-being results.

Our definition of psychological needs is quite narrow and restrictive relative to other theoretical uses of the need construct (e.g., Murray, 1938). We use the concept of needs to pertain only to factors essential for growth and well-being so as to differentiate needs from the more encompassing and pervasive phenomena of human wants, goals, or desires – some of which are need-related and some of which are not. As an example of this distinction between needs and wants, think of a person who, currently driving a well-functioning Volkswagen, states that he "needs" a new Mercedes. He really means that he "wants" or "desires" rather than "needs" this luxury car. By our definition, since the added luxury is not essential to his growth or integrity, he is not expressing a true need. Some human wants and desires, of course, are good instruments of basic needs, whereas others serve to distract from need fulfillment, or in a misinformed manner to compensate for the frustration of basic needs.

Specifically, we have argued that human psychological development is moved primarily by three basic needs, namely those for autonomy, competence, and relatedness. Regarding autonomy, humans have a basic need to be the origins of action (deCharms, 1968) and experience their behavior as volitional or "stemming from the self" (Deci & Ryan, 1991). They also manifest a need for effectance or competence (White, 1963; Koestner & McClelland, 1990), a propensity that has been quite widely researched and acknowledged (often to the neglect of other needs). Finally, the need for relatedness or belonging provides another basic propensity at work in development. From the time of birth, persons strive to maintain connectedness to others and to attain a sense of secure belonging, a nutriment that has been shown to be critical to psychological health (Baumeister & Leary, 1995). Angyal (1965) described this need for relatedness in its broadest form as *homonomy,* a striving for oneness with something larger than self, which, depending on cultural circumstances, can be either synergistic with or antagonistic to autonomy.

Failure to satisfy these basic psychological needs in ongoing action – because the environment either frustrates their fulfillment or places them in dynamic competition with one another – sets the stage for psychological distress and psychopathology (Ryan, Deci, & Grolnick, 1995). By contrast, need-fulfilling activities tend to produce great psychological satisfaction, and therefore are apt to be experienced as volitional and autonomous (Sheldon, Ryan, & Reis, 1997). As we conceptualize it, when humans act in accord with their nature they also tend to experience their action as unconflicted and volitional – it is felt as coming from the self. Further, when social conditions support the fulfillment of basic psychological needs, then alienation, helplessness, introjection, and other problems of autonomy are less likely to occur. Support for psychological needs, in short, facilitates the natural growth tendencies in humans, leading to both greater self-actualization and community (Ryan, 1993, 1995).

By explicitly positing fundamental psychological needs, self-determination theory supplies some basic tools for social criticism. To the extent that well-being is considered a function of need satisfaction, research can then focus on those aspects of the social environment that facilitate or forestall the satisfaction of psychological needs, and how they promote or hinder personality development and integration. We therefore judge the humanity of a social context or culture in terms of both *how* it accomplishes its socialization (e.g., Does a culture socialize through controlling or autonomy-supportive means?) and *what* it socializes its adherents to do (e.g., Are people taught to seek goals that do not satisfy or that interfere with the fulfillment of basic psychological needs?). Correspondingly, we argue that variations in methods of socialization produce different qualities of internalization, and culturally transmitted values can be more or less congruent with and fulfilling of human nature. Integration in personality and in culture is thus optimized when both the "how" and the "what" of socialization within a culture are maximally supportive of the fulfillment of basic psychological needs (see Ryan, Sheldon, Kasser, et al., 1996).

I have made these few comments about our own work inappropriately, in the sense that it is not my task here to present self-determination theory, but rather to comment on the three theories presented. However, I explicated the idea of needs and their dynamics within social contexts because, as I critically review these theories, I evaluate them in terms of what needs they implicate to be at the base of human motivations and desires, and what these theorists have to say about optimizing, indeed humanizing, social conditions. These are critical questions because they bear on the most important of today's issues. Insofar as empirical models begin to explicate not only what it is that moves people toward specific actions but also what makes them more whole and more human, then they are also raising the right question's of how practically to arrange parenting activities, classrooms, workplaces, and, more generally, cultures. Conversely, if knowledge and theories do not engender suggestions for change and optimal cultural designs, then, frankly, what good are they?

Kuhl and Fuhrmann's Analysis of Volition

Chapter 1, by Kuhl and Fuhrmann, is based on work for which I feel a great affinity. The constructs of volition and autonomy, which have been foundational constructs in our own work on self-determination (Deci & Ryan, 1985, 1987), represent a central focus for Kuhl and Fuhrmann as well.

To my knowledge, there are very few researchers in the world who are currently grappling with the problems of volition and true self-regulation. This may sound like a strange claim in today's psychology, which is dominated by constructs concerning intentionality, self-efficacy, and goal-directed action. Yet contemporary studies of goal-directed action rarely attend to the fact that not all intentional acts are necessarily autonomous, or "come from the self." Despite this neglect, it is clear that distinguishing those intentional actions that are autonomous from those that are not is critical for understanding differences in the quality of behavioral regulation and the experiences attending it.

The conceptual distinction between intentionality and autonomy was made long ago within phenomenological studies (e.g., Pfander, 1908/1967), and within empirical psychology it can be traced back to deCharms's (1968) elaborations on Heider's (1958) classic attributional theories. Heider's (1958) "naive psychology" was concerned with factors that influence the phenomenal construal of events and the behavior that follows from them.

According to Heider, one variable that makes a great deal of difference is whether individuals perceive their own (or others') actions as intentional or *personally caused,* as opposed to nonintentional or *impersonally caused.* DeCharms (1968) subsequently distinguished between those personally caused behaviors that have an *internal* versus *external perceived locus of causality.* That is, some intentionally enacted or personally caused behaviors may feel as if they are compelled by forces experienced as external to the self (e.g., social demands, introjected regulations), whereas other actions are experienced as emanating from the self, or as self-determined. In deCharms's analysis, as in ours, not all intentional actions are truly volitional (Deci & Ryan, 1991).

In Chapter 1, when Kuhl and Fuhrmann take on the task of "decomposing volition" and examine the component processes involved in what they label *volitional competence,* they use the term *volition* to apply to all intentional or personally caused behaviors. Nonetheless, they arrive in their analyses at the same fundamental distinction that deCharms had in mind. In Kuhl and Fuhrmann's terminology there are two distinct modes of volition: *self-regulation* and *self-control.* The ability to regulate attention, shut out distractors, and amplify confidence and optimism – indeed most all of the competencies that allow individuals to master a task or reach a goal competently – can be seen at work in either type of regulation. Yet, importantly, their model also acknowledges and describes how the absence of an "internal perceived locus of causality" is associated with a diminished quality of behavior. Specifically, they argue that the absence of autonomy in behavior is evident in the "suppressive organization" of action. For instance, they have begun empirically to demonstrate how, when one part of the person dominates other parts, as in compliance or introjection, there is a loss of efficiency and vitality in action. Their theory thus corresponds to the clinical observation that nonautonomous self-control can be a source of both dis-ease and inefficiency over time (e.g., Perls, 1973; Ryan, 1982; Shapiro, 1981). Intentional goal-directed behavior can be organized by a "totalitarian ego" in Greenwald's (1982) sense (self-control), or by a more democratic ego that doesn't suppress other motives, thoughts, or desires, but rather captures the dedicated interest and resources of the individual through integration (self-regulation). The latter process exemplifies self-determination (Deci & Ryan, 1985).

As a psychologist, I often wear different hats in that I am both a practicing clinician and a researcher. I see much of my job as a clinician as one of helping people move away from self-controlled forms of regulation toward more autonomous forms. To do so, I try to produce the circumstances in which, to use Kuhl and Fuhrmann's terminology, holistic self-feeling can be accessed, and integrated self-representations can emerge. These interpersonal conditions include, in my view, providing a noncontrolling atmosphere, emotional support for self-discovery, and empathy. Empathy in particular, in the form of actively taking the internal frame of reference of the person (Ryan, 1993; Ryan & Solky, in press), helps a person to access and integrate more fully the various, often competing, motives and needs at work, and to move toward optimal self-regulation as Kuhl and Fuhrmann describe it. More generally, the map of regulatory processes laid out by Kuhl and Fuhrmann is unusual for empirically based models in its clinical applicability and phenomenological richness.

In their Volitional Competence Inventory (VCI), Kuhl and Fuhrmann attempt to specify and assess the elements of competence required for integrated volition to occur. Even under the best of motivational circumstances, individuals must engage the machinery of their minds and bodies in the service of their endeavors, and there are many potential breaking points in this process. For instance, a person desiring to carry out an autonomous act may have difficulty when lacking energy owing to fatigue – such as composing a theoretical commentary while jet-lagged, or trying to care for a child when physically ill. Or a person may have difficulty carrying out a volitional act when skills are absent. Or a person may have difficulty completing an intention when fighting with relevant introjects. The VCI thus has great heuristic value for diagnosing problems in motivation. Philosophers from Rorty to Ricouer have struggled with the meaning of *akratic behavior,* or "weakness of will." The VCI provides a taxonomy of many of its various forms.

At the same time, knowing what it takes to have volitional competence does not tell psychologists much about the question of what social and developmental conditions facilitate the occurrence of volitional acts, particularly those characterized by true self-regulation. Indeed, I was struck by the extent to which Kuhl and Fuhrmann accounted for akrasia or volitional incompetence by citing *internal* mechanisms such as a lack of accessibility of holistic self-representations, high activity of a punishment system, or individual differences between state orientation and action orientation. I do not dispute that such internal factors are markers of motivational problems, but I worry that there might be too much emphasis on the internal sources of motivational difficulties to the neglect of the social-contextual influences that typically have brought them about. Ultimately, the preponderance of causes of human alienation and tonic self-control lie not in human physiology, which in most cases will support *either* integrated or fractionated functioning, but in social conditions that shunt individuals toward one mode of functioning versus another.

The VCI should prove extremely useful in studying how both varied biologic and social conditions may differentially affect specific components of the volitional process. Indeed, the VCI is an elaborate tool that could be used to operationalize autonomous regulation, in order to study its variations under different social-contextual conditions. In self-determination work, our emphasis has been more on the social conditions that facilitate, as opposed to undermine, autonomy than on the mechanisms and processes through which autonomy operates. By contrast, Kuhl and Fuhrmann's work has focused more exactingly on the mechanisms of regulation, and less on the effects of social conditions. Perhaps it is time we worked to combine the two and benefit from the synergism. Of course, that is one of the goals of this volume – to link independently developed paradigms that apply to human motivation across development.

Heckhausen and Schulz's Theory of the Primacy of Control

I now turn to Chapter 2, by Heckhausen and Schulz, who presented a life-span theory of *personal control*. As a theorist who has been occupied with the distinction between intention and volition (or autonomous versus controlled behavior), I have found traditional control theories to be problematic. Partly, my critical view of many control constructs stems from their behavioristic origins, where the focus has been on control over outcomes – most typically reinforcements (e.g., Bandura, 1977; Rotter, 1954; Seligman, 1975). Control-based theories have often ignored the fact that there are many behaviors that are not "outcome-driven" at all, behaviors such as intrinsically motivated play, or engagement in relationally oriented dialogue, in which control over separable outcomes is often neither necessarily a focus of interest nor a central concern.

In addition, because of their emphasis on behavior/outcome contingencies, many control theories have been culturally noncritical. They do not often question *what* individuals want to control and *why* they want those outcomes. For example, Bandura's (1989) social-cognitive theory assumes that as long as an individual experiences self-efficacy with respect to "valued" outcomes, he or she will be in a state of adaptation and health. Little regard is given to why or how an individual arrives at certain values or rewards, and there is certainly no comparative sense that some goals may be less good for that individual than other goals (see Ryan, Sheldon, Kasser, et al., 1996). Thus the Bandurian worldview, a control theory par excellence, easily becomes an ideological support for individualistic acquisitiveness, as in the "objectivist" views of Locke and Latham (1990). Insofar as self-efficacy per se becomes promoted to a psychological ideal, without concern over what an individual competently pursues, or how such pursuits relate to real human needs, then all capacity for social criticism has been vanquished.

Heckhausen and Schulz's control theory, however, is more complicated regarding these issues than the "efficacyisms" dominating American social-cognitive approaches. Their focus is not on rewards, but rather on adaptation. They define the benefits of control in terms of the functional yield of different regulatory strategies under changing conditions. Furthermore, their theory is enriched by its life-span perspective, which inherently raises questions concerning how different goals may be differentially relevant at different points in the life span, or in different social-contextual circumstances (Baltes & Baltes, 1990). Heckhausen and Schulz view the focus of control over the life span as affected by an ever-shifting configuration of capacities, resources, and interests, arguing that the tools of efficacy itself, as well as the focus of its exercise, change at different points in development.

Among their primary points, Heckhausen and Schulz differentiate between two major types of control: *primary control,* when an individual acts directly on the external world to attain outcomes; and *secondary control,* which represents the modification of an individual's internal structures to accommodate to circumstances that do not afford primary control. This distinction, which they attribute to Rothbaum, Weisz, and Snyder (1982), parallels one made decades earlier by Reich (1929), who contrasted alloplasm (changing the world) and autoplasm (changing the self) in reaction to perceived challenges. Reich had a clear preference for alloplasm, because for him most of the autoplastic accommodations made within cultures are repressive in nature. Clearly, he believed that, other things aside, individuals prefer primary to secondary control.

For quite different reasons, Heckhausen and Schulz also give a special priority to alloplastic or primary control, which they describe as having a *functional primacy* in development. However, they also acknowledge and appreciate that individuals need a variety of control strategies, some more oriented to changing the world, and others more oriented toward adjustment, compensation, or accommodation, as each type carries certain functional advantages for different circumstances and developmental epochs. Detecting the relative strength of these two types of control across varied goal domains, developmental periods, and social-contextual circumstances is both intriguing and potentially generative.

What intrigues me even more is the proposition, central to Heckhausen and Schulz's theory, that control strategies are themselves regulated by a higher-order process of *optimization,* in which the control processes are made servant to long-term outcomes. But just what are the long-term outcomes that are being optimized? I have already laid out my own view of what healthy humans optimize in development – namely, their experiences of autonomy, competence, and relatedness. Therefore, in the self-determination viewpoint, goals and strategies are evaluated in terms of their serviceability with regard to human needs. For Heckhausen and Schulz, however, a different goal of optimization processes is hypothesized – namely, the maximization of the individual's long-term *potential for primary control.*

The idea that people fundamentally prefer primary over secondary control is a provocative and potentially testable premise – a rarity in contemporary theorizing. Furthermore, the hypothesis can be linked to adaptation in the dual sense that being able to control outcomes directly through taking action on the environment (primary control) may yield both ontogenetic and evolutionary advantages. However, the maximization hypothesis does not argue simply that primary control is a useful thing; it argues that primary control is an end in itself, a basic organismic preference or teleology.

Heckhausen and Schulz's assumption of the functional primacy of primary control can be viewed as consistent with the idea of a basic organismic need for competence or effectance, though they do not use that term. Drawing on the foundation of White (1959), they argue that "an underlying assumption of all control-related theories is the idea that humans desire to produce behavior-event contingencies" (Heckhausen & Schulz, 1995, p. 285). This human desire may refer to the need for competence as we describe it, but they specifically focus on effectance related to control over outcomes and do not focus on situations where separable outcomes are not a focus (e.g., intrinsically motivated actions). Nonetheless it is clear that outcome control is one forum through which competence strivings (needs?) do express themselves, and primary control may be an especially satisfying type of competence to effect. I suspect that Heckhausen and Schulz would agree with the idea that failure to experience control (to feel competence), even independent of the rewards control brings, has very negative effects on growth and well-being.

Nonetheless, the claim that organisms have a basic propensity to maximize primary control has, I think, many problems, not the least of which is that primary control per se is not invariantly advantageous. Control over outcomes, even when it is primary, does not necessarily imply or entail healthy self-regulation. As both our work (Deci & Ryan, 1985) and that of Kuhl (1987; Kuhl & Kazen, 1994) indicate, an individual can exercise control through autonomous self-regulatory processes or because of external or internal heteronomous pressures. Certainly, the latter forms of primary control may be optimized to the individual's detriment.

Additionally, people can seek control for all kinds of reasons and focus on all kinds of outcomes. For example, placing emphasis on the primary control of "extrinsic" outcomes such as money, fame, or appearance can often be pathonomic rather than adaptive. Tim Kasser and I have found that people who place high relative values on such outcomes as money, fame, and appearance often manifest poor mental health and adjustment even when perceived efficacy is high (Kasser & Ryan, 1993, 1996). Further, when we compare people's relative sense of efficacy with respect to specific outcomes, we find that those who experience more control and competence with respect to money, fame, or looks, versus, say, love, growth, and generativity (i.e., more "intrinsic" aspirations) tend to be less self-actualized, report less vitality, and be more susceptible to depression and anxiety. They also come from home environments unsupportive of psychological needs (Kasser, Ryan, Zax, et al., 1995).

The point here is that it is critical to ask: "Primary control over *what,* and for what reasons (*why*)?" From the viewpoint of self-determination theory, control processes, even primary ones, can be as much servant to alienation and introjection as to human liberation, relatedness, and well-being (Ryan, Sheldon, Kasser, et al., 1996).

Finally, I wish to state yet one other reservation about the idea that the psychic system functions to maximize long-term primary control. The concept of primary control does not seem all that well suited to explicating how individuals fulfill relatedness needs. One of the most noteworthy characteristics of humanity is people's social, interdependent, nature. People strive to care for others, as well as be cared for. Often, individuals willingly give up control to others, and/or freely rely and depend on them (Ryan, 1995; Ryan & Solky, 1996). They do so not only to free up their resources for primary control activities elsewhere, but because doing so often directly fulfills human needs. Engaging in secondary control within relationships is thus not merely compensatory, but often a great treasure, psychologically. An individualistic perspective on control may miss this reflection of human tendencies to relatedness.

Therefore I, for one, view control, whether it be primary or secondary, as an *instrument of human needs rather than an end in itself.* This of course is my own metapsychological bias; it is one that suggests that humans often can gain control and lose themselves in the process. I think that people's humanity is more centrally defined by their strivings for relatedness, autonomy, and effectance than by their desire for primary control, and that control strategies of all types are optimally regulated so as to serve basic needs within development. Wholeness and community rather than primary control is, in this view, the principal endgame of development.

Whether or not one agrees with the strong version of Heckhausen and Schulz's functional primacy hypothesis, an individual's desire to engage the world and shape his or her own environment is minimally a central and persistent striving in human life, one that is given up only with difficulty. As Heckhausen and Schulz point out, the normative life event of aging often carries with it an inevitable recognition that primary control capacities can dissipate. I am reminded of an interview I read recently with the Delany sisters, two black women raised in America, who had both passed the century mark in age. One of them, Bessie, commented that "It took me a hundred years to figure out I can't change the world. I can only change Bessie. And, honey, that ain't easy either" (Delany, Delany, & Hearth, 1993). Increasing acceptance of the authentic limitations of primary control is perhaps one of the most complex gifts supplied by old age. I think this gift comes about not only because people become more incapacitated with age (which is true only in some respects – see Carstensen, 1993) and must accommodate this fact, but also because people (ideally) grow in wisdom. Wisdom includes appreciating the limits of one's powers and an acceptance of oneself as a part of a much larger process of social change and history. Wisdom requires a heavy dose of secondary control.

Because development carries with it variations in people's preferences for and capabilities to enact primary or secondary control, it is clear that tracing the trajectory of these two classes of control will bear much empirical fruit. Some forms of control will clearly be more functionally important in different phases of development and the challenges that accompany these phases. I expect that such variations will be associated not only with age differences but also with differences in exposure to trauma, different types of socialization, different cultural contexts and beliefs, and myriad other factors. There is a rich fabric to be woven from these conceptual threads, and a generative program of research lies ahead.

Higgins and Loeb on Regulatory Focus and the Motivation of Action

Finally, I turn to Chapter 3, by Higgins and Loeb. The chapter represents their attempt to apply a "social-cognitive" framework to the understanding of different regulatory or motivational styles. This is an endeavor similar to our own work (e.g., Deci & Ryan, 1991) in which we attempt to understand these issues in an organismic/phenomenological perspective. So often when we meet, we are struggling with similar conceptual issues through our quite distinct theoretical lenses, their lens being a social-cognitive one, whereas my paradigmatical preferences lie in the organismic/phenomenological camp. Our intellectual kinship is of no benefit to Professor Higgins in this particular context, since it simply makes me feel freer to be critical of his work, since I know he will tolerate (perhaps even enjoy) my doing so.

Higgins and Loeb have presented here ideas that have an important place within Higgins's own theorizing about personality. The model described in Chapter 3 synthesizes prior work on self-discrepancy theory (Higgins, 1987) with emerging thinking concerning approach versus avoidance forms of action regulation. Higgins and Loeb specifically explore how tendencies toward a positive versus negative regulatory focus may be shaped by the way in which individuals are socialized by early caregivers.

Higgins and Loeb argue that parents who hope and wish for their child to have certain attributes, and who orient their child to these hopes and wishes with loving support, foster the development of *ideal self-guides* that are associated with a positive-outcome focus in behavioral regulation. Such parents are labeled *promotion-oriented* – they are trying to nurture active goal-seeking. By contrast, parents whose focus is primarily on preventing the occurrence of bad outcomes tend to regulate their child's behavior toward the ends of ensuring safety and fulfilling obligations. These *prevention-oriented* parents are described as using more sanctions and punishments to enforce such obligatory action, and ultimately they foster a more *ought-guided self* in the child, oriented more toward avoiding negative outcomes than to achieving ideals. Thus Higgins and Loeb account for the etiology of more approach versus avoidant tendencies as an individual difference in human personalities.

An increasing number of contemporary theorists are building models founded upon an approach versus avoidance motivation dichotomy. Historically, the approach–avoidance distinction emerged within the Lewinian tradition (Hoppe, 1930, as cited in Lewin, Dembo, Festinger, et al., 1944). Recently, the distinction has reemerged within varied theoretical contexts, including studies of achievement motivation (Elliot, 1997; Elliot & Harackiewicz, 1996; H. Heckhausen, 1991), self-regulatory systems (Carver & White, 1994), and neuroanatomical systems subserving action regulation (Depue, 1995; Gray, 1987). Kuhl and Fuhrmann (Chapter 1, this volume) also make use of this dichotomous systems approach. Each varies a bit, but the overall message is that the quality of action and experience changes if regulation operates through approach versus avoidance systems. Engagement of approach motivation appears to be associated with the experience of positive affect, and with certain types of improved performance. Avoidance-oriented regulation has many drawbacks, the most central of which is the tendency toward more negative affect and the drain on performance capabilities that comes with it. There is no doubt that the evidence of both physiologically distinct approach and avoidance subsystems and differences in outcomes associated with this distinction point to important phenomena.

One of the most impressive contributions of the work Higgins and Loeb present in Chapter 3 is the attempt to construct a *social psychology* of people's tendency to be occupied with approach versus avoidance regulatory forms. Locating the source of individual differences in approach/avoidance tendencies in the dynamics of early interactions with caregivers frees some of the approach/avoidance theorizing from mere reductionism; the motivational system that tends to get activated is traced to social-contextual rather than exclusively biologic influences.

Furthermore, in their sociogenetic account of the development of individual differences in tendencies toward approach (positive regulatory focus) or avoidance (negative regulatory focus), Higgins and Loeb are, I believe, also highlighting the power of *relatedness needs* in the formation or shaping of personality. As they state in Chapter 3 of this volume, "Children are motivated to learn what to do in order to obtain the nurturance and security they need from their caretakers." The need to stay connected to early caregivers is, in Higgins and Loeb's model, such a basic need that it serves as the prime force shaping the acquisition of regulatory forms. Obviously, Higgins and Loeb do not emphasize the idea of psychological needs – and frankly the idea of basic needs doesn't fit into a social-cognitive tradition all that well. Nonetheless, it is clear in this model that children are assumed to seek parental love, support, pride, and nurturing acts, and these sought-after caregiver inputs are so critical or desirable that they "condition" the child's regulatory style.

Higgins and Loeb's emphasis on the degree to which children will strive to do whatever will maintain connectedness with parents is one shared by those with organismic perspectives on development. For example, Rogers (1951) made a similar claim when he argued that the need for positive regard is the basis for the adoption of values and strivings, whether they be organismically congruent or not. In the same vein, we have posited a basic relatedness need as an important motivational basis for all internalization processes. However, because social-cognitive approaches cannot, in principle, posit a true self, as most organismic approaches do (see Ryan, Deci, & Grolnick, 1995), the issue of whether the strivings that individuals adopt from their parents are congruent, autonomous, or integrated as opposed to incongruent, introjected, or poorly assimilated is not fully addressed.

I presume that Higgins and Loeb's prevention-focused parents (because they use controlling methods that forestall active integration) would foster more *introjected* forms of regulation, to use the terminology of self-determination theory. On the other hand, promotion-oriented parents (because they use more benign, noncontrolling socialization techniques) would facilitate greater *identification* with and *integration* of transmitted values. However, the relative autonomy or congruence of internalized strivings is not a central consideration in Higgins's work as it is in both Rogers's theory (1951) and our work on self-determination (Deci & Ryan, 1985); both the latter approaches view development in terms of an overarching organismic integrative and actualizing process. By contrast, in social-cognitive approaches, including Higgins's, each adopted regulatory form is in a certain sense a different self, and each of these multiple selves is a regulatory program that is cued up by habitual use and/or situational variables (Ryan, 1995). Furthermore, there are no "natural" pushes provided by social-cognitive models; goals and strivings are seen as induced or conditioned by social forces rather than by intrinsic motives or needs. Therefore, there is no focus on the inherent conflicts between fundamental needs and social proscriptions – a focus central to organismic thinking on internalization. Finally, as I understood the prevention- and promotion-focus approaches, neither contains an idea of *unconditional* love or regard – a love for the child that is independent of whether he or she avoids mishaps or strives for the ideals of significant others. We have found that it is unconditional love that most truly fulfills the need for relatedness (Ryan, 1993), whereas conditional regard, in both our work and that of Rogers (1951), is an inherently compromised form of nurturance. Still, even as I highlight these assumptive differences between an organismic perspective and Higgins and Loeb's model, I am struck by the extent to which, among social-cognitive approaches, Higgins and Loeb's model comes the closest to specifying an idea of what are optimal as opposed to degraded forms of goal socialization. Additionally, this is one of the few theories to date, organismic or otherwise, that offers a compelling account of how socialization influences the development of individual differences in approach versus avoidance tendencies.

A second contribution of Higgins and Loeb's model is its differentiation within promotion and prevention forms of regulation of the issue of outcome valence. The resulting fourfold classification scheme allows for discrimination between phenomenologically contrasting types of both positive affect – namely, the happy satisfaction of succeeding at gaining a positive outcome, as opposed to the "positive" relief of successfully avoiding a negative outcome – and negative affect – namely, the sadness of failing to attain a desired positive outcome, versus the tension and pressure of failing to avoid a negative outcome. Their model, therefore, has the promise of moving beyond the two-dimensional model of affect derived from factor-analytic approaches (e.g., Watson & Tellegen, 1985) that may be insensitive to the situationally driven distinctiveness of emotional states. Indeed, Higgins and Loeb's regulatory-focus/valence classification discriminates between emotional outcomes that are both intuitively and empirically separable, even though closely connected within circumplex or two-factor models of affective states.

I cannot leave my commentary on Higgins and Loeb's model without stating some "meta" reservations concerning approach – avoidance theorizing, not necessarily as Higgins and Loeb employ it, but in a more general sense. First, there is a temptation to regard the distinction as basic by virtue of the fact that it corresponds to two distinct neurological systems. However, the existence of neurological underpinnings does not, by itself, speak to what is determinative of what individuals do. It may be a constraining factor but not a determinative one. Therefore, it should never be considered a fact that because a motive operates through a given physiological structure, it is determined by it. Structure does not cause motives as much as human motives and meanings *entrain* underlying structures in their service. The goals and motives individuals enact, I believe, have more to do with needs they are trying to fulfill than with the tools they have to fulfill them. No physiological structures have been discovered that correspond distinctly with needs for autonomy, competence, or relatedness (nor are there likely to be). However, this makes these needs no less fundamental. Indeed if people were to examine *what* it is they try to approach, and/or *what* it is they try to avoid, they are still forced to come back to an understanding of the substance of human needs and desires. What gives human life meaning will be found not by examining the brain, but by examining experience.

Second, whether an approach–avoidance taxonomy is founded on physiological or conceptual foundations, multiple hazards lie in contrasting a "good" approach system versus a "bad" avoidance system. The principal hazard, in my mind, is that of failing to evaluate critically what society promotes in childrearing, or what children are socialized to approach. Should parents, through loving pride and conveyance of hopes and encouragement (the factors Higgins and Loeb see as generative of ideal self-guides) urge children to approach high status, an eternally youthful appearance, selfish acquisition, or enormous power? Is being "approach- (or positive-regulation) oriented," even with all its attendant performance benefits and positive affect, good no matter what people perceive as their goals? What happens when a strong approach motivation for say, achievement, status, or money, overrides the need for relatedness or love? This brings me back to the thought that approach systems still can be good or poor servants of human needs (Ryan, Sheldon, Kasser, et al., 1996). There is no escaping the necessity of looking critically within approach motives and evaluating what goals and outcomes functionally fulfill and optimize the development and well-being of individuals, and the humanity of the cultures in which they are participants.

Human Needs as a Focus
for Motivational Psychology: A Reprise

In concluding my comments, I return to the idea that mechanisms of control, competencies, goals, beliefs, habits, and culturally internalized behavioral regulations can all be studied in their own right – but sooner or later psychologists must ask the question of how well they serve organismic needs. The concept of needs refers to nutriments essential to growth and integrity. Few would dispute physical needs, but historically many have disputed the idea that there are psychological needs. Yet pervasive evidence shows that obstacles to the fulfillment strivings for competence, relatedness, and autonomy all result in diminished well-being (Ryan & Frederick, 1997) and greater pathology across stages of development (Ryan, Deci, & Grolnick, 1995). Therefore, there are some basic inputs requisite to psychological growth that seem unassailable, and their essentialness constitutes these inputs as true needs.

Exploration of overarching conceptualizations of what moves people to act across developmental phases of life makes clear that processes of volition, control, and regulatory focus are all implicated. Optimally, these processes come into play as useful servants of human needs, both psychological and physical. It is these basic human needs that (in my view) supply both the basis of meaning within human existence and a teleology for personal and social development.

As I reviewed Chapters 1, 2, and 3, I focused on each of them with this self-determination theory approach to psychological needs in mind. I emphasized in particular the relationship of Kuhl and Fuhrmann's work

(Chapter 1) to the need for autonomy, Heckhausen and Schulz's work (Chapter 2) to the need for competence, and Higgins and Loeb's work (Chapter 3) to the need for relatedness. In subjecting these theories to my own conceptual procrustean bed, I have undoubtedly hacked at some valuable theoretical limbs with an awfully blunt instrument, and my brief critiques and argumentative meandering in no way do full justice to these thoughtful presentations. I hope that any ax-wielding I have done has been in the service of promoting an interesting theoretical dialogue and has facilitated self-critical thinking among all of us involved in the study of motivation and development. I learned a lot from these exchanges, and I have these authors in particular to thank for so constructively engaging with me in this dialogue, and allowing us all to share in their thinking.

References

Angyal, A. (1965). *Neurosis and treatment: A holistic theory.* New York: Wiley.

Baltes, P. B., & Baltes, M. M. (1990). Psychological perspectives on successful aging: The model of selective optimization with compensation. In P. B. Baltes & M. M. Baltes (Eds.), *Successful aging: Perspectives from the behavioral sciences* (pp. 1–34). New York: Cambridge University Press.

Bandura, A. (1977). Self-efficacy: Toward a unifying theory of behavioral change. *Psychological Review, 84,* 191–215.

(1989). Human agency in social-cognitive theory. *American Psychologist, 44,* 1175–1184.

Baumeister, R., & Leary, M. R. (1995). The need to belong: Desire for interpersonal attachments as a fundamental human motivation. *Psychological Bulletin, 117,* 497–529.

Carstensen, L. L. (1993). Motivation for social contact across the life span. In J. Jacobs (Ed.), *Nebraska symposium on motivation: Developmental perspectives on motivation* (Vol. 40, pp. 209–254). Lincoln: University of Nebraska Press.

Carver, C. S., & White, T. L. (1994). Behavioral inhibition, behavioral activation, and affective responses to impending reward and punishment. The BIS/BAS scales. *Journal of Personality and Social Psychology, 67,* 319–333.

deCharms, R. (1968). *Personal causation: The internal affective determinants of behavior.* New York: Academic Press.

Deci, E. L., & Ryan, R. M. (1985). *Intrinsic motivation and self-determination in human behavior.* New York: Plenum Press.

(1987). The support of autonomy and the control of behavior. *Journal of Personality and Social Psychology, 53,* 1024–1037.

(1991). A motivational approach to self: Integration in personality. In R. Dienstbier (Ed.), *Nebraska symposium on motivation. Vol. 38: Perspectives on motivation* (pp. 237–288). Lincoln: University of Nebraska Press.

Delany, S., Delany, A. E., & Hearth, A. H. (1993). *Having our say: The Delany sisters' first 100 years.* New York: Kodansha International.

Depue, R. A. (1995). *Neurobehavioral systems, personality, and psychopathology.* New York: Springer-Verlag.

Elliot, A. J. (1997). Integrating the "classic" and "contemporary" approaches to achievement motivation: A hierarchical model of approach and avoidance achievement motivation. In M. Maehr & P. Pintrich (Eds.), *Advances in motivation and achievement* (Vol. 10, pp. 143–179). Greenwich, CT: JAI Press.

Elliot, A. J., & Harackiewicz, J. M. (1996). Approach and avoidance achievement goals and intrinsic motivation: A mediational analysis. *Journal of Personality and Social Psychology, 70,* 461–475.

Greenwald, A. G. (1982). Is anyone in charge? Personalysis versus the principle of personal unity. In J. Suls (Ed.), *Psychological perspectives on the self* (Vol. 1, pp. 151–181). Hillsdale, NJ: Erlbaum.

Gray, J. A. (1987). *The psychology of fear and stress* (2d ed.). London: Cambridge University Press.

Heckhausen, H. (1991). *Motivation and action* (P. K. Leppmann, Trans.). New York: Springer-Verlag.

Heckhausen, J., & Schulz, R. (1995). A life-span theory of control. *Psychological Review, 102,* 284–304.

Heider, F. (1958). *The psychology of interpersonal relations.* New York: Wiley.

Higgins, E. T. (1987). Self-discrepancy theory: A theory relating self and affect. *Psychological Review, 94,* 319–340.

Kasser, T., & Ryan, R. M. (1993). A dark side of the American dream: Correlates of financial success as a central life aspiration. *Journal of Personality and Social Psychology, 65,* 410–422.

———(1996). Further examining the American dream: Differential correlates of intrinsic and extrinsic goals. *Personality and Social Psychology Bulletin, 22,* 280–287.

Kasser, T., Ryan, R. M., Zax, M., & Sameroff, A. J. (1995). The relations of maternal and social environments to late adolescents' materialistic and prosocial values. *Developmental Psychology, 31,* 907–914.

Koestner, R., & McClelland, D. C. (1990). Perspectives on competence motivation. In L. A. Pervin (Ed.), *Handbook of personality: Theory and research* (pp. 527–548). New York: Guilford Press.

Kuhl, J. (1987). Action control: The maintenance of motivational states. In F. Halisch & J. Kuhl (Eds.), *Motivation, intention, and volition* (pp. 279–291). New York: Springer.

Kuhl, J., & Fuhrmann, A. (1998). Decomposing self-regulation and self-control: The Volitional Components Inventory. In J. Heckhausen & C. S. Dweck (Eds.), *Motivation and self-regulation across the life span.* New York: Cambridge University Press.

Kuhl, J., & Kazen, M. (1994). Self-discrimination and memory: State orientation and false self-ascription of assigned activities. *Journal of Personality and Social Psychology, 66,* 1103–1115.

Lewin, K., Dembo, T., Festinger, L., & Sears, P. S. (1944). Level of aspiration. In J. McV. Hunt (Ed.), *Personality and the behavior disorders* (Vol. 1, pp. 333–378). New York: Ronald Press.

Locke, E. A., & Latham, G. P. (1990). *A theory of goal setting and task performance.* Englewood Cliffs, NJ: Prentice-Hall.

Murray, H. A. (1938). *Explorations in personality.* New York: Oxford University Press.

Perls, F. S. (1973). *The Gestalt approach and eyewitness to therapy.* Ben Lomond, CA: Science and Behavior Books.

Pfander, A. (1967). *Phenomenology of willing and motivation* (H. Spiegelberg, Trans.). Evanston, IL: Northwestern University Press. (Original work published 1908)

Reich, W. (1929). Dialectical materialism and psychoanalysis. In L. Baxandall (Ed.) (1972). *Sex-Pol: Essays 1929–1934* (pp. 1–74). New York: Vintage Books.

Rogers, C. (1951). *Client centered therapy.* Boston: Houghton Mifflin.

Rothbaum, F., Weisz, J. R., & Snyder, S. S. (1982). Changing the world and changing the self: A two-process model of perceived control. *Journal of Personality and Social Psychology, 42,* 5–37.

Rotter, J. B. (1954). Social learning and clinical psychology. Englewood Cliffs, NJ: Prentice-Hall.

Ryan, R. M. (1982). Control and information in the intrapersonal sphere: An extension of cognitive evaluation theory. *Journal of Personality and Social Psychology, 43,* 450–461.

(1993). Agency and organization: Intrinsic motivation, autonomy and the self in psychological development. In J. Jacobs (Ed.), *Nebraska symposium on motivation: Developmental perspectives on motivation* (Vol. 40, pp. 1–56). Lincoln: University of Nebraska Press.

(1995). Psychological needs and the facilitation of integrative processes. *Journal of Personality, 63,* 397–427.

Ryan, R. M., Deci, E. L., & Grolnick, W. S. (1995). Autonomy, relatedness, and the self: Their relation to development and psychopathology. In D. Cicchetti & D. J. Cohen (Eds.), *Developmental psychopathology. Vol. 1: Theory and methods* (pp. 618–655). New York: Wiley.

Ryan, R. M., & Frederick, C. M. (1997). On energy, personality and health: Subjective vitality as a dynamic reflection of well-being. *Journal of Personality, 65,* 529–565.

Ryan, R. M., Sheldon, K. M., Kasser, T., & Deci, E. L. (1996). All goals were not created equal: An organismic perspective on the nature of goals and their regulation. In P. M. Gollwitzer, & J. A. Bargh (Eds.), *The psychology of action: Linking motivation and cognition to behavior* (pp. 7–26). New York: Guilford Press.

Ryan, R. M., & Solky, J. A. (1996). What is supportive about social-support? On the psychological needs for autonomy and relatedness. In G. R. Pierce, B. R. Sarason, & I. G. Sarason (Eds.), *Handbook of social support and the family* (pp. 249–267). New York: Plenum Press.

Seligman, M. E. P. (1975). *Helplessness: On depression, development, and death.* San Francisco: Freeman.

Shapiro, D. (1981). *Autonomy and rigid character.* New York: Basic Books.

Sheldon, K. M., Ryan, R. M., & Reis, H. T. (in press). What makes for a good day? Competence and autonomy in the day and in the person. *Personality and Social Psychology Bulletin.*

Watson, D., & Tellegen, A. (1985). Toward a consensual structure of mood. *Psychological Bulletin, 98,* 219–235.

White, R. W. (1959). Motivation reconsidered: The concept of competence. *Psychological Review, 66,* 297–333.

(1963). *Ego and reality in psychoanalytic theory.* New York: International Universities Press.

PART TWO

Social Determinants
of Motivation

5   Social Motivation and Perceived Responsibility in Others: Attributions and Behavior of African American Boys Labeled as Aggressive

Sandra Graham

Abstract

The study of motivation and control typically focuses on personal motivation and self-perceptions of control. For example, how individuals react to and cope with their own achievement failure is an example of personal motivation. However, it also is useful to consider this topic in an interpersonal, rather than intrapersonal context, and to examine how perceptions of control in others influence social motivational outcomes, both prosocial (e.g., helping, friendship) and antisocial (e.g., aggression). Guided by this broader social motivational framework, I will discuss a series of studies that my colleagues and I have conducted on aggressive children's attributions of control and beliefs about others' responsibility for ambiguously caused provocation. Of particular importance is how such perceptions influence the aggressive child's propensity to engage in hostile retaliation. This research focuses on African American middle elementary and early adolescent boys of low socioeconomic status. Among the topics addressed in these studies are: (1) the cognitive (i.e., attributional) and socialization (maternal beliefs) antecedents of aggressive boys' beliefs about others' control; (2) their understanding of impression management strategies that individuals use to alter perceptions of responsibility and control; (3) and an intervention approach designed to change biased perceptions about others' responsibility for (control over) negative outcomes.

Introduction

The study of aggression is integrally related to perceived control and to the linked constructs of responsibility and intentionality. In this case, however,

This chapter was written while the author was supported by grants from the National Science Foundation No. DBS-9211982.

the focus is on perceived control in others rather than self-perceptions of control. Most of the chapters in this volume examine control beliefs as an intrapsychic phenomenon, influencing personal motivation. My goal is to investigate perceived control in an interpersonal context and to show how this belief system influences social motivation. Considering an achievement example where control beliefs might be relevant, I would be studying personal motivation if I examined how students react to and cope with their own impending failure. I define social motivation as, for example, how teachers react to such failing students, with praise versus blame or help versus neglect.

In this chapter, I describe a program of research on peer-directed aggression among African American youth where personal motivation (what we think about ourselves) and social motivation (what we think about others) are differentiated. This focus on aggression is consistent with my broader goal of understanding the factors that contribute to chronic school failure among ethnic minority children. I believe that far too many minority children perform poorly in school not because they lack basic intellectual competencies or even specific learning skills, but because they feel hopeless, have low expectations, or give up in the face of failure. These are prototypical personal motivational concerns where self-perceptions of control are relevant. At the same time, far too many minority children perform poorly in school because they have few friends, are quick to blame others, and often elicit anger from their teachers and peers. These also are prototypical motivational concerns, of a social rather than personal nature, in which perceptions of control in others are relevant. In my research with African American youth, I attempt to understand both personal motivation and social motivation within the context of a general theoretical framework that is applicable to both. That framework is attribution theory, or causal beliefs about why particular outcomes occur (see reviews in Weiner, 1986, 1995).

I begin with an overview of the basic principles of an attributional theory of motivation. Next I apply these principles as I describe a series of studies with aggressive African American boys that my colleagues and I have carried out over the past few years. Some of these investigations span more than one stage in the life course inasmuch as the attributions of mothers of aggressive boys also are examined. In keeping with the theme of this volume, I conclude the chapter by highlighting some of the implications of the presented work for a social (attributional) motivational analysis of perceived control across the life span.

Attribution Theory

Causal attributions are answers to "why" questions, such as "Why did I get a poor grade on the exam?" or "Why did the person in front of me step on my toe?" These examples intentionally describe negative outcomes because individuals are more likely to ask "why" given failure rather than success, unexpected versus anticipated events, and atypical as opposed to usual outcomes. Causal search is therefore functional because it may help the individual impose order on an uncertain environment.

Although causal search can lead to an infinite number of attributions, in the achievement domain a few salient causes for success and failure tend to be endorsed: ability, which includes both aptitude and acquired skills; exertion, which entails both short- and long-term effort; task difficulty or ease; luck; mood; and help or hindrance from others. Among these causal factors, ability and effort appear to be most dominant. That is, when explaining achievement outcomes, individuals attach the most importance to their perceived competencies and how hard they try.

All causes can then be classified according to their perceived underlying dimensions. To illustrate what is meant by a dimension, consider the following example from the physical world. If I give a person a collection of square objects and round objects of different colors and instruct her to sort them into two piles, most likely she will place the square objects in one pile and the round objects in another. Shape is therefore perceived as an underlying property of these objects.

Causal attributions also have basic properties, but in this case they are of a psychological rather than physical nature. Three such properties, or *causal dimensions,* have been identified with some certainty: *locus,* or whether a cause is internal or external to the individual; *stability,* which designates a cause as constant or varying over time; and *controllability,* or whether a cause is subject to volitional influence. For example, ability (aptitude) is typically perceived as internal, stable, and uncontrollable. That is, low aptitude as a cause for failure resides within the individual, is constant over time, and is not subject to volitional control. This is in contrast to lack of effort, which is also internal, but more often perceived as unstable and under an individual's personal control.

Each of these dimensions has both psychological and behavioral consequences. In this chapter I focus on the set of interrelated principles linking the controllability dimension to emotions and to subsequent behavior toward others (i.e., to social motivation). According to this formulation, beliefs about control influence behavior toward others through the mediating influences of responsibility inferences and the emotions of pity and anger. To illustrate with research from the domain of helping behavior, when a person's need state is perceived as uncontrollable, that individual is not held responsible; the absence of responsibility tends to elicit pity and prosocial actions such as help. Thus people pity those with disabilities and want to help because they are perceived as not responsible for their plight. In contrast, attributing someone's need state to controllable factors gives rise to the inference that the person is responsible. This is because perceived responsibility presumes freedom of choice, a concept that is embodied in the notion of personal control. Inferences that the person is responsible for negative events often elicit anger, and help tends to be withheld. Furthermore, a very reliable finding in this attribution literature is that emotions of pity and anger, more so than attributions of controllability and inferences about responsibility, directly influence helping behavior (e.g., Schmidt & Weiner, 1988). Thus, attribution theorists propose a particular thought-emotion-action sequence in which causal thoughts and inferences about responsibility determine feelings, and feelings, in turn, guide behavior (see Weiner, 1995).

Because aggression, like helping, is also partly the consequence of perceived controllability and responsibility in others, the same attribution principles and temporal sequence relating causal beliefs to emotion and behavior should be applicable to both domains. Applied to the study of peer-directed aggression, this sequence can be represented as:

$$outcome \rightarrow antecedent\ cues \rightarrow perceived\ controllability \rightarrow$$
$$inference\ about\ responsibility \rightarrow anger \rightarrow aggression$$

An illustration of this sequence is as follows: A child experiences a negative outcome instigated by a peer, such as being pushed while waiting in line, and it is unclear whether the peer's behavior was intended or not. There may be certain antecedent cues that determine perceived controllability and responsibility inferences. To the degree that the peer provocateur is perceived as responsible, feelings of anger would likely be invoked, and anger, in turn, would likely be directly related to retaliation. In contrast, to the degree that the provocateur is perceived as not responsible, anger would be mitigated and it is less likely that hostile behavior would be endorsed. That is the motivational sequence. Thoughts guide feelings, and feelings, in turn, guide behavior.

As an attribution theorist, I believe that this sequence captures a general principle relating emotion to causal thinking and action. If it is a general principle, then it ought to apply to many social motivational domains, including aggression. Therefore, one can ask if the thinking-feeling-action linkages suggested here account for the causal reasoning and behavior of aggressive children. Developmental social psychologists who study peer aggression have documented a direct linkage between attributions and behavior. For example, Dodge and others have shown that aggressive children display an attributional bias to perceive others as acting with hostile intent, and these attributional preferences have been related to subsequent aggressive behavior (see Crick & Dodge, 1994). However, developmentalists working in the area of peer-directed aggression have not yet considered the role of emotion as an instigator of behavior; nor have they placed the attributional findings within the framework of a general theory of social motivation. Therefore, from the point of view of theory testing, this is a reasonable question to pursue.

Peer-Directed Aggression from an Attributional Perspective

With this theoretical framework as background, in the following sections I report five investigations that my colleagues and I have undertaken to examine peer-directed aggression among African American youth. I do have a bias toward studying a particular phenomenon at the conceptual level. In addition, as I describe the studies, I often refer to beliefs about the *intentions* of another person. I do this to be consistent with the terminology used in the peer aggression literature. At a theoretical level, however, intentionality pertains to an action, controllability attributions are judgments about the cause of that act, and responsibility inferences are beliefs about the actor. These conceptual distinctions notwithstanding, the constructs of intentionality, controllability, and responsibility tend to be used interchangeably in everyday language because of their shared meaning.

Study 1: The Consequences of Controllability Attributions and Responsibility Inferences

In our first study (Graham, Hudley, & Williams, 1992), which laid the groundwork for those that followed, we set out to document the understanding of our proposed thought-emotion-action linkages in a group of ethnic minority early adolescents labeled as aggressive. From about 300 seventh and eighth graders attending junior high school in an economically depressed community of metropolitan Los Angeles, we identified a group of 44 aggressive young black adolescents and a matched group of nonaggressives, using the standard peer nomination and teacher rating procedures from the peer aggression literature.

These children read a series of short scenarios in which they were asked to imagine that they experienced a negative outcome that was initiated by a hypothetical peer provocateur. For example, in one scenario, participants read the following:

> Imagine that you are lined up to get on the school bus to take a field trip with your class. Kids are getting on the bus one at a time. Just as you get to the front of the line, this other kid you know steps in front of you to claim the last seat on the bus.

We then manipulated the intent (responsibility) of the peer provocateur to be either prosocial, accidental, ambiguous, or hostile. In the ambiguous scenario, participants were told that "the other kid looks at you and then walks up the steps of the bus." In the hostile condition, the causal information stated that the hypothetical peer started laughing as he cut in and entered the bus.

For each story, we asked: "Did the kid do this on purpose?" and "How much anger would you feel?" These questions were answered on seven-point rating scales. We then asked participants to tell us the likelihood that they would engage in each of six behaviors that ranged along a continuum from prosocial ("do something nice for this other kid") to hostile ("have it out right then and there"). These stories and rating scales were administered to small groups of respondents by one of three African American female experimenters.

Table 5.1 shows the data from aggressive and nonaggressive subjects. It is evident that aggressive subjects were more likely than nonaggressives to believe that the hypothetical peer acted with hostile intent. This was particularly true in the ambiguous scenarios, which is consistent with the findings of Dodge and others. Aggressives also reported feeling more anger and having a greater preference for aggressive behaviors.

In this study, we were particularly interested in the temporal relations between perceived intentionality, anger, and aggressive action tendency. Our motivational sequence illustrates how thoughts determine feelings and feelings, in turn, guide behavior. To examine this sequence where emotion mediates the relation between thought and behavior, we used structural equation modeling. We also tested our model against other possible sequences involving thought, feeling, and behavior (see Graham, Hudley, & Williams, 1992 for a more detailed discussion of these alternative models). In causal modeling techniques, support for a model would be revealed by a nonsignificant chi-square; that is, the tested model adequately reproduces (does not differ significantly from) the relations in the sample data. In this case,

Table 5.1. *Mean ratings on intentionality, emotions, and aggressive action as a function of status group and causal condition*

Variable	Causal condition				
	Prosocial	Accidental	Ambiguous	Hostile	*M*
Intentionality					
Nonaggressive	3.6	3.6	4.2	6.4	4.4
Aggressive	3.9	3.9	5.2	6.5	4.9
Anger					
Nonaggressive	3.9	4.4	5.4	6.6	5.1
Aggressive	3.8	5.1	5.7	6.6	5.3
Get even					
Nonaggressive	2.6	3.6	4.7	6.2	4.3
Aggressive	3.6	4.5	5.1	6.1	4.8
Have it out					
Nonaggressive	2.5	3.2	4.2	5.8	3.9
Aggressive	3.2	3.9	4.9	6.0	4.5

Note: Rating scales range from 1 to 7. High numbers indicate greater perceived intentionality, reported emotion, and likelihood of aggressive action.
Source: Data from Graham, Hudley, and Williams (1992).

our analysis revealed a nonsignificant chi-square only for the hypothesized model, and this was true in both status groups. Substantively we interpret our findings to mean that when aggressive and nonaggressive children reason about social dilemmas with negative consequences, much of the relationship between what they think and the way they intend to behave can be accounted for by how they feel. Individuals' thoughts tell them how to feel, and their feelings tell them what to do. That is the motivational sequence.

The findings of this study encouraged us to pursue the topic further and to think about attributional change. Aggressive children are biased toward perceiving peer provocation as intentional, especially in situations of attributional ambiguity. If attributions to intentionality instigate a set of reactions that leads to aggression, then it might be possible to train aggression-prone children to see peer provocation as less intended. This would be likely to mitigate anger as well as the tendency to react with hostility.

Study 2: An Attributional Change Program

My colleague Cynthia Hudley and I developed a school-based attributional intervention to alter the intent attributions of children labeled as aggressive (Hudley & Graham, 1993). The intervention was a six-week, twelve-session program designed for children in the upper elementary grades. Through a variety of activities, children were given training in how accurately to detect intentionality from social cues and to assume nonmalicious intent in situations of ambiguity.

The participants in this study were African American fifth- and sixth-grade boys labeled as aggressive according to the criteria used in the previous study. A third of these boys were randomly assigned to the experimental intervention; one-third participated in an attention-training program of the same scope and duration as the experimental intervention, but not related to attributional change; and one-third of the boys constituted the control group. The experimental and attention-training groups met twice weekly for six weeks in small groups of four to six during the regular school day. The programs were run by two African American female experimenters with extensive experience in classroom teaching.

We collected pre- and postmeasures of children's intentionality attributions, emotional reactions of anger, and aggressive action tendency in hypothetical social dilemmas much like those used in the previous study. Prior to the intervention, none of the three groups differed on any of these variables. That is, all the aggressive boys inferred malicious intent on the part of the peer provocateur, they felt very angry, and they intended to behave aggressively. Following the intervention, only the boys in the experimental group altered their judgments in the direction of less intentionality, less anger, and less endorsement of hostile behavior. We also had pre- and postmeasures on teacher ratings of aggression. These findings, too, supported the efficacy of the attributional intervention. Compared to their counterparts in the attention-training and control conditions, intervention group subjects were rated as less aggressive by their teachers one month following the intervention.

The above data derive only from hypothetical situations and ratings of behavior by others. Since this was a real intervention, we would hope that its effects might generalize to situations of actual behavior. Obviously we could not create the kinds of social dilemmas depicted in the hypothetical scenarios, and we did not have the resources (or the patience) for a large-scale observation study of naturally occurring peer provocation. Therefore, we compromised by using a laboratory analog task in the second part of the study that would simulate ambiguously caused peer provocation. About one month after the experimental intervention ended, all the subjects participated in a problem-solving task that supposedly was unrelated to the earlier intervention. The task required the subject to communicate with an unseen peer who was seated on the other side of a barrier. Using simple grid maps, the peer was to give directions to the subject so that he could complete a

Table 5.2. *Attributions to intent, reported anger, and verbal behavior in the analog task, by treatment group*

Variable	Treatment group		
	Experimental	Attention training	Control
Intentionality	2.3	4.5	4.7
Angry	1.7	2.5	2.6
Behavior (% total)			
Neutral	61%	29%	31%
Complaining	20%	25%	31%
Criticizing	19%	29%	23%
Insulting	0%	17%	15%

Note: Rating scales for intentionality and anger range from 1 to 7. High numbers indicate greater perceived intent and more intense anger.
Source: Data from Hudley and Graham (1993).

maze, with the goal of winning a prize. In fact, however, the task was designed to block goal attainment. Unbeknownst to either child, the peer's map was different from the subject's. Thus incorrect directions were necessarily given, the maze was not completed, and no prize was awarded. After the first trial, when it was clear that the subject had not completed the maze, he was asked a series of questions about the outcome. Embedded in these questions were attributions about the peer's intent and feelings of anger toward that peer.

These data are shown in Table 5.2 as a function of treatment group during the intervention. High numbers indicate that aggressive children believed that the peer purposely gave misleading directions. Notice that the children who participated in the attributional intervention were significantly less likely to infer malicious intent on the part of the peer. They also expressed less anger toward the peer, although here the differences between groups is much smaller.

What about behavior? During the experiment, an observer also unobtrusively recorded the verbal behaviors of the subject during the frustrating task. These behaviors were classified into one of four types:

1. *Neutral:* nonjudgmental statements to the peer or adult experimenter
2. *Complaining::* negative comments to the experimenter about his own performance (e.g., "I can't do this")
3. *Criticizing:* remarks to the unseen peer about his performance (e.g., "You obviously don't know how to read a map")

4. *Insulting:* negative personal comments to the peer (e.g., "You're dumb")

If the boys who participated in the attributional intervention inferred less hostile intent and reported less anger, then they would also be likely to engage in less of the kind of verbally aggressive behavior, such as criticizing and insulting, that might accompany goal frustration in this context. The behavioral data in Table 5.2 show that this was indeed the case. Neutral comments were by far the preferred verbal behavior of experimental subjects, and not one of these children resorted to insult. With the nontrained aggressive subjects, in contrast, about one in every six verbalizations was an insult. Therefore, it is clear that the manipulation worked in this actual behavioral context.

We were encouraged by these findings. We identified a particular population of young African American males labeled as aggressive. We were able to conceptualize their status in terms of a motivational sequence relating feelings of anger to biased intent attributions and subsequent behavior. By influencing their causal thinking, we were able to show changes in the feelings and behaviors that theoretically follow such thoughts. Even in the achievement change literature it has proved difficult to produce both cognitive and behavioral changes based on attributional interventions. I think our study is one of few that have documented the success of an attributional intervention with children in the social domain.

Study 3: Social Cognitive Antecedents of Biased Attributions to Intent

Thus far I have been discussing the consequences of biased attributions to intent. Now I want to move backward in the temporal sequence that I presented earlier to the antecedents of perceived hostile intent in others. One might then ask: Where do these beliefs come from? That is, what factors lead an aggressive child to infer prematurely or inappropriately that a peer did something negative to him or her "on purpose"?

Here, my colleagues and I were guided by the belief that there might be stable individual differences between aggressives and nonaggressives in the way they have learned mentally to represent, or categorize and interpret, the behavior of others. The school bus scenario presented earlier is an example of ambiguous peer provocation. A mental represention of this event as intentionally caused may be the most accessible, or readily usable, causal construct stored in the memory of the aggressive child, whose own life experiences are probably replete with instances of assigning and receiving blame. Cognitive psychologists who study construct accessibility sometimes use the metaphor of the "memory bin," where mental constructs that individuals use to judge others are stored in layers (see Srull & Wyer, 1989). The ones that are most likely to be used are those that have made their way to the top of the "bin" as a result of recent or frequent use in the past. For the aggressive child, the perception that negative events occur "on purpose" resides at the top of the memory bin and is therefore readily accessible.

To study construct accessibility, cognitive social psychologists use a procedure known as *priming*. As this label suggests, individuals can be primed to interpret information in a particular way. For example, in one prototypical study, subjects were primed to think about the trait of "adventurous" versus "reckless" (Higgins, Rholes, & Jones, 1977). Those primed for "adventurous" were more likely to evaluate positively someone described as "driving in a demolition derby" or "crossing the Atlantic in a sailboat" than were those primed for "reckless." The recent activation of a construct in one context influenced subsequent judgments about ambiguous behavior.

We adapted the priming methodology for use with aggressive and nonaggressive early adolescent males (Graham & Hudley, 1994). We wanted to test our hypothesis that there might be individual differences between aggressives and nonaggressives in the accessibility of perceptions of hostile intent. In this study, participants were randomly assigned either to a condition that primed the perception of negative intent, benign intent, or to a no-priming control condition. A sentence memorization task was used to prime the relevant constructs. For example, subjects in the negative-intent condition read and studied sentences such as, "The cheerleader kept her team from winning the competition because she was too lazy to practice her routines." In the benign-intent condition, the same sentence read, "The cheerleader kept her team from winning the competition because she was so nervous, she couldn't remember her routines." Following the priming task, in a supposedly unrelated task, subjects were presented with a scenario describing hypothetical peer provocation. They then made inferences about the peer's intent, their feelings of anger and blame toward the peer, and the likelihood that they would endorse aggressive retaliation.

Figure 5.1 shows the judgments for intentionality, anger, and blame as a function of status group and priming condition. These data reveal two noteworthy findings. First, the differences in judgment extremity for aggressives and nonaggressives in the negative-intent condition were not significant. Therefore, it was possible to "create" an attributional bias in nonaggressive children by priming them to perceive others as acting with negative or hostile

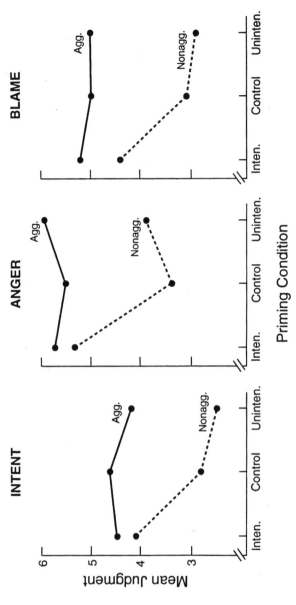

Figure 5.1. Attributions to intent and judgments about anger and blame as a function of status group and priming condition (from Graham & Hudley, 1994).

intent. Second, for aggressive children the priming manipulations had virtually no effect. Their judgments were equally extreme no matter what we did. We can conclude that what we conceptualized as a trait – that is, a chronic propensity to perceive others as acting with hostile intent – was more powerful than our situational manipulation that tried to prime benign intent.

These data have some clear implications for intervention. When discussing the attributional intervention, I spoke positively about the effects of attributional change. However, the effects were short-lived. When we followed the children in the Hudley and Graham intervention after a six-month interval, there were no differences between treatment groups in teacher ratings of hostile behavior, and peer nominations for aggression were virtually unchanged from what they had been prior to the intervention. I do not think that these disappointing long-term results occurred because we were dealing with the wrong variable. Rather, it is clear to me that chronically accessible constructs are not easily amenable to change.

How far back in a causal chain do we need to go to find the causes of chronically accessible constructs? I believe that aggressive children might be socialized early in life to be quick to assign blame. Also, much of this socialization occurs inside the home. For example, the causal construct *negative intent* is likely to become more accessible to the child whose family members display low thresholds for categorizing one another's negative behavior as purposeful rather than unintended, just as the trait construct *considerate* will emerge as more accessible for the youngster whose parents frequently make reference to the thoughtful behavior of others.

Because most of the African American boys in our studies live in single-parent homes where the mother is head of household, the priming study led us to think more about the role of mothers as socializers of belief patterns pertinent to aggression. Our insights gained from working with African American mothers, as well as our understanding of the socialization literature, led us to think that some mothers of aggressive boys may unknowingly be socializing their offspring to perceive the world as a hostile place. This may be based, in part, on maternal attitudes and beliefs that have been acquired as a result of dealing with the adult stressors of single parenthood and/or economic hardship. It might also reflect these mothers' *own* life histories of being reared in contexts of racial prejudice, and social and economic disadvantage. A number of developmental psychologists have written about how the multiple stressors of poverty, single parenthood, and racism can have a negative impact on the general coping strategies as well as parenting styles of some low-income African American mothers (e.g., McLoyd & Wilson, 1991). Therefore, the degree to which negative life circumstances have led mothers to adopt a blameful stance in situations of interpersonal conflict may be reflected in the degree to which their children exhibit these same differences.

Study 4: Socialization Antecedents of Biased Attributions to Intent

In the next study, we began to explore these socialization arguments and to take our analysis to a new stage in the life course. Here we examined the responsibility inferences of mothers of aggressive and nonaggressive children to see if they also differ in the tendency to infer hostile intent in others in situations of attributional ambiguity (Graham & Hudley, 1995). From samples of aggressive and nonaggressive boys identified in our ongoing research, we recruited forty African American mothers with an aggressive son and thirty African American mothers with a nonaggressive son. Both groups of mothers tended to be poorly educated and living at the poverty level, and they were rearing several children alone ($M = 3.4$ children per household).

In individual interviews, each mother was presented with two types of scenario. One type involved negative outcomes involving her son (i.e., not doing chores at home, being accused of cheating at school) in which it was unclear whether the boy's behavior was intended or not. Each mother then rated how responsible her son was for the behavior, how much anger, blame, and sympathy she would feel, and the likelihood that she would punish him.

The second type of scenario involved ambiguous peer provocation in which the mothers themselves were the targets of the transgression. For example, mothers read scenarios such as:

> Imagine that you are walking in a long line that is going into a crowded event – such as a game or a live concert. Everyone has to wait a long time and then go through the doors at the same time. You know, those situations where people can get really impatient. In fact, the person right behind you was complaining loudly and starting to show signs of impatience. As you are walking through the doors, you notice that a disturbance breaks out and the person behind you in line is involved. People are arguing, some pushing and shoving occurs, but it is hard to tell what the argument is about or who started it. Just then, the person in back of you suddenly falls forward, causing both of you to fall down, and you bump your knee.

Notice that this scenario is conceptually analogous to the kind that we use in our studies that differentiate aggressive and nonaggressive boys. The mothers then made inferences about the hypothetical peer's intent, the degree of anger and blame they would experience, the amount of sympathy

Table 5.3. *Means and standard deviations for each dependent variable, combined across the four adult ambiguous scenarios*

	Group				
	Mothers of aggressive sons		Mothers of nonaggressive sons		
Variable	*M*	SD	*M*	SD	*F*(1, 68)
Responsibility	4.7	0.9	4.2	1.1	5.13
Blame	4.5	1.1	4.1	0.9	3.93
Anger	4.1	1.4	3.4	1.0	5.09
Sympathy	3.2	1.2	3.9	1.1	6.06
Action tendency					
Hostile	4.1	1.4	3.3	1.4	6.82
Neutral	2.6	0.1	3.3	1.4	4.54
Prosocial	4.5	0.2	5.2	1.2	5.50

Note: Rating scales range from 1 to 7. High numbers indicate more perceived responsibility, blame, anger, sympathy, and greater action tendency. Univariate *F*-values are all significant at $p \leq 0.05$.

they would feel, and the likelihood that they would engage in behavior that was retaliatory (confront the person); neutral (do nothing, just forget it); or prosocial (in this case, offer to help the person get up).

First we examined mothers' ratings on intentionality, blame, anger, sympathy, and severity of endorsed punishment for their son, given ambiguously caused negative outcomes. The results showed that mothers of aggressive sons inferred significantly more hostile intent on the part of their sons, they felt more anger, less sympathy, blamed them more, and they endorsed harsher punishment. This replicates other attributional data showing that mothers of aggressive boys take a more blameful stance toward their sons than do mothers of nonaggressive boys (e.g., Baden & Howe, 1992).

More important for our purposes, Table 5.3 shows the data for hypothetical adult peer provocation. When they reasoned about their own situations of ambiguous provocation, mothers of aggressive sons were also more likely than mothers of nonaggressive sons to infer that their adult peers acted with hostile intent. They were also more angry, blameful, less sympathetic, and more endorsing of hostile behavior. Thus, the mothers presented with these scenarios involving ambiguous adult peer provocation responded in much the same way as aggressive and nonaggressive boys in studies of childhood peer aggression.

To examine the relations between mothers' causal beliefs and the aggressive status of their sons, we created separate indexes capturing response extremity (in the direction of perceived negative intent, anger, blame, hostility) based on mothers' responses to the scenarios involving their sons and adult peers, respectively. Mothers' scores on these indexes were then correlated with their sons' aggressive status, as measured by the sons' standardized score on peer nominations for aggressive behavior. Both maternal indexes were significantly correlated with child aggressive status. That is, the more extreme the mother's interpretation of her son's ambiguous behavior, the more aggressive he was perceived to be by his peers ($r = 0.42, p < 0.001$), and the more extreme the mother's response to adult provocation, the more aggressive he was thought to be ($r = 0.29, p < 0.05$). In other words, a mother's blameful stances in relation to her son and adult peer provocateurs were predictive of the severity of perceived aggressiveness in her son.

These data relate back to construct accessibility: the causal construct *negative intent* is likely to become more accessible to the child whose mother displays a low threshold for categorizing her son's ambiguous behavior and the ambiguous behavior of others as hostile rather than unintended. I believe that these results take the psychology community one step closer to documenting how maternal beliefs and behavior can be an antecedent to child aggressive status. (Also see Pomerantz & Ruble, Chapter 6, this volume, for a discussion of parental control practices that are associated with aggression in children).

Of course, I must be cautious in interpreting our findings, given the correlational nature of the analysis. It may be, as I speculate here, that aggressive children have learned to model their caregivers' style of dealing with an environment perceived as hostile, and this socialization process then partly accounts for why the children themselves engage in antisocial behavior. It also may well be that mothers of aggressive children are more easily angered because of the stress of rearing a difficult child, and this negative mood state then biases their perceptions of the causes of others' behavior (e.g., Dix, Reinhold, & Zambarano, 1990; Peterson, Ewigman, & Vandiver, 1994). As yet, psychologists know very little about the processes by which biased beliefs concerning hostile intent might be transmitted intergenerationally, or how they might become more chronic across stages of the life course. These are fruitful areas for future research.

Study 5: Consequences of Controllability Attributions and Responsibility Inferences in the Use of Excuses

Now I return to the motivational sequence that I began. Thus far I have discussed how these thinking-feeling-action linkages provide insight into how aggressive boys (and their mothers) perceive others. There is yet another way to view this sequence. As actors, or potential provocateurs, people also initiate negative outcomes that have an impact on others. Most individuals learn social skills early in life that teach them to alter potentially negative impressions that others have of them: They learn to shift causal responsibility away from themselves. This mitigates anger from others and the likelihood that they will behave aggressively toward the individual.

A good example of how this process operates is in the domain of excuse-giving. For example, Jack makes plans to meet a friend and then doesn't show up because he decides to do something else. When Jack sees his friend the next time, he is not likely to reveal the truth, which is, "I didn't want to meet you." Rather, he is more likely to say something that implies nonresponsibility, such as, "I was too ill to come." The use of excuses is based on a naive analysis of the linkages that I have been examining throughout this chapter. People make excuses in order to alter perceptions of responsibility (or intentionality) and their linked emotions and behavioral reactions (Weiner, Amirkhan, Folkes, et al., 1988).

In our next study, we examined the development of excuse-giving in aggressive and nonaggressive African American boys (Graham, Weiner, & Benesh-Weiner, 1995). This kind of approach – in which we look at how aggressive children manage the impressions that others have of them – has not been explored in the peer aggression literature. We recruited a sample of younger (third- to fifth-grade) and older (sixth- to eighth-grade) aggressive and nonaggressive African American boys. In the first part of the study, we told the boys to imagine that they had agreed to meet either their mother or a peer after school, and then failed to show up because they had decided to get together with their friends. In other words, we provided our respondents with a controllable cause for social transgression. We then asked them whether they would admit this true and controllable cause to their mother or peer, or whether they would make something up.

Among nonaggressives, the findings revealed that younger children were much more likely than older children to reveal the true cause for their failure to show up (i.e., the older nonaggressives were more likely to make up an excuse). Both groups of aggressives, in contrast, showed response patterns similar to the younger nonaggressives.

In the next part of the study, we manipulated the reason for this social misconduct to be either controllable (i.e., "You decided to go to someone's house" or "You forgot") or uncontrollable (i.e., "You were sick in the nurse's office," or "Your jacket got stolen and you had to look for it after school"). For each reason, we asked respondents three questions: (1) Would

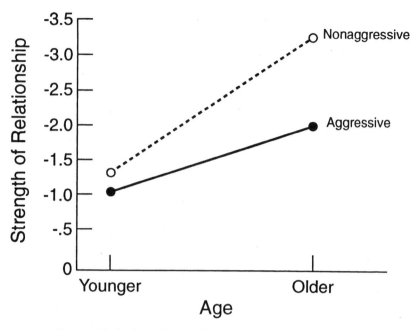

Figure 5.2. Social understanding in excuse giving as a function of age and status group (from Graham et al., 1995).

you tell your Mom (peer) why you did not show up? (2) Would she think you were responsible? and (3) How angry would she be? These questions were answered on seven-point rating scales.

We calculated a combined index of these ratings showing the relationship between perceived responsibility for the transgression, inferred anger, and likelihood of revealing the true cause (see Figure 5.2). Stronger relationships indicate greater "social awareness," that is, the respondents understand that perceived responsibility and anger from others "go together," and they use this understanding to decide when to reveal and when to withhold the reasons for social misconduct. Figure 5.2 shows that with increasing age, children understood the anger-mitigating function of excuses. This is consistent with what is known about older children becoming more sophisticated social information processors. However, there were also effects of aggressive status: As indicated in the free-responses data, the older aggressive boys showed less understanding, or social awareness, than their same-age nonaggressive counterparts. Thus, the age-related increase in understanding of the anger-mitigating function of excuses is less evident in aggressive African American boys.

Such data shed light on how the cycle of aggressive responding becomes exacerbated in boys labeled as aggressive. Not only are they quick to assign blame, react with anger, and respond with hostility toward others, but they also seem to lack some of the social skills that allow them to control others' potential anger toward them in situations of social misconduct.

Summary

I began this program of research with a simple set of principles relating causal thoughts to emotions and action. By working with these principles, my colleagues and I have been able to: show how aggressive children organize their thinking about peer provocation; suggest a viable direction for intervention; gain some insight into the chronicity of biased beliefs about control, responsibility, or the intentions of others; examine some of the socializing influences on these beliefs; and begin to explore how aggressive children manage the impressions that others have about them.

Implications for a Life-Span Perspective

Thus far I have (cleverly) sidestepped a central theme of this volume, which is that each chapter addresses a life-span perspective on motivation and self-regulation. This poses a challenge to the attribution theorist. There are vast but separate bodies of literature on attributional processes in adults and on the development of attributional concepts in children (see Dweck, Chapter 10, this volume). However, there is relatively little research that bridges these two traditions to examine attributional processes within a life-span perspective.

In terms of this chapter, one way to think about a life-span perspective is to consider whether perceptions of control and responsibility in others, as well as their hypothesized relations to emotion and social behavior, change across the life course. Based on other research that my colleagues and I have conducted, my speculation is that the basic linkages are understood very early in life and undergo little developmental change. For example, in our one attempt to study changes in attributional reasoning across the life span (Graham & Weiner, 1991), we gave children and adults, who ranged from 5 to 95 years of age, scenarios involving a hypothetical stimulus person who needed help. The person's need state was manipulated to be either controllable or uncontrollable. For each scenario, respondents indicated whether the person was responsible for his or her need state, how much anger and pity they would feel toward the needy person, and the likelihood that they would help that individual. We found that all age groups tested, from 5-year-olds to 95-year-olds, inferred more responsibility on the part of the person whose need state was manipulated to be controllable: They felt more anger, less pity, and they were less willing to help. Furthermore, consistent with the motivational sequence suggested by attribution theory, the relationships between these variables were the same in all age groups. That is, for 5-year-olds as well as 95-year-olds, emotions of anger and pity mediated the relationship between beliefs about responsibility in others and helping behavior.

In another recent study guided by our attributional framework (Graham & Hoehn, 1995), we moved to even younger respondents in an investigation of children's perceptions of stigmatized others. We presented 4-, 5-, and 6-year-olds with scenarios describing a male peer who was either aggressive or shy/withdrawn. The children were then asked to tell us whether the peer was responsible for his behavior, whether they would feel anger or pity, and whether they would want this person as a friend. Again consistent with attributional principles, we found that even 5-year-olds inferred that aggressive children were more responsible for their behavior than were shy/withdrawn peers, they felt more anger and less pity, and they were less likely to want an aggressive classmate as a friend. Among 4-year-olds, in contrast, the differentiations were much less clear. Thus, from our perspective, it appears that sometime between the ages of 4 and 5, children acquire a very clear meaning of what it means for someone to do something "on purpose," and they use this understanding in a variety of contexts involving interpersonal evaluation and behavior toward others.

In sum, I believe that the concept of perceived responsibility in others is a prevalent psychological construct in American society – at least as central as self-perceptions of control. It is a construct that is acquired early in life, utilized across all stages of the life course, and useful for organizing a vast number of phenomena in social motivation research. From a life-span perspective, it would be worthwhile to examine both the salience of perceptions of control at different stages of development and the intensity of affective reactions to others' transgressions that are perceived as controllable. For example, older people may be relatively more forgiving or more tolerant of deviance than their younger counterparts, which would then have implications for the activation of attribution-emotion-action sequences. Even though the basic linkages between variables are the same across age groups, mean differences may exist that are important for predicting behavior.

Yet another issue pertinent to a life-span perspective concerns the possibility of intergenerational transmission of biased beliefs about others' responsibility. As I intimated in the study of mothers of aggressive and nonaggressive African American boys, a caregiver's style of dealing with her own adult world perceived as hostile may unintentionally be communicated to and modeled by her son. This raises issues about contextual variables influencing the development of motivation constructs across different life stages, as well as factors that may interrupt or distort "normal" development (see Cantor & Sanderson, Chapter 7, this volume). Recognizing the importance of context and the idea of different trajectories for different individuals is fundamental to a multidetermined and multidirectional life-span approach to development (e.g., Baltes & Reese, 1984).

I suspect that our aggression research has much to gain from greater attention to a life-span perspective. First, this perspective provides a rich theoretical framework for continued investigation of socialization determinants of beliefs about hostile intent. Second, the fluidity and flexibility of development implied by a life-span approach encourages the belief that intervention may be efficacious at almost any age. For example, rather than focusing exclusively on aggressive children as targets of attributional change (Hudley & Graham, 1993), it might be useful to think about parent intervention as a pathway to reducing aggressive behavior across more than one generation. These are indeed fruitful questions for the future as psychologists broaden the theoretical net in their search to understand complex social problems such as aggression.

References

Baden, A., & Howe, G. (1992). Mothers, attributions, and expectancies regarding their conduct-disordered children. *Journal of Abnormal Child Psychology, 20,* 467–485.

Baltes, P., & Reese, H. (1984). The life-span perspective on developmental psychology. In M. Bornstein & M. Lamb (Eds.), *Developmental psychology: An advanced textbook* (pp. 493–531). Hillsdale, NJ: Erlbaum.

Cantor, N., & Sanderson, C. A. (1998). The functional regulation of adolescent dating relationships and sexual behavior: An interaction of goals, strategies, and situations. In J. Heckhausen & C. S. Dweck (Eds.), *Motivation and self-regulation across the life span.* New York: Cambridge University Press.

Crick, N., & Dodge, K. (1994). A review and reformulation of social-information processing mechanisms in children's social adjustment. *Psychological Bulletin, 115,* 74–101.

Dix, T., Reinhold, D., & Zambarano, R. (1990). Mothers' judgments in moments of anger. *Merrill-Palmer Quarterly, 36,* 465–485.

Graham, S., & Hoehn, S. (1995). Children's understanding of aggression and withdrawal as social stigmas: An attributional analysis. *Child Development, 66,* 1143–1162.

Graham, S., & Hudley, C. (1994). Attributions of aggressive and nonaggressive African American early adolescents: A study of construct accessibility. *Developmental Psychology, 30,* 365–373.

(1995, March). *Attributional bias in mothers of aggressive and nonaggressive African American boys.* Paper presented at the meeting of the Society for Research in Child Development, Indianapolis, IN.

Graham, S., Hudley, C., Williams, E. (1992). Attributional and emotional determinants of aggression among African American and Latino early adolescents. *Developmental Psychology, 28,* 731–740.

Graham, S., & Weiner, B. (1991). Testing judgments about attribution-emotion-action linkages: A life-span approach. *Social Cognition, 9,* 254–276.

Graham, S., Weiner, B., & Benesh-Weiner, M. (1995). An attributional analysis of the development of excuse-giving in aggressive and nonaggressive African American boys. *Developmental Psychology, 31,* 274–284.

Higgins, E., Rholes, W., & Jones, C. (1977). Category accessibility and impression formation. *Journal of Personality and Social Psychology, 13,* 141–154.

Hudley, C., & Graham, S. (1993). An attributional intervention to reduce peer-directed aggression among African American boys. *Child Development, 64,* 124–138.

McLoyd, V., & Wilson, L. (1991). The strain of living poor: Parenting, social support, and child mental health. In A. C. Huston (Ed.), *Children in poverty: Child development and public policy* (pp. 105–135). New York: Cambridge University Press.

Peterson, L., Ewigman, B., & Vandiver, T. (1994). Role of parental anger in low-income women: Discipline strategy, perceptions of behavior problems, and the need for control. *Journal of Clinical Child Psychology, 23,* 435–443.

Pomerantz, E., & Ruble, D. (1998). The multidimensional nature of control: Implications for the development of sex differences in self-evaluation. In J. Heckhausen & C. S. Dweck (Eds.), *Motivation and self-regulation across the life span.* New York: Cambridge University Press.

Schmidt, G., & Weiner, B. (1988). An attribution-affect-action theory of behavior: Replications of judgments of help giving. *Personality and Social Bulletin, 14,* 610–621.

Srull, T., & Wyer, R. (1989). Person memory and judgment. *Psychological Review, 96,* 58–83.

Weiner, B. (1986). *An attributional theory of motivation and emotion.* New York: Springer-Verlag.

(1995). *Judgments of responsibility: A foundation for a theory of social conduct.* New York: Guilford Press.

Weiner, B., Amirkhan, J., Folkes, V., & Verette, J. (1988). An attributional analysis of excuse giving: Studies of a naive theory of emotion. *Journal of Personality and Social Psychology, 52,* 316–324.

6 The Multidimensional Nature of Control: Implications for the Development of Sex Differences in Self-Evaluation

Eva M. Pomerantz and Diane N. Ruble

Abstract

What environmental conditions promote perceptions that one can control or cope with failures and adversities in one's life? Much research on motivation has emphasized the importance of conditions that minimize external control. However, many of the forms of control shown to have negative consequences in this research have been suggested to have positive consequences in the research on parental socialization, particularly that on authoritative control (see Lewis, 1981). How can this apparent contradiction be explained? In this chapter, we first review previous conceptualizations and operationalizations of control in the area of parental socialization, highlighting some of the weaknesses of the operationalizations of control in this area. Next, we argue that research on control in the area of motivation and in the area of parental socialization may be discrepant not only for methodological reasons, but also for substantive ones. We propose that control may be a multidimensional construct, and that this perspective on the nature of control provides an understanding of how control may have both positive and negative consequences. Here, we present evidence from our own research suggesting that control may indeed convey dual messages to children, and that this is increasingly likely as children progress through elementary school. We then highlight the explanatory power of our analysis of control for the development of sex differences in self-evaluation. We present evidence from our own research that some forms of parental control may be used more with daughters than with sons, and that these forms of control may foster negative self-evaluation in children.

We are grateful to Ed Deci, Carol Dweck, Sarah Mangelsdorf, Karen Rudolph, and Jill Saxon for their helpful feedback on an earlier draft of this chapter. The preparation of this chapter and the research presented in it were supported by NIMH grants (nos. MH01202 and MH37215) to Diane N. Ruble.

159

Control in the Parental Socialization Area

A Brief History

There has been considerable disagreement in the parental socialization literature over what constitutes control and what its consequences are. In his 1964 review, based on factor analyses of parent interviews and questionnaires, Becker proposed two central dimensions of parenting: restrictiveness versus permissiveness, and warmth versus hostility.[1] The restrictive end of the restrictive versus permissive dimension was characterized by "many restrictions and strict enforcement of demands in the areas of sex play, modesty behavior, table manners, toilet training, neatness, orderliness, care of household furniture, noise, obedience, aggression to sibs, aggression to peers, and aggression to parents" (Becker, 1964, p. 174). The permissive end was characterized by fewer restrictions and less strict enforcement. Becker crossed the two dimensions to yield four constellations of parenting, and concluded that each of the four had distinct consequences. Consistent with research on control in the area of motivation, permissiveness combined with warmth appeared to foster positive characteristics in children, such as creativity, extroversion, and independence. The other three constellations were associated with more negative outcomes, such as delinquency, shyness, submissiveness, and lack of creativity.

Two decades later, in their comprehensive review of research on parental socialization, Maccoby and Martin (1983) argued that although the research did indeed suggest that there were two central dimensions of parenting, based on the work of Baumrind (1967, 1971; Baumrind & Black, 1967), the dimensions might better be thought of as demanding/controlling versus undemanding/low in control attempts and accepting/responsive/child-centered versus rejecting/unresponsive/parent-centered. Instead of delineating the characteristics associated with the ends of each dimension, Maccoby and Martin depicted those associated with each of the four constellations, suggesting that each constellation may represent not the low and high ends of the two dimensions but, instead, qualitatively distinct characteristics resulting from their interaction.

With the relabeling of the two dimensions, Maccoby and Martin's review yielded results quite different from those of Becker. Whereas Becker's review had suggested that the constellation including low control ("permissiveness," in Becker's terms) and high acceptance ("warmth," in Becker's terms) yielded the most positive outcomes for children, Maccoby and Martin's review, and particularly the research of Baumrind, suggested that the authoritative constellation, comprising high control and high acceptance, yielded the most positive outcomes. Although not all the research was consistent, the authoritative constellation tended to be associated with positive outcomes, such as heightened self-esteem, social skills, independence, and moral development. The indulgent constellation (low control and high acceptance), which Becker had concluded had positive effects, was generally associated with decrements in self-esteem, social competence, and moral development as well as increased aggression in children.

Although control has been of major interest to investigators for over three decades, it is still not clear what underlies the inconsistencies in its impact. For example, are the inconsistencies a result of research on qualitatively different forms of control that foster distinct outcomes (see Grusec & Lytton, 1988)? Could it be that the forms of control included in the authoritative parenting constellation lead to positive outcomes only in the family context? Is it that, in general, parents' use of control has become less severe over time, so that permissiveness prior to 1964 was equal to the moderate levels of control included under the label of authoritative parenting introduced in the seventies (see Ruble & Thompson, 1992)? Are there other reasons for the discrepancies? In an attempt to clarify the cause of these inconsistencies, we review the research on parents' use of control with their children. We begin with research on the authoritative constellation, and suggest that it may be difficult to draw conclusions about the impact of control from this research. Subsequently, we briefly review the research on more specific forms of parental control proposed to be beneficial to children, highlighting methodological problems in this literature. In the next section, we offer an analysis of the multidimensional nature of control, suggesting that the forms of control associated with the authoritative constellation may have both positive and negative consequences, and present some of our own data in support of this proposal.

The Authoritative Constellation

Baumrind's Research. Baumrind (1967, 1971; Baumrind & Black, 1967) conceptualized authoritative parenting as characterized by parents' efforts to direct children in a "rational and issue-oriented manner." The major elements Baumrind outlined were: articulated standards and expectations for mature behavior; firm enforcement of rules and standards, using commands when necessary; reciprocal communication between parents and children; acknowledgment of rights of parents and children; and valuing of independence as well as "disciplined conformity" (see also Maccoby & Martin,

1983). Empirically, Baumrind defined authoritative parenting as high firm enforcement, high encouragement of independence and individuality, and low passive acceptance. Thus, the authoritative constellation included elements of both autonomy-granting and controlling behavior on the part of parents, although Baumrind emphasized the importance of parents' use of firm enforcement.

Baumrind (1967, 1971) reported that preschool children with authoritative parents were better adjusted than preschool children with parents characterized by other constellations (e.g., indulgent). For example, in Baumrind's (1971) study, boys of authoritative parents were significantly more likely to be friendly, cooperative, tractable, and achievement-oriented, but not independent, than boys of parents characterized by other constellations. Girls of authoritative parents were likely to be only more achievement-oriented. To determine if the control component is indeed a primary cause of the positive outcomes associated with the authoritative constellation, the key comparison would be between the authoritative constellation and the indulgent constellation (low firm enforcement, high encouragement of independence and individuality, and high passive acceptance).[2] Only a few parents in Baumrind's research, however, fit this category. Hence, Baumrind never made the essential comparison between groups differing in control but not in other dimensions.

More Recent Research. Baumrind's work spurred a considerable amount of research examining the impact of authoritative parenting on children, especially during the toddler and adolescent years. This work has generally, but not always, indicated that the authoritative constellation is associated with positive outcomes in children. Much of this research, however, has conceptualized and, consequently, operationalized authoritative parenting in a manner that is somewhat different from that of Baumrind. A review of this literature suggests that although parental control is often an element of authoritative parenting, it plays a far smaller part than Baumrind proposed. In one discussion of authoritative parenting among adolescents, the authoritative constellation was described as "parental warmth, inductive discipline, nonpunitive punishment practices, and consistency in child rearing" (Lamborn, Mounts, Steinberg, et al., 1991, p. 1049), with no mention of firm enforcement. Indeed, many influential research programs have used operationalizations of authoritative parenting that focus more on other aspects of the constellation than on firm enforcement (e.g., Dekovic & Janssens, 1992; Dornbusch, Ritter, Leiderman, et al., 1987; Kochanska, 1991, 1995). Consequently, it is difficult to tell if the positive child outcomes linked to these operationalizations have anything to do with parents' use of firm control.

Recent research on authoritative parenting, however, has also used operationalizations that emphasize control (e.g., Steinberg, Elemen, & Mounts, 1989; Steinberg, Lamborn, Dornbusch, et al., 1992). For example, all four of the parenting constellations introduced by Maccoby and Martin (authoritative, authoritarian, indulgent, and neglectful) have been examined in adolescents by crossing measures of children's perceptions of their parents' warmth and involvement with their perceptions of their parents' supervision and strictness (Lamborn, Mounts, Steinberg, et al., 1991). The strictness and supervision dimension has been assessed by asking adolescents how much their parents attempt to know and how much they really know about their lives (e.g., where they go at night, what they do with their free time). Authoritative parenting operationalized in this manner appears to have a number of positive outcomes for adolescents. Lamborn and colleagues (1991) found that adolescents who perceived their parents as authoritative were generally more likely than those who perceived their parents as authoritarian, indulgent, or neglectful to have higher psychosocial competence (i.e., self-reliance, work orientation, perceived social competence) and school competence (i.e., grades, orientation toward school, perceived academic competence). They were also less likely to have externalizing problems (i.e., school misconduct, drug use, delinquency). There were very few differences for internalizing problems (i.e., depression, anxiety, somatic problems), however. Significantly, this study made the comparisons between the authoritative and indulgent constellations that Baumrind was unable to make. Although children of authoritative parents were less likely than those of indulgent parents to be doing poorly in school and to have externalizing problems, there were practically no significant differences between the two groups in terms of psychosocial development and internalizing problems. Thus, the control dimension of authoritative parenting may foster only some positive outcomes in children.

Conclusions. Although authoritative parenting appears to be associated with a number of positive child outcomes, it is often not clear whether the positive outcomes are due to control or to other elements of the constellation. Whereas research on motivation has generally focused on specific forms of control, such as the use of rewards or surveillance, research on parental socialization has tended to focus on control in the context of larger constellations of parenting. It is, therefore, not clear what it is about the authoritative constellation that leads to positive child outcomes (see Bugental

& Goodnow, in press; Darling & Steinberg, 1993): Is the central determinant of child outcomes control, autonomy-granting, responsiveness, the sum of these variables, or their interaction? One reason for the apparent discrepancies concerning the impact of control is that in the parental socialization research, forms of control thought to be beneficial are often embedded among a number of other behaviors that themselves might lead to positive outcomes. Some studies, however, have looked directly at control, and we turn to those next.

Research on Specific Forms of Parental Control

Although research has examined control largely in the context of authoritative parenting, a good deal of research has also examined directly the forms of control thought to be associated with authoritative parenting. The most common approach to the direct assessment of specific forms of control has been to examine parental control in the domains of monitoring, decision-making, supervision, and structure (e.g., Fuhrman & Holmbeck, 1995; Ginsberg & Bronstein, 1993; Grolnick & Ryan, 1989; Kurdek, Fine, & Sinclair, 1995; Steinberg, Elemen, & Mounts, 1989). However, researchers have also examined parental control in terms of the use of rewards as well as in other domains (e.g., Coopersmith, 1967; Deci, Driver, Hotchkiss, et al., 1993; Ginsberg & Bronstein, 1993; Grolnick & Ryan, 1989). The research examining specific forms of parental control thought to be associated with the authoritative constellation suggests that parental control has positive effects on children's development. For example, parental decision-making has been shown to be associated with heightened school performance, perceptions of competence, and psychosocial competence as well as decreased internalizing problems in adolescents (e.g., Fuhrman & Holmbeck, 1995; Steinberg, Elemen, & Mounts, 1989). However, there is also some evidence suggesting that parents' use of controlling behavior in these domains has no effect – or negative effects – on children. For example, parental decision-making has been shown to be unrelated to externalizing problems in adolescents (Fuhrman & Holmbeck, 1995) and has been found in at least one study to be associated with decrements in school performance (Brown, Mounts, Lamborn, et al., 1993). Similarly, parental supervision has been shown to be associated with low grades and low intrinsic motivation in children (Ginsberg & Bronstein, 1993), with one study finding its impact on children dependent on a number of factors (Kurdek & Fine, 1994). How are we to interpret these ambiguous findings? The research on parental control in specific domains is limited by some significant methodological drawbacks that may contribute to the mixed results. We want to highlight these, because they are important features of our own research that we describe later.

First, it is often not clear whether some of the measures used to assess parental control in specific domains actually assess control. For example, measures assessing monitoring often ask children how much their parents really know about their lives or ask parents directly how much they know, and then compare their answers to what is actually happening in children's lives. Research using such measures has found that monitoring appears to inhibit externalizing problems (e.g., Barber, Olsen & Shagle, 1994; Brown, Mounts, Lamborn, et al., 1993), especially for boys (Crouter, MacDermid, McHale, et al., 1990; Patterson & Stouthamer-Loeber, 1984), and to a lesser degree internalizing problems and their potential precursors (e.g., Barber, Olsen, & Shagle, 1993; Brown, Mounts, Lamborn, et al., 1993; Crouter, MacDermid, McHale, et al., 1990). These results need to be interpreted with caution, however. Although the measures of monitoring may reflect parents' knowledge about their children's lives, they may not reflect controlling behavior because it is unclear how parents' knowledge was obtained. That is, it is ambiguous whether intrusive methods were actually used in procuring the information. Significantly, one study focusing explicitly on parents' use of intrusive monitoring found that such monitoring was associated with children's social maladjustment in school (Ladd & Golter, 1988).

Second, unlike the laboratory research on control, research carried out in the family context has generally not examined the impact of *actual* control. Instead, much of this research has relied on parents' and children's reports. Parents are asked either to indicate their beliefs about the use of control or to provide summary reports. But correlations between parents' socialization beliefs and behaviors are quite low (see Holden & Edwards, 1989; McGillicuddy-DeLisi, 1985, for reviews). On a daily basis, parents may not always be able to act as they would like because of children's demands, reductions in their own cognitive capacity due to the stress of daily life, or competing socialization goals (see Bugental & Goodnow, in press). Parents' summary reports may suffer from the same problems as belief measures because such reports may be based on beliefs. Another common method of assessing parental control is by asking children, usually adolescents, about their perceptions of their parents' orientation toward control. Children's perceptions of parental control may also be biased. For example, children who are functioning at an optimal level and are content with their family life may desire to portray their parents as conforming to models of good parenting. The reliance on these types of measures is particularly problematic in light of a recent meta-analysis indicating that parent and child reports of parental caregiving are less predictive of children's externalizing behavior than are measures of parents' actual behavior (Rothbaum & Weisz, 1994).

Finally, caution is also warranted because research has generally not adjusted for children's behaviors that may elicit parental control (for exceptions, see Steinberg, Lamborn, Dornbusch, et al., 1992; Stice & Barrera, 1995). It is possible that children who are doing well (e.g., getting good grades, high in self-esteem, intrinsically motivated) may respond with behavior that leads parents to engage in behavior that appears to be controlling. For example, children who are highly motivated to do well in school may be more likely to ask their parents for help in making school-related decisions or to check to see if they have made any mistakes on their homework. Conversely, children who are doing poorly (e.g., acting out, using drugs, extrinsically motivated) may engage in behavior that causes parents to withdraw controlling behavior (see Stice & Barrera, 1995). For example, children who often act out may be particularly difficult when parents exert control over them. Consequently, in an effort to avoid difficult situations, parents may refrain from using control with such children.

The Multidimensional Nature of Control

The Valence Distinction

So far, we have argued that the major reasons for the conflicting findings on the impact of control are methodological: either control is not part of the construct or it does not really reflect controlling behavior on behalf of parents. We hasten to add, however, that the confusion in the literature is by no means only methodological. Comparing the motivation and parental socialization literatures highlights the fact that control may convey a number of quite distinct messages. The motivation literature has emphasized the negative messages of external control. Extensive pilot testing goes into laboratory studies to ensure that controlling features are salient. In contrast, over the past three decades, parental socialization research has emphasized the positive messages associated with parents' use of control. Nevertheless, even within the parental socialization literature, the control examined by investigators would be expected to have some of the negative features identified by research on motivation, and these features may impart a number of distinct messages that negatively affect feelings of self-determination and competence. In this section, we describe this multidimensional nature of control.

Positive Messages. As the literature on parental socialization has suggested, control may convey positive messages. Control may communicate involvement (Baumrind, 1991; Coopersmith, 1967). For example, when parents monitor children's school performance, they may convey to children that they want to be involved in their lives and are committed to their well-being. In one of the few empirical investigations of the processes by which control has an impact on individuals, Steinberg and colleagues (1992) found that adolescents' perceptions of their parents as involved in their school experience mediated the positive relation between adolescents' perceptions of parental authoritativeness and school performance.

Control may also communicate the standards for appropriate behavior, and consequently provide guidance to individuals who are not fully knowledgeable about what society requires of them. For example, when parents make decisions for children about schoolwork, they may indicate to children what is necessary for academic success. Coopersmith (1967) has proposed that firm and demanding parents, who establish and enforce rules, are equipping their children with definitions about how to interpret the world to maximize success and minimize anxiety. He has also argued that such control fosters an appreciation in children of the needs and demands of others. To the extent that control provides individuals with information about what the standards are for appropriate behavior, individuals may be less likely to engage in the socially unacceptable behavior characteristic of externalizing problems (see Higgins, 1991).

Negative Messages. As suggested by the social and personality literature, control may also convey a number of negative messages, even in the family context. First, consistent with the arguments of Lepper (1983; Lepper, Greene, & Nisbett, 1973) and Deci and Ryan (1980, 1985, 1987), control may cause individuals to feel that they are controlled by external forces. This, in turn, may lead to decreased feelings of self-determination and competence, thereby undermining intrinsic motivation. For example, parents who make decisions for their children about school, may cause children to feel that they are pursuing interests that have been imposed on them instead of ones that emanate from the self, and children may be less intrinsically motivated.

Second, control may convey that performing well, and not mastery, is important (e.g., Harackiewicz, Manderlink, & Sansone, 1984, 1992; Harackiewicz, Sansone, & Manderlink, 1985). Control may communicate not only what the standards for appropriate behavior are, but also that it is important to meet these standards (Higgins, 1991). For example, when parents reward children for doing well in school, they may emphasize that performance is important. The heightened importance attached to meeting performance standards may lead to several negative outcomes for children. For example, individuals may become anxious about performing well. This may interfere with instrumental behaviors (Wine, 1991) and, as performance deteriorates, lead to negative self-evaluative and affective processes. In addition, control, and the accompanying performance cues, may indicate to children that they are expected to meet externally set standards (Deci & Ryan, 1980, 1985, 1987) and that their self-worth is contingent upon doing so (Burhans & Dweck, 1995; Dweck, Chapter 10, this volume). This may increase individuals' motivation to perform well. However, when standards are difficult to meet, and therefore are not achieved quickly, individuals with strong standards may be more likely to feel that they have failed (Costanzo, Miller-Johnson, & Wencel, 1995; Burhans & Dweck, 1995; Dweck, Chapter 10, this volume; Higgins & Loeb, 1991, Chapter 3, this volume).

Finally, control may communicate to individuals directly that they are incompetent and not capable of solving problems on their own (Nolen-Hoeksema, Wolfson, Mumme, et al., 1995). For example, when parents help children with their homework without being requested to do so, they may convey to children that they are not capable of confronting challenges on their own. This may be particularly detrimental when individuals fail, as they may attribute the failure to internal causes, such as a lack of ability, instead of external causes, such as the difficulty of the task.

The messages of control that have been labeled as negative may not actually lead to negative outcomes in all contexts. In fact, some of these messages may sometimes foster positive outcomes. Our analysis suggests that the negative messages associated with control are most likely to lead to negative outcomes when standards are difficult to meet and failure is encountered. Indeed, both internal attributions for failure and strong standards have been linked to depressive symptoms during times of failure, but not success (e.g., Higgins, Shah, & Friedman, 1997; Hilsman & Garber, 1995). Unfortunately, the effects of parental control have rarely been examined in such contexts. School transitions, such as that between elementary and junior high school, have been suggested to be characterized by environments in which performance standards are difficult to meet (Eccles & Midgley, 1989). Hence, parental control may be particularly detrimental during such times. Consistent with this suggestion, the one study that has examined the effect of parental control during a school transition has found that parental decision-making is associated with decrements in children's self-esteem

(Lord, Eccles, & McCarthy, 1994). It will be important for future research to examine the effect of control on individuals in multiple contexts.

Developmental Differences. Children's awareness of the positive and negative messages associated with parental control may change as children progress through elementary school. Two developments during the elementary school years may lead older children to be particularly sensitive to the negative messages associated with parental control. First, as children grow older, they increasingly conceive of ability as stable and unchangeable across time and situations (for a review, see Rholes, Newman, & Ruble, 1990). Such an understanding leads children to be more sensitive to ability-related information (e.g., Miller, 1985; Pomerantz & Ruble, 1997; Rholes, Jones, & Wade, 1988; for reviews, see Rholes, Newman, & Ruble, 1990; Ruble, 1994). Consequently, children who conceive of ability as stable may be particularly aware that parental control is indicative of incompetence. Consistent with this proposal, research has indicated that during elementary school the meaning children attach to teachers' behavior changes, such that older children are more likely than younger children to glean information about incompetence from teachers' seemingly positive behavior (e.g., Barker & Graham, 1987; Lord, Umezaki, & Darley, 1990; Pomerantz & Ruble, 1997). For example, research conducted by Graham & Barker (1990) has shown that older, but not younger, elementary school children view teachers' help as indicative of child incompetence. Similar processes may operate in terms of children's conceptions of parental control. Second, as children progress through elementary school, issues of autonomy may become increasingly important to them. Hence, they may attend to the negative messages conveyed by control to a greater degree.[3]

Empirical Evidence for the Valence Distinction. To examine directly the possibility that parental control may communicate both positive and negative messages to children, we (Pomerantz & Eaton, 1998) asked 231 children in the second through fifth grades why parents might engage in controlling behavior with their children. Specifically, we asked children why parents might help their kids with their homework without being asked to do so (helping), why parents might check their kids' homework (monitoring), and why parents might make decisions for their kids (decision-making). In addition, children indicated how it makes kids feel when their parents engage in these forms of control and why it makes them feel that way. Consistent with our proposal that parental control may convey dual messages to children, over 75 percent of children indicated that parental control conveys both positive and negative messages. Specifically, although children were likely to conceive of parental control as indicating a concern for children's well-being, they were also likely to say that parental control made them feel bad because it suppressed their autonomy. As children progressed through elementary school, however, they became increasingly aware of the negative messages associated with parental control, especially those related to incompetence. Indeed, older children were more likely than younger children to say that parental control makes kids feel incompetent. Moreover, as anticipated, such conceptions were associated with children's conceptions of ability as stable and their awareness of signals of incompetence in teachers' behavior.

To test the hypothesis that the impact of parental control on children depends on children's conceptions of such behavior, we also asked children how often their parents engaged in control in terms of helping, monitoring, and decision-making and assessed children's self-esteem. Consistent with the dual-message perspective, perceptions of frequent parental control were associated with low self-esteem only among children who conceived of control as indicative of incompetence. It appears that children's conceptions of the messages conveyed by control play a key role in the impact parental control has on them. The pattern of results suggests that the inconsistencies in past research in terms of the consequences of control may be due in part to differences in the messages associated with control.

The Domain Distinction

As we suggested in our introduction, we view control as manifesting itself in a number of domains. Despite the large body of theory and research concerned with control, little attention has actually been given to the distinct messages conveyed by control exerted in different domains. Such distinctions, however, may be fundamental to elucidating the contingencies of the impact of control. Specifically, the particular message conveyed by control may depend upon the specific domain in which control manifests itself, and the message may determine the consequences of control. For example, some forms of control, such as monitoring, may lead to negative self-evaluative processes by conveying to individuals that they are not capable of overcoming problems on their own. However, other forms of control, such as disciplining, may not convey information relevant to self-evaluative processes, and therefore may not affect such processes.

The Autonomy Granting–Controlling Distinction

The distinction between autonomy-granting and controlling behavior may be meaningful in elucidating inconsistencies in the impact of control. Whereas controlling behavior may be defined as the use of external pressures to guide or push an individual toward a particular outcome, autonomy-granting behavior may be defined as the encouragement of the individual to engage in behaviors or pursue outcomes that emanate from the self. Although we have suggested that including autonomy-granting and controlling behavior in the authoritative constellation is problematic in terms of identifying the effects of control, we agree with Baumrind (1971) and others (e.g., Lamborn, Mounts, Steinberg, et al., 1991; Steinberg, Lamborn, Dornbusch, et al., 1992) that it is important to consider the use of autonomy-granting and controlling behavior together. Unfortunately, little empirical work has actually examined the relation between autonomy-granting and controlling behavior. If the two co-occur, however, it may be important to tease apart controlling behavior exerted in conjunction with autonomy-granting behavior and controlling behavior exerted alone. Whereas the latter may convey negative messages, the former may convey positive messages (see Baumrind, 1971; Deci & Ryan, 1987; Lepper, 1983). For example, when parents help children with a problem without being requested to do so, they may communicate to children that they do not think they are capable of solving problems on their own. Parents who engage in this same type of behavior, but only after encouraging children to try to solve the problem on their own, may not communicate negative information about children's capabilities but, instead, may communicate positive information.

Our argument differs from that of Baumrind's in that Baumrind suggested that the actual nature of parents' controlling behavior changes when it is exerted in conjunction with autonomy-granting behavior. Thus, for example, demands issued by an authoritarian parent might be communicated in a loud, angry voice, whereas demands issued by an authoritative parent might be communicated in a low, rational voice. In contrast to Baumrind, however, we suggest that parents' use of controlling behavior in conjunction with autonomy-granting behavior and their use of controlling behavior alone appear to be the same on the surface, but that the message conveyed by each is different. This proposal suggests that research examining controlling behavior and not autonomy-granting behavior may be misleading. Controlling behavior may reflect both controlling behavior in conjunction with autonomy-granting behavior and controlling behavior alone, and the two may have quite distinct messages.

Conclusions

We have suggested that control is a multidimensional construct in terms of the messages it conveys and that this perspective has implications for understanding the consequences of control. First, controlling behavior in a particular domain appears to communicate both positive and negative messages. Second, controlling behavior in different domains may convey distinct messages and, therefore, have distinct consequences. Third, we have suggested that if autonomy-granting and controlling behavior are thought of as separate, albeit related, unipolar constructs instead of opposite ends of a bipolar continuum, control may convey distinct messages dependent on how it is conveyed (i.e., in conjunction with autonomy-granting versus alone). This analysis presents a more complex picture of control than has been articulated in the past and suggests that the impact of control may depend on a number of factors that have generally been ignored in past research. Specifically, inconsistencies in the impact of control may be due to emphasis on one message of control over another (e.g., involvement versus incompetence), failure to examine the impact of control in a variety of situations (e.g., during school transitions) and developmentally, attention to forms of control that convey one message versus another in terms of content, and rough indexes of control that do not take into account how control has been conveyed (e.g., in conjunction with autonomy-granting versus alone). One of the most interesting implications of such an analysis concerns the etiology of sex differences in self-evaluative processes. It is to this topic that we turn next.

Parental Control and the Development of Sex Differences in Self-Evaluation

It has been well documented that females are more likely than males to engage in negative self-evaluative processes (for reviews, see Deaux, 1976; Lenney, 1977; Roberts, 1991), and this difference appears to be evident as early as elementary school (for a review, see Ruble, Greulich, Pomerantz, et al., 1993). Specifically, females appear to be more likely than males to engage in maladaptive attributions (e.g., attributing failure to ability) and learned helplessness. Females are also more likely to have low expectations for their future performance and low self-perceptions of competence for novel and stereotypically male tasks. Given the link between control and self-evaluative processes (e.g., Nolen-Hoeksema, Wolfson, Mumme, et al., 1995; for reviews, see Deci & Ryan, 1980, 1985, 1987) and the claim by a number of investigators that parents are more controlling with their daughters than with their sons (e.g., Blechman, 1981; Block, 1973, 1978, 1983; Higgins, 1991; Hoffman, 1972; Hops, Sherman, & Biglan, 1990; Huston, 1983; Maccoby, 1990), parental control may play a central role in the development of sex differences in self-evaluative processes.

Despite the fact that numerous investigators have argued that parents are more controlling with daughters than with sons, the empirical evidence for this claim is quite ambiguous (for reviews, see Block, 1983; Huston, 1983; Maccoby & Jacklin, 1974; Siegal, 1987). Most recently, based on the results of their meta-analysis, Lytton and Romney (1991) concluded that parents do not use control differentially with girls and boys. A close examination of the literature, however, indicates that this conclusion may be premature. First, most studies have used global definitions of control (e.g., Armentrout, 1975; Baumrind, 1971; Grolnick & Ryan, 1989). Such global definitions are problematic because parents may be more controlling in some behavioral domains (e.g., helping, monitoring) with daughters than with sons, but may not differentiate between the two in other domains (e.g., disciplining, rule-enforcing). Grouping together multiple forms of control may obscure gender socialization patterns (see Block, 1978, 1983). Second, previous research may be ambiguous because control has generally been operationalized as a bipolar construct; consequently, parental autonomy-granting behavior has been ignored. It is possible that gender socialization processes may take place in the context of parental autonomy-granting but not controlling behavior or in some combination of parental autonomy-granting and controlling behavior (e.g., controlling behavior in conjunction with autonomy-granting behavior) that is not detected by examining mean levels of controlling behavior. Finally, prior research may be equivocal because it has not examined parents' behavior in their everyday interactions with their children. Instead, research has tended to rely on measures assessing parents' beliefs or their behavior in artificial laboratory situations (e.g., Block, 1978; Hunter, 1984). This is problematic, as parents may believe in treating daughters and sons equally, but may be unable to act on these beliefs in their daily interactions, because they are often preoccupied with other issues (e.g., what to make for dinner, being on time, a problem at work).

Empirical Evidence for the Role of Parental Control
in Sex Differences in Self-Evaluation

Because of the potential importance of parents' differential use of control for the development of sex differences in self-evaluative processes, it is valuable to take a closer look at the question of whether gender socialization processes are evident in parents' use of control with their children. We (Pomerantz, 1995; Pomerantz & Ruble, 1998) recently examined the hypothesis that parents use specific forms of control more with daughters than with sons, and that these forms of control heighten children's vulnerability to engaging in negative self-evaluative processes. In a cross-sectional study with 91 second through fifth graders and their mothers, we examined forms of control that we thought were particularly likely to convey messages that would lead children to be vulnerable to engaging in negative self-evaluative processes. Specifically, we examined maternal autonomy-granting and controlling behavior in the domains of helping, monitoring, decision-making, praising, and disciplining. Although parental autonomy-granting and controlling behavior in the disciplining domain was not expected to differ as a function of children's sex or to affect children's self-evaluative processes, this domain was included because it has been the center of much research on parental control (for reviews, see Grusec & Goodnow, 1994; Maccoby & Martin, 1983; Rothbaum & Weisz, 1994).

We wanted to obtain assessments of mothers' tendencies to be autonomy-granting and controlling with their children that would be representative of how they interact on a daily basis and that would not be biased by their beliefs. Our central measure, therefore, was a daily checklist that asked mothers about their specific interactions with their children. The checklist assessed both autonomy-granting and controlling behavior in all five domains and was designed so that autonomy-granting and controlling behavior could co-occur within each domain. Mothers completed the checklist for 10 to 21 days every night before going to bed. To adjust for children's behavior that might elicit autonomy-granting and controlling behavior (e.g., child asks mother for help with homework, child performs well in school), mothers were asked not only about their own behavior each day, but also about that of their children.

In our operationalization of control, we followed our analysis of the negative messages conveyed by control. Specifically, controlling behaviors were those that were likely to make children feel that they were controlled by external forces (e.g., mother says child's behavior makes her feel proud, gives child a reward for doing well in school); were likely to convey to children that performance standards are important (e.g., mother makes decisions for child about a topic for a school assignment); or were likely to communicate to children that they are not capable of solving problems on their own (e.g., mother helps child with homework either upon being requested or without being requested).[4] Conversely, autonomy-granting behaviors were those that (1) were likely to make children feel that their behavior emanated from themselves (e.g., mother attributes child's good performance in school to child's ability or enjoyment of the task); (2) were likely to convey to children that mastery, and not performance, is important (e.g., mother encourages child to make own decision about topic for school assignment); or (3) were likely to communicate to children that they are capable of solving problems on their own (e.g., mother encourages child to solve difficulties with homework on own when child requests help).

Consistent with our proposal that autonomy-granting and controlling behavior are not opposite ends of a bipolar continuum but instead may co-occur within each domain, autonomy-granting and controlling behavior were not strongly correlated (mean correlation = -0.15). Because of the small correlations between autonomy-granting and controlling behavior, it seemed quite likely that the two might be used in conjunction with one another by at least some mothers. Therefore, in addition to examining mothers' overall levels of autonomy-granting and controlling behavior, we examined four patterns of their autonomy-granting and controlling behavior in each of the domains. Specifically, we examined how often mothers used controlling behavior in conjunction with autonomy-granting behavior (e.g., encouraged child to do her homework on her own and then helped her with it), controlling behavior alone (e.g., helped child with homework immediately upon being asked), autonomy-granting behavior alone (e.g., encouraged child to do her homework on her own and did not help her with it), and no response (e.g., did not respond to child's request for help).

Differential Use of Control. Consistent with our predictions, although children's behavior did not differ as a function of their sex, mothers of boys were significantly more likely to be autonomy-granting than mothers of girls in the domains of helping, monitoring, decision-making, and praising, but not disciplining. There were, however, no differences between mothers of boys and mothers of girls in their tendency to be controlling. However, analyses examining mothers' engagement in the patterns of autonomy-granting and controlling behavior identified above revealed that mothers were significantly more likely to engage in controlling behavior in conjunction with autonomy-granting behavior with boys than with girls in the domains of helping, monitoring, decision-making, and praising. Conversely, mothers were more likely to engage in controlling behavior alone with girls than with boys in these domains. This pattern of gender socialization was not due to a tendency for mothers simply to interact more with boys than with girls, because there were no differences in mothers' tendency to engage in autonomy-granting behavior alone or to not respond. Prior research may not have detected differences in parents' use of control with their daughters and sons because it did not examine parental autonomy-granting behavior and, relatedly, did not explore how parents might use autonomy-granting and controlling behavior together. Moreover, our analyses indicated that gender socialization was evident in some behavioral domains (helping, monitoring, decision-making, praising) but not others (disciplining), suggesting that it is valuable to look separately at different forms of control when examining gender socialization processes.

Consequences of Control. What are the consequences of mothers' differential use of autonomy-granting and controlling behavior for children's self-evaluative processes? We examined three self-evaluative outcomes that corresponded to the three negative messages of control outlined above: extrinsic motivation for schoolwork, strength of performance standards in school, and attributions for failure in school and an experimental situation. Consistent with predictions, the autonomy-granting and controlling behavioral patterns in which gender socialization was evident were associated with children's attributions for failure. Specifically, the less mothers used controlling behavior in conjunction with autonomy-granting behavior, and the more they used controlling behavior alone, the more children blamed themselves for their failure, by attributing it either to lack of ability or to lack of effort. Moreover, path analyses indicated that mothers' differential engagement in these socialization patterns mediated the tendency of girls to make significantly more internal attributions for failure than boys. Also, consistent with predictions, this same pattern of gender socialization (decreased controlling behavior in conjunction with autonomy-granting behavior and increased controlling behavior alone) was associated with stronger performance standards among children. Girls and boys, however, had equally strong standards for performance. Contrary to expectations, the pattern of autonomy-granting and controlling behavior used more with girls than with boys was associated with heightened intrinsic motivation in children. It appears that the effects of mothers' use of controlling behavior in conjunction with autonomy-granting behavior were due to the use of the *combination* of the two behaviors. This combination had an effect on children opposite to that of controlling behavior alone. Moreover, autonomy-granting behavior alone had no effect on children. Finally, consistent with the suggestion that the messages conveyed by autonomy-granting and controlling behavior may vary by domain, the two behaviors in the disciplining domain were not associated with children's self-evaluation.

Conclusions

We have suggested that control is a multidimensional construct and that this view helps to clarify some of the inconsistencies in the literature regarding the impact of control. This perspective is illustrated to some extent by the research presented here. First, it appears that the distinction between autonomy-granting and controlling behavior is a meaningful one. In the data we presented, mothers of girls and mothers of boys differed in their overall use of autonomy-granting behavior but not in their overall use of controlling behavior. Furthermore, mothers appeared to use the two together; and the frequency of simultaneous use differed as a function of children's sex. In addition to providing insight into the etiology of sex differences in self-evaluative processes, this last pattern of results suggests why some studies (e.g., Baumrind, 1967, 1971; Crouter, MacDermid, McHale, et al., 1990) have found that parental control has a more positive impact on boys than on girls. Although overall parental control may not have differed in these studies as a function of children's sex, parents may have engaged in more controlling behavior in conjunction with autonomy-granting behavior with boys, and more controlling behavior alone with girls. Thus, the message conveyed by parental control may have been very different for girls and boys, and consequently, may have had very different effects.

General Conclusions

It appears that the inconsistencies in the literature in terms of the impact of control may actually reflect the complex nature of control and the messages it communicates. We have suggested that control is a multidimensional construct and that such a perspective is beneficial in terms of elucidating the processes by which control may lead to adaptive as well as maladaptive outcomes for individuals. In our own research we found this perspective very valuable in elucidating parental gender socialization processes in terms of control. Although we have highlighted a number of dimensions on which control may vary, there are still other dimensions that may be important to understanding the contingencies of control. For example, the degree to which control has a positive- versus negative-outcome focus (see Higgins & Loeb, Chapter 3, this volume) may be an important dimension of control. An integral aspect of our multidimensional perspective is that it suggests that the impact of control on individuals may vary as they progress through the multiple contexts of the life span. It is important for future research to examine directly how such contexts may moderate the effects of control on individuals.

Notes

1. Becker also suggested a third dimension – anxious-emotional involvement versus calm detachment – but his review of the literature rested on the restrictiveness versus permissiveness and warmth versus hostility dimensions. Research following Becker's review has generally attended to the latter two dimensions, with some variations. The anxious-emotional involvement versus calm-detachment dimension, however, may be an important dimension for investigators to examine, as it may moderate the impact of parental control. Specifically, control exerted by anxious parents may communicate messages to children quite different from those provided in a calm and detached fashion.
2. Baumrind actually labeled this constellation as *permissive*. Consistent with Maccoby and Martin's terminology, and that of later research, we refer to this constellation as *indulgent*.
3. Although children may become increasingly sensitive to the negative messages of control as they get older, this does not mean that some young children are not sensitive to these negative messages. Indeed, the children identified by Dweck (Burhans & Dweck, 1995; Dweck, Chapter 10, this volume) as being particularly vulnerable to criticism at an early age may be quite sensitive to the negative messages of control at an early age.
4. Originally, we differentiated between moderate and high levels of control, with moderate levels of control representing behaviors in response to children's behaviors (e.g., mother helps child with homework upon being requested), and high level of control representing behaviors not in response to children's behavior (e.g., mother helps child with homework, without child requesting help). There were, however, no differences between the two levels. There were also theoretical reasons to combine the two levels, as they both communicated the same messages to children.

References

Armentrout, J. A. (1975). Repression-sensitization and MMPI correlates of retrospective reports of parental child-rearing behaviors. *Journal of Clinical Psychology, 31,* 444–448.

Barber, B. K., Olsen, J. E., & Shagle, S. C. (1994). Associations between parental psychological and behavioral control and youth internalized and externalized behaviors. *Child Development, 65,* 1120–1136.

Barker, G. P., & Graham, S. (1987). Developmental study of praise and blame as attributional cues. *Journal of Educational Psychology, 79,* 62–66.

Baumrind, D. (1967). Child care practices anteceding three patterns of preschool behavior. *Genetic Psychology Monographs, 75,* 43–88.

(1971). Current patterns of parental authority. *Developmental Psychology Monograph, 1* (4, Pt. 2).

(1991). The influence of parenting style on adolescent competence and substance use. *Journal of Early Adolescence, 11,* 56–95.

Baumrind, D., & Black, A. E. (1967). Socialization practices associated with dimensions of competence in preschool boys and girls. *Child Development, 38,* 291–327.

Becker, W. C. (1964). Consequences of different kinds of parental discipline. In M. L. Hoffman & L. W. Hoffman (Eds.), *Review of child development research* (Vol. 1, pp. 169–208). Chicago: University of Chicago Press.

Blechman, E. A. (1981). Competence, depression, and behavior modification with women. In M. Hersen, R. M. Eisler, & P. M. Miller (Eds.), *Progress in behavior modification* (Vol. 12, pp. 227–263). New York: Academic Press.

Block, J. H. (1973). Conceptions of sex role: Some cross-cultural and longitudinal perspectives. *American Psychologist, 28,* 512–526.

(1978). Another look at sex differentiation in the socialization behaviors of mothers and fathers. In J. Sherman & F. L. Denmark (Eds.), *The psychology of women: Future directions of research* (pp. 29–87). New York: Psychological Dimensions.

(1983). Differential premises arising from differential socialization of the sexes: Some conjectures. *Child Development, 54,* 1335–1354.

Brown, B. B., Mounts, N., Lamborn, S. D., & Steinberg, L. (1993). Parenting practices and peer group affiliation in adolescence. *Child Development, 64,* 467–482.

Bugental, D. B., & Goodnow, J. J. (in press). Socialization processes. In N. Eisenberg (Ed.), *Handbook of child psychology. Vol. 3: Social, emotional, and personality development* (5th ed.). New York: Wiley.

Burhans, K. K., & Dweck, C. S. (1995). Helplessness in early childhood: The role of contingent self-worth. *Child Development, 66,* 1719–1738.

Coopersmith, S. (1967). *The antecedents of self-esteem.* San Francisco: Freeman.

Costanzo, P., Miller-Johnson, S., Wencel, H. (1995). Social development. In J. March (Ed.), *Anxiety disorders in children and adolescents* (pp. 82–108). New York: Guilford Press.

Crouter, A. C., MacDermid, S. M., McHale, S. M., & Perry-Jenkins, M. (1990). Parental monitoring and perceptions of children's school performance and conduct in dual- and single-earner families. *Developmental Psychology, 26,* 649–657.

Darling, N., & Steinberg, L. (1993). Parenting style as context: An integrative model. *Psychological Bulletin, 113,* 487–496.

Deaux, K. (1976). Sex: A perspective on the attribution process. In J. H. Harvey, W. J. Ickes, & R. F. Kidd (Eds.), *New directions in attribution research* (Vol. 1, pp. 335–352). Hillsdale, NJ: Erlbaum.

Deci, E. L., Driver, R. E., Hotchkiss, L., Robbins, R. J., Wilson, I. M. (1993). The relation of mothers' controlling vocalizations to children's intrinsic motivation. *Journal of Experimental Child Psychology, 55,* 151–162.

Deci, E. L., & Ryan, R. M. (1980). The empirical exploration of intrinsic motivational processes. In L. Berkowitz (Ed.), *Advances in experimental social psychology* (Vol. 13, pp. 39–80). New York: Academic Press.

(1985). *Intrinsic motivation and self-determination in human behavior.* New York: Plenum Press.

(1987). The support of autonomy and the control of behavior. *Journal of Personality and Social Psychology, 53,* 1024–1037.

Dekovic, M., & Janssens, M. A. M. (1992). Parents' child-rearing style and child's sociometric status. *Developmental Psychology, 28,* 925–932.

Dornbusch, S. M., Ritter, P. L., Leiderman, P. H., Roberts, D. F., & Fraleigh, M. J. (1987). The relation of parenting style to adolescent school performance. *Child Development, 58,* 1244–1257.

Dweck, C. S. (1998). The development of early self-conceptions: Their relevance for motivational processes. In J. Heckhausen & C. S. Dweck (Eds.), *Motivation and self-regulation across the life span.* New York: Cambridge University Press.

Eccles, J. S. & Midgley, C. (1989). Stage/environment fit: Developmentally appropriate classrooms for adolescents. In R. E. Ames & C. Ames (Eds.), *Research on motivation in education* (Vol. 3, pp. 139–186). San Diego, CA: Academic Press.

Fuhrman, T., & Holmbeck, G. N. (1995). A contextual-moderator analysis of emotional autonomy and adjustment in adolescence. *Child Development, 66,* 793–811.

Graham, S., & Barker, G. P. (1990). The down side of help: An attributional developmental analysis of helping behavior as a low ability cue. *Journal of Educational Psychology, 82,* 7–14.

Ginsberg, G. S., & Bronstein, P. (1993). Family factors related to children's intrinsic/extrinsic motivational orientation and academic performance. *Child Development, 64,* 1461–1474.

Grolnick, W. S., & Ryan, R. M. (1989). Parent styles associated with children's self-regulation and competence in school. *Journal of Educational Psychology, 81,* 143–154.

Grusec, J. E., & Goodnow, J. J. (1994). Impacts of the parental discipline methods on the child's internalization of values: A reconceptualization of current points of view. *Developmental Psychology, 30,* 4–19.

Grusec, J. E., & Lytton, H. (1988). *Social development: History, theory, and research.* New York: Springer-Verlag.

Harackiewicz, J. M., Manderlink, G., & Sansone, C. (1984). Rewarding pinball wizardry: Effects of evaluation and cue-valence on intrinsic interest. *Journal of Personality and Social Psychology, 47,* 287–300.

(1992). Competence processes and achievement motivation: Implications for intrinsic motivation. In A. K. Boggiano & T. S. Pittman (Eds.), *Achievement and motivation: A social-developmental perspective* (pp. 115–137). New York: Cambridge University Press.

Harackiewicz, J. M., Sansone, C., & Manderlink, G. (1985). Competence, achievement orientation, and intrinsic motivation: A process analysis. *Journal of Personality and Social Psychology, 48,* 493–508.

Higgins, E. T. (1991). Development of self-regulatory and self-evaluative processes: Costs, benefits, and tradeoffs. In M. R. Gunnar & L. A. Sroufe (Eds.), *Self processes and development: The Minnesota symposium on child psychology* (Vol. 23, pp. 125–166). Hillsdale, NJ: Erlbaum.

Higgins, E. T., & Loeb, I. (1998). Development of regulatory focus: Promotion and prevention as ways of living. In J. Heckhausen & C. S. Dweck (Eds.), *Motivation and self-regulation across the life span.* New York: Cambridge University Press.

Higgins, E. T., Shah, J., & Friedman, R. (1996). Emotional responses to goal attainment: Strength of regulatory focus as moderator. *Journal of Personality and Social Psychology, 72,* 515–525.

Hilsman, R., & Garber, J. (1995). A test of the cognitive diathesis-stress model of depression in children: Academic attributional type, perceived competence, and control. *Journal of Personality and Social Psychology, 69,* 370–380.

Hoffman, L. W. (1972). Early childhood experiences and women's achievement motives. *Journal of Social Issues, 28,* 129–155.

Holden, G. W., & Edwards, L. A. (1989). Parental attitudes toward child rearing: Instruments, issues, and implications. *Psychological Bulletin, 106,* 29–58.

Hops, H., Sherman, L., & Biglan, A. (1990). Maternal depression, marital discord, and children's behavior: A developmental perspective. In G. R. Patterson (Ed.), *Depression and aggression in family interactions* (pp. 185–208). Hillsdale, NJ: Erlbaum.

Hunter, F. T. (1984). Socializing procedures in parent-child and friendship relations during adolescence. *Developmental Psychology, 20,* 1092–1099.

Huston, A. C. (1983). Sex-typing. In E. M. Hetherington (Ed.), *Handbook of child psychology. Vol. 4: Socialization, personality, and social development* (4th ed., pp. 387–467). New York: Wiley.

Kochanska, G. (1991). Socialization and temperament in the development of guild and conscience. *Child Development, 62,* 250–263.

 (1995). Children's temperament, mothers' discipline, and security of attachment: Multiple pathways to emerging internalization. *Child Development, 66,* 597–615.

Kurdek, L. A., & Fine, M. A. (1994). Family acceptance and family control as predictors of adjustment in young adolescents: Linear, curvilinear, or interactive effects? *Child Development, 65,* 1137–1146.

Kurdek, L. A., Fine, M. A., & Sinclair, R. J. (1995). Social adjustment in sixth graders: Parenting transitions, family climate, and peer norm effects. *Child Development, 66,* 430–445.

Ladd, G. W., & Golter, B. S. (1988). Parents' management of preschooler's peer relations: Is it related to children's social competence? *Developmental Psychology, 24,* 109–117.

Lamborn, S. D., Mounts, N. S., Steinberg, L., & Dornbusch, S. M. (1991). Patterns of competence and adjustment among adolescents from authoritative, authoritarian, indulgent, and neglectful families. *Child Development, 62,* 1049–1065.

Lenney, E. (1977). Women's self-confidence in achievement settings. *Psychological Bulletin, 84,* 1–13.

Lepper, M. R. (1983). Social control processes and the internalization of social values: An attributional perspective. In E. T. Higgins, D. N. Ruble, & W. W. Hartup (Eds.), *Social cognition and social development: A sociocultural perspective* (pp. 294–330). Cambridge: Cambridge University Press.

Lepper, M. R., Greene, D., Nisbett, R. E. (1973). Undermining children's intrinsic interest with extrinsic rewards: A test of the "overjustification" hypothesis. *Journal of Personality and Social Psychology, 28,* 129–137.

Lewis, C. C. (1981). The effects of parental firm control: A reinterpretation of findings. *Psychological Bulletin, 90,* 547–563.

Lord, S., Eccles, J. S., & McCarthy, K. A. (1994). Surviving the junior high school transition: Family processes and self-perceptions as protective and risk factors. *Journal of Early Adolescence, 14,* 162–199.

Lord, C. G., Umezaki, K., & Darley, J. M. (1990). Developmental differences in decoding the meanings of the appraisal actions of teachers. *Child Development, 61,* 191–200.

Lytton, H., & Romney, D. M. (1991). Parents' differential socialization of boys and girls: A meta-analysis. *Psychological Bulletin, 109,* 267–296.

Maccoby, E. E. (1990). Gender and relationships: A developmental account. *American Psychologist, 45,* 513–520.

Maccoby, E. E., & Jacklin, C. N. (1974). *The psychology of sex differences.* Stanford, CA: Stanford University Press.

Maccoby, E. E., & Martin, J. (1983). Socialization in the family context: Parent child interaction. In E. M. Hetherington (Ed.), *Handbook of child psychology. Vol. 4: Socialization, personality, and social development* (4th ed., pp. 1–101). New York: Wiley.

McGillicuddy-DeLisi, A. V. (1985). The relationship between parental beliefs and children's cognitive level. In I. E. Sigel (Ed.), *Parental belief systems* (pp. 7–24). Hillsdale, NJ: Erlbaum.

Miller, A. T. (1985). A developmental study of the cognitive basis of performance and improvement after failure. *Journal of Personality and Social Psychology, 49,* 529–538.

Nolen-Hoeksema, S., Wolfson, A., Mumme, D., & Guskin, K. (1995). Helplessness in children of depressed and nondepressed mothers. *Developmental Psychology, 31,* 377–387.

Patterson, G. R., & Stouthamer-Loeber, M. (1984). The correlation of family management practices and delinquency. *Child Development, 55,* 1299–1307.

Pomerantz, E. M. (1995). *The role of parental autonomy granting and control in the development of sex differences in self-evaluative processes.* Unpublished doctoral dissertation. New York University, New York.

Pomerantz, E. M., & Eaton, M. A. M. (1998). *Developmental differences in children's conceptions of parental control.* Manuscript submitted for publication.

Pomerantz, E. M., & Ruble, D. N. (1997). Distinguishing multiple dimensions of conceptions of ability: Implications for self-evaluation. *Child Development, 53,* 322–339.

—— (1998). The role of maternal control in the development of sex differences in child's self-evaluative factors. *Child Development, 69,* 458–478.

Rholes, W. S., Jones, M., & Wade, C. (1988). Children's understanding of personal dispositions and its relationship to behavior. *Journal of Experimental Child Psychology, 45,* 1–17.

Rholes, W. S., Newman, L. S., & Ruble, D. N. (1990). Understanding self and other: Developmental and motivational aspects of perceiving persons in terms of invariant dispositions. In E. T. Higgins and R. M. Sorrentino (Eds.), *Handbook of motivation and cognition: Foundations of social behavior* (Vol. 2, pp. 369–407). New York: Guilford Press.

Roberts, T. (1991). Gender and the influence of evaluation on self-assessments in achievement settings. *Psychological Bulletin, 109,* 297–308.

Rothbaum, F., & Weisz, J. R. (1994). Parental caregiving and child externalizing behavior in nonclinical samples: A meta-analysis. *Psychological Bulletin, 116,* 55–74.

Ruble, D. N. (1994). A phase model of transitions: Cognitive and motivational consequences. In M. Zanna (Ed.), *Advances in experimental social psychology* (Vol. 26, pp. 163–214). New York: Academic Press.

Ruble, D. N., Greulich, F., Pomerantz, E. M., & Gochberg, B. (1993). The role of gender-related processes in the development of sex differences in self-evaluation and depression. *Journal of Affective Disorders, 29,* 97–128.

Ruble, D. N., & Thompson, E. P. (1992). The implications of research on social development for mental health: An internal socialization perspective. In D. N. Ruble, P. R. Costanzo, & M. E. Oliveri (Eds.), *The social psychology of mental health: Basic mechanisms and applications* (pp. 81–125). New York: Guilford Press.

Siegal, M. (1987). Are sons and daughters treated more differently by fathers than by mothers? *Developmental Review, 7,* 183–209.

Steinberg, L., Elemen, J. D., & Mounts, N. S. (1989). Authoritative parenting, psychosocial maturity, and academic success among adolescents. *Child Development, 60,* 1424–1436.

Steinberg, L., Lamborn, S. D., Dornbusch, S. M., & Darling, N. (1992). Impact of parenting practices on adolescent achievement: Authoritative parenting, school involvement, and encouragement to succeed. *Child Development, 63,* 1266–1281.

Stice, E., & Barrera, M. (1995). A longitudinal examination of the reciprocal relations between perceived parenting and adolescents substance use and externalizing behaviors. *Developmental Psychology, 31,* 322–334.

Wine, J. (1971). Test anxiety and direction of attention. *Psychological Bulletin, 76,* 92–104.

7   The Functional Regulation of Adolescent Dating Relationships and Sexual Behavior: An Interaction of Goals, Strategies, and Situations

Nancy Cantor and Catherine A. Sanderson

Abstract

This chapter focuses on showing how the interaction between personal goals and daily life situations is associated with functional self-regulation, using as a model a particular life period, namely adolescence, and a particular age-graded task, namely social dating. First, we examine how individual differences, such as attachment styles and ego identity, and subcultural factors, such as ethnicity and gender, are associated with the relative predominance of intimacy and interdependence as a goal in social dating. Second, we focus on how an intimacy goal in turn is associated with particular predictable patterns of task pursuit in daily life, including preferences for different types of situations, the use of specific strategies for goal pursuit, and the elicitation of distinct types of support. Third, we consider how particular aspects of dating situations, such as one's partner's orientation toward intimacy, become especially significant affordances for functional behavior, such as dating satisfaction and the regulation of safer sexual behavior, for individuals with predominant intimacy goals. Finally, we suggest the relevance of this life task model of functional behavior for diverse life tasks across the life span.

Introduction

A life task perspective in personality psychology posits that in order to understand individuals' behavior in daily life, one needs to understand the

The research reported in this chapter was supported by a National Science Foundation Graduate Fellowship to Catherine A. Sanderson. We wish to acknowledge the assistance of Annmarie Cano, Marlorie Stinfel, and Fiona Vajk in conducting this research, and to thank Colleen DiIorio for access to the Southern college student data. Portions of this chapter were presented at the 1995 annual meetings of the American Psychological Society and the Society for Personality and Social Psychology.

broader life problems or tasks that they are working on as well as the specific strategies that they are implementing to work on them (Cantor & Kihlstrom, 1987). Life tasks represent what individuals in a particular age-graded subculture are currently working on and devoting energy and thought to, such as "getting a job," "being a good parent," and "finding a romantic partner," and can be seen as the problems that individuals are attempting to solve in daily life (Cantor, 1994). Many Western cultures, for example, set forth independence from family as a broad task for college-age young adults, and many students do in fact report working on this task (see Zirkel, 1992; Zirkel & Cantor, 1990).

Although cultural groups expect individuals to address certain tasks in given life periods (Erikson, 1950; Havighurst, 1972), individuals are re-markably flexible in the ways that they adapt these tasks to their own goals, interests, and experiences and those emphasized by their subcultural (Cantor & Fleeson, 1994; Emmons, 1989; Little, 1989; Veroff, 1983). For example, in the task of social dating, an adolescent who is focused on gaining inde-pendence from parents and establishing identity could pursue the task with self-focused identity goals, whereas one who is focusing on establishing in-timacy with others could perceive the task as an opportunity to gain emo-tional support (see Bakan, 1966; Cantor & Malley, 1992). Similarly, the meaning that male and female adolescents, or adolescents in different eth-nic groups or from different socioeconomic or geographic backgrounds, give to the task of social dating may differ (see Mays & Cochran, 1988; Winett, 1995). Although most individuals take on these broader, socially defined life tasks, they do so in ways that reflect their own distinct needs as well as the values specified by their subculture. Life tasks therefore repre-sent the intersection between broad age-graded tasks and the specific mean-ing and goals that individuals bring to these tasks.

We believe that in order to understand how individuals effectively regu-late behavior, it is critical to understand the goals they bring to a given task and how these goals are in turn associated with distinct strategies for task pursuit: Functional behavior occurs when individuals who give a particular meaning to the task are in an environment that encourages the use of their preferred strategies for task pursuit. For example, the coping literature (Tay-lor & Aspinwall, 1996) has shown that successful coping depends in part on a match between individuals' coping strategies and the specific situa-tional contingencies. Moreover, adaptive coping may often involve indi-viduals' proclivity to structure their daily lives actively in ways that afford the pursuit of goals and strategies within their repertoire (Brandtstädter & Renner, 1990; Gollwitzer, 1993; Heckhausen & Schulz, 1995). Similarly, we suggest that the functional self-regulation of behavior is related to the meaning that individuals bring to a task (e.g., their personal goals), their corresponding methods of task pursuit in daily life, and the extent to which they find situations that encourage the fulfillment of their goals. In this way, whether situations allow for the functional regulation of behavior depends critically on what an individual is trying to do in a given life task.

A Life Task Model for Functional Self-Regulation

This chapter shows how the life task perspective can be used to elucidate effective behavior, and specifically the association of the interaction between personal goals and daily life situations with functional self-regulation (see Cantor, 1994). We have chosen here to describe our model in terms of a particular life period, adolescence, and an age-graded task that most adolescents pursue, social dating (see Havighurst, 1972; Kelly & Hansen, 1987). Although social dating is one of many normative tasks in adolescence (e.g., serious school work, decisions for the future), it may be a particularly involving one because this is typically the first life period in which individuals are "allowed" to engage seriously in social dating and sexual activity (a component of many adolescent dating relationships) (Christopher & Cate, 1984). During adolescence individuals spend increasing amounts of time with peers, and specifically with opposite-sex peers: Whereas high school freshmen spend 4 percent of their time in opposite-sex dyads, for example, high school seniors spend 24 percent of their time in such pairs (Csikszentmihalyi & Larsen, 1984). Furthermore, adolescents receive multiple, and at times conflicting, messages from friends, parents, and society about appropriate rules for dating and sexual behavior (Gilligan, 1982; Simmons & Blyth, 1987). The regulation of dating and sexual behavior therefore represents a key *problem* for adolescents within the dating task, much as taking a test and meeting new people are seen as major problems within the academic and social domains, respectively (see Harlow & Cantor, 1994; Norem & Cantor, 1986). Although the problem of regulating sexual behavior is most salient for late adolescents (e.g., college students, who represent the bulk of the participants in our research), as individuals engage in sexual activity at earlier ages the regulation of such behavior is becoming a concern throughout adolescence and hence research is increasingly focusing on younger adolescents. Consequently, we believe that social dating in adolescence is a very fertile arena of life task activity in which to observe the impact of personal goals, strategic pursuit, and situational affordances on self-regulation.

In the present chapter, we describe our life task model of functional be-havior following the heuristic guide presented in Figure 7.1 (adapted from Cantor & Fleeson, 1991). As shown in path A of Figure 7.1, we assume that *individual differences* are associated with different personal goals that indi-viduals pursue. Individuals, after all, bring various global preferences, ori-entations, and styles to their life tasks, and these orientations are likely to influence the goals they set within a given task, such as social dating (see Clark, Muchant, Ouellete, et al., 1987; Hazan & Shaver, 1987). Individuals with a strong need for intimacy, for example, are likely to spend consider-able time thinking about interpersonal processes and pursuing goals related to this need (McAdams & Constantian, 1983). Similarly, research has shown that those who have a secure working model of attachment bring a focus on intimacy and closeness to a variety of their life tasks (for a review, see Shaver & Hazan, 1993). Finally, individuals who are preoccupied with establishing an independent, coherent personal identity, as Erikson (1950) suggested that adolescents must do, are likely to bring these concerns to bear on how they pursue many of their specific tasks, including the task of social dating.

The personal goals that individuals bring to their life tasks may also be influenced by the values and priorities emphasized in their given *subcul-ture,* as indicated in path B of Figure 7.1. Considerable cross-cultural work has demonstrated that different cultures hold different values, which in turn are associated with different personal goals (Markus & Kitayama, 1991; Schwartz, 1992; Triandis, 1989; see also Veroff, 1983). An adolescent from a subculture that emphasizes collectivism is more likely to pursue goals of interdependence in social dating, for example, whereas one from a subcul-ture emphasizing individualism may focus more on enhancing self-reliance and independence in social dating. Gender as a subculture is also associated with the distinct meaning given to one's self-concept and the pursuit of cer-tain types of goals (see Gilligan, 1982; Markus & Oyserman, 1988). Markus and colleagues (Markus & Oyserman, 1988) suggest that women are more likely to have a communal or collectivist view of the self, whereas men are more likely to have an individual or independent view of the self, and these differences are likely to be reflected in the social dating goals of men and women in adolescence (see also Reis, Senchak, & Solomon, 1985). We be-lieve that these subcultural factors help to shape the types of personal goals that individuals develop by influencing the priority that individuals give to various goals (e.g., interdependence versus independence) within a life task such as social dating.

The distinct personal goals that individuals bring to their age-graded life

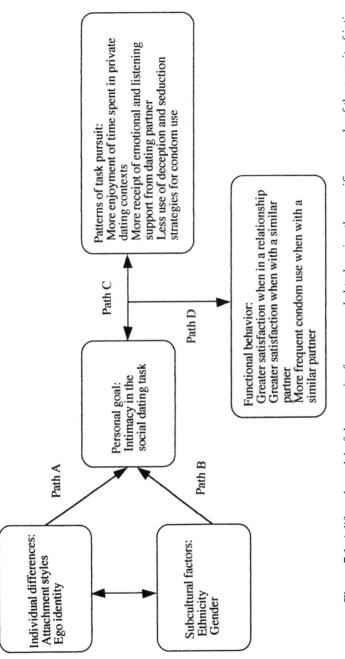

Figure 7.1. A life task model of the pursuit of an age-graded task, using the specific example of the pursuit of intimacy goals in social dating in adolescence. (*Source:* Adapted with permission from Cantor & Fleeson, 1995.)

tasks are in turn associated with the *patterns of task pursuit,* including the what, when, where, and how of task pursuit, as portrayed in path C of Figure 7.1. Specifically, individuals with a specific goal have particular task pursuit strategies, such as choosing to enter particular environments, seeing particular activities and situations as task-relevant, and appraising their work on tasks in ways that reflect their goals (see Cantor, Norem, Niedenthal, et al., 1987). For example, a teenager who is pursuing an intimacy goal within the social dating life task may particularly enjoy pursuing this task with a single partner in a private context and seek primarily emotional support from that partner. Even in casual dating contexts, the same teenager may still be intent on establishing trust by being unusually self-revealing and self-disclosing. We believe that the goals that individuals bring to their life tasks such as social dating are associated systematically with characteristic methods of strategic pursuit and structuring of daily life activity (see Cantor & Fleeson, 1991).

Finally, as shown in path D of Figure 7.1, the ongoing *outcome* of individuals' work on a given life task is a result of the link between personal goals and specific situations, because situations differentially afford goal pursuit (Cantor, 1994). Snyder and his colleagues (for a review, see Snyder, 1993), for example, analyzed patterns of volunteerism and found that individuals gravitate toward specific activities and situations that are relevant to their own personal motivations and that sustaining volunteer activity, in turn, depends on how well the volunteer situation allows for goal fulfillment. Similarly, in the present context, adolescents who take on the social dating goals task with a predominant personal goal of intimacy, for example, are likely to find it easier to engage in safer sex and simultaneously fulfill this intimacy goal in relatively "private" social dating contexts (i.e., long-term relationships with an intimacy-focused partner) that encourage open communication, trust, and self-disclosure (i.e., their broader social dating goals).

Although we have drawn the model from left to right to suggest a linear process by which functional behavior occurs, we expect that the model is bidirectional and that many of the paths likely run in both directions. Experiences in task pursuit in particular may influence one's personal goals in a life task: Positive experience in a close relationship, for example, could well encourage the pursuit of an intimacy goal even on the part of an adolescent with substantial anxiety about social closeness. Moreover, we have certainly simplified the links in this model, especially with regard to indirect sources of influence. For example, subcultures may influence goal-setting indirectly by constraining the situational opportunities provided to group members; Pomerantz and Ruble (Chapter 6, this volume) suggest that this occurs in the academic goal-setting affordances that parents provide to girls (e.g., controlling, performance-oriented) versus boys (e.g., autonomy-granting, mastery-oriented). Therefore, we intend for this model to serve not as an empirical or causal mapping – we are not proposing a path analysis model of functional behavior – but rather as an abstract mapping of how these various factors may be associated with functional behavior, which will ideally lead to future research on the complex causal relationship between these multiple factors. Furthermore, although we emphasize *positive* affordances for functional behavior in accordance with personal goals, it is also critical to consider in future research negative affordances that encourage dysfunctional behavior. Graham (Chapter 5, this volume), for example, compellingly documents affordances in single-parent families that may inadvertently provoke inferences that the world is a hostile place, encouraging a low threshold for retaliatory aggression in children.

In the next section we follow the basic flow of Figure 7.1, providing selective examples of research focused on the pursuit of intimacy and interdependence as a goal in social dating in adolescence. First, we examine how individual differences are associated with the relative predominance of intimacy and interdependence as a goal in social dating. Second, we consider how subcultural factors affect intimacy goals. Third, we focus on how an intimacy goal in turn is associated with particular predictable patterns of goal pursuit in daily life; that is, ways of conducting a dating relationship. In this discussion, we consider how particular aspects of dating situations, such as the intimacy goals of one's partner, become especially significant affordances for dating satisfaction and the regulation of safer sex, when an individual has those predominant intimacy goals. In so doing, we hope to illustrate how the life task approach is a natural way to integrate individual differences and social-cultural factors into an analysis of situational affordances for self-regulation in an age-graded context.

The Pursuit of Social Dating in Adolescence

Individual Differences and Personal Goals

Although most adolescents pursue the dating task, it is likely that different adolescents bring particular goals to bear on their work in this task (Cantor, Acker, & Cook-Flannagan, 1992; Zirkel, 1992). For example, one adolescent may see the dating task as an opportunity to gain independence from family, whereas another may see this task as an opportunity to share intimate thoughts and feelings. The prevailing cultural meaning of social dating has emphasized the pursuit of intimacy (see Hazan & Shaver, 1987; McAdams, 1984), and specifically the fulfillment of goals related to self-disclosure and mutual dependence. Despite this emphasis on intimacy and closeness with a single other, however, not all adolescents may be ready for such exclusive intimacy. Erikson (1950), for example, posited that adolescents first focus on the life crisis of identity formation, and then approach the task of intimacy; adolescents who are still struggling with identity issues may not yet be ready to focus more intently on exclusive intimacy. Furthermore, adolescents who lack the base of a secure attachment model are likely to have more difficulty in focusing primarily on intimacy and trust in dating relationships. Nonetheless, they will be working on addressing the age-graded task of social dating, although they may do it with the goals of self-definition and self-exploration more predominantly in mind.

In order to examine adolescents' orientations toward intimacy specifically in the social dating task, we created the thirteen-item Social Dating Goals scale based on prior literature (see Hazan & Shaver, 1987; Marcia, 1966). The goal of intimacy involves disclosing thoughts and feelings, mutual dependence, and emotional attachment, and therefore items were created that assessed these general concerns within the particular context of dating ("In my dating relationships, I try to share my most intimate thoughts and feelings," and "In my dating relationships, I try to date those I can count on"). Because we believed that those not yet ready to focus on intimacy in social dating would be working more on identity issues, we also included items that assessed identity concerns in social dating (e.g., "In my dating relationships, I try to keep my individual identity," and "In my dating relationships, I try to maintain a strong sense of independence"). The items assessing identity concerns were reverse-scored prior to the summation of the scale, and hence this scale measures one's degree of intimacy goals. The Social Dating Goals scale meets the standard criteria for determining unidimensionality, and has been used in multiple studies with high school and college students (Sanderson & Cantor, 1995; L. T. Volenski, personal communication, March 10, 1995).

As reported in Sanderson and Cantor (1995), the Social Dating Goals scale is predictably associated with general scales measuring degree of identity resolution: It is significantly positively correlated with interpersonal achievement and ideological ego achievement, and significantly negatively correlated with interpersonal diffusion and ideological ego diffusion, suggesting that adolescents who focus primarily on intimacy goals in dating have more successfully "resolved" their current identity issues (i.e., they have formed a more unified identity) and are perhaps therefore more ready to focus on intimacy issues. Furthermore, this scale is also predictably associated with scales measuring the general security of interpersonal attachment: It is significantly positively correlated with secure attachment and significantly negatively correlated with anxious attachment, indicating that those who report pursuing stronger intimacy goals have reached a more secure intimacy status and are able to engage in mutuality with a romantic partner.

There is no association between social dating goals and scores on avoidant attachment, demonstrating that those with weaker intimacy goals are not particularly fearful of or disinterested in close relationships in general, and are thus not necessarily likely to avoid social dating as a task, even though they may not look for interdependence or exclusive intimacy. In fact, when we examined the association between social dating goals and patterns of dating and sexual behavior in a variety of research projects with late adolescents (Sanderson & Cantor, 1995), these data consistently showed that individuals with stronger intimacy goals report having longer dating relationships compared to those with weaker intimacy goals (twenty-two months compared to twelve months, respectively, in one study), but they also reported having fewer casual dating and sexual partners. In other words, those with predominant intimacy goals were pursuing dating more typically in close, exclusive relationships, whereas those less focused on intimacy were as actively engaged in dating but with many casual partners.

These different dating situations – a steady relationship versus casual dating partners – can also be seen as differentially encouraging the adoption of intimacy dating goals, because experience in a compatible relationship could lead an adolescent with such proclivities to focus more on intimacy in dating, whereas finding enjoyment from interacting with several different kinds of partners could draw that same adolescent toward goals of self-exploration in dating (i.e., bidirectional path C in Figure 7.1). Similarly, these dating situations are also likely differentially to afford a comfortable means of engaging with a partner in safer-sex regulation for an adolescent with strong intimacy goals (path D in Figure 7.1). In fact, in an analysis of individuals' dating goals and their dating situation, we (Sanderson & Cantor, 1995) found that the predominance of intimacy goals interacted with dating situations in the prediction of safer sexual behavior (see Figure 7.2). Specifically, those with strong intimacy goals who were in steady dating relationships had the lowest levels of risky sexual behavior, whereas those with strong intimacy goals who were in casual dating relationships had the highest levels of risky sexual behavior. The serious relationship is a dating

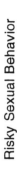

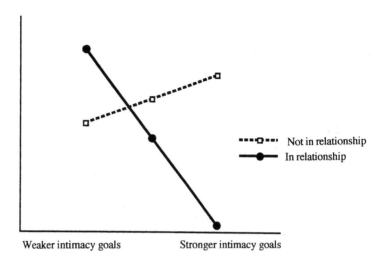

Figure 7.2. The relationship between risky sexual behavior and intimacy dating goals for participants in each dating situation. (*Source:* Adapted with permission from Sanderson & Cantor, 1995.)

context that affords direct communication and the establishment of trust in sexual activity (see Miller, Bettencourt, DeBro, et al., 1993); the casual dating situation, on the other hand, encourages self-reliance and even hedonistic self-exploration. Individuals who focus on issues of interpersonal trust and sharing may find this latter dating situation to be particularly difficult as they try not only to manage safer sex but also to fulfill their intimacy goals.

Subcultural Factors and Personal Goals

As depicted in path B of Figure 7.1, the adoption of strong intimacy goals in social dating should also be significantly linked to membership in various subcultural and cultural groups. Analyses of cultural values and frameworks for living have shown significant variations across cultures in the priority placed on interdependence or independence as an overarching goal in daily life relations (e.g., Markus & Kitayama, 1991; Singelis, 1994). Moreover, as Veroff (1983) compellingly argued, subcultural factors such as ethnicity and gender can also be an important influence on an individual's emphasis on interdependence or on self-reliance in daily life. Cross-cultural differences in collectivism/individualism, for example, also appear *among* different ethnic groups of a single population: For example, African American college students in the United States have a greater focus on collectivism and interdependence than white students (Baldwin & Hopkins, 1990). Many theorists have argued that gender constitutes another subculture oriented around connection (for women) and independence (for men) (e.g., Markus & Oyserman, 1988). Furthermore, there is evidence that these subcultural differences are associated with differential value placed on cooperation and unity as opposed to self-reliance, specifically in dating and sexual behavior (see Jemmott & Jones, 1993; Mays & Cochran, 1988). Amaro (1995), for example, proposes that human immunodeficiency virus (HIV) risk-reduction messages for women should take into account the importance of connection in women's lives. This work suggests that different ethnicity and gender subcultures within the broad adolescent population may well give differential emphasis to intimacy and interdependence goals in social dating and sexual activity.

In order to examine the role of various subcultural factors in influencing goals and tactics related to dating and sexual behavior, we used data from a study on HIV risk–associated behavior that was collected from approximately 1,300 college students at 6 different colleges in Georgia (see DiIorio, 1998). This study included a number of measures related to condom use and HIV prevention, including patterns of sexual behavior, tactics for preventing HIV infection, and orientation toward interpersonal discussion about condom use with one's sexual partner. Given the range of respondents from different subcultures (47 percent white, 41 percent African American, 22 percent other; 60 percent female, 40 percent male), these data allowed us to examine the relationship of gender and ethnicity to goals and tactics for HIV prevention. Specifically, we examined the association of subculture with orientation toward discussing HIV prevention (a measure of individuals' orientation toward interdependence and mutuality with a sexual partner), tactics for preventing HIV infection, and predictors of safer sexual behavior. We expected that in this sample, individuals from those subcultures that are known to place a greater emphasis on interdependence and mutuality – namely, women and African Americans – would have a greater orientation toward interpersonal discussion and more inclination to use tactics for preventing HIV infection that involved cooperating with a partner. We also expected that individuals from these relatively more interdependent subcultures would be more influenced by their degree of interpersonal orientation (in terms of regulation of behavior) than would those from more independent-focused subcultures, because this orientation is emphasized and valued in these particular subcultures.

As predicted, there were subcultural differences in individuals' orientation

A

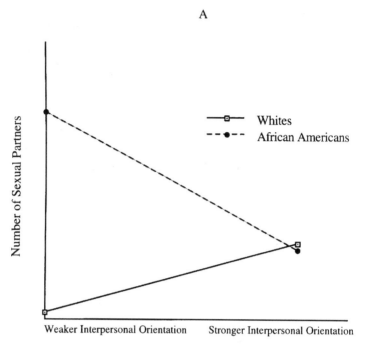

Figure 7.3 (*above and opposite*). (A) Number of sexual partners as a function of race and interpersonal orientation. (B) Frequency of condom use as a function of gender and interpersonal orientation.

toward discussing safer sex and HIV prevention with a sexual partner. First of all, women and African Americans had significantly higher scores on interpersonal orientation toward discussion. Second, subcultural factors were also associated with the use of different strategies for preventing HIV infection. African American and white women were more likely than men to report using partner-focused, interdependent strategies for preventing HIV infection, namely, limiting their number of sexual partners, discussing safer sex with their partner, and having sex only with people they knew well. Contrary to our predictions, African Americans, compared to the sample of white people, were not more likely to report using these partner-focused strategies for HIV prevention. Interestingly, African American students reported using condoms more frequently than did white students. It is possible that the greater prevalence of HIV infection in the African American community (see Jemmott & Jones, 1993) has led to the relatively higher awareness of risks and, in turn, to the more frequent use of this highly effective strategy.

B

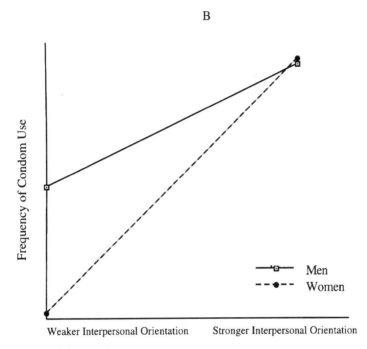

Figure 7.3. (*cont.*)

These differences in interpersonal orientation as a function of subculture have important implications for self-regulation; they suggest that for individuals in different subcultures, degree of interpersonal orientation may be differentially relevant to engaging in safer sex. In fact, in this sample, subculture moderated the association of interpersonal orientation with patterns of safer sexual behavior. Among male and female white students, interpersonal discussion orientation had little effect on number of partners, whereas for African American students, weaker interpersonal orientation was associated with an increase in the number of partners in the last month (see Figure 7.3). Specifically, African Americans in this study seemed to be particularly debilitated (e.g., have more sexual partners) when they were not oriented toward discussion. Similarly, while for both genders stronger interpersonal orientation was associated with increased condom use, this effect was considerably stronger for both African American and white women (see Figure 7.3). In addition, women who were low on interpersonal discussion orientation had the lowest reported frequency of condom use. Interestingly, the interaction of ethnicity and interpersonal orientation influenced the number of sexual partners, whereas the interaction of gender and interpersonal orientation influenced the frequency of condom use. The differential effects of these interactions as a function of the outcome measure were unexpected. They may be due in part to the greater use of condoms in general among African Americans than among the white population and the greater frequency of limiting sexual partners among women than among men (i.e., ceiling effects).

These findings suggest, as predicted, that individuals in different subcultures give different meanings to the task of managing safer sex in dating and, specifically, that those in more interdependent subcultures (African Americans and women) have a greater orientation toward discussing safer sex with a sexual partner. Furthermore, individuals whose subcultures emphasize interdependence were particularly influenced in their safer sexual behavior by their degree of interpersonal orientation. Interpersonal orientation may therefore become a significant mediator of self-regulation for individuals whose subcultures place particular value on interdependence.

Intimacy Dating Goals and Patterns of Dating in Daily Life

In the next phase of our model, as shown in path C of Figure 7.1, we move from the relatively abstract links of individual differences and subcultural values to the more concrete playing out of intimacy dating goals in daily life relationships. As Gollwitzer (1993) noted in his analysis of goal implementation, another critical feature of successful task pursuit is the recognition of the need to plan where, when, and with whom to engage in a task (Mischel, Cantor, & Feldman, in press). Individuals who are particularly adept at structuring their social world in order to gain what they need are likely to have more effective self-regulation. For example, as Heckhausen and Schulz's (Chapter 2, this volume) model of adaptive coping suggests, an adolescent with intimacy dating goals is likely to need to exert both primary (e.g., find a small set of friends with similar intimacy goals) and secondary (e.g., shift the criterion for closeness and intimacy to include relatively "public" moments) control in order to adjust comfortably to the typical group-oriented, casual dating scene at college (see also Rothbaum, Weisz, & Snyder, 1982). Therefore, we believe that individuals with predominant intimacy dating goals try to structure their dating lives in a variety of ways to best allow for the fulfillment of these relatively private intimacy goals within the relatively public environment of college dating. Those with intimacy goals are likely to use particular characteristic patterns of and methods for task pursuit, including *where* they pursue dating, *what* they seek from their dating partners, and how they manage safer sex within these dating relationships.

In order to examine how individuals with predominant intimacy goals structure their daily lives, we conducted a life-sampling questionnaire study with 100 college students (Cantor & Sanderson, 1995). This study included the Social Dating Goals scale described previously (Sanderson & Cantor, 1995), and measures of the enjoyment of time spent in various dating situations (e.g., at parties, alone with one's partner in a dorm room, attending athletic events), the amount of various types of social support participants reported receiving from different people (e.g., boy/girlfriend, friends, professors), and the use of various strategies for regulating condom use (e.g., deception, reward, seduction). Since our particular focus in this chapter is on how individuals regulate their dating relationships, the analyses we report will include only those 52 students who were in a steady dating relationship at the time of this study.

Dating Situations with Partner. As portrayed in path C of Figure 7.1, we believe that individuals go to some lengths to structure their lives to afford goal-relevant experiences (see Cantor, 1994). Exclusive dating relationships, for example, are likely to provide the best arena for fulfilling goals related to self-disclosure, mutual dependence, and open communication; correspondingly, adolescents with predominant intimacy dating goals spend more time in such relationships (Sanderson & Cantor, 1995). Similarly, dating contexts that provide private time with one's dating partner should best provide the opportunities for fulfilling intimacy goals (e.g., self-disclosure). Silbereisen and colleagues (Silbereisen, Noack, & von Eye, 1992), for example, found that adolescents who were trying to establish a relationship sought out more public contexts, such as malls, whereas those who had already established such a relationship sought out more private contexts, such as homes. We therefore expected that in our life sampling study, stronger intimacy goals would be associated with more enjoyment of time spent in such private dating contexts.

As predicted, our analyses demonstrated that dating goals significantly positively predicted enjoyment of time spent in "alone with partner" situations and time spent in "alone with partner in the presence of others" situations. There was no association between social dating goals and enjoyment of time spent in situations with one's partner and many other people. These findings suggest how individuals with predominant intimacy goals systematically pursue the dating task in particular daily life situations that can be predicted by their apparent utility for goal fulfillment. Although all the subjects in these analyses were in steady dating relationships, intimacy goals were still associated with enjoyment of time spent in various dating situations, even controlling for the overall time spent with their partner and whether or not they were sexually active with their dating partner. These patterns make sense because goals related to self-disclosure and open communication are likely to be easier to fulfill in the context of these dating situations than in more public dating situations.

Social Support from Dating Partner. Another critical aspect of a dating relationship is the kinds of social support and help that a person values and reports receiving from a partner, as portrayed in path C of Figure 7.1. Whereas all dating relationships probably consistently provide support, individuals may well differ in how they structure a relationship optimally to fulfill personal goals (e.g., Cohen & Wills, 1985; Harlow & Cantor, 1995). House and Kahn (1985), for example, distinguish between four categories of social support: emotional (demonstrations of love and affection), appraisal (providing feedback about daily life activities), instrumental (actions that facilitate the fulfillment of daily tasks and goals), and informational (opinions and advice that are useful in problem-solving tasks). Although all the participants in this study were currently involved in a serious relationship, we expected them to differ in the kinds of support they valued and received from a partner, as a function of the predominance of intimacy as a dating goal. Specifically, we expected those with predominant intimacy goals, who were attempting to fulfill goals related to open communication and mutual dependence with a dating partner, to value and report receiving greater emotional and listening support from their dating partners. However, we did not assume that they would report receiving more esteem-enhancing or informational support, because these types of support are not uniquely relevant to intimacy goals.

Our findings supported these predictions by showing that greater intimacy dating goals were significantly positively associated with receiving emotional and listening support from one's dating partner, even controlling for total time spent with one's dating partner and the amount of support provided by one's family members and close friends (who, along with one's dating partner, were the greatest providers of support in this sample). There was no significant association between dating goals and receiving esteem-enhancing or informational support from one's dating partner. Furthermore, there was no significant association between social dating goals and any type of support from family or friends, with one exception: Social dating goals were associated with listening support received from one's family. Therefore, those with stronger intimacy goals reported receiving more goal-relevant support specifically from their dating partners than from people in general. Although these data do not speak to the accuracy of individuals' reports (e.g., whether they were actually receiving more social support), it is nonetheless valuable to know that they have these perceptions about their environment and specifically about their relationship with their dating partners.

Strategies for Safer Sex with Partner. As also shown in path C of Figure 7.1, an additional very important part of many adolescent dating relationships is the negotiation of safer sexual behavior (Christopher & Cate, 1984). Once again, we expected those with predominant intimacy goals to try to regulate sexual activity in a manner consonant with their broader relationship goals of trust and interdependence. Within the domain of sexual behavior regulation, commonly used taxonomies of strategies for condom use (e.g., DeBro, Campbell, & Peplau, 1994; McCormick, 1979) distinguish between direct (e.g., expressing concern about protection) and indirect (e.g., deceiving a partner into using a condom) strategies for implementing condom use, which can also be seen as relationship-enhancing (e.g., directly communicating with a partner about condom use) or relationship-harming (e.g., indirectly "tricking" a partner into condom use). Following our basic model, in the life-sampling study we expected those participants with strong intimacy goals to use more direct, relationship-enhancing strategies for regulating sexual behavior because they were trying to build communication and trust in their dating relationships. Furthermore, they were particularly unlikely to use more indirect, relationship-harming strategies for regulating condom use because such strategies were likely to disrupt their pursuit of intimacy goals.

Based on their self-reported preferences for different strategies for condom use (see DeBro, Campbell, & Peplau, 1994), we found, as predicted, that intimacy dating goals were significantly negatively associated with the use of both seduction and deception, above and beyond the effects of sexual activity, gender, and condom use self-efficacy. In other words, individuals with predominant intimacy dating goals were less likely to use the indirect strategies of seduction and deception for implementing condom use than were those with less strong intimacy goals. Although we expected that social dating goals would also be positively associated with the use of direct, relationship-enhancing strategies (i.e., emotion/reward and risk avoidance), these hypotheses were not supported, perhaps because almost everyone in a dating relationship in this sample used these strategies quite frequently. Nonetheless, in general our findings suggest that individuals use strategies for regulating behavior that correspond to their broader dating goals. An individual with stronger intimacy goals is very unlikely to use indirect strategies because this approach is not consistent with their broader goal of increasing open communication and mutual dependence. In fact, the use of such strategies could ultimately harm this broader goal by decreasing trust and intimacy with a partner. On the other hand, an individual with less strong intimacy goals may prefer to use these more self-focused, indirect strategies for regulating condom use largely because such strategies do not demand direct interpersonal negotiation, even if they do involve somewhat deceptive behavior.

Functional Patterns of Self-Regulation

Thus far we have focused on how individuals who bring a specific meaning and goal to the social dating task, namely intimacy, engage in task pursuit in distinct ways. In turn, these characteristic patterns of task pursuit have practical implications because they identify contexts for dating that are likely to give those with strong intimacy goals positive affordances for self-regulation (see Cantor, 1994). Miller and colleagues (Miller, Bettencourt, DeBro, et al., 1993) have shown that different dating situations (e.g., a long-term relationship versus a one-night stand) are associated with the use of different strategies (e.g., reward versus deception) for implementing condom use. For example, long-term relationships are likely to provide positive affordances for safer sex for those individuals who endorse relationship-enhancing strategies in daily life, such as those with predominant intimacy goals. As portrayed in Figure 7.1, we believe that the functional regulation of behavior emerges when individuals with distinct goals, such as intimacy in social dating, are in situations that provide or afford opportunities, such as those for establishing trust in a steady relationship, to fulfill those goals (e.g., Baron & Boudreau, 1987; Cantor, 1994; Read & Miller, 1989).

In the previous section, we showed how individuals with predominant intimacy goals enjoy spending time in more private dating situations, receive more listening and emotional support from their dating partners, and are less likely to use indirect, potentially relationship-harming strategies for regulating safer sex than are those with less strong intimacy goals. Building on these findings, in this next section we examine situations that provide affordances that are therefore likely to be particularly important to those with stronger intimacy goals, namely the presence (or absence) of a steady dating relationship, and the similarity of the dating goals of one's dating partner. We hypothesize that a steady dating relationship and consonant partner goals would make it easier for a person with strong intimacy goals to fulfill those goals. In particular, we examine the ways in which these two types of situational affordances (dating status and partner goals) interact with intimacy dating goals to enhance or inhibit relationship satisfaction (e.g., how satisfied are individuals with their pursuit of this task?) and safer sexual behavior (e.g., how effectively can individuals regulate their sexual activity within this dating context?).

Relationship Satisfaction

First, in considering the correlates of relationship satisfaction, we expect that individuals who are pursuing intimacy goals within the dating task will find it easiest, and therefore most satisfying, to work on these goals in long-term relatively stable dating situations that allow for mutual dependence and open communication. On the other hand, individuals who are attempting to fulfill intimacy goals by relying on a casual dating partner may be disappointed and frustrated when they find that such a partner is not always dependable and trustworthy.

In order to examine this issue, we analyzed data from participants in our life-sampling study on their satisfaction with their dating/romantic life. (The satisfaction data were gathered between one and five months after participants completed the original life-sampling questionnaire, and hence represent an independent data point.) These analyses demonstrated that there was a main effect for relationship status, with those currently in a dating relationship having greater dating satisfaction than did those who were not in a relationship, and a main effect for social dating goals, with stronger intimacy goals predicting greater dating satisfaction. These main effects, however, were qualified by an interaction between relationship status and dating goals, which revealed that for those individuals in a dating relationship, stronger intimacy goals were associated with greater satisfaction. For those not in a dating relationship, on the other hand, there was no association between dating goals and dating satisfaction – although there was a slight trend suggesting that those with stronger intimacy goals had *less* dating satisfaction when they were not in a relationship.

In addition to examining dating satisfaction as a function of both individuals' dating goals and their current relationship status, we were also interested in studying the influence of another type of situational affordance, namely, one's partner's goals in such relationships. We believed that individuals with predominant intimacy goals would most easily be able to fulfill these goals if they were in a relationship with a partner who shared these goals, and hence could provide the desired level of emotional and listening support in a situation that encouraged open communication and mutual dependence. We were therefore interested in examining relationship satisfaction as a function of both individuals' relationship goals and the degree of similarity between one's own and one's partner's goals.

In order to examine this issue, we conducted a study of twenty young married couples (Cano, Sanderson, & Cantor, 1995). Each spouse completed a questionnaire that included a measure of marital satisfaction (see Spanier, 1976) and a revised version of the Social Dating Goals Scale that specifically assessed goals within the marital relationship. These findings indicated that individuals who had relationship goals similar (regardless of their degree of intimacy) to those of their spouses (matched) reported more marital satisfaction (see Figure 7.4). Moreover, among individuals with dissimilar goals (mismatched), those who also had stronger intimacy goals than those with more discrepancy between their own and their spouses' goals, had the least marital satisfaction: Apparently, individuals with stronger intimacy goals are particularly debilitated (e.g., less satisfied) when they have a spouse with weaker intimacy goals (see also Sanderson & Cantor, 1997).

Regulation of Sexual Behavior

Relationship satisfaction is a commonly used measure of well-being and functional behavior (see Bradbury & Fincham, 1988); however, another behavior of particular relevance within the dating task for adolescents is that of regulating safer sexual behavior. Our own prior research has shown how the pursuit of intimacy dating goals is associated with regulating sexual behavior more effectively in close dating relationships than in casual dating contexts (Cantor & Sanderson, 1995). Although this research focused on the association between the dating context and patterns of sexual behavior, individuals' beliefs about their dating partners' preferences may also be associated with particular methods of regulating safer sex and therefore may represent another important component of the dating situation. Specifically, we hypothesized that an individual who does not think that his or her partner is comfortable with discussing condom use may be less likely actually to implement condom use than might an individual who thinks that her or his partner is more open to discussion of condom use; this is likely to be particularly true for those with a greater interpersonal discussion orientation themselves.

In order to address the influence of one's partner on condom use, we again used data from the Southern college student sample (DiIorio, 1998). This

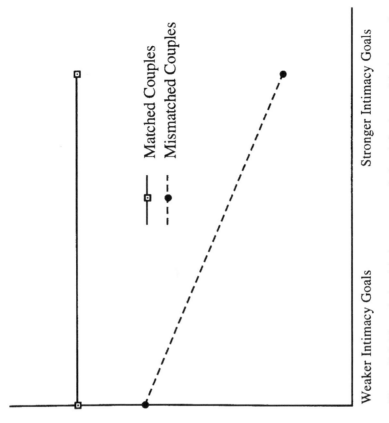

Figure 7.4. The relationship between marital satisfaction and intimacy relationship goals for couples with matching and mismatching intimacy goals.

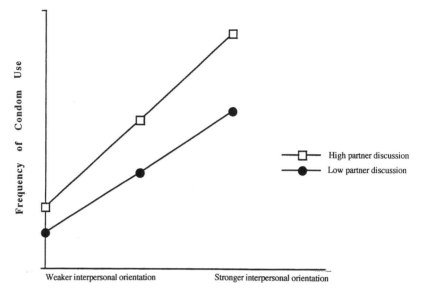

Figure 7.5. The relationship between condom use and interpersonal discussion orientation for participants with partners high and low in discussion orientation.

study included measures of one's own orientation toward the interpersonal discussion of HIV prevention, and also of individuals' beliefs about their dating partner's orientation toward such discussion. Although these data obviously do not assess the accuracy of individuals' perceptions of their partner's comfort, the participants' perceptions may in fact be important influences on their own condom use behavior. These findings revealed main effects of both own and perceived partner's interpersonal orientation toward discussion, indicating in both cases (own and partner's) that greater discussion orientation is associated with increased condom use. However, these main effects were qualified by a significant interaction (see Figure 7.5). The interpretation of this interaction revealed that individuals who are more comfortable with discussion are even more influenced by their perceptions of their partner's comfort with discussing condom use than are those who are less comfortable with discussion. In other words, although all individuals are more likely to use condoms when their partners are very comfortable with discussion, the stronger interpersonal orientation individuals (e.g., more intimacy-focused) are the most likely to use condoms when they believe that their partner is also high in discussion-orientation. Those who are weaker on interpersonal discussion orientation (e.g., more independence-focused) are not as influenced by their perceptions of their partner's comfort with discussing condom use, presumably because they do not typically attempt to regulate safer sex through discussion and hence are not as heavily affected by their beliefs about their partner's comfort with discussion. These findings again show that behavior regulation is a function of both individuals' personal concerns and the affordances in their specific dating situation – in this case, their perceptions of their partner's orientation toward discussing safer sex.

Implications for Functional Self-Regulation

The model we propose in this chapter, and the research presented to support this model, describes functional behavior as the result of interaction between personal goals and situational affordances: the what, where, how, and with whom of task pursuit. Specifically, we believe that functional behavior emerges from the interaction between the particular meaning and personal goal that individuals bring to specific age-graded life tasks (e.g., the pursuit of intimacy in social dating) and the affordances presented by their specific daily life situations (e.g., their dating context and dating partner). This model takes into account both individual-difference variables and subcultural factors by considering how both of these factors could influence the formation of the personal goals that individuals bring to their life tasks.

As portrayed in paths A and B of Figure 7.1, we believe that both individual differences and subcultural factors have an impact on the meaning and goals that adolescents pursue in the dating task. Adolescents with secure working models of attachment and a more resolved ego identity, for example, are likely to approach dating with predominant intimacy goals. Similarly, adolescents from more typically interdependent subcultures (African Americans and women) are likely to approach sexual activity in dating with more interdependent goals. These findings suggest that both individual differences and subcultures relate to the personal goals that adolescents bring to social dating. Although we focused on examining how subcultural differences could directly relate to the personal goals that individuals bring to their life tasks, it is probable that subcultures also exert an influence on personal goals indirectly either by shaping individual differences (e.g., in preferences, needs, styles), or by providing selective opportunities for task pursuit (e.g., situations, partners, timing), which in turn have an impact on personal goals (see Veroff, 1983).

These different meanings and goals that individuals bring to their life tasks are in turn associated with particular patterns of task pursuit (see path

C of Figure 7.1). We have shown that adolescents who approach social dating with an intimacy goal, for example, enjoy spending time in contexts alone with their dating partner, report obtaining particular types of goal-relevant social support from their partner, and avoid using goal-disrupting strategies for behavior regulation. The goal of intimacy is only one example of a meaning that individuals can give to a specific life task, and these data indicate that individuals are reasonably good at structuring their lives in ways that afford these goal-relevant experiences. This research provides additional support for many other studies demonstrating that individuals seek out situations that provide goal-relevant affordances (e.g., Emmons, Diener, & Larsen, 1986; Niedenthal & Mordkoff, 1991). Alternatively, positive experience in these situations may also contribute to the predominance of their intimacy dating goals (see bidirectional path in Figure 7.1). For example, over a period of time, an individual who enjoys the open communication and mutual dependence found in private dating situations is likely to develop stronger intimacy goals in dating.

Finally, as shown in path D of Figure 7.1, functional behavior emerges as a result of the particular goals that individuals pursue in a given life task and the extent to which their daily life situations afford the fulfillment of these goals. Again using the goal of intimacy as an example, we have shown that adolescents who are pursuing intimacy in dating and who are in a steady relationship that affords the fulfillment of such goals have greater dating satisfaction and engage in less risky sexual behavior than those who lack such an intimacy focus. Similarly, those with strong intimacy goals who have a partner with similar goals have greater relationship satisfaction and use condoms more consistently. These data indicate that functional behavior is a result of one's personal needs and situational affordances (see Cantor, 1994).

Functional Behavior Across the Life Span and Life Tasks

Throughout this chapter we have described our model using a single example – the life stage of adolescence, the task of social dating, and the goal of intimacy. Although we believe that this model can also be used to predict patterns of functional behavior across the life span and across life tasks, we also believe that the particularly influential individual-difference dimensions and subcultural prescriptions that we have emphasized here in our analysis of social dating in adolescence may vary in importance across the life span and also across life tasks.

First, with respect to changing life periods, the influence that particular individual differences such as attachment styles or particular subcultural factors such as gender roles have on the meaning that individuals bring to their close relationship tasks may well diminish across the life span. Older adults are *generally* more selective in their close contact with individuals in their social networks (Carstensen, 1993); therefore *individual differences* in preferences for intimacy may be less relevant to and predictive of behavior in the social relationships of older adults. Similarly, the female subculture in late adulthood may not place the emphasis on interdependence that it does earlier in life: Gender roles have been shown to decrease in importance for women over the life span as sex role specialization decreases (see Helson & Moane, 1987). In fact, it might be the case that for older adults, the goals served in close relationships for both men and women involve a mixture of socioemotional support (Carstensen, Chapter 13, this volume) and integration into a routine of daily life activities outside the home (Harlow & Cantor, in press). If this is so, then the affordances for goal pursuit may involve quite a delicate balance between private closeness and public activity, and they may be more difficult to find, perhaps, than the preferred contexts for social dating in adolescence.

Second, even within the social dating task of adolescence there may be dimensions of meaning other than interdependence/independence that guide task pursuit in daily life. Snyder's work on self-monitoring (see Snyder & Simpson, 1984), for example, has shown that individuals who differ in their orientation toward public versus private standards for regulating behavior have different preferences for dating partners and different patterns of dating. An adolescent who has a relatively public orientation may bring a desire to "look good in the eyes of others" to his or her pursuit of social dating, and therefore may attempt to date high-status individuals in highly public situations (e.g., bring the high school athletic star to the prom), whereas one with a more private, self-focus, may bring his or her own internal values to their pursuit of social dating and attempt to find a partner who best exemplifies those attitudes and values. This sensitivity to social norms as opposed to self-norms in self-regulation (see Abrams, 1994; Cheek, 1989; Fenigstein, Scheier, & Buss, 1975) may therefore be another dimension that influences how individual adolescents shape their personal goals within the age-graded social dating task.

Finally, in generalizing this approach to other life tasks that adolescents face (e.g., doing school work, making friends), other particularly relevant dimensions of meaning may exist; yet we predict that functional behavior will derive from the match between personal goals and situational affordances. In achievement tasks, for example, individual differences in self-directedness or autonomy (e.g., Deci & Ryan, 1987) are correlated with task- versus ego-focused goals with implications for what constitutes matching situations, such as the kinds of effective social support (e.g., Harlow & Cantor, 1995; Pomerantz & Ruble, Chapter 6, this volume) and the use of social comparison information (Butler, 1992) that best affords functional behavior (e.g., task persistence under free choice conditions; Ryan, Koestner, & Deci, 1991). Similarly, Dweck and her colleagues (Dweck & Leggett, 1988) have documented in detail the implications of individual differences in theories of intelligence for the setting of achievement goals (mastery versus performance) and patterns of task pursuit (e.g., persistence in the face of obstacles) that define, in turn, positive affordances for achievement and success (e.g., level of challenge of task). Thus, although the particular goals and situational affordances most relevant to functional behavior may vary across life tasks and life periods, the person x situation fit in life task pursuit should always play a key role (Cantor, 1994; Higgins, 1990; Read & Miller, 1989; Snyder, 1993).

References

Abrams, D. (1994). Social self-regulation. *Personality and Social Psychology Bulletin, 20,* 473–483.

Amaro, H. (1995). Love, sex, and power: Considering women's realities in HIV prevention. *American Psychologist, 50,* 437–447.

Bakan, D. (1966). *The duality of human existence.* Boston: Beacon Press.

Baldwin, J. A., & Hopkins, R. (1990). African American and European American cultural differences as assessed by the worldviews paradigm: An empirical analysis. *The Western Journal of Black Studies, 14,* 38–52.

Baron, R. M., & Boudreau, L. A. (1987). An ecological perspective on integrating personality and social psychology. *Journal of Personality and Social Psychology, 53,* 1214–1221.

Bradbury, T. N., & Fincham, F. (1988). Individual difference variables in close relationships: A contextual model of marriage as an integrative framework. *Journal of Personality and Social Psychology, 54,* 713–721.

Brandtstädter, J., & Renner, G. (1990). Tenacious goal pursuit and flexible goal adjustment: Explication and age-related analysis of assimilative and accommodative strategies of coping. *Psychology and Aging, 5,* 58–67.

Butler, R. (1992). What young people want to know when: Effects of mastery and ability goals on interest in different kinds of social comparisons. *Journal of Personality and Social Psychology, 62,* 934–943.

Cano, A., Sanderson, C. A., & Cantor, N. (1995, August). *Relationship goals and marital satisfaction.* Poster session presented at the 103rd Annual Meeting of the American Psychological Association, New York.

Cantor, N. (1994). Life task problem solving: Situational affordances and personal needs. *Personality and Social Psychology Bulletin, 20,* 235–243.

Cantor, N., Acker, M., & Cook-Flannagan, C. (1992). Conflict and preoccupation in the intimacy life task. *Journal of Personality and Social Psychology, 63,* 644–655.

Cantor, N., & Fleeson, W. (1994). Social intelligence and intelligent goal pursuit: A cognitive slice of motivation. *Nebraska Symposium on Motivation* (Vol. 41, pp. 125–179). Lincoln: University of Nebraska Press.

—— (1991). Life tasks and self-regulatory processes. *Advances in Motivation and Achievement, 7,* 327–369.

Cantor, N., & Kihlstrom, J. F. (1987). *Personality and Social Intelligence.* Englewood Cliffs, NJ: Prentice-Hall.

Cantor, N., & Malley, J. (1992). Life tasks, personal needs, and close relationships. In G. J. O. Fletcher & F. D. Fincham (Eds.), *Cognition in close relationships* (pp. 101–125). Hillsdale, NJ: Erlbaum.

Cantor, N., Norem, J. K., Niedenthal, P. M., Langston, C. A., & Brower, A. M. (1987). Life tasks, self-concept ideals, and cognitive strategies in a life transition. *Journal of Personality and Social Psychology, 53,* 1178–1191.

Cantor, N., & Sanderson, C. A. (1995, June). The interaction between personality and social processes: A life-sampling study with students in dating relationships. Paper presented at the 5th Annual Convention of the Society for Personality and Social Psychology, New York.

Carstensen, L. L. (1993). Motivation for social contact across the life span: A theory of socioemotional selectivity. In J. E. Jacobs (Ed.), *Developmental perspectives on motivation: Nebraska symposium on motivation* (Vol. 40, pp. 209–254). Lincoln: University of Nebraska Press.

—— (1998). A life-span approach to social motivation. In J. Heckhausen & C. S. Dweck (Eds.), *Motivation and self-regulation across the life span.* New York: Cambridge University Press.

Cheek, J. M. (1989). Identity orientations and self-interpretation. In D. M. Buss & N. Cantor (Eds.), *Personality psychology: Recent trends and emerging directions* (pp. 275–285). New York: Springer-Verlag.

Christopher, F. S., & Cate, R. M. (1984). Factors involved in premarital decision making. *Journal of Sex Research, 20,* 363–376.

Clark, M. S., Muchant, C. G., Ouellete, R., Powell, M., & Milberg, S. (1987). Relationship type, recipient mood, and helping. *Journal of Personality and Social Psychology, 53,* 94–103.

Cohen, S., & Wills, T. A. (1985). Stress, social support, and the buffering hypothesis. *Psychological Bulletin, 85,* 310–357.

Csikszentmihalyi, M., & Larsen, R. (1984). *Being adolescent: Confusion and growth in the teenage years.* New York: Basic Books.

DeBro, S., Campbell, S., & Peplau, L. (1994). Influencing a partner to use a condom. *Psychology of Women Quarterly, 18,* 165–182.

Deci, E. L., & Ryan, R. M. (1987). The support of autonomy and the control of behavior. *Journal of Personality and Social Psychology, 53,* 1024–1037.

DiIorio, C. (1998). A social cognitive–based model for condom use among college students. Manuscript under review.

Dweck, C. S., & Leggett, E. L. (1988). A social-cognitive approach to personality and motivation. *Psychological Review, 95,* 256–273.

Emmons, R. A. (1989). The personal strivings approach to personality. In L. A. Pervin (Ed.), *Goal concepts in personality and social psychology* (pp. 87–126). Hillsdale, NJ: Erlbaum.

Emmons, R. A., Diener, E., & Larsen, R. J. (1986). Choice and avoidance of everyday situations and affect congruence: Two models of reciprocal interactionism. *Journal of Personality and Social Psychology, 51,* 815–826.

Erikson, E. H. (1950). *Childhood and society.* New York: Norton.

Fenigstein, A., Scheier, M. R., & Buss, A. H. (1975). Public and private self-consciousness: Assessment and theory. *Journal of Consulting and Clinical Psychology, 43,* 522–527.

Gilligan, C. (1982). *In a different voice.* Cambridge, MA: Harvard University Press.

Gollwitzer, P. M. (1993). Goal achievement: The role of intentions. In W. Stroebe & M. Hewstone (Eds.), *European review of social psychology* (Vol. 4, pp. 141–185). London: Wiley.

Graham, S. (1998). Social motivation and perceived responsibility: Attributions and behavior of African American boys labeled as aggressive. In J. Heckhausen & C. S. Dweck (Eds.), *Motivation and self-regulation across the life span.* New York: Cambridge University Press.

Harlow, R., & Cantor, N. (1994). The social pursuit of academics: Side-effects and "spillover" of strategic reassurance seeking. *Journal of Personality and Social Psychology, 66,* 386–397.

Harlow, R. E., & Cantor, N. (1995). To whom do people turn when things go poorly? Task orientation and functional social contexts. *Journal of Personality and Social Psychology, 69,* 329–340.

Havighurst, R. J. (1972). *Human development and education.* New York: Longmans, Green.

Hazan, C., & Shaver, P. R. (1987). Romantic love conceptualized as an attachment process. *Journal of Personality and Social Psychology, 52,* 511–524.

Heckhausen, J., & Schulz, R. (1995). A life-span theory of control. *Psychological Review, 102,* 284–304.

Helson, R., & Moane, G. (1987). Personality change in women from college to midlife. *Journal of Personality and Social Psychology, 53,* 176–186.

Higgins, E. T. (1990). Personality, social psychology, and person-situation relations: Standards and knowledge activation as a common language. In L. A. Pervin (Ed.), *Handbook of personality: Theory and research* (pp. 301–338). New York: Guilford Press.

House, J. S., & Kahn, R. L. (1985). Measures and concepts of social support. In

S. Cohen & S. L. Syme (Eds.), *Social support and health.* Orlando, FL: Academic Press.

Jemmott, J. B. III, & Jones, J. M. (1993). Social psychology and AIDS among ethnic minority individuals: Risk behaviors and strategies for changing them. In J. Pryor & G. Reeder (Eds.), *The social psychology of AIDS infection* (pp. 183–224). Hillsdale, NJ: Erlbaum.

Kelly, J. A., & Hansen, D. J. (1987). Social interactions and adjustment. In V. B. Van Hasselt & M. Hersen (Eds.), *Handbook of adolescent psychology* (pp. 131–146). New York: Pergamon Press.

Little, B. (1989). Personal projects analysis: Trivial pursuits, magnificent obsessions, and the search for coherence. In D. M. Buss & N. Cantor (Eds.), *Personality psychology: Recent trends and emerging directions* (pp. 15–31). New York: Springer-Verlag.

Marcia, J. E. (1966). Development and validation of ego identity status. *Journal of Personality and Social Psychology, 3,* 551–558.

Markus, H. R., & Kitayama, S. (1991). Culture and the self: Implications for cognition, emotion, and motivation. *Psychological Review, 98,* 224–253.

Markus, H. R., & Oyserman, D. (1988). Gender and thought: The role of the self-concept. In M. Crawford & M. Hamilton (Eds.), *Gender and thought* (pp. 100–127). New York: Springer-Verlag.

Mays, V. M., & Cochran, S. D. (1988). Issues in the perception of AIDS risk and risk reduction activities by Black and Hispanic/Latina women. *American Psychologist, 43,* 949–957.

McAdams, D. P. (1984). Human motives and personal relationships. In V. J. Derlega (Ed.), *Communication, intimacy, and close relationships* (pp. 41–70). Orlando, FL: Academic Press.

McAdams, D. P., & Constantian, C. A. (1983). Intimacy and affiliation motives in daily living: An experience sampling analysis. *Journal of Personality and Social Psychology, 45,* 851–861.

McCormick, N. B. (1979). Come-ons and put-offs: Unmarried students' strategies for having and avoiding sexual intercourse. *Psychology of Women Quarterly, 4,* 194–211.

Miller, L. C., Bettencourt, B. A., DeBro, S. C., & Hoffman, V. (1993). Negotiating safer sex: Interpersonal dynamics. In J. Pryor & G. Reeder (Eds.), *The social psychology of AIDS infection* (pp. 85–123). Hillsdale, NJ: Erlbaum.

Mischel, W., Cantor, N., & Feldman, S. (1996). Principles of self-regulation: The nature of willpower and self-control. In E. T. Higgins & A. W. Kruglanski (Eds.), *Social psychology: Handbook of basic principles* (pp. 329–360). New York: Guilford.

Niedenthal, P. M., & Mordkoff, J. T. (1991). Prototype distancing: A strategy for choosing among threatening situations. *Personality and Social Psychology Bulletin, 17,* 483–493.

Norem, J. K., & Cantor, N. (1986). Defensive pessimism: "Harnessing" anxiety as motivation. *Journal of Personality and Social Psychology, 51,* 1208–1217.

Pomerantz, E., & Ruble, D. (1998). The multidimensional nature of control: Implications for the development of sex differences in self-evaluation. In J. Heckhausen & C. S. Dweck (Eds.), *Motivation and self-regulation across the life span.* New York: Cambridge University Press.

Read, S. J., & Miller, L. C. (1989). Interpersonalism: Toward a goal-based theory of persons in relationships. In L. A. Pervin (Ed.), *Goal concept in personality and social psychology* (pp. 413–472). Hillsdale, NJ: Erlbaum.

Reis, H., Senchack, M., & Solomon, B. (1985). Sex differences in the intimacy of social interaction: Further exploration of potential explanations. *Journal of Personality and Social Psychology, 48,* 1204–1217.

Rothbaum, F., Weisz, J. R., & Snyder, S. S. (1982). Changing the world and changing the self: A two-process model of perceived control. *Journal of Personality and Social Psychology, 42,* 5–37.

Ryan, R. M., Koestner, R., & Deci, E. L. (1991). Ego-involved persistence: When free-choice behavior is not intrinsically motivated. *Motivation and Emotion, 15,* 185–206.

Sanderson, C. A., & Cantor, N. (1995). Social dating goals in late adolescence: Implications for safer sexual activity. *Journal of Personality and Social Psychology, 68,* 1121–1134.

Sanderson, C. A., & Cantor, N. (1997). Creating satisfaction in steady dating relationships: The role of personal goals and situational affordances. *Journal of Personality and Social Psychology, 73,* 1424–1433.

Schwartz, S. H. (1992). Universal in the content and structure of values: Theoretical advances and empirical tests in 20 countries. *Advances in Experimental and Social Psychology, 25,* 1–65.

Shaver, P. R., & Hazan, C. (1993). Adult romantic attachment: Theory and evidence. In D. Perlman & W. Jones (Eds.), *Advances in personal relationships* (Vol. 4, pp. 29–70). London: Jessica Kingsley.

Silbereisen, R. K., Noack, P., & von Eye, A. (1992). Adolescents' development of romantic friendship and change in favorite leisure contexts. *Journal of Adolescent Research, 7,* 80–93.

Simmons, R. G., & Blyth, D. A. (1987). *Moving into adolescence: The impact of pubertal change and school context.* New York: Aldine de Gruyter.

Singelis, T. M. (1994). The measurement of independent and interdependent self-construals. *Personality and Social Psychology Bulletin, 20,* 580–591.

Snyder, M. (1993). Basic research and practical problems: The promise of a "functional" personality and social psychology. *Personality and Social Psychology Bulletin, 19,* 251–264.

Snyder, M., & Simpson, J. A. (1984). Self-monitoring and dating relationships. *Journal of Personality and Social Psychology, 47,* 1281–1291.

Spanier, G. (1976). Measuring dyadic adjustment: New scales for assessing the quality of marriage and similar dyads. *Journal of Marriage and the Family, 38,* 15–27.

Taylor, S. E., & Aspinwall, L. G. (1996). Mediating processes in psychosocial stress: Appraisal, coping, resistance, and vulnerability. In H. B. Kaplan (Ed.), *Psychosocial stress: Perspectives on Structure, Theory, Life Course, and Methods* (pp. 71–110). New York: Academic Press.

Triandis, H. C. (1989). The self and social behavior in differing cultural contexts. *Psychological Review, 96,* 506–520.

Veroff, J. (1983). Contextual determinants of personality. *Personality and Social Psychology Bulletin, 9,* 331–343.

Winett, R. A. (1995). A framework for health promotion and disease prevention programs. *American Psychologist, 50,* 341–350.

Zirkel, S. (1992). Developing independence in a life transition: Investing the self in the concerns of the day. *Journal of Personality and Social Psychology, 62,* 506–521.

Zirkel, S., & Cantor, N. (1990). Personal construal of a life task: Those who struggle for independence. *Journal of Personality and Social Psychology, 58,* 172–185.

8   Commentary: Strategies for Studying Social Influences on Motivation

Ellen A. Skinner

Abstract

The purpose of this chapter is to suggest strategies to aid researchers as they explore the social factors that contribute to children's motivation. These suggestions are based on three general principles: (1) children actively participate in the processes by which social factors shape their motivation; (2) the social context includes multiple dimensions and multiple levels; and (3) the elements in the equation, namely the social context and children's motivation, as well as the mechanisms that connect them, change with development. From this perspective, children are assumed to be active in selecting, initiating, interpreting, and provoking interactions with multiple and changing social partners and their proxies. A strong theoretical perspective on how these interpretations – for example, experiences of self-determination or helplessness – influence children's motivation then allows researchers to move "backward" to an identification of the broad dimensions of social interactions (such as autonomy support or chaos) that are expected to have an impact on children's interpretations. As a next step, researchers can try to analyze the multiple pathways through which social partners communicate these dimensions to children. In describing each of these steps, I suggest how sensitization to the possibility that these processes are developmental may guide the direction of research. I then use the work described in Chapters 5, 6, and 7 of this volume to illustrate how these principles can add to the study of the social factors that shape children's motivation.

Support from research grant no. HD11914 from the National Institute of Child Health and Human Development, from Training Grant no. 527594 from the National Institute of Mental Health, and from a Faculty Scholars Award from the William T. Grant Foundation are gratefully acknowledged.

Introduction

Parents and educators know that children's motivation is shaped by their social contexts. They know that social relationships and social interactions influence children's exertion, interest, enthusiasm, and persistence in the face of failure. Despite this common knowledge, however, psychologists sometimes seem hard pressed to provide a detailed and comprehensive empirical account of the specific social factors that contribute to children's motivation, including precisely how these factors exert their effects and whether they change with development.

To be sure, fifty years of concentrated research has made significant inroads into these important questions (see Eccles, Wigfield, & Schiefele, 1998, for a review). Early phases of research examined correlations between global dimensions of parenting, such as warmth and control, and child motivational outcomes, such as locus of control and achievement motivation (Lefcourt, 1982). A second strand involved the experimental analysis of effects of very specific manipulations, such as noncontingency, repeated failure, rewards, and competition (Deci & Ryan, 1985; Seligman, 1975). And from the beginning, application-oriented research has been conducted – in parenting and especially in education – in which researchers have attempted to train parents to be contingent, responsive, and sensitive (Riksen-Walraven, 1978) or have helped institute cooperative learning–oriented or mastery-oriented curricula in classrooms, and then have examined the effects on children's control or intrinsic motivation (Ames & Ames, 1985).

Perhaps it is surprising that even after all this important work, the literature provides only partial conclusions about the social contributors to motivation. The early global work led to confusion about the precise contextual dimensions that were involved. For example, confusion still exists about the effects of one of the main dimensions of parenting: warmth. In a review of the research on social antecedents of locus of control up to 1982, Lefcourt stated that the dimension of parenting that showed the most consistent positive effects on locus of control was parental "warmth." In contrast, in 1983, Crandall and Crandall published the results of arguably the best study of parental influences on locus of control: a longitudinal study in which parent interactions with children had been observed in early childhood, and in which locus of control was assessed in early adolescence. In this study, maternal warmth was *negatively* correlated with locus of control; Crandall and Crandall (1983) hypothesized that perhaps warmth discouraged children from taking internal responsibility for failure, whereas relatively less maternal involvement allowed children more opportunities to experience the effects of their actions. One conclusion about work examining the connections between global parenting antecedents and child motivational outcomes is that it was useful in providing a big picture, but the picture seemed somewhat unfocused.

On the other hand, experimental work has consistently been clear and precise on conceptual dimensions; however, it can be difficult to translate some experimental manipulations into actual interactions in families, in schools, or with peers. For example, where can one find the noncontingency that may produce helplessness in school? Is it in interactions with the teacher? In attempts to comply with the rules of the classroom? In the challenges provided by the materials and activities of schoolwork? Or is it somewhere in previous interactions with parents? It is possible to critique this work as a whole by pointing out that it provided many very clear pieces but left researchers unsure about what the entire puzzle looked like.

Finally, when considering the results of application research, it is fair to conclude that these intervention studies produced many successes. However, effects tended to be global: It was unclear why or for whom they were working. These interventions also introduced researchers to the complex issues surrounding *unintended side effects.* For example, a token economy might promote a sense of control through its high contingencies, but what are its effects on self-determination and intrinsic motivation? Or, cooperative learning might have advantages for effort and for peer relations, but does it have disadvantages for an individual's estimates of his or her own competence and ability?

The goal of this chapter is not to review the research on social antecedents of motivation (see, e.g., Eccles, Wigfield, & Schiefele, 1998) but instead to suggest new avenues for approaching these old questions. Suggestions attempt to build on the strengths of earlier work, while keeping in mind its shortcomings. These "new" strategies are based on three principles that together form a set of core assumptions about the individual and social nature of motivation, which can be seen in many strands of current research on the development of children's motivation (Connell & Wellborn, 1991; Deci & Ryan, 1985; Dweck, 1991; Harter, 1978; Skinner, 1995; Weisz, 1983, 1986). The unique contribution of this chapter is that it attempts to articulate these principles and to examine their usefulness in guiding the study of the social influences of motivation (see Table 8.1).

Because the chapters in Part II of this volume provide cutting-edge examples of the best work in this area, I will use them, along with other current research, to illustrate the strategies proposed. The three principles,

Table 8.1. *Three general principles to guide research on social influences on motivation*

1. Individuals actively participate in the processes by which social factors shape their motivation.
   a. They seek and select social partners and situations and initiate interactions.
   b. They interpret social interactions and relationships.
   c. They provoke reactions from social partners.
2. The social context includes multiple dimensions and multiple levels.
   a. The general ways in which social contexts influence motivation are captured by theoretically derived dimensions (e.g., structure).
   b. The specific ways these are communicated to individuals are many and exist at multiple levels.
   c. The communications that influence motivation may be contradictory.
3. The elements in the equation, namely the social context and children's motivation, as well as the mechanisms that connect them, change with development.
   a. Individuals develop, normatively and differentially.
   b. Contexts change, normatively and differentially.
   c. The mechanisms that mediate the effects of social factors on motivation may change with development as well.

which I will discuss in turn, are: (1) Children actively participate in the processes by which social factors shape their motivation; (2) the social context includes multiple dimensions and multiple levels; and (3) the elements in the equation, namely the social context and children's motivation, as well as the mechanisms that connect them, change with development.

Children Actively Participate in the Processes by Which Social Factors Shape Their Motivation

The first assumption simply alerts researchers to the fact that between the two phenomena that they wish to connect – that is, between social forces and children's motivation – is an active participating individual, the child. The first major implication is the idea that social relationships and interactions are perceived and interpreted by children, and it is these interpretations that in turn diminish or bolster their motivation. The second major implication is the idea that children are also active in provoking reactions from the social context.

Children as Participants

Common to most theories of motivation is the assumption that children actively interpret their social interactions and attempt to discover what these interactions reveal about themselves and about how the social world works. These are not usually considered to be fleeting, situation-specific perceptions, but instead to consist of experiences that accumulate and become organized as sets or systems of beliefs. In fact, children seem to bring preconceived notions (sometimes referred to as biases or styles) with them into many situations. These contribute greatly to children's experiences of social interactions and may even override concurrent opposing situational cues.

Theories differ with regard to the perceptions and interpretational processes they postulate as mediating the relationship between social interactions and children's motivation. The chapters in this volume provide excellent examples of a variety of theoretical perspectives. Grounded in attribution theory, Graham's work begins with a child who is aware of and busily interpreting cues from social partners about the *causes* of performance, such as ability and effort, or about the *intentionality* of negative acts. This strong theoretical approach has allowed for a well-guided search for the kinds of social interactions and cues that may communicate causal information to children. In her earlier work, Graham (1984) has examined the subtle effects of emotional cues (i.e., anger and pity) on causal attributions with the perhaps surprising finding that following failure, teacher anger communicates to the child that a controllable cause, such as lack of effort, was responsible for the outcome, whereas a sympathetic reaction can lead the child to infer that an uncontrollable cause, such as ability, was responsible. In Chapter 5 of this volume, Graham uses an attributional analysis to suggest hypotheses about the patterns of parental praise and blame that are likely to communicate to children the intentionality of negative acts.

In Cantor and Sanderson's work, the active adolescent is also depicted clearly. According to these authors, although adolescents generally take on the life tasks assigned by their cultural and subcultural groups, each adolescent nevertheless creates his or her own set of goals within those life tasks, and these goals guide the specific strategies used to work on the tasks. For example, within the general culturally assigned task of social dating, Cantor and Sanderson (Chapter 7, this volume) examine how different goals (e.g., establishing identity versus intimacy) influence the kinds of dating relationships that adolescents seek out and how they behave within those relationships.

In Pomerantz and Ruble's work, the active individual is also clearly present – in this case, the child experiencing him- or herself as incompetent, or forming high standards, or depending on external approval. This view of the child's inner workings led to a differentiated view of the social contextual dimensions of parenting and teaching. One of Pomerantz and Ruble's greatest contributions has been the careful analysis of a dimension sometimes referred to as "control," which is typically considered to range from permissiveness to restrictiveness. Predictions about the effects of this dimension seem contradictory, because two different strands of research lead to two different conclusions about its effects on motivation. According to learned helplessness theories, low parental control is detrimental because noncontingency produces helplessness and passivity in children. In contrast, researchers studying intrinsic motivation conclude that high parental control is harmful to children's motivation because it undermines their intrinsic interest in activities.

Pomerantz and Ruble (Chapter 6, this volume) suggest one solution to this problem when they distinguish two aspects of the dimension "permissiveness to restrictiveness." They separate one aspect "in the form of rules and standards . . . central to children's healthy functioning as it provides children with information about how to meet adult standards and engage in appropriate behavior" from a second aspect that "communicates to the individual being regulated that his or her actions do not stem from the self, but instead are the consequences of external pressures, and that he or she is not capable of controlling the surrounding environment" (Chapter 6, this volume).

A similar distinction has been introduced by the originators of cognitive evaluation theory (Deci & Ryan, 1985; Ryan, 1982), and we have also adapted it for use in our own work (Skinner & Wellborn, 1994). Cognitive evaluation theory states that children have a need to be both competent, or effective in their interactions with the environment, *and* autonomous, or self-determined in their goals and actions (Deci & Ryan, 1985). From this perspective, permissive versus restrictive is not a useful bipolar dimension, because one pole of the dimension – namely, permissiveness – should be beneficial to autonomy because it allows children freedom, whereas the other pole of the dimension – namely, restrictiveness – should be beneficial to competence because it provides consistency and contingency.

However, beginning with the child's perspective, and asserting that children need support for both autonomy *and* competence, it becomes clear that permissiveness versus restrictiveness actually combines two different dimensions. If permissiveness, or freedom, supports autonomy then its opposite (which undermines autonomy) is not restrictiveness, or firm limit-setting, but instead is *coercion*. And, if the structure of restrictiveness supports the experience of competence, then its opposite, which can produce helplessness, is not permissiveness but *chaos*. According to this perspective, children need both freedom (in order to exercise autonomy) *and* structure (in order to develop competence). Of course, if authoritative parenting is high on structure *and* autonomy support, then they can't really be opposite poles of the same dimension.

Children as Initiators

A second implication of the notion that children are active participants in the social interactions and relationships that shape their motivation is the idea that children, through their own characteristics and behaviors, *provoke* reactions from the social context. When children are passive, bored, angry, aggressive, or anxious, then social partners – including parents, peers, and teachers – respond to these cues (e.g., Skinner & Belmont, 1993).

Social reactions typically magnify initial individual differences, for better or for worse (Kindermann & Skinner, 1992). Aggressive children provoke more hostile reactions from peers and adults. Rebellious children provoke more coercion and arbitrary limit-setting from teachers. Anxious children solicit more help and are awarded easier tasks and more pity. Children with low motivation select peers who are likewise low in engagement (Kindermann, 1993). Children who are already highly enthusiastic and interested receive more autonomy support and more challenging tasks from teachers (Skinner & Belmont, 1993).

The picture that Cantor and Sanderson paint of adolescent social dating suggests an even more active role for the individual. For example, adolescents who have self-focused identity goals actually tend to seek out or create multiple, shorter-lasting, more superficial dating relationships. In fact, Cantor and Sanderson (Chapter 7, this volume) argue that adolescents have a proclivity to structure their daily lives so that they afford pursuit of their self-chosen goals and maximize the effectiveness of the strategies in their own repertoire. In the area of social dating, it would be reasonable to hypothesize that the reactions of social partners might also magnify an adolescent's initial goal orientation. If an adolescent is self-focused and wants to use social dating as a means of exploration, he or she will likely seek out like-minded adolescents who will encourage these goals. Or, if the adolescent hooks up with adolescents who desire more intimacy, the behavior of the self-directed adolescent (i.e., engaging in multiple, more superficial relationships) would be likely to drive away partners who could potentially teach the adolescent about the possibilities and values of intimacy.

Reactions that magnify individual differences are typical. However, it would be useful if researchers could not only document the reciprocal role of the child in shaping the social context, but also search out "unnatural"

but developmentally corrective *compensatory* reactions from social partners. Who are the teachers who know how to provide autonomy support to
oppositional or reactive children? Who are the parents who can support an
anxious child in challenging situations? What can interventions do to foster these compensatory social relationships, which may help to prevent the
"motivationally poor" from becoming poorer? Research exploring these
questions will allow a fuller understanding of the active role individuals
play in their own motivational development.

One controversial, but potentially interesting, way of characterizing the
full nature of children's active role in shaping their motivation is the concept
of *psychological needs*. Analogous to the concept of physiological needs of
hunger and thirst, psychological needs refer to the experiences children require for their healthy psychological development. These needs, which are
hypothesized to be inborn and innate – a part of "human nature" – lead children to seek out opportunities for their fulfillment, to respond with joy and
enthusiasm to opportunities that exercise them, and to become despondent
and disaffected when placed in environments that discourage them.

Proponents of the notion of needs often refer to them as sources of children's intrinsic motivation. For example, in 1959, White reviewed evidence
that children come with an innate need to experience themselves as effective in their interactions with the environment. The concept of *effectance
motivation* underlies many theories of motivation today (e.g., Harter, 1978)
and is one explanation for the strong motivational consequences of perceived competence and control (Skinner, 1995). Other motivational theories
suggest that children also are born with the need to experience themselves
as autonomous (Deci & Ryan, 1985) and as connected to others (Ainsworth,
1979, 1989). Recent motivational perspectives suggest that all three needs
may be sources of children's motivation (Connell & Wellborn, 1991; Deci
& Ryan, 1985).

Needs theories place the ultimate source of motivation inside children
and so, in some sense, assign a relatively smaller role to social factors. According to this perspective, children – even infants – do not require social
contexts to socialize them to desire achievement or affiliation; children are
born with these desires. These theories suggest that children's innate needs
dictate the kinds of experiences that contexts must provide if they are to allow children the opportunity to "motivate themselves." Needs, in a very real
way, dictate the possible roles and routes for social partners in shaping children's motivation. In this sense, needs theories assign more power to individuals than do theories that suggest that sources of motivation are external
to the child.

The Social Context Includes
Multiple Dimensions and Multiple Levels

A focus on the active individual, which allows researchers to work "backward" from children's experience to analyze the kinds of social interactions that are expected to influence them, also produces a more differentiated view of the social context and its dimensions. From previous experimental work, it is clear that a strong theoretical orientation that specifies both the experience of the child and its general antecedents is extremely useful in this analysis. However, from the early global work on parenting comes the suggestion that careful thought is needed to determine how some of these theoretical dimensions then operate – not in the lab, but in interactions in the real world.

Social Contextual Dimensions

A focus on the child's experience provides a bridge between social factors and motivational outcomes, but it is only a first step in specifying the variety of pathways through which social contexts and interactions in everyday life can shape motivation. An important next step is to identify (usually theoretically) the general contextual dimensions that are expected to shape children's experiences, and then to figure out how these would be manifest in specific social contexts, such as schools, family homes, or dating relationships.

Motivational theories currently seem strong in their capacity to specify theoretically the general contextual dimensions that influence specific experiences. For example, if the target is children's experience of themselves as self-determining, the general contextual dimension referred to as *autonomy support versus coercion* can be identified as central in allowing (or not allowing) children opportunities to be self-determining (Deci & Ryan, 1985; Grolnick & Ryan, 1989; Ryan, 1982). Theoretically, this dimension describes the extent to which the social context allows children freedom and respects their wishes and desires as opposed to attempting to control, manipulate, or force them into complying with someone else's agenda.

In a parallel fashion, theories that are based on children's experience of themselves as competent generally conclude that a contextual dimension often referred to as *structure versus chaos* is central in providing opportunities for children to experience themselves as effective (Connell & Wellborn, 1991; Skinner, 1991, 1995). This dimension describes the extent to which social contexts are consistent and contingent, and the extent to which these contexts provide information about the pathways for reaching desired outcomes and avoiding undesired outcomes as well as support children in their attempts to follow those pathways.

Also clear are the theoretical dimensions that provide children opportunities to experience themselves as related, connected, or belonging (Ainsworth, 1979, 1989; Connell & Wellborn, 1991; Deci & Ryan, 1985). These opportunities are usually captured by the dimension of *warmth and involvement versus hostility and neglect,* and refer to the extent to which social partners communicate affection and caring versus dislike and rejection, and the extent to which they are emotionally and physically available versus emotionally distant or physically absent.

Social Interactions

In contrast to the clarity of these theoretical dimensions is the difficulty of determining the multiplicity of social avenues through which they are communicated to children. For example, when considering how children can be "coerced" by social contexts, it becomes clear that virtually limitless routes are available, both intentional and unintentional. Studies have documented that seemingly trivial word choices such as "should" and "you better" can rob children of their perceived freedom (Deci, Driver, Hotchkiss, et al., in press). At the opposite end of the spectrum, seemingly vast ingrained social patterns, such as gender role stereotypes, can constrain children from acting on their actual desires and interests (Pomerantz & Ruble, Chapter 6, this volume).

Research programs have been painstakingly tracing the many and varied pathways through which broad social contextual dimensions such as involvement, structure, and autonomy support make their way into children's daily lives. They focus on how experiences of belongingness, abandonment, control, helplessness, self-determination or "pawn-dom" are co-constructed by the child and his or her social partners in the contexts of the real world. The recognition that the social context has many levels allows researchers to examine a wide variety of social partners and their proxies – in rules, materials, physical space, time constraints, schedules, and curricula. Researchers attempt to determine what these partners actually do to, with, or for children. How do children interpret these interactions? What do children take away from them?

Not surprisingly, this orientation has led to more detailed, process-oriented observations, including studies by contributors to this volume (see Dweck, Chapter 10, this volume; Graham, Chapter 5, this volume;

and Pomerantz & Ruble, Chapter 6, this volume; e.g., Dweck, Davidson, Nelson, et al., 1978) and others (e.g., Hokoda & Fincham, 1995; Pintrich & Blumenfeld, 1985). These observations are complemented by analyses of children's interpretations of their interactions. Such research programs are beginning to produce a sequential view of how interactive and reciprocal processes might unfold. For example, in Graham's research, the process begins with parents whose interpretations of social interactions are colored by a blaming, accusatory bias and children who perhaps are a bit more active temperamentally. These parents mete out harsh, seemingly arbitrary punishment to their children, accompanied by blame; this pattern is probably unmitigated by children's excuses or explanations. As a result, children experience the world as hostile and begin to interpret even ambiguous social acts as hostile, ignoring contradictory cues. In turn, these children react to peers with aggression and retaliation, and provide no explanations. This turns out to be an effective strategy for provoking aggression and retaliation even from originally nonaggressive peers. If this strategy is enacted in school, it can also provoke anger, blame, and harsh limit-setting from otherwise supportive teachers. Consequently, the child concludes that the world is indeed a very hostile place.

Interaction Among Contextual Dimensions

An additional challenge to motivational theories stems from the fact that children's motivation is shaped by many experiences and that the social contextual interactions that support these experiences may, in combination, be contradictory. In trying to support children in one way, people within the social context may inadvertently undermine some other aspect of children's experience that itself has an effect on motivation. The possibility of trade-offs and unintended side effects has been brought to the attention of researchers through application-oriented research and interventions.

The three theoretical dimensions described earlier can provide examples of how challenging it can be to provide children with optimal support for motivation – in this case, an optimal combination of involvement, structure, and autonomy support. Intrinsic motivation theorists have pointed out that too much structure can unintentionally become coercive, when children experience the provision of information about strategies as pressure to enact them. Similarly, too much parental involvement can become intrusive as children attempt to establish their own goals and exercise their own competencies. Conversely, too much autonomy support can be experienced as chaotic or negligent if children wish for more guidance and closeness.

At this point, I do not believe that the end poles of any of these dimensions are necessarily defined by the other dimensions; that is, I do not believe that "too much" structure becomes coercion. However, I do hold that when parents and teachers attempt to provide children with involvement, structure, or autonomy support, they should also be aware of the effects of their behavior on the other dimensions as well. If adults focus only on one dimension in promoting motivation, they may end up inadvertently undermining a complementary source.

Alternatively, social contexts can be contradictory because they consist of multiple social partners, each with their own agendas, demands, and reactions to children's behavior. For example, Cantor and Sanderson point out that "Adolescents receive multiple, and at times conflicting, messages from friends, parents, and society about appropriate rules for dating and sexual behavior" (Chapter 7, this volume). Even within the peer context, adolescents may experience conflicting demands as when, for example, friends resent the time taken by new romantic relationships, or romantic partners attempt to sever old friendship ties (Zimmer-Gembeck, 1998).

Development and Social Influences on Motivation

For the most part, the study of children's motivation and its social antecedents has been conducted by personality and social psychologists from a perspective that emphasizes individual differences. Developmentalists seemed largely content with the important task of documenting normative developmental changes in cognitive, perceptual, and social processes connected to motivation, such as changes in the use of causal schemes, social comparison information, or perceptions of one's own ability (e.g., H. Heckhausen, 1982, 1984).

Relatively recently, however, some theorists have attempted to bring together these lines of work (e.g., Connell & Wellborn, 1991; Harter, 1978; Skinner, 1995). These theorists suggest to individual-difference researchers that the elements they have been studying (namely, the social context and children's motivation), as well as the mechanisms that connect them, change with development. They also suggest to developmentalists that some of the normative changes they are studying may in some sense open the door to new sources of social influences on individual differences in children's motivation.

The Developing Person

If one answer to the riddle of social influences on motivation begins with the understanding of children's interpretations of social interactions, then changes in how these social interactions are processed should inform the study of social contributors. Excellent examples of this work can be found in the study of developmental changes in how causal information is processed, and how this affects the kind of social cues that lead to attributions at different ages (e.g., Graham, Chapter 5, this volume). Recently, reviews have appeared that attempt to describe the developmental changes that influence children's motivation, for example, their achievement motivation (Eccles, Wigfield, & Schiefele, 1998) or their perceptions of control (Skinner, 1995).

As yet, surprisingly little has been studied about how social context communications are experienced by children of different ages. It is obvious, for example, that the same behaviors that communicate parental love to infants (e.g., cuddling, nuzzling) are inappropriate expressions of warmth for older children. This common knowledge has resulted in assessments of social factors that are developmentally appropriate; consequently, when assessing the same construct (e.g., limit-setting) at different ages, psychologists should examine different behaviors. However, this methodology also prevents the direct examination of developmental differences in the kinds of social interactions that communicate motivational supports to children (Kindermann & Skinner, 1992). How are warmth and affection best communicated to adolescents? What is the best way to provide structure for infants? How can parents support the autonomy of 2-year-olds? These questions must be answered in the construction of developmentally adapted interventions to improve children's motivation.

Development will also continue to be a theme in individual-differences work on motivation as researchers attempt to trace the origins of individual differences. If some children come to social interactions with attributional biases or preferred goals and strategies, developmentalists already want to know about the history of experiences that contributed to these individual differences. Clear examples of how a cumulative history of interactions can produce a bias that shapes future interactions can be found in Pomerantz and Ruble's discussion (Chapter 6, this volume) of how early styles of interpretation lead to later vulnerability when negotiating transitions. Likewise, Graham (Chapter 5, this volume) makes clear predictions about how children's early interactions with parents who blame can lead to later biases that themselves create more hostile interactions, this time with peers.

The "Developing" Context

In considering social influences on motivation, it is also possible to imagine how contexts can themselves undergo both normative and individual change over time. For example, Pomerantz and Ruble (Chapter 6, this volume) describe how normative school transitions result in age-graded opportunities and demands. Normatively, because of regular shifts in classroom structure during middle school and junior high school, students have less frequent and less intense contact with teachers, so the level of teacher involvement with students normatively declines during adolescence (Eccles, Midgley, Wigfield, et al. 1993; Roeser, Midgley, & Urdan, 1996). As another example, in typical classrooms in the United States, the basis of student feedback changes from evaluations based on participation and effort to evaluations based on successful completion of academic tasks. This normative shift changes the source of contingencies that shape children's perceived control from teacher behavior to academic performance (Skinner, Zimmer-Gembeck, & Connell, 1995, in press).

Contexts are also instrumental in shaping differential development by providing different opportunities, expectations, demands, and translations for different people. Pomerantz and Ruble are examining these processes in girls; Graham examines their effects on African American children, especially boys.

Mechanisms of Development

The processes that mediate between social factors and children's motivation may themselves change with age. Because mechanisms are usually the last aspect of a process to be studied, relatively little is known empirically about this possibility. However, whenever these processes have been examined directly, evidence has been found to support the notion that mediators "develop" or at least change with development. It makes sense to include the possibility in future research.

For example, one social factor that influences children's interest and persistence in difficult tasks is the provision of help. An understanding of the developmental course of children's interpretation of parent help (e.g., H. Heckhausen, 1984; J. Heckhausen, 1988) suggests that at very young ages, before the age of 2, children's motivation for challenging tasks is augmented by adult provision of help. However, after children form a conception of personal competence based on individual performance, adult help interferes with motivation.

Another example can be found in our own work on perceived control as a mediator of the effects of social context (interactions with teachers) on children's engagement in the classroom. As part of a longitudinal study, we have detected developmental shifts in the aspects of perceived control that appear to regulate children's motivation (Skinner, Zimmer-Gembeck, & Connell, 1995, in press). In the third grade, for example, a belief in powerful others as causes of school success and failure undermines children's engagement. However, by the seventh grade, the aspect of perceived control most detrimental to engagement changes to low perceptions of ability. As these mediators change, the aspects of the social context that are central predictors of motivation change as well. Corresponding to beliefs in powerful others, the primary predictor of the development of engagement in third grade is interactions with teachers (specifically the provision of structure and involvement). By seventh grade, however, when perceived ability is the primary regulator of motivation, children's own academic performance becomes a more central predictor of motivation in school. In sum, the assumption that the child, the social context, and the mechanisms that connect them change with age can set the stage for a more detailed empirical examination of how these developmental shifts may unfold.

Conclusion

The goal of this chapter was to suggest strategies that may aid researchers in the exploration of the social factors that contribute to children's motivation. Three general principles, as well as past research on the topic, have been used as a basis for these suggestions. Taken together, they paint a picture of children who are active participants in the social interactions that shape their motivation. Children can be seen as initiating, interpreting, and provoking interactions with social partners. A strong theoretical perspective on how these interpretations (e.g., experiences of self-determination or helplessness) influence children's motivation then allows researchers to move "backward" to an identification of the broad dimensions of social interactions (i.e., autonomy support or chaos) that are likely to influence children's interpretations. As a next step, researchers can try to analyze the multiple pathways through which social partners – and other aspects of the social context, such as rules, materials, and assigned tasks – may communicate these dimensions to children.

As researchers take each of these steps, their increasing awareness of the possibility that these processes are developmental can lead them to expand their research programs in several directions. They may continue to investigate the developmental antecedents of individual differences in children's style of interpreting social interactions. They may explore how normative developments in children's processing of motivationally relevant information could change with age. They may study age differences in how children experience communications of motivational supports (such as warmth and freedom). They may analyze how normative changes in children's treatment by schools and parents have an impact on children's motivation. They may examine whether the mechanisms that connect social context and child motivation themselves develop.

The exciting research programs described in Chapters 5, 6, and 7 indicate that results in many of these areas of study will soon be forthcoming. I would like to end my commentary by suggesting that the focus on social contributors to motivation also points the way to a new challenge in this area: a focus on the social contributors to these social contributors. When some sort of catalog of the social factors that shape children's motivation has been assembled, researchers will be able to provide parents and teachers with a rough map of the pathways through which they can support children's motivation.

However, researchers will then want to know how they can support parents and teachers in their efforts to support children. Why do some teachers support autonomy? Why are some parents chaotic? Why do some teachers stereotype children by race and by sex? How do some parents manage to magnify their children's strengths and still compensate for their weaknesses? Many theories assume that the prime determinant of parent or teacher style of interaction with children is the personality of the parent or teacher. Many interventions assume that parents and teachers lack knowledge, and that once informed of the results of research, they will be better able to provide motivationally friendly environments. Some developmental theories even assume that adults are doomed to recapitulate their own childhoods. However, it seems unlikely that the complex interplay that characterizes children in their attempts to interact successfully and satisfyingly with their social partners will turn out to be any less complex when the target is parents or teachers. Perhaps some of the general principles espoused in this chapter – about active individuals, complex contexts, and developmental change – may be useful in charting the new territory in this area of research.

References

Ainsworth, M. D. S. (1979). Infant-mother attachment. *American Psychologist, 34,* 932–937.

(1989). Attachments beyond infancy. *American Psychologist, 44,* 709–716.

Ames, C., & Ames, R. (1985). *Research on motivation in education. Vol. 2: The classroom milieu.* San Diego: Academic Press.

Cantor, N., & Sanderson, C. A. (1998). The functional regulation of adolescent dating relationships and sexual behavior: An interaction of goals, strategies, and situations. In J. Heckhausen & C. S. Dweck (Eds.), *Motivation and self-regulation across the life span.* New York: Cambridge University Press.

Connell, J. P., & Wellborn, J. G. (1991). Competence, autonomy and relatedness: A motivational analysis of self-system processes. In M. Gunnar & A. Sroufe (Eds.), *Minnesota Symposium on Child Psychology* (pp. 43–77). Chicago: University of Chicago Press.

Crandall, V. C., & Crandall, B. W. (1983). Maternal and childhood behaviors as antecedents of internal-external control perceptions in young adulthood. In H. M. Lefcourt (Ed.), *Research with the locus of control construct. Vol. 2: Developments and social problems* (pp. 53–103). New York: Academic Press.

Deci, E. L., Driver, R. E., Hotchkiss, L., Robbins, R. J., & Wilson, I. M. (in press). The relation of mothers' controlling vocalizations to children's intrinsic motivation. *Journal of Experimental Child Psychology.*

Deci, E. L., & Ryan, R. M. (1985). *Intrinsic motivation and self-determination in human behavior.* New York: Plenum Press.

Dweck, C. S. (Ed.). (1991). Self-theories and goals: Their role in motivation, personality, and development. In R. A. Dienstbier (Ed.), *Nebraska Symposium on Motivation, 1990.* Lincoln: University of Nebraska Press.

(1998). The development of early self-conceptions: Their relevance for motivational processes. In J. Heckhausen & C. S. Dweck (Eds.), *Motivation and self-regulation across the life span.* New York: Cambridge University Press.

Dweck, C. S., Davidson, W., Nelson, S., & Enna, B. (1978). Sex differences in learned helplessness: (II) The contingencies of evaluative feedback in the classroom and (III) An experimental analysis. *Developmental Psychology, 14,* 268–776.

Eccles, J. S., Midgley, C., Wigfield, A., Buchanan, C. M., Reuman, D., Flanagan, C., & MacIver, D. (1993). Development during adolescence: The impact of stage-environment fit on adolescents' experiences in schools and families. *American Psychologist, 48,* 90–101.

Eccles, J. S., Wigfield, A., & Schiefele, U. (1998). Motivation to succeed. In W. Damon (Series Ed.) and N. Eisenberg (Vol. Ed.), *Handbook of child psychology. Vol. 4: Socialization, personality, and social development* (pp. 1017–1095). New York: Wiley.

Graham, S. (1984). Communicating sympathy and anger to Black and White children: The cognitive (attributional) consequences of affective cues. *Journal of Personality and Social Psychology, 47,* 40–54.

(1998). Social motivation and perceived responsibility: Attributions and behavior of African American boys labeled as aggressive. In J. Heckhausen & C. S. Dweck (Eds.), *Motivation and self-regulation across the life span.* New York: Cambridge University Press.

Grolnick, W. S., & Ryan, R. M. (1989). Parent styles associated with children's self-regulation and competence: A social contextual perspective. *Journal of Educational Psychology, 81,* 143–154.

Harter, S. (1978). Effectance motivation reconsidered: Toward a developmental model. *Human Development, 21,* 36–64.

Heckhausen, H. (1982). The development of achievement motivation. In W. W. Hartup (Ed.), *Review of child development research* (Vol. 6, pp. 600–668). Chicago: University of Chicago Press.

(1984). Emergent achievement behavior: Some early developments. In M. Maehr (Ed.), *Advances in motivation and achievement* (pp. 1–32). Greenwich, CT: JAI.

Heckhausen, J. (1988). Becoming aware of one's competence in the second year: Developmental progression within the mother-child dyad. *International Journal of Behavioral Development, 11,* 305–326.

Hokoda, A., & Fincham, F. D. (1995). Origins of children's helpless and mastery achievement patterns in the family. *Journal of Educational Psychology, 87,* 375–385.

Kindermann, T. A. (1993). Natural peer groups as contexts for individual development: The case of children's motivation in school. *Developmental Psychology, 29,* 970–977.

Kindermann, T. A., & Skinner, E. A. (1992). Modeling environmental development: Individual and contextual trajectories. In J. B. Asendorpf & J. Valsiner (Eds.), *Framing stability and change: An investigation into methodological issues* (pp. 155–190). Newbury Park, CA: Sage.

Lefcourt, H. M. (1982). *Locus of control: Current trends in theory and research.* New York: Wiley.

Pintrich, P. R., & Blumenfeld, P. C. (1985). Classroom experience and children's self-perceptions of ability, effort, and conduct. *Journal of Educational Psychology, 77*(6), 646–657.

Pomerantz, E., & Ruble, D. (1998). The multidimensional nature of control: Implications for the development of sex differences in self-evaluation. In J. Heckhausen & C. S. Dweck (Eds.), *Motivation and self-regulation across the life span.* New York: Cambridge University Press.

Riksen-Walraven, J. M. (1978). Effects of caregiver behavior on habituation rate and self-efficacy in infants. *International Journal of Behavioural Development, 1,* 105–130.

Roeser, R., Midgley, C., & Urdan, T. C. (1996). Perceptions of the school psychological environment and early adolescents' psychological and behavioral functioning in school: The mediating role of goals and belonging. *Journal of Educational Psychology, 88,* 408–422.

Ryan, R. M. (1982). Control and information in the intrapersonal sphere: An extension of cognitive evaluation theory. *Journal of Personality and Social Psychology, 43,* 450–461.

Seligman, M. E. P. (1975). *Helplessness: On depression, development, and death.* San Francisco: Freeman.

Skinner, E. A. (1991). Development and perceived control: A dynamic model of action in context. In M. Gunnar & L. A. Sroufe (Eds.), *Minnesota symposium on child psychology* (pp. 167–216). Hillsdale, NJ: Erlbaum.

(1995). *Perceived control, motivation, and coping.* Beverly Hills, CA: Sage.

Skinner, E. A., & Belmont, M. J. (1993). Motivation in the classroom: Reciprocal effects of teacher behavior and student engagement across the school year. *Journal of Educational Psychology, 85,* 571–581.

Skinner, E. A., & Wellborn, J. G. (1994). Coping during childhood and adolescence: A motivational perspective. In D. Featherman, R. Lerner, & M. Perlmutter (Eds.), *Life-span development and behavior.* Hillsdale, NJ: Erlbaum.

Skinner, E. A., Zimmer-Gembeck, M. J., & Connell, J. P. (1995, March). *Individual trajectories of perceived control from third to seventh grade: Relations to children's engagement versus disaffection.* Poster presented at the Meetings of the Society for Research in Child Development, Indianapolis, IN.

Skinner, E. A., Zimmer-Gembeck, M. J., & Connell, J. P. (in press). Individual differences and the development of children's perceived control. *Monographs of the Society for Research in Child Development.*

Weisz, J. R. (1983). Can I control it? The pursuit of veridical answers across the life span. In P. B. Baltes & O. G. Brim, Jr. (Eds.), *Life-span development and behavior* (pp. 233–300). New York: Academic Press.

(1986). Understanding the development of the understanding of control. In M. Perlmutter (Ed.), *Minnesota Symposium on Child Psychology* (Vol. 18, pp. 219–278). New York: Academic Press.

White, R. W. (1959). Motivation reconsidered: The concept of competence. *Psychological Review, 66,* 297–333.

Zimmer-Gembeck, M. J. (1998). *Negotiation and reorganization of peer relationships during adolescence: The emergence of romantic relationships and quality of peer relationships.* Unpublished dissertation, Portland State University, Portland, OR.

PART THREE

Functional and Dysfunctional Control-Related Behavior in Childhood

9   Ruminative Coping with Depression

Susan Nolen-Hoeksema

Abstract

Most people have periods in which they become at least moderately depressed: they feel sad, they lose their motivation and interest in their usual activities, they slow down and are chronically fatigued, and so on. For most people, these periods last only a few days and their symptoms never become debilitating. For others, these periods last weeks or months, and their symptoms become worse with time. I suggest that the ways people initially try to regulate or cope with their symptoms of depression can affect the severity and duration of these symptoms. Specifically, people who have a ruminative style of responding to their initial symptoms of depression will have longer and more severe episodes of depressed mood than people who have more active, less ruminative response styles. A ruminative response style for depression is defined as the tendency to focus passively and repetitively on one's symptoms of depression and on the possible causes and consequences of those symptoms without taking action to relieve them. Ruminative responses to depression exacerbate and prolong periods of depression through at least three mechanisms. First, rumination enhances the negative effects of depressed mood on thinking, making depressive interpretations of events and negative memories more accessible and more likely to be used in ongoing deliberations about one's life. Second, rumination interferes with complex interpersonal problem-solving, in part because it enhances pessimistic, distorted thinking. Third, rumination inhibits people from engaging in everyday instrumental behaviors that could enhance their sense of control and lift their moods.

I present data from several laboratory and naturalistic studies supporting these arguments. Specifically, both laboratory and naturalistic studies have shown that people who tend to engage in ruminative responses to depression, or who are induced to ruminate while in a depressed mood, evidence longer and more severe periods of depressed mood than do people who do not ruminate. These studies also support the arguments that ruminative responses to depressed mood enhance negative thinking, interfere with complex interpersonal problem-solving, and interfere with the initiation of instrumental behaviors. Women tend to engage in ruminative responses to their depressed moods more than men do, and this may partially explain the greater rate of significant depressions in women compared to men. I discuss factors that might cause children or adolescents to develop a ruminative response style, and the links between the development of a ruminative response style and the emergence of gender differences in depression in early adolescence.

Ruminative Coping with Depression

Over the last twenty years, a large literature has emerged on how people cope with discrete, identifiable events in the environment (Carver, Scheier & Weintraub, 1989; Folkman & Lazarus, 1986; Moos & Billings, 1982). Two general categories of coping responses have been described: *Problem-focused* coping includes behaviors intended to solve concrete problems; *emotion-focused* coping includes a wide variety of behaviors and thoughts focused on the moods brought about by an event.

Problem-focused coping is often viewed as the most effective type of coping, at least as long as there is a controllable problem to be solved (Folkman, 1984; Moos & Billings, 1982). Some studies have found that persons who use active problem-solving coping strategies show lower levels of depression and anxiety both immediately after and long after experiencing a stressor (Billings & Moos, 1981; Mitchell, Cronkite, & Moos, 1983).

When no problem or event can be clearly linked to an individual's depressed mood, coping behaviors focused on relieving the depressed mood are considered appropriate (Folkman, 1984). The thrust of much of the coping literature has been that avoiding negative emotions aroused by an event is a maladaptive response (Aldwin & Revenson, 1987; Billings & Moos, 1981; Holahan & Moos, 1987). There is increasing evidence, however, that people who focus chronically on their negative moods, rather than engaging in structured problem-solving or using pleasant, reinforcing activities to distract themselves from their moods, are also at risk for prolonged and serious bouts of depression (Blaney, 1986; Ellis & Ashbrook, 1988; Ingram, 1990; Lewinsohn, Hoberman, Teri, et al., 1985; Musson & Alloy, 1988; Pyszczynski & Greenberg, 1987; Smith & Greenberg, 1981).

We have been investigating a specific style of self-focused coping, labeled the *ruminative coping style* (Nolen-Hoeksema, 1991). Ruminative responses to depression are behaviors and thoughts that passively focus one's attention on one's depressive symptoms and on the implications of these symptoms. Examples can include sitting alone thinking about how tired and unmotivated one feels, worrying that one's depression will interfere with one's job, and passively reviewing all the things wrong in one's life that might be contributing to the depression. People engaging in ruminative responses may worry about the causes and consequences of their depression, but they do not take action to change their situation, and they spend much of their time thinking about how bad they feel. In support of this distinction between ruminative responses and problem-solving, correlational studies have shown that people who have ruminative, self-focused responses are significantly less likely to engage in active, structured problem-solving (Carver, Scheier, & Weintraub, 1989; Nolen-Hoeksema, 1991). Rumination may be viewed as one form of state orientation or overcontrol, as discussed by Kuhl and Fuhrman (Chapter 1, this volume).

Ruminative responses to depression can be most clearly contrasted with distracting responses, defined as the purposeful turning of one's attention away from one's symptoms of depression onto pleasant or neutral activities. Effective distracting responses are engrossing and have a high probability of positive reinforcement to the person (Lewinsohn, 1974). Examples of distracting responses include engaging in an activity with friends, working on a hobby, or concentrating on one's work. Are people who use distracting responses simply avoiding their problems? We have found that people who use pleasant activities to lift their moods are more likely to engage in active problem-solving once their mood has lifted than do people with a more ruminative response style (Nolen-Hoeksema, Morrow, & Fredrickson, 1993; Nolen-Hoeksema, Parker, & Larson, 1994). Also, we have found no relationship between the tendency to use pleasant activities to lift a mood and the tendency to engage in reckless, dangerous activities (e.g., heavy drinking) in response to a stressor.

Ruminative responses may prolong depressed mood, and distracting responses relieve depressed mood, through at least three mechanisms (see also Lewinsohn, Hoberman, Teri, 1985; Musson & Alloy, 1988). First, because ruminative responses involve focusing on depressed mood and thinking about its implications, they make the negative thoughts and memories associated with, and primed by, the depressed mood more available (Blaney, 1986; Bower, 1981; Teasdale, 1985). This increases the likelihood that the depressed ruminator will make negative interpretations of current events, and have negative expectations for the future. This negative thinking feeds the depression. Second, ruminative responses interfere with complex problem-solving, again because they promote pessimistic thinking and impair concentration. In turn, because the individual's problems go unsolved, his or her depression is maintained. Third, ruminative responses interfere with instrumental behavior because they impair concentration and attention, and because they lead the individual to be more pessimistic about his or her ability to carry out tasks (Brockner & Hulton, 1978; Coyne, Metalsky, & Lavelle, 1980; Lewinsohn, Hoberman, Teri, et al., 1985; Musson & Alloy, 1988). In turn, decrements in instrumental behavior cause new problems for the individual, fueling his or her depression. In contrast, distracting activities interrupt the effects of depressed mood on thinking, and may provide direct positive reinforcement to the individual. The depressed mood can subside at least slightly, so if the individual then attempts to problem-solve, he or she can do so without the biasing effects of depressed mood on thinking and concentration.

Rumination and the Duration of Depressed Moods

Does rumination lead to longer periods of depressive symptoms, and distraction to shorter periods? Two methodological problems to be overcome in studies addressing this question are the need to control for the fact that more severely depressed people have more depressive symptoms to ruminate about, and the need to control for third variables that may affect both the tendency to ruminate and the duration of depressive symptoms. In a series of laboratory studies, we handled these problems by randomly assigning both moderately depressed subjects and comparison groups of nondepressed subjects to engage in rumination or distraction; we then observed the effects on their moods (Lyubomirsky & Nolen-Hoeksema, 1993; Lyubomirsky & Nolen-Hoeksema, 1995; Morrow & Nolen-Hoeksema, 1990; Nolen-Hoeksema & Morrow, 1993). In the rumination induction, subjects focused on their current feelings and personal characteristics. In the distraction induction, subjects focused on geographical locations and objects. We attempted to overcome the demand characteristics that often arise in studies of mood and thinking by convincing subjects that they were participating in a series of several unrelated experiments on thinking and imagination. We accomplished this by using an elaborate cover story, many filler tasks, and multiple experimenters.

In seven separate studies, the rumination task maintained or increased the depressed moods of the depressed subjects, and the distraction task led to significant decreases in depressed mood (Lyubomirsky & Nolen-Hoeksema, 1993, 1995; Morrow & Nolen-Hoeksema, 1990; Nolen-Hoeksema &

Morrow, 1993). In fact, depressed subjects who participated in the distraction condition showed decreases in depressed mood to a level similar to that in the nondepressed groups. In contrast, as we expected, the rumination and distraction tasks had no effect on the moods of the nondepressed subjects. This was because the rumination task was not inherently depression-inducing: The items in this task were rated as neutral in affective tone, as were the items in the distraction task. Moreover, I argue that rumination is detrimental only in the context of a depressed mood, because it works in large part by enhancing the effects of depressed mood on thinking and behavior.

These laboratory studies allowed us to control extraneous variables that might covary with the tendency to ruminate and with the severity and duration of depressed mood. However, these studies do not directly address the claim that individual differences in rumination and distraction help to explain individual differences in the duration and severity of naturally occurring depressive symptoms. We conducted three longitudinal, correlational studies to test this claim directly. The longitudinal design of these studies allowed us to use response styles to predict changes in levels of depressive symptoms over time, controlling for the severity of subjects' symptoms at the time we measured their response styles.

In the "diary" study, we asked seventy-nine subjects to track their moods and responses to these moods every day for a month (Nolen-Hoeksema, Morrow, Fredrickson, et al., 1993). (Subjects also tracked personal events other than moods, and therefore did not guess our primary interest in mood.) We found that most people were consistent in the types of responses they had to everyday depressed moods; that is, they appeared to have either a ruminative style or a distracting style of responding to their moods. Moreover, people with a more ruminative style had longer periods of depressed mood, even after we statistically controlled for the severity of their moods (for similar results, see Wood, Saltzberg, Neale, et al., 1990).

One alternative explanation for the results of the diary study, however, is that the tendency to ruminate and lengthy depressed moods are both the result of certain types of stressful events – perhaps uncontrollable, severely negative events. To rule out this alternative explanation, in our other naturalistic studies we have observed groups of people who faced a common, uncontrollable negative event. The 1989 earthquake that hit the San Francisco Bay Area was an uncontrollable, negative event. By chance, we were able to conduct one of the only prospective studies of people's reactions to a natural disaster (Nolen-Hoeksema & Morrow, 1991). Two weeks before the earthquake, we happened to have obtained measurements of 139 students' levels of depressive symptoms and response styles. We remeasured their depression levels 10 days and again 7 weeks after the earthquake. We also obtained information about the kinds of stress that subjects experienced concerning the earthquake (e.g., personal injury, damage to their homes) so that we could control for the different levels of stress subjects experienced. The analyses showed that subjects with a more ruminative, less distracting style of responding to their depressive symptoms before the earthquake were more depressed 10 days and again 7 weeks after the earthquake. This was true even after we statistically controlled for their levels of depressive symptoms before the earthquake, and for the amount of stress they experienced as a result of the earthquake. People who said they tend to focus on their feelings when they are down rather than engaging in activities to lift their moods subsequently showed more depressive symptoms after the earthquake, regardless of how distressed they were when the earthquake hit or how much damage and hardship the earthquake caused them.

Bereavement is another stressor that is uncontrollable and highly distressing. Most bereaved people experience at least some level of depression, and a substantial minority become clinically depressed (Osterweis, Solomon, & Green, 1984). However, large individual differences in the duration and severity of these symptoms. In structured interviews with people who lost a loved one to a terminal illness, we assessed levels of depressive symptoms, response styles, and several other psychosocial variables, one month and again six months following the loss (Nolen-Hoeksema, Parker, & Larson, 1994). Clinical psychologist interviewers assessed depression levels according to the Hamilton Rating Scale for Depression (Hamilton, 1960). This study also allowed us to investigate whether certain personality and environmental variables might account for the relationship between a ruminative response style and longer depressions. For example, perhaps subjects who are socially isolated or have poor relationships with others are both prone to ruminate and prone to depression. Or perhaps people who are dispositionally pessimistic tend to ruminate and tend to remain depressed. Or perhaps people who face many stressors in addition to the death of their loved one (e.g., job loss, divorce) have more to ruminate about and experience longer periods of depression.

We found that people with a more ruminative style of responding to their depressed moods at one month tend to be more depressed at six months (Nolen-Hoeksema, Parker, & Larson, 1994). This was true even after we statistically controlled not only for subjects' levels of depression at one month, but also for their perceived quality of their social support, dispositional pessimism, and stressors experienced in addition to the loss. The results of this study suggest that the ways people respond to their bereavement-related depressive symptoms predict how long these symptoms last, even after controlling for a host of third variables. Indeed, people's response styles appear to be better predictors of their adjustment to bereavement than are factors traditionally thought to be important to adjustment, such as people's past relationship to the deceased and their current level of social support.

In sum, several laboratory studies and longitudinal, correlational studies support the basic prediction that ruminative responses to depressed mood are associated with longer and more severe periods of depressive symptoms, and that distracting responses are associated with shorter and less severe periods of depressive symptoms. Laboratory studies have tested this prediction while maintaining experimental control over third variables, and correlational studies have tested the prediction in ecologically valid settings. The next question then is, "How does a ruminative response prolong and worsen depressed mood, and how does a distracting response relieve depressed mood?"

Effects of Rumination on Thinking, Behavior, and Problem-Solving

We have addressed this question in a series of laboratory studies that tested predictions about the effects of rumination and distraction on thinking, instrumental behavior, and problem-solving among depressed people. In these studies, depressed and nondepressed subjects underwent either the rumination or distraction induction described earlier. All subjects then completed some measure of negative thinking, interpersonal problem-solving skills, or willingness to engage in positive, reinforcing behaviors. Our predictions were that the depressed people who were made to ruminate would show more negative thinking, poorer problem-solving skills, and less motivation to engage in positive behaviors than would the depressed people who were made to distract. In contrast, the rumination and distraction tasks were expected to have no effects on the thinking, problem-solving, or behavior of the nondepressed subjects, because rumination must interact with an existing depressed mood in order to have its deleterious effects.

Our predictions were upheld. First, we found that the depressed subjects who were made to ruminate subsequently made more pessimistic, self-defeating attributions for hypothetical negative events and chose more depressed/distorted interpretations of events than did the depressed subjects who were made to distract or either of the nondepressed groups (Lyubomirsky & Nolen-Hoeksema, 1995). In contrast, the depressed subjects who were made to distract were no more pessimistic, negative, or distorted in their interpretations of hypothetical events than were the nondepressed groups. As predicted, the rumination and distraction inductions had no effect on the nondepressed groups. Second, the depressed subjects who were made to ruminate subsequently were more pessimistic about their futures than were the depressed subjects who were made to distract, or either of the nondepressed groups (Lyubomirsky & Nolen-Hoeksema, 1995; Pyszczynski, Hamilton, Herring, et al., 1989; Pyszczynski, Holt, & Greenberg, 1987). In contrast, the depressed subjects who were made to distract were as optimistic about their futures as the nondepressed subjects. These studies strongly suggest that the relationship between negative cognitions and depressed mood may be mediated by rumination and distraction. That is, depressed people who tend to ruminate (or who are made to ruminate in the context of an experiment) will demonstrate negative thinking, and depressed people who tend to distract (or who have been distracted in the context of an experiment) will not engage in negative thinking. Negative cognitions are likely to have a causal influence on the severity and duration of people's depressed mood. However, our studies, and studies by other researchers (Fennell & Teasdale, 1984; Persons & Miranda, 1992), clearly reveal a complex interplay between negative cognitions, depressed mood, and styles of responding to depressed mood.

In another set of studies (Lyubomirsky & Nolen-Hoeksema, 1993), we examined the effects of rumination and distraction on the views of depressed and nondepressed subjects concerning pleasant, mood-lifting activities (e.g., going out for coffee with a friend, playing a favorite sport). Although the depressed subjects who were made to ruminate said they knew that such activities would be enjoyable if they engaged in them, they rated themselves significantly less likely to engage in these activities if given the chance than did the depressed subjects who were made to distract, or either of the nondepressed groups. The depressed subjects in the distraction condition rated themselves as likely to engage in pleasant activities as the nondepressed groups rated themselves. Only a few minutes of distracting themselves encouraged the depressed subjects to engage in activities that would be likely to help lift their mood.

Finally, and most important, we have examined the effects of rumination and distraction on depressed and nondepressed subjects' skills at solving interpersonal problems often related to depressed mood (Lyubomirsky & Nolen-Hoeksema, 1995). We found that the depressed subjects who were made to ruminate subsequently gave poorer-quality solutions to hypothetical interpersonal problems than did the depressed subjects who were made to distract before doing the problem-solving task, or either of the nondepressed groups. The depressed/rumination group also made attributions for these problems that were more pessimistic than the attributions made by the other three groups. The depressed subjects who were made to distract were as optimistic in their attributions, and provided solutions to the problems that were as high in quality, as the nondepressed groups. It is clear, then, that when depressed people self-focus and ruminate in an attempt to solve their problems, they may generate poorer solutions to these problems than they are capable of generating.

Given that rumination appears to worsen or maintain depressed mood, and that it appears to contribute to negative thinking, poor problem-solving, and low motivation, why do some depressed people continue to ruminate? We have begun to examine the self-perpetuating properties of depressive rumination. In experimental studies, we have found that rumination appears to make depressed people feel they have greater insight into themselves and their problems (Lyubomirsky & Nolen-Hoeksema, 1993). In our studies, the depressed people who were made to ruminate subsequently rated themselves as more "in touch" with their own personalities, their current life situation, and "how the world works" than were the depressed people who were made to distract for a few minutes before rating their insightfulness. This sense of gaining insight may encourage rumination, as the depressed person seeks an understanding of and solution to his or her problems. Yet, as we know from our other studies, depressed people who ruminate actually are worse at problem-solving than are depressed people who distract themselves prior to problem-solving.

Gender Differences in Rumination and Depression

Among adults, women are about twice as likely as men to be depressed (Nolen-Hoeksema, 1990; Weissman & Klerman, 1977). This is true whether depression is indexed as a diagnosable unipolar mood disorder or as high levels of depressive symptoms on self-report questionnaires. This gender difference in depression appears to emerge sometime in early adolescence (Brooks-Gunn & Petersen, 1991; Nolen-Hoeksema, 1990; Nolen-Hoeksema & Girgus, 1994; Rutter, 1986).

In turn, both self-report and observational studies of adults have found that women are more likely than men to show the ruminative style of coping with depressive symptoms described above (Butler & Nolen-Hoeksema, 1994; Ingram, Cruet, Johnson, et al., 1988; Nolen-Hoeksema, Morrow, & Fredrickson, 1993; Nolen- Hoeksema, Parker, & Larson, 1994). For example, Nolen-Hoeksema and colleagues (1993) asked male and female college students to record their experiences of depressed mood, and what they did in response to these moods, each day for a month. Women were significantly more likely than men to report engaging in ruminative, self-focused responses to their depressed moods, such as thinking about how tired and alone they felt. In an observational laboratory study of college students that did not rely on subjects' self-reports, Butler and Nolen-Hoeksema (1994) found that among men and women in a sad mood, women were more likely to choose to focus on their mood.

Increasing evidence shows that among children and adolescents, girls are more likely than boys to show a ruminative style of responding to their depressed moods. Girgus and colleagues (Girgus, Nolen-Hoeksema, & Seligman, 1991) asked prepubescent children what they would do in response to distressing events (e.g., another child rejecting them). Girls were more likely than boys to endorse ruminative coping responses such as "think about what happened" and "go somewhere to be alone." Koenig and Juhasz (1991) administered the same instrument used to assess ruminative responses in the adult studies described above to male and female adolescents. The females were significantly more likely than the males to report using ruminative responses to cope with their depressed moods. Similarly, Compas and colleagues (Compas, Malcarne, & Fondacaro, 1988) found that adolescent girls were more likely than adolescent boys to use ruminative coping strategies in dealing with academic stressors.

Can gender differences in ruminative coping explain the emergence of gender differences in depression during adolescence? Probably not, because some studies indicate that girls are more likely than boys to have a ruminative coping style even before gender differences in depression emerge in adolescence (Girgus, Nolen-Hoeksema, & Seligman, 1991). Nolen-Hoeksema and Girgus (1994) suggest that girls' greater tendency toward an emotion-focused, passive, and ruminative style of coping interacts with certain challenges that girls face more often than boys in early adolescence.

What are the distress-inducing challenges that girls face more often than boys? Some clues have emerged from a recent study of adolescent worries (Nolen-Hoeksema, 1995). The subjects were 615 students in the sixth grade (69 males, 84 females), eighth grade (68 males, 73 females), and tenth grade (148 males, 165 females) in public schools. We asked these subjects about their tendencies to "worry" about a variety of specific topics. In four domains, girls reported worrying more than boys.

First, girls appear to worry more than boys about personal appearance. A large number of previous studies also show that girls dislike the physical changes their bodies undergo at puberty more than boys dislike their physical changes (Simmons & Blyth, 1987). In turn, girls' more negative body image appears to lead them to experience more periods of moderate depressive symptoms compared to boys (Allgood-Merten, Lewinsohn, & Hops, 1990; Teri, 1982).

Second, the girls in our study were concerned about personal safety. Other studies suggest that the rates of sexual abuse among girls increase substantially in early adolescence, and many abuse victims continue to be abused throughout their adolescent years (Russell, 1984). Girls are two to three times more likely than boys to be the victims of sexual abuse (Finkelhor, 1984). In turn, rape and sexual abuse are associated with greatly increased risk for depression, particularly in female victims, both shortly after the abuse and long after (Kilpatrick, Resick, & Veronen, 1981; Wirtz & Harrell, 1987).

Third, girls in our study were concerned about issues of personal worth and being a "good person." Beginning in early adolescence, girls may be presented with societal expectations that restrict their choices of careers and lifestyles and may find their accomplishments and talents undervalued relative to those of boys (Coleman, 1961; Gove & Herb, 1974; Rosen & Aneshensel, 1976; Simmons & Blyth, 1987). Parents' expectations for their daughters are lower, and they allow their daughters less independence relative to sons in early adolescence (Block, 1978; Eccles, Jacobs, & Harold, 1990; Simmons & Blyth, 1987). These expectations may leave many girls wondering how to achieve a sense of self-worth and competence, and with a concomitant vulnerability to distress.

Fourth, the girls in our study were concerned about a variety of issues having to do with interpersonal relationships. Although investment in interpersonal relationships can enrich the lives of both girls and boys, a number of theorists have argued that anyone who invests too much self-esteem in interpersonal relationships is at risk for depression (Chevron, Quinlan, & Blatt, 1978; Gove & Herb, 1974; Kessler & McLeod, 1984; Lenny, 1977). This may be because such relationships are not controllable. Maccoby (1990) has argued that the increase in interactions with the opposite sex that occurs in early adolescence as girls and boys begin dating is more distressing for girls than for boys because boys' interaction style is more aggressive and domineering than that of girls.

According to our study, the domains in which there are no gender differences in worries, or in which boys tend to worry more than girls, are domains in which it may be easier to exert control and thereby overcome worries. These domains included school problems, future careers, sports, and other hobbies or activities.

Girls, more than boys, face a set of biological and social challenges in adolescence that may contribute directly to frequent periods of distress. There are large individual differences in girls' reactions to these challenges, however. Nolen-Hoeksema and Girgus (1994) suggest that girls who enter early adolescence with a ruminative coping style are most at risk for developing serious depressions in reaction to challenges of this period.

This model suggests continuity between the gender differences in depression found in adolescents and the gender differences in depression found in adults, as many of the challenges that are more prevalent in the lives of adolescent girls continue to be more prevalent in the lives of adult women. In addition, both girls and boys who experience long or frequent periods of depression in adolescence are at risk for experiencing episodes in adulthood for at least two reasons. First, depression interferes with performance. Consequently, girls and boys who are depressed during much of their adolescence may undermine opportunities they would otherwise have to accomplish important goals (e.g., their low grades in high school may prevent them from getting into a good college). Unsatisfying careers or unfulfilled goals may then contribute to depressive episodes in adulthood (Carver & Scheier, 1990). Second, depressed mood appears to influence people's thinking to the extent that negative memories and interpretations of events are more available and influence decision-making (see Bower, 1981; Blaney, 1986). Girls and boys who are depressed often during adolescence may develop more negative self-concepts and make poorer decisions about important areas of their lives, putting them at risk for future depressions during adulthood.

Origins of Response Styles

Children may learn a ruminative style by modeling their parents, because they have not developed more active coping strategies, through the messages they receive from others, because they feel little control over their environment, or because they are physiologically overreactive to stress. First, some parents model a ruminative style (Compas, 1987; Krohne, 1979). Studies of children of clinically depressed parents, many of whom may have a ruminative response style, show that these children have problems in regulating their negative moods (Field, Sandberg, Garcia, et al., 1985; Zahn-Waxler, McKnew, Cummings, et al., 1984). For example, we (Nolen-Hoeksema, Wolfson, Mumme, et al., 1995) found that 5- to 7-year-old children of depressed mothers were more likely to show passive, helpless responses to frustration situations than were children of nondepressed mothers. Moreover, children whose mothers showed more ruminative styles of responding to depressed mood were more likely to have passive, helpless styles of responding to challenge.

Second, children might develop ruminative, passive styles because they have not been taught a repertoire of more adaptive strategies for handling negative affect, such as benign distraction or appropriate problem-solving (Baumrind, 1977; Cohn & Tronick, 1983; Kopp, 1982; Patterson, 1982; Shure & Spivack, 1978). In an important series of studies, Dweck found that children who became helpless in the face of frustration rather than remaining problem-focused also became mired in ruminative self-focus and negative affect (Dweck, Chapter 10, this volume). Higgins and Loeb (Chapter 3, this volume) suggest that poor self-regulatory skills, such as the tendency to fall into rumination, may develop in children whose caretakers are either hostile and rejecting or overprotective and intrusive. In support of this argument, our study of depressed and nondepressed mothers and their children found that mothers' styles of responding to their children when they were frustrated predicted children's problem-solving and affect-regulation skills (Nolen-Hoeksema, Wolfson, Mumme, et al., 1995). Specifically, we found that mothers who were intrusive, and did not allow their children to solve many of their own problems, did not teach their children to respond to negative affect by trying new approaches to a problem; they were unsupportive and critical when their children failed, and their children had poorer problem-solving skills and tended to become helpless and passive when upset.

Third, the literature on sex-role socialization suggests that parents' expectations of what types of emotional expression are appropriate for their male and female children may influence children's styles of affect regulation (Block, 1978). Parents seem particularly concerned that their sons not show feminine-stereotyped characteristics, such as displays of emotionality (Maccoby & Jacklin, 1974). Rather, boys are encouraged to "be strong" and "act like a little man." Sanctions against males showing depressive behaviors continue into adulthood. Siegel and Alloy (1990) found that depressed men were evaluated much more negatively by their roommates than were depressed women. The male tendency to engage in distracting responses to depressed mood may result, in part, from conformity to sanctions against emotionality in males. There is little evidence that adults explicitly reinforce passive, ruminative responses to distress in girls (Maccoby & Jacklin, 1974). Adults may simply not encourage distraction and mastery-oriented responses in girls as often as they do in boys. Pomerantz and Ruble (Chapter 6, this volume) found that parents grant more autonomy to boys than to girls; as a result, girls may feel that they have less control over their environment and, consequently, may turn to rumination.

In addition, because females often are told that they are naturally emotional, they may come to believe that their depressed moods are unavoidable and cannot be dismissed easily (see Nolen-Hoeksema, 1990). Or, because of sex-role socialization, females may be more likely than males to believe that ruminating will give them some secondary control over their negative circumstances (see Heckhausen & Schulz, Chapter 2, this volume) by providing them with insights about themselves and their emotions. Such beliefs decrease the probability that females will take action to distract themselves from their moods or to change their situation.

Fourth, our study of adolescent worries suggests that the issues that girls tend to worry more about than boys are personal appearance, being a good person, personal safety, and interpersonal relationships. These are domains in which it may be quite difficult for girls (or boys) to exert control and thereby reduce worry. In contrast, the domains in which there are no gender differences in worries, or in which boys tended to worry more than girls, including school problems, future careers, sports, and other hobbies or activities, are domains in which it may be easier to exert some control and thereby overcome worries. This result suggests that girls become caught in worrying, ruminative cycles of thought because the domains that concern them are ones in which it is difficult to problem-solve and to feel as though they have gained control.

Finally, biological factors may also play a role in the development of styles of responding to depressed mood. Some people appear to have greater physiological reactivity to stress than other people (Davidson & Fox, 1989; Depue & Monroe, 1986; Gottman & Levenson, 1988). More reactive children may find their negative emotional states more compelling, and thus may be more likely to focus on those states (Lewis & Michalson, 1983). If they frequently become upset when others do not, they may also begin to question their negative emotionality. Focusing on emotion and questioning it may develop into a ruminative style of responding to negative mood – at least in some people who are reactive.

These suggestions concerning the origin's of response styles are highly speculative and require empirical testing. The development of styles of affect regulation seems a particularly important area for future research.

Conclusions

I have argued that one determinant of the duration of a depressive episode is the type of responses individuals engage in when depressed. People who engage in ruminative responses when depressed tend to remain depressed and may become more severely depressed than people who try to distract themselves from their symptoms. Further, women's tendency to have a more ruminative response style than men may help to explain why they are more likely to be depressed and to report longer periods of depression than do men. Existing laboratory and field studies have supported these predictions. Much research remains to be done, however, and suggestions for future research have been given throughout this chapter.

The response styles theory represents a shift from a focus on the determinants of individual differences in the onset of depression to a focus on determinants of individual differences in the duration of depression. Even among people whose depressions appear to be attributable to similar causes, there appear to be large individual differences in the duration of depression (Windholz, Marmar, & Horowitz, 1985). A greater understanding of the reasons for protracted periods of depression will inform clinicians in their efforts to help depressed individuals manage their symptoms and avoid demoralization from the depression itself (Teasdale, 1985). Perhaps, then, those individuals can more effectively address the reasons they initially became depressed.

References

Aldwin, C. M., & Revenson, T. A. (1987). Does coping help? A reexamination of the relation between coping and mental health. *Journal of Personality and Social Psychology, 53,* 337–348.

Allgood-Merten, B., Lewinsohn, P. M., & Hops, H. (1990). Sex differences and adolescent depression. *Journal of Abnormal Psychology, 99,* 55–63.

Baumrind, D. (1977, March). *Socialization determinants of personal agency.* Paper presented at the meeting of the Society for Research in Child Development, New Orleans, LA.

Billings, A. G., & Moos, R. H. (1981). The role of coping responses and social resources in attenuating the stress of life events. *Journal of Behavioral Medicine, 4,* 157–189.

Blaney, P. H. (1986). Affect and memory: A review. *Psychological Bulletin, 99,* 229–246.

Block, J. H. (1978). Another look at sex differentiation in the socialization behaviors of mothers and fathers. In J. Sherman & F. Denmark (Eds.), *Psychology of women: Future directions of research* (pp. 29–87). New York: Psychological Dimensions.

Bower, G. H. (1981). Mood and memory. *American Psychologist, 36,* 129–148.

Brockner, J., & Hulton, A. J. B. (1978). How to reverse the vicious cycle of low self-esteem: The importance of attentional focus. *Journal of Experimental Social Psychology, 14,* 564–578.

Brooks-Gunn, J., & Petersen, A. C. (1991). Studying the emergence of depression and depressive symptoms during adolescence. *Journal of Youth and Adolescence, 20,* 115–119.

Butler, L. D., & Nolen-Hoeksema, S. (1994). Gender differences in depressed mood in a college sample. *Sex Roles, 30,* 331–346.

Carver, C. S., & Scheier, M. F. (1990). Origins and functions of positive and negative affect: A control-process view. *Psychological Review, 97,* 19–35.

Carver, C. S., Scheier, M. F., & Weintraub, J. K. (1989). Assessing coping strategies: A theoretically based approach. *Journal of Personality and Social Psychology, 56,* 267–283.

Chevron, E. S., Quinlan, D. M., & Blatt, S. J. (1978). Sex roles and gender differences in the expression of depression. *Journal of Abnormal Psychology, 87,* 680–683.

Cohn, J. F., & Tronick, E. Z. (1983). Three-months-old infants' reaction to simulated maternal depression. *Child Development, 54,* 185–193.

Coleman, J. S. (1961). *The adolescent society: The social life of the teenager and its impact on education.* New York: Free Press.

Compas, B. E. (1987). Coping with stress during childhood and adolescence. *Psychological Bulletin, 101,* 393–403.

Compas, B. E., Malcarne, V. L., & Fondacaro, K. M. (1988). Coping with stressful events in older children and young adolescents. *Journal of Consulting and Clinical Psychology, 56,* 405–411.

Coyne, J. C., Metalsky, G. I., & Lavelle, T. L. (1980). Learned helplessness as experimenter-induced failure and its alleviation with attentional redeployment. *Journal of Abnormal Psychology, 89,* 350–357.

Davidson, R. J., & Fox, N. A. (1989). Frontal brain asymmetry predicts infants' response to maternal separation. *Journal of Abnormal Psychology, 98,* 127–131.

Depue, R. A., & Monroe, S. M. (1986). Conceptualization and measurement of human disorder in life stress research: The problem of chronic disturbance. *Psychological Bulletin, 99,* 36–51.

Dweck, C. S. (1998). The development of early self-conceptions: Their relevance for motivational processes. In J. Heckhausen & C. S. Dweck (Eds.), *Motivation and self-regulation across the life span.* New York: Cambridge University Press.

Eccles, J. S., Jacobs, J. E., & Harold, R. D. (1990). Gender role stereotypes expectancy effects and parents' socialization of gender differences. *Journal of Social Issues, 46,* 183–201.

Ellis, H. C., & Ashbrook, P. W. (1988). Resource allocation model of the effects of depressed mood states on memory. In K. Fiedler & J. Forgas (Eds.), *Affect, cognition and social behavior* (pp. 1–21). Toronto, Canada: Hogrefe.

Fennell, M. J. V., & Teasdale, J. D. (1984). Effects of distraction on thinking and affect in depressed patients. *British Journal of Clinical Psychology, 23,* 65–66.

Field, T., Sandberg, D., Garcia, R., Vega-Lahr, N., Goldstein, S., & Guy, L. (1985).

Pregnancy problems, postpartum depression, and early mother-infant interactions. *Developmental Psychology, 21,* 1152–1156.

Finkelhor, D. (1984). Child sexual abuse: New theory and research. Beverly Hills, CA: Sage.

Folkman, S. (1984). Personal control and stress and coping processes: A theoretical analysis. *Journal of Personality and Social Psychology, 46,* 839–852.

Folkman, S., & Lazarus, R. S. (1986). Stress processes and depressive symptomatology. *Journal of Abnormal Psychology, 95,* 107–113.

Girgus, J. S., Nolen-Hoeksema, S., & Seligman, M. E. P. (1991, August). *Why do girls become more depressed than boys in early adolescence?* Paper presented at the American Psychological Association, San Francisco, CA.

Gottman, J. M., & Levenson, R. W. (1988). The social psychophysiology of marriage. In P. Noller & M. A. Fitzpatrick (Eds.), *Perspectives on marital interaction* (pp. 182–189). Clevedon, England: Multilingual Matters Ltd.

Gove, W., & Herb, T. (1974). Stress and mental illness among the young: A comparison of the sexes. *Social Forces, 53,* 256–265.

Hamilton, M. (1960). A rating scale for depression. *Journal of Neurology, Neurosurgery, & Psychiatry, 23,* 56–62.

Heckhausen, J., & Schulz, R. (1998). Developmental regulation in adulthood: Selection and compensation via primary and secondary control. In J. Heckhausen & C. S. Dweck (Eds.), *Motivation and self-regulation across the life span.* New York: Cambridge University Press.

Higgins, T., & Loeb, I. (1998). Development of regulatory focus: Promotion and prevention as ways of living. In J. Heckhausen & C. S. Dweck (Eds.), *Motivation and self-regulation across the life span.* New York: Cambridge University Press.

Holahan, C. J., & Moos, R. H. (1987). Personal and contextual determinants of coping strategies. *Journal of Personality and Social Psychology, 52,* 946–955.

Ingram, R. E. (1990). Self-focused attention in clinical disorders: Review and a conceptual model. *Psychological Bulletin, 107,* 156–176.

Ingram, R. E., Cruet, D., Johnson, B. R., & Wisnicki, K. S. (1988). Self-focused attention, gender, gender role, and vulnerability to negative affect. *Journal of Personality and Social Psychology, 55,* 967–978.

Kessler, R. C., & McLeod, J. D. (1984). Sex differences in vulnerability to undesirable life events. *American Sociological Review, 49,* 620–631.

Kilpatrick, D., Resick, P., & Veronen, L. (1981). Effects of a rape experience: A longitudinal study. *Journal of Social Issues, 37,* 105–122.

Koenig, L. J., & Juhasz, J. A. (1991, August). *Dealing with depression: Rumination and the perseveration of transient dysphoria among adolescents.* Paper presented at the American Psychological Association, San Francisco, CA.

Kopp, C. B. (1982). Antecedents of self-regulation: A developmental perspective. *Developmental Psychology, 18,* 199–214.

Krohne, H. W. (1979). Parental child-rearing behavior and the development of anxiety and coping strategies in children. In I. G. Sarason & C. D. Spielberger (Eds.), *Stress and anxiety* (Vol. 7, pp. 233–245). Washington, DC: Hemisphere.

Kuhl, J., & Fuhrmann, A. (1998). Decomposing self-regulation and self-control: The Volitional Components Inventory. In J. Heckhausen & C. S. Dweck (Eds.), *Motivation and self-regulation across the life span.* New York: Cambridge University Press.

Lenny, E. (1977). Women's self-confidence in achievement settings. *Psychological Bulletin, 84,* 1–13.

Lewinsohn, P. M. (1974). A behavioral approach to depression. In R. J. Friedman & M. M. Katz (Eds.), *The psychology of depression: Contemporary theory and research.* Washington, DC: Winston-Wiley.

Lewinsohn, P. M., Hoberman, H., Teri, L., & Hautzinger, M. (1985). An integrative theory of depression. In S. Reiss & R. Bootzin (Eds.), *Theoretical issues in behavior therapy* (pp. 331–359). New York: Academic Press.

Lewis, M., & Michalson, L. (1983). *Children's emotions and moods.* New York: Plenum Press.

Lyubomirsky, S., & Nolen-Hoeksema, S. (1993). Self-perpetuating properties of depressive rumination. *Journal of Personality and Social Psychology, 65,* 339–349.

    (1995). Effects of self-focused rumination on negative thinking and interpersonal problem solving. *Journal of Personality and Social Psychology, 69,* 176–190.

Maccoby, E. E. (1990). Gender and relationships: A developmental account. *American Psychologist, 45,* 513–520.

Maccoby, E. E., & Jacklin, C. N. (1974). *The psychology of sex differences.* Stanford, CA: Stanford University Press.

Mitchell, R. E., Cronkite, R. C., & Moos, R. H. (1983). Stress, coping, and depression among married couples. *Journal of Abnormal Psychology, 92,* 433–448.

Moos, R. H., & Billings, A. G. (1982). Conceptualizing and measuring coping resources and processes. In L. Goldberger & S. Breznitz (Eds.), *Handbook of stress: Theoretical and clinical aspects* (pp. 212–230). New York: Free Press.

Morrow, J., & Nolen-Hoeksema, S. (1990). Effects of responses to depression on the remediation of depressive affect. *Journal of Personality and Social Psychology, 58,* 519–527.

Musson, R. F., & Alloy, L. B. (1988). Depression and self-directed attention. In L. B. Alloy (Ed.), *Cognitive processes in depression* (pp. 193–220). New York: Guilford Press.

Nolen-Hoeksema, S. (1990). *Sex differences in depression.* Stanford, CA: Stanford University Press.

    (1991). Responses to depression and their effects on the duration of depressive episodes. *Journal of Abnormal Psychology, 100,* 569–582.

    (1995). Gender differences in coping with depression across the life span. *Depression, 3,* 81–90.

Nolen-Hoeksema, S., & Girgus, J. S. (1994). The emergence of gender differences in depression during adolescence. *Psychological Bulletin, 115,* 424–443.

Nolen-Hoeksema, S., & Morrow, J. (1991). A prospective study of depression and posttraumatic stress symptoms after a natural disaster: The 1989 Loma Prieta earthquake. *Journal of Personality and Social Psychology, 61,* 115–121.

———— (1993). The effects of rumination and distraction on naturally occurring depressed moods. *Cognition and Emotion, 7,* 561–570.

Nolen-Hoeksema, S., Morrow, J., & Fredrickson, B. L. (1993). Response styles and the duration of episodes of depressed mood. *Journal of Abnormal Psychology, 102,* 20–28.

Nolen-Hoeksema, S., Parker, L., & Larson, J. (1994). Ruminative coping with depressed mood following loss. *Journal of Personality and Social Psychology, 67,* 92–104.

Nolen-Hoeksema, S., Wolfson, A., Mumme, D., & Guskin, K. (1995). Helplessness in children of depressed and nondepressed mothers. *Developmental Psychology, 31,* 377–387.

Osterweis, M., Solomon, F., & Green, M. (Eds.). (1984). *Bereavement: Reactions, consequences, and care.* Washington, DC: National Academy Press.

Patterson, G. R. (1982). *A social learning approach. Vol. 3: Coercive family process.* Eugene, OR: Castalia Publishing Co.

Persons, J. B., & Miranda, J. (1992). Cognitive theories of vulnerability to depression: Reconciling negative evidence. *Cognitive Therapy and Research, 16,* 485–502.

Pomerantz, E., & Ruble, D. (1998). A multidimensional perspective of social control: Implications for the development of sex differences in self-evaluation and depression. In J. Heckhausen & C. S. Dweck (Eds.). *Motivation and self-regulation across the life span.* New York: Cambridge University Press.

Pyszczynski, T., & Greenberg, J. (1987). Self-regulatory perseveration and the depressive self-focusing style: A self-awareness theory of reactive depression. *Psychological Bulletin, 201,* 122–138.

Pyszczynski, T., Hamilton, J., Herring, F., & Greenberg, J. (1989). Depression self-focused attention and the negative memory bias. *Journal of Personality and Social Psychology, 57,* 351–357.

Pyszczynski, T., Holt, K., & Greenberg, J. (1987). Depression, self-focused attention, and expectancies for positive and negative future life events for self and others. *Journal of Personality and Social Psychology, 52,* 994–1001.

Rosen, B. C., & Aneshensel, C. S. (1976). The chameleon syndrome: A social psychological dimension of the female sex role. *Journal of Marriage and the Family, 38,* 605–617.

Russell, D. E. H. (1984). *Sexual exploitation.* Beverly Hills, CA: Sage Library of Social Research.

Rutter, M. (1986). The developmental psychopathology of depression: Issue and perspectives. In M. Rutter, C. E. Izard, & P. B. Read (Eds.), *Depression in young people.* New York: Guilford Press.

Shure, M. B., & Spivack, G. (1978). *Problem-solving techniques in child rearing.* San Francisco: Jossey-Bass.

Siegel, S. J., & Alloy, L. B. (1990). Interpersonal perceptions and consequences of depressive–significant other relationships: A naturalistic study of college roommates. *Journal of Abnormal Psychology, 99,* 361–373.

Simmons, R. G., & Blyth, D. A. (1987). *Moving into adolescence: The impact of pubertal change and school context.* New York: Aldine De Gruyter.

Smith, T. W., & Greenberg, J. (1981). Depression and self-focused attention. *Motivation and Emotion, 5,* 323–332.

Teasdale, J. D. (1985). Psychological treatments for depression: How do they work? *Behavior Research and Therapy, 23,* 157–165.

Teri, L. (1982). Depression in adolescence: Its relationship to assertion and various aspects of self-image. *Journal of Clinical Child Psychology, 11,* 101–106.

Weissman, M. M., & Klerman, G. L. (1977). Sex differences in the epidemiology of depression. *Archives of General Psychiatry, 34,* 98–111.

Windholz, M. J., Marmar, C. R., & Horowitz, M. J. (1985). A review of the research on conjugal bereavement: Impact on health and efficacy of intervention. *Comprehensive Psychiatry, 26,* 433–447.

Wirtz, P. W., & Harrell, A. V. (1987). Effects of postassault exposure to attack-similar stimuli on long-term recovery of victims. *Journal of Consulting and Clinical Psychology, 55*(1), 10–16.

Wood, J. V., Saltzberg, J. A., Neale, J. M., Stone, A. A., & Rachmiel, T. B. (1990). Self-focused attention, coping responses, and distressed mood in everyday life. *Journal of Personality and Social Psychology, 58,* 1027–1036.

Zahn-Waxler, C., McKnew, D. H., Cummings, M., Davenport, Y. B., & Radke-Yarrow, M. (1984). Problem behaviors and peer interactions of young children with a manic-depressive parent. *American Journal of Psychiatry, 141,* 236–240.

10   The Development of Early Self-Conceptions: Their Relevance for Motivational Processes

Carol S. Dweck

Abstract

This chapter focuses on self-conceptions and motivational processes in young children, a topic of interest for several reasons. First, greater understanding of motivational processes in young children can provide insight into the origins of adaptive and maladaptive functioning. Second, from a theoretical and empirical standpoint, it is a topic that has been somewhat shrouded in mystery. That is, although maladaptive motivational patterns had been identified and studied in older children for quite some time, these patterns had not been found in younger children (below the age of about 8 or 9), and, in fact, were widely believed not to exist. In this chapter, I first describe the adaptive and maladaptive motivational patterns that characterize older children, contrasting the mastery-oriented pattern of challenge-seeking and effective persistence with the helpless pattern of risk avoidance and impairment in the face of difficulty. I show how these patterns are related to the conceptions about their intelligence that children hold. I then discuss why younger children were believed to be exclusively mastery-oriented, and present a series of studies from our laboratory demonstrating that they are not. Indeed, a sizable proportion of young children (as young as preschool and kindergarten age) exhibit every aspect of the helpless pattern. Moreover, this pattern is linked to children's self-conceptions: not to their conceptions about their intelligence, but to their conceptions about their goodness and badness – the domain of greatest relevance to children in this age group.

Motivational Patterns in Older Children

Mastery-Oriented and Helpless Motivational Patterns

In our studies of students ranging from late grade school through college, we identified two distinct motivational patterns (Diener & Dweck, 1978,

257

1980; Dweck & Reppucci, 1973; Licht & Dweck, 1984; Zhao & Dweck, 1994). One is a more adaptive mastery-oriented pattern in which students confront challenge with relish, and show intensified effort, sustained optimism, and effective strategizing when they confront obstacles. The other is the more maladaptive helpless pattern in which students avoid challenges that pose the risk of errors or failure, and show self-blame (denigration of their intellectual ability), negative affect, and impaired problem-solving strategies in the face of difficulty.

One might think that brighter students would be the ones who typically display the more mastery-oriented pattern and that the less advanced students would be the ones who avoid challenge, blame themselves for failure, and more readily give up when they encounter problems. Yet our studies show repeatedly that these motivational patterns are not related to students' intelligence or achievement, at least not in the grade school years and at least not within the normal range of intellectual ability. Many of the very brightest students exhibit the helpless pattern when they face difficulty (although they may not yet face much real difficulty in school), and many students with weaker skills look quite mastery-oriented (see, e.g., Licht & Dweck, 1984). This means that these patterns are not based on the "reality" of actual ability or actual academic outcomes, but rather require a psychological explanation. We first sought this explanation by investigating students' goals in achievement situations.

Achievement Goals

Specifically, we theorized that achievement situations might mean different things to different students (Dweck & Elliott, 1983; Elliott & Dweck, 1988; see also Dweck & Leggett, 1988). Some students might see these situations as tests of their ability, while others might see them as opportunities to learn something new. That is, some might be pursuing what we call *performance goals:* the goal of obtaining positive judgments of one's ability and avoiding negative ones, the goal of looking smart. Others might be pursuing *learning goals:* the goal of increasing one's ability, the goal of becoming smarter. We then showed that focusing on performance goals made children vulnerable to the helpless pattern in the face of failure, particularly when they did not have confidence in their ability at the task (Elliott & Dweck, 1988). That is, an emphasis on proving or measuring their ability (especially when they doubted that ability) made it more likely that when they failed, students would fall into a helpless pattern of self-blame, negative affect, and impaired performance. In contrast, an emphasis on learning goals was found to foster the mastery-oriented pattern, even in students who thought they had low ability at the task. That is, when their goal was to increase their ability, students were not hindered by thinking they were not already good at the task. Thus students' achievement goals were found to set up the helpless and mastery-oriented patterns (see also Ames, 1987; Nicholls, 1984). However, it was still not clear why some students favor performance goals and others favor learning goals. To understand this, we were led to consider students' theories about their intelligence.

Theories of Intelligence

In this research (Bandura & Dweck, 1985; Dweck & Leggett, 1988), we found that students' beliefs about the nature of their intelligence did indeed predict their achievement goal preferences. Specifically, some students believed that their intelligence was a fixed trait, that they had only so much intelligence and that there was nothing they could do to change that. We called this an *entity* theory of intelligence because here intelligence is conceived of as a static entity. Students who held this belief were the ones who favored performance goals over learning goals. That is, they wanted to prove that the fixed intelligence they had was adequate. They wanted to look smart and not look dumb, and they were willing to give up potentially valuable learning opportunities that held the risk of error.[1]

In contrast, other students believed that their intelligence was a malleable quality, one that they could cultivate and develop. We called this an *incremental* theory because here intelligence is conceived of as something that can be increased through effort. Students who held this view favored learning goals over performance goals. That is, they preferred goals that would allow them to increase their level of ability over goals that would simply validate their existing ability level.

In a study by Dweck, Dinces, and Tenney (see Dweck & Leggett, 1988), we experimentally manipulated children's theories of intelligence (by means of vivid and compelling reading passages) in order to determine whether these theories could have a direct causal effect on students' goals. The results showed that students exposed to the entity theory passage were significantly more likely to choose performance over learning goals than were the students who read the incremental theory passage. These findings suggest, first, that students' theories of intelligence are malleable and, second, that they can exert a causal effect on the goals students pursue.

In several studies, we have shown that students' theories of intelligence also predict their helpless versus mastery-oriented response to difficulty.

For example, in one study (Henderson & Dweck, 1990), we tracked students over the transition to junior high school, a time when they were encountering increasingly difficult schoolwork and more stringent grading practices. We found that students holding an entity theory showed, as a group, clear decrements in their class standing, whereas students holding an incremental theory showed clear gains. Those holding an entity theory were also more likely to show anxiety or apprehension about their schoolwork and to attribute their difficulties to a lack of ability.

In a study by Zhao and Dweck (1994), college students responded to academic failure scenarios by relating what they would think, how they would feel, and what they would do in response to the failures depicted. Those students with an entity theory of their intelligence reported significantly more self-denigration, intelligence-blaming, and severe negative affect, along with significantly fewer constructive strategies than did students with an incremental theory.

In summary, our work with older students has shown two quite distinct patterns of reaction to challenge and failure. It has also shown that these patterns are predicted by the theories of intelligence that students hold. Those who believe in fixed intelligence appear to see failure as measuring that intelligence and are vulnerable to helplessness when they fail. Those who believe in malleable intelligence appear to be focused on learning, and they maintain a mastery-oriented stance in the face of failure.

It is interesting to speculate about the relation between these motivational patterns and those discussed by other authors in this volume. For example, does the entity theory encourage a more ruminative coping style (see Nolen-Hoeksema, Chapter 9, this volume) and more of a state orientation than action orientation (Kuhl & Fuhrmann, Chapter 1, this volume), as students focus on what failure implies about their adequacy rather than on the actions they can take to address the problem? In a related vein, is the entity theory framework, in which failure can carry strong negative meaning, more likely to be associated with an avoidance versus approach orientation (Kuhl & Fuhrmann, Chapter 1, this volume) and with a negative- versus positive-outcome focus (Higgins & Loeb, Chapter 3, this volume), compared to the incremental theory framework? Further, do the two theories differ in the extent to which they foster primary versus secondary control (Heckhausen & Schulz, Chapter 2, this volume)? It seems likely that the entity theory framework, with its belief in basic attributes that are not under one's control and its greater tendency to foster a helpless response, would not foster primary control beliefs to the same degree as the incremental theory framework. It is also useful to relate our work to that of Ryan and Deci (see Ryan, Chapter 4, this volume) on intrinsic motivation. Does the entity theory, with its emphasis on documenting one's ability, undermine intrinsic motivation compared to the incremental theory, with its emphasis on learning and mastery? It is clear that there are many ways in which our research makes contact with the work of the other authors in this volume, and this raises many potentially fruitful questions for further research.

Young Children's Theories of the Self

Thus far I have examined students' theories of intelligence and the impact these theories can have on their motivational patterns, but we have discussed only students from late grade school on. What about younger children? Do they have theories about themselves, and do they suffer vulnerabilities? For quite some time many researchers did not think so.

As researchers, we saw that thinking of their intelligence as a fixed trait and then blaming it when they failed appeared to create vulnerability for older children. We believed that children younger than 8 or 9 were too inexperienced or too cognitively unsophisticated to reason in this way (Dweck & Elliott, 1983; Miller, 1985; Nicholls, 1978a; 1984; Rholes, Blackwell, Jordan, et al., 1980; Stipek, 1984). The logic was as follows: If young children do not conceive of intelligence as a fixed trait – or if they do not even have an understanding of intelligence, for that matter – then they will not blame their fixed intelligence and feel inadequate when they fail. Some researchers argued that young children think of ability as being the same as effort (e.g., Nicholls, 1978b), and that consequently they should be particularly energized by difficulty, as are older mastery-oriented children who focus on effort in the face of failure. In other words, many researchers thought that the helpless response required sophisticated concepts that young children did not have.

If one adds to this the fact that young children as a group often appear to be more optimistic and resilient in the face of obstacles (e.g., Miller, 1985; see also Stipek, 1984), one has a portrait of young children as protected from vulnerability during their most crucial, formative years. It makes good sense that this should be so. It would not do at all to have the young of our species give up in the face of obstacles as they confronted the most important tasks of their lives, such as learning to walk and talk. These are tasks that are fraught with obstacles, yet most children do not refuse to locomote or speak for fear of making mistakes. If this invulnerability lasted a long time, it would help children as they approached and mastered their first years of school. But it does not.

Our research has now shown that children as young as preschoolers display every aspect of the helpless pattern: self-blame, lowered expectations, negative emotions, lack of persistence, and impaired strategies (Cain & Dweck, 1995; Hebert & Dweck, 1985; Heyman, Dweck, & Cain, 1992; Smiley & Dweck, 1994; see also Burhans & Dweck, 1995; Lewis, Alessandri, & Sullivan, 1992; Stipek, Recchia, & McClintic, 1992). Why have we been able to see this repeatedly when it was so unclear before? There are several reasons.

One reason is that in the new studies, we gave young children tasks that were meaningful to them and ones on which they understood clearly what success and failure were. Older students who are prone to helpless responses react negatively whenever they know they have failed to meet a standard; young children need visible evidence that they have failed to complete a task (for example, a picture puzzle with pieces that are not all in place). Also, when they are questioned about these failures, it is important that the evidence of the failure (e.g., an incomplete puzzle) is present, because young children may have trouble pondering past, now invisible, outcomes and remembering what they thought and how they felt.

Perhaps an even more important reason that we were able to identify the helpless pattern in young children is that we began to believe that it was actually there. We realized that we had not been thinking about the issue in quite the right way: Maybe children do not have to understand intelligence at all in order to show a helpless response. Perhaps intelligence is the issue for older students in achievement situations, but maybe younger children bring different issues to these situations. After all, younger children are being socialized intensively. They are constantly being told what is good and bad, right and wrong, appropriate and inappropriate. Maybe this is the issue for them as they confront a failure. Maybe some young children believe that they are *bad* or *unworthy* when they fail, and it is this belief rather than a belief that their intelligence is inadequate that triggers the helpless response in them (see Stipek, Recchia, & McClintic, 1992; Yussen & Kane, 1985).

I turn now to the research that has documented the helpless pattern in young children and that has linked it to their beliefs about their goodness. I also describe our current research, which is beginning to reveal where these beliefs and reactions may come from.

Evidence of the Helpless Response in Young Children

In our first study demonstrating the helpless response in young children, we focused on preschoolers aged 3½ to 5 years old (Hebert & Dweck, 1985;

see Dweck, 1991). We gave the children colorful jigsaw puzzles of popular cartoon characters. However, some of these puzzles were too complicated for them to complete within the allotted time. We could then assess such factors as their persistence, their emotions, and their expectations for future success in the face of this difficulty. We also asked them to role-play parents' and teachers' reactions to their puzzle performance so that we could begin to determine whether the young children who were helpless saw their failures as meaning that they were bad or punishment-worthy.

More specifically, we gave the children in our study four puzzles to solve; the first three they worked on were ones that they were unable to complete.[2] While the children worked on the puzzles, we recorded their spontaneous statements, and after they finished working on the four puzzles, we asked them a number of questions.

Persistence

First, we measured the children's desire to persist in the face of difficulty. To do this, we told children that we had a little extra time and they could choose any one of the puzzles to work on again. We wanted to know how many children would choose to redo the puzzle they had already completed, which we considered to be the nonpersistent choice because the child was not attempting to confront or master the difficulty, and how many would choose to reattempt one of the incomplete puzzles, which we considered the persistent choice. We found that 37 percent of the children were nonpersistent – that is, they chose to redo the one puzzle they had already successfully completed instead of trying to grapple with one of the harder ones.

Was it the case, perhaps, that these children found the success puzzle to be challenging and were choosing it for that reason? In two other studies that used the same procedure (Cain & Dweck, 1995; Smiley & Dweck, 1994), we asked children the reasons for their choice. *Not one* nonpersister in either study gave a challenge-seeking or learning-oriented reason for his or her selection. On the contrary, the great majority of nonpersisters gave very clear challenge-avoidant reasons, saying, for example, that they chose the puzzle because it was easy or because they already knew how to do it. The persistent children gave clear challenge-seeking reasons for their choice. They said, for example, that they wanted to try the harder puzzle, or they wanted to see if they could figure it out.

To buttress this finding, we (Smiley & Dweck, 1994) asked children to make yet another puzzle choice. In other words, we asked them to tell us which puzzle they wanted to work on following their first-choice puzzle.

We were surprised and fascinated to find that the great majority of the nonpersisters repeated their choice of the same, already-solved puzzle. This means that they wanted to work on the same puzzle three times rather than confront a more difficult one. In contrast, most of the persistent children selected a different unsolved puzzle when asked to make a second choice.

Could it be that the nonpersistent children were simply not as good at solving puzzles as the persistent children? In the study by Cain and Dweck (1995) and the one by Smiley and Dweck (1994), we asked all the children beforehand (in a previous session) to solve puzzles that were very similar to the ones we used later in the study, and found that persisters and nonpersisters were completely equivalent in their puzzle performance. This finding shows that any differences in the children's response to difficulty does not stem from different levels of ability at the task.

We then sought to determine whether children who made the nonpersistent choice showed other aspects of the helpless response. Did they show more negative thoughts and feelings, and did they feel incapable of achieving future success?

Negative Thoughts and Feelings

When we examined the children's spontaneous statements, we found that the nonpersistent children did indeed make significantly more negative statements about themselves and their performance than did the persistent children (Hebert & Dweck, 1985; Smiley & Dweck, 1994). They also expressed significantly more negative emotion than did the persistent children (Cain & Dweck, 1995; Hebert & Dweck, 1985; Smiley & Dweck, 1994). Thus, in terms of their focus on negative aspects of themselves and their actions, and in terms of their descent into negative feelings, these children's reactions closely resembled the helpless responses of the older children.

Negative Expectations

As with older children who showed helpless responses, the young nonpersistent children in all three studies fell into extremely low expectations for their future performance. For example, in one study (Hebert & Dweck, 1995) we asked children: "If you had lots of time right now, do you think you could finish any of these puzzles, or are you just not good enough at puzzles?" The clear majority of nonpersisters (71 percent) believed that they wouldn't be able finish any of the puzzles even if they had lots of time. In contrast, the majority of the persistent children (64.3 percent) believed they could succeed with more time.

In the same vein, pointing to the incomplete puzzles, we asked the children: "If you tried very hard right now, your very hardest, do you think you could do any of these puzzles? Yes or no?" Although overall children responded more optimistically to this question, there were very strong differences between the nonpersisters and persisters in the extent of their optimism. Less than half of the nonpersisters (46.4 percent) believed that their best effort would yield success, whereas the great majority of the persisters (81.5 percent) expected success to follow from their efforts. Again, these findings with younger children directly mirror what we found for older children. After failure, the nonpersisters lost faith in their abilities and did not believe that their efforts would be fruitful. The persisters continued to believe that further effort would bring them success.

These findings make it clear that young children can display all the various facets of the helpless response. Like older children, a sizable number of young children respond to failure with negative thoughts about themselves and their performance, lowered confidence in their ability to succeed, negative feelings, and decreased persistence. Even if children in this age group have little understanding of intelligence, its nature, its properties, and its implications, they can still react to failure with a full-blown helpless response.

Helpless Responses to Criticism

As suggested earlier, we suspected that young children's helpless responses might arise not so much in intellectual achievement situations where they make mistakes as in social contexts where they receive praise and criticism. We wondered, then, whether young children would have helpless responses when they received criticism.

Initial Positive Appraisal

In a study by Heyman et al. (1992), we asked kindergarten children to pretend that they were creating something as a nice surprise for their teacher. By using dolls (representing themselves) and props, they pretended to build a house of blocks, to write the numbers one through ten, and to paint a picture of a family.[3] In each case, we asked them to pretend that just as they were about to bestow the surprise on their teacher, they noticed a flaw or mistake in their work. They noticed, for example, that the house had no windows or that they had omitted the number eight from the array of numbers or that they had forgotten to paint feet on one of the children in the family. Here is an example of one of the stories they acted out as the researcher read it to them:

> You spend a lot of time painting a picture of a family to give to your teacher. You pick out colors you think are nice and carefully draw each person. As you are about to give it to your teacher you say to yourself, "Uh-oh, one of the kids has no feet." But you worked really hard on the picture and want to give it to her. You say, "Teacher, here's a picture for you."

Interestingly, when we stopped a story at this point and asked the children to evaluate their work, they almost all gave their creation an extremely high rating (94.4 percent gave their product a 5 or a 6 on a 6-point scale). The small mistake did not really bother them. However, when we continued the stories and had the (toy) teacher react with criticism to the child's pretend creation, a different reaction emerged. That is, when the teacher criticized the flaw and expressed disappointment in the child, a helpless response was evident in a number of the children.

Response to Criticism

Many of the children gave their work a lower rating after receiving criticism (39.3 percent now rated their work at 4 or below), and these children showed the other features of the helpless response as well. That is, even though these children were quite pleased with their flawed creations before the teacher criticized them, they now denigrated their product and reacted in a helpless manner. Compared to the children who continued to give their work high ratings, these children reacted as described below.

- *Lower persistence:*   When asked if they were willing to pursue the activities in the story on a future occasion, these children were much more likely than their more mastery-oriented peers to say they would prefer to do something else instead.
- *Less constructive solutions to the problem:*   When children were asked to role-play how they would end the story, these children were less likely than the others to come up with happy endings or with constructive ways to correct the product and solve the problem. They often left both the child and the teacher dolls mired in negative feelings. For example, one child role-played the teacher reiterating her negative evaluation ("I still hate those numbers"), and another portrayed herself going to throw her work in the

garbage. Their more mastery-oriented peers, in contrast, gave lots of suggestions for how to remedy the situation and they generally ended the story with everyone feeling pleased.

The fact that there were so many helpless responses on this measure was surprising and extremely revealing. This was a role-playing situation, in which children did not *actually* have to fix their products or *really* address the issue with the teacher – they simply had to wave the dolls in the air and *say* that the product was fixed and the teacher was happy. Yet, many children failed to do even this. It was as though they had been paralyzed by the criticism.

- *More negative emotions:* When children were asked to choose faces representing their feelings about everything that happened in each episode, these children were far more likely than the others to report feeling sad or angry, and far less likely to report feeling happy.
- *More self-blame and negative self-evaluations:* These children showed far more self-denigration and self-blame after criticism than the other children did, a finding that will be discussed in more detail below. What is more, they were much more likely to think that the teacher had acted appropriately in criticizing them. We told children: "Really think about everything that happened with the painting. If you were the teacher, what would you say to [child's name]?"

 Compared to the more mastery-oriented children, almost twice as many of these children (41 percent versus 21.5 percent) acted out negative evaluations such as,"You are very bad" or "How could you do this? This is not a very good building. I don't like it." Almost twice as many mastery-oriented children (64.6 percent versus 33.3 percent) acted out positive evaluations such as,"That is a good girl," "You did a good job. I'm proud of you," or "That's a very nice picture. Why don't you put some feet on that picture?" When given a chance to rethink and perhaps rectify what had happened to them, many of the children who responded helplessly instead ended up affirming the validity of the criticism they had received.

Once again, we can see that young children do in fact show each facet of the helpless response. When they experience failure or criticism, a sizable number of them show clear signs of low persistence or impaired strategies, negative emotions, and negative self-evaluation. We proposed earlier that helpless responses in young children might be associated with feelings of badness or low self-worth. We now set out to test this idea.

Helpless Responses and Expectations of Punishment

The first way we approached this question of whether vulnerable children feel "bad" when they make mistakes, was to see whether those children expect punishment or disapproval for their errors. In a study described earlier in this chapter (Hebert & Dweck, 1985), children could not complete three of the four puzzles they were given to work on. In this study, some children showed clear helpless responses to the difficulty, while others showed highly mastery-oriented ones. The question was whether these two groups of children would differ in their anticipation of disapproval and punishment for what they had done.

With their work arrayed before them (the three incomplete and one completed puzzle), the children in this study were asked to role-play the reactions of the adults in their lives. For example, we showed them an adult female doll and said: "This is your mother. She looks at what you've done. [The doll was moved as if it were scanning the puzzles.] What does she say? What does she do?"

After the child's initial response, we followed up with a sequence of more specific probes, with the doll representing the child saying: "Are you happy with me?" "Are you mad at me?" "Will you punish me?" "What should I do now?"

There were four episodes in which children could role-play adults' reactions. In the first three, they role-played reactions from their teacher, their mother, and their father. In the last episode, the child role-played the mother looking over the work and calling the father on the telephone to report her assessments.

When we compared the reactions of the children who showed a helpless response (37 percent) with those who showed a mastery-oriented response, dramatic differences were apparent. The children who showed the helpless response (of low persistence, negative thoughts, and negative feelings) were far more likely than the mastery-oriented children to portray criticism and punishment when they role-played adults' reactions to their work. A full 50 percent of them role-played punishment in the majority of the four episodes, while only 18.5 percent of the mastery-oriented children did so (with a great many of the mastery-oriented children role-playing no punishment at all). Here is a sampling of what the helpless-response group role-played as the adults' reactions to their work: "He's punished 'cause he can't do them and he didn't finish"; "You better do nothing but sit in your room"; "Daddy's gonna be very mad and spank her."

As can be seen, there was a great deal of emphasis on the failures and on the notion that the child was bad and deserving of punishment. The responses of the mastery-oriented group had a fundamentally different quality. These children did make many references to issues of goodness, but the emphasis was on what they did well and, interestingly, on strategies (such as additional effort) that they could use to improve their performance. Here is a sampling of what the mastery-oriented group portrayed their parents and teachers as saying: "He didn't work hard enough. He can try again after lunch"; "He worked hard but he just didn't finish them. He wants to try them again later"; "Our little girl did very good. I'm proud of her and I'm going to hug her."

These were the first findings suggesting that children who are vulnerable to a helpless response do indeed feel more punishment-worthy when they fail – or at least that they expect to be viewed this way by the important adults around them. Another of our studies (Heyman, Dweck, & Cain, 1992) yielded very similar findings. In this study, we asked children to role-play how their parents would react to their flawed product. We said: "If you went home and your parents knew about what happened at school with the painting [or the house or the numbers], what would they do or say?" Almost twice as many children in the helpless-response group (47.5 percent versus 24.6 percent of the children in the mastery-oriented group) spontaneously said that their parents would respond with disapproval of them or their work. The children in the mastery-oriented group, in contrast, were more likely to say that their parents would respond by praising them or their work (46.2 percent versus 25 percent of the children in the helpless-response group).

In this context, it is interesting to revisit the findings on how the children in this study (Heyman, Dweck, & Cain, 1992) said they would have responded if they were the teacher. These findings are relevant here for two reasons: First, they provide further support for the point that the children in the helpless-response group enact more disapproval of themselves and their products (e.g.,"You are very bad," "I hate those numbers") and that the children who are more mastery-oriented enact more supportive responses. Second, on the parent reaction measure, children may simply have been telling us how they thought their parents *would* respond; on this measure, however, they were telling us how they thought the teacher *should* respond. In other words, they were telling us more directly what they thought they deserved for what they had done.

In summary, the findings from these studies provide initial support for the idea that children who are vulnerable to the helpless response think of themselves as bad or punishment-worthy when they experience failure or criticism. However, we wanted more direct evidence that children in the

helpless-response group felt they were bad when they failed or were criticized – and so we asked them directly.

Helpless Responses and Judgments of the Self

In the study by Heyman, Dweck, and Cain, we assessed the extent to which
children saw their criticized performance as a reflection of their goodness
and adequacy. After each story with criticism, we said to them:

> Think about everything that happened with the painting [or the numbers
> or the house]. Did everything that happened make you feel like you were
> good or not good at painting? [Child's answer] Did everything that hap-
> pened make you feel like you were a good or not a good girl [or boy]? Did
> it make you feel like you were a nice or not nice girl? Did it make you feel
> like you were a smart or not smart girl [or boy]?

The question was whether children in the helpless-response group felt
less good and less adequate than the children in the mastery-oriented
group – that is, whether the criticism led them to call the basic qualities of
the self into question. Our findings showed that for every one of the four
self-judgments, the children in the helpless-response group rated themselves far more negatively than the children in the mastery-oriented group. A
majority of the children in the helpless-response group said not only that they
felt not good at the task or not smart (61.9 percent), but also that they felt they
were not good children (52.5 percent). Moreover, even though the whole
story was explicitly focused on their making a nice present for the teacher,
38.1 percent of them reported feeling that they were not nice children.

These responses were in sharp contrast to the children in the mastery-
oriented group. About 20 percent of them reported feeling that they were
not good at the task, and that was the extent of their negative response. Less
than 10 percent reported feeling not smart or not good, and almost none of
them said they felt they were not nice.

These findings provided direct evidence that young children who show the
helpless pattern feel they are bad or unworthy when they encounter criticism.
Their self-condemnation goes far beyond the particular task for which they
are criticized. In contrast, the children showing the mastery-oriented response
see the identical criticism as having much more limited implications. Some
think it casts doubt on their ability at the task, but very few think it means anything about their goodness as a person. For children who show the helpless
reaction, criticism speaks to very basic and general qualities of the self.

Can it be that children who are more vulnerable to self-doubt are simply less competent than their peers? If so, then maybe an adult's criticism carries a greater ring of truth for them. To check for this possibility, we asked children's teachers to rate each child's overall academic ability on a five-point scale from "very low" to "very high." We found no difference between the groups in the level at which teachers rated their competence: Children in the helpless-response group received an average rating of 4.19 from their teachers, and children in the mastery-oriented group received an average rating of 4.06. Therefore, as with the older students we discussed earlier, the group differences in self-judgments and negative reactions do not stem from ability differences.

Thus far we have seen that young children, contrary to the beliefs of many researchers, can display all aspects of the helpless reaction. As with older students, their helpless reactions are accompanied by negative self-judgments. Are these children similar to their older counterparts in other ways? In particular, we began to wonder whether the helpless reaction in young children is linked to a belief in fixed traits the way it is in older children – however, in young children it would be linked to a belief in goodness/badness, rather than intelligence, as a fixed quality.

Helpless Reactions and the Belief in Fixed Badness

It is difficult to elicit meaningful answers from young children when one asks them to think about abstract qualities, such as goodness or badness, and to ponder whether these qualities are fixed or malleable. This made it impossible for us to give them the kind of implicit theory measure we give to older children. So we formulated a different kind of question to ask the young children in our study (Heyman, Dweck, & Cain, 1992). Instead of asking about goodness/badness in the abstract, we described a child's concrete actions. Also, instead of asking whether the child could change or not, we asked if he or she would always be that way: "Imagine a new boy [girl] is in your class. S/he steals your crayons, scribbles on your paper, and spills your juice. Then s/he teases you and calls you names. Do you think this new boy [girl] will always act this way?"

The children understood exactly what we were asking and were quite emphatic in their answers. However, the helpless-response and mastery-oriented groups differed from each other. Only 24.6 percent of the children in the mastery-oriented group thought that a child who performed negative actions on one occasion would always perform negative actions. In contrast, 50 percent of the children in the helpless-response group took the "once bad, always bad" position.

This question was asked of children in a previous session that was separate from the one in which the teacher criticism was role-played. Thus, it is not simply the case that the children in the helpless-response group are easily overcome when they are criticized. Instead, they seem to be more likely than their mastery-oriented counterparts to hold general beliefs that go along with, and perhaps heighten, their vulnerability. That is, much like older students who am vulnerable to the helpless reaction, these children seem to believe that stable traits are being judged when children are evaluated.

In a real sense, then, the model developed to describe the patterns of older students applies to young children as well. In both age groups, those who believe in fixed or stable traits are more likely to blame those traits and show a helpless response when they meet with negative feedback.

Possible Origins of Helpless and Mastery-Oriented Patterns in Young Children

Our ideas about the origins of these patterns came from several places. First, we looked at the role-playing of the young children studied. Although their role-played dramas cannot be taken as literal reflections of what goes on in their lives, they can reveal clues about what might distinguish the experiences of children with helpless responses from the experiences of children with mastery-oriented responses. You will remember that the children with helpless responses tended to role-play more parental punishment and criticism. The parental reactions they portrayed often implied not only that their work was deficient, but also that they themselves were blameworthy. In contrast, the children with mastery-oriented responses tended to show their parents praising the positive aspects of their work and, perhaps even more important, suggesting strategies to correct the deficient aspects.

Other clues came from the achievement motivation literature, which describes the benefits of focusing students on strategies and effort rather than on their traits (e.g., Anderson & Jennings, 1980; Dweck, 1975) and from child-rearing literature that stresses the importance of criticizing the behavior and not the child when responding to transgressions (e.g., Hoffman, 1988).

Kamins and I (1996) tested several hypotheses about the kinds of critical feedback that would lead to helpless and mastery-oriented response patterns in young children. In this study (modeled on Heyman, Dweck, & Cain, 1992), kindergarten children pretended to perform a series of tasks for their teacher, using props and toy figures. When they finished each one, the (pretend) teacher criticized the work as incomplete or inadequate and then delivered one of four kinds of feedback. In one condition, the teacher gave feedback that conveyed a judgment of the (pretend) child as a whole, "I'm very disappointed in you." This condition was predicted to be the one most likely to create a helpless reaction on a subsequent task. In the second condition, the criticism was directed only at the behavior ("That's not what I call doing it the right way"). The third provided criticism of the behavior with an explanation ("That wasn't the right way to do it because . . ."). The fourth condition was the one predicted to be most likely to create a mastery-oriented response, and, after pointing out the flaw in the work, it focused the child on strategies: "Maybe you could think of another way to do it."

Following the series of scenarios with feedback, all children then enacted a final scenario in which their mistake was pointed out, but no further feedback was provided. The question was: How would the children respond to their mistake as a function of the feedback they had received for their previous errors? What we found was that the children who had received the more global, person-oriented criticism showed a significantly more helpless reaction on virtually every measure when compared to the group receiving strategy-oriented criticism, or when compared to the other three groups combined. The strategy feedback group, in contrast, was the most mastery-oriented.

First, the children in the person-oriented feedback condition rated their work more negatively than those in the other conditions. Second, they exhibited significantly more global negative self-judgments, for example, saying more often that they felt like they were not a good boy/girl. Third, they reported significantly more negative affect. Fourth, they suggested significantly fewer constructive strategies for fixing their mistakes. The person-oriented feedback created a full helpless response in the children who experienced it.[4]

The groups differed on yet another measure, and this was somewhat surprising to us. They differed on whether they thought badness was a stable quality, as well as whether a child who did poorly on his or her schoolwork was a bad child. These were beliefs that helpless children in our previous research had held (Heyman, Dweck, & Cain, 1992), but we did not expect our manipulation in this study to create these beliefs directly. It may be that the person-oriented feedback created in children the impression that the adult was looking into them and judging deep, permanent qualities. In contrast, the strategy-oriented feedback may have created the impression that people's actions are correctable and that they should not be judged by what they do at any given time. (See Pomerantz and Ruble, Chapter 6 of this volume, for parental control techniques that are likely to foster different control beliefs in children.)

Clearly, the results from this study need to be replicated, refined, and extended before firm conclusions can be drawn. Nonetheless they are suggestive, and support the hypothesis that person-oriented judgments can encourage children to be self-judgmental and to respond to criticism with helplessness and feelings of badness.

The question of whether certain ways of giving *praise* might set children up for a helpless response to failure or criticism is also very intriguing. Thus, in another set of studies (Kamins & Dweck, 1996; Mueller & Dweck, in press), we are testing the hypothesis that certain types of person-oriented praise (e.g., praise directed at children's underlying traits on the basis of their behaviors or outcomes) may lead children to doubt those very traits and become vulnerable when they subsequently fail or are criticized – although the praise may make the children feel good while they are succeeding. These feedback practices may also lead children to avoid challenges in order to maintain the praise. If this is the case, then the implications for practices that promote motivational vulnerability versus hardiness will be provocative, especially since there is a widespread belief in our society that such praise builds self-esteem and promotes adaptive achievement patterns.[5] Indeed, the intriguing finding reported by Little (Chapter 11, this volume) – that American children's high control beliefs do not predict their achievement – may result from just this type of feedback, that is, feedback that can make children feel good about themselves in the immediate situation but that does not promote adaptive achievement patterns.

Questions for the Future

A great many issues remain to be investigated. One fascinating question involves the fate of young children's feelings of badness over the course of their subsequent development. If vulnerable young children have a more or less undifferentiated sense of a good/bad self, what happens when they begin to differentiate individual attributes of the self (e.g., intelligence, personality) over the grade school years (Benenson & Dweck, 1986)? Are they then protected from a sense of global badness when they meet with failure or criticism? Is the damage circumscribed by an emerging understanding of distinct qualities?

Some recent findings may speak to this question. Heyman (1995) followed up the kindergarten children from the 1992 study (Heyman, Dweck, & Cain, 1992); the children were now in second grade. A series of questions documented that these children no longer confused issues of goodness with issues of intellectual ability. For example, virtually none of the children now said that children who do poorly on their schoolwork are bad. Nonetheless, a sizable proportion of the children who in kindergarten had shown the helpless pattern in kindergarten continued to engage in global self-blame, including feelings of badness, when they made mistakes. Moreover, children who in kindergarten had held the belief in stable badness were more likely to hold a belief in stable intellectual skills in second grade. Thus, for at least some of the children, the recognition of distinct domains does not eliminate feelings of badness when they err. It would be interesting to follow these children over a longer period of time, as well as to know more about the children who did show changes in their patterns from kindergarten to second grade. In short, the grade school years are a time of transition in children's understanding of their social and intellectual attributes. It is therefore important to learn more about the ways in which their changing understanding can affect their motivational patterns.

Other findings relevant to the issue of whether feelings of badness or low self-worth persist in older individuals who encounter failure come from a study mentioned earlier (Zhao & Dweck, 1994). In this study, college students were asked to imagine they were experiencing important academic failures. After each scenario, they reported what they would think, how they would feel, and what they would do. The participants in this study were divided into three groups. One group consisted of students who scored above 12 on the Beck Depression Inventory, indicating clear dysphoria or mild to moderate depression. The two other groups were considered nondepressed (i.e., scored below 12 on the depression inventory), and were divided into entity and incremental theorists of intelligence. The responses of the latter two groups were then compared to each other and to those of the depressed group. On almost every variable assessed, the nondepressed entity theorists resembled the depressed individuals and differed significantly from the incremental theorists. As mentioned earlier, the entity theorists showed greater denigration of their intelligence, a greater incidence of severe negative affect, and less use of constructive strategies than did the incremental theorists. However, like the depressed group, the entity theorists also showed a significantly greater amount of global self-condemnation. In response to the failure scenarios, they said things like "I would feel like a total failure as a person" or "I would feel worthless." These findings suggest that the global self-blame seen in our young helpless-response children may persist in some individuals, particularly those who subscribe to a belief in fixed traits.

Another interesting set of questions relates to the life-span implications of our analysis. I have argued that young children's vulnerability reveals itself in the realm of goodness/badness because these are the issues they are grappling with in their lives. Indeed, even the role-playing of the mastery-oriented young children was filled with comments relating to goodness. Older children, while not abandoning issues of goodness, appear to be grappling with and vulnerable to issues relating to their intellectual ability and to their social success with their peers. The question that remains is whether each age/stage of life has its unique issues that create unique sensitivities and vulnerabilities (see Cantor & Sanderson, Chapter 7, this volume). If we take Erikson's (1950) analysis of the issues that are paramount at the various life phases, we are led to ask whether adolescents would be particularly vulnerable to feedback that relates to issues of identity, whether young adults would be particularly vulnerable to issues of intimacy, and so on (see Cantor & Sanderson, Chapter 7, this volume).

Along these lines, it would also be useful to determine whether vulnerability is related to the development of certain types of beliefs in the new focal domains. Do fixed beliefs (e.g., "You either have it or you don't," "You're either good at it or your aren't") predict vulnerability at each point in development, or are there some developmental stages at which a recognition of fixed limitations would be adaptive? My suspicion is that it will always be adaptive to believe one can cultivate the attributes, or that one has control over the goals, that are focal at a particular stage of life (see Heckhausen & Schulz, Chapter 2, this volume; Brandtstädter, Rothermund, & Schmitz, Chapter 14, this volume).

In conclusion, this chapter has identified helpless and mastery-oriented patterns of motivation in young children. These patterns look highly similar to the patterns observed in older children, except that young children's issues center on their concerns about their goodness: Young children prone to helpless responses believe that failure or criticism means that they are bad – and they believe that badness is a stable attribute. I have discussed the possible origins of these beliefs and patterns as well as their implications for motivational vulnerabilities at different points in the life span.

Notes

1. A few things should be noted about the entity theory. First, the strict definition of an entity theory is the belief that one's intelligence is not under one's control. Believing it to be fixed is the most common form this belief takes. However, if an individual believes that his or her intelligence will wane over time no matter what is done, this is also an entity theory, since the individual does not believe in personal control over the attribute. Second, although students who hold this theory may believe that intelli-

gence is fixed, their reading of its level may vary as they confront successes and failures. That is, since intelligence is a construct and is never directly knowable, individuals who wish to judge its adequacy must estimate this from performance outcomes. Third, individuals may hold different implicit theories for different attributes, believing, for example, that intelligence is malleable but personality is a fixed trait.

2. We later showed them how to solve these puzzles and gave them a great deal of praise for having tried so hard, so that all the children would leave the session feeling they had mastered the task. Also, if any children became upset, we concluded the failure trials and immediately gave them puzzles they could solve. Despite the puzzle difficulty, virtually all the children ended the session feeling proud of their performance.

3. We used this pretend situation to control for children's skill at the tasks and also because we did not want to criticize the children or their creations directly.

4. Again, great care was taken to ensure that all children left the situation with a positive experience and mastery training. For example, all the stories were repeated with constructive solutions and positive endings.

5. These studies have now been completed. Our hypothesis that trait-oriented or person-oriented praise can create challenge avoidance and motivational vulnerability (including self-blame and helpless responses to setbacks) has received strong confirmation.

References

Anderson, C. A., & Jennings, D. L. (1980). When experiences of failure promote expectations of success: The impact of attributing failure to ineffective strategies. *Journal of Personality, 48,* 1393–1407.

Ames, C. (1987). The enhancement of student motivation. In J. Nicholls (Ed.), *Advances in motivation and achievement: Enhancing motivation* (Vol. 5, pp. 123–148). Greenwich, CT: JAI.

Bandura, M., & Dweck, C. S. (1985). *The relationship of conceptions of intelligence and achievement goals to achievement-related cognition, affect, and behavior.* Unpublished manuscript, Harvard University.

Benenson, J. F., & Dweck, C. S. (1986). The development of trait explanations and self-evaluations in the academic and social domains. *Child Development, 57,* 1179–1187.

Brandtstädter, J., Rothermund, K., & Schmitz, U. (1998). Maintaining self-integrity and efficacy in later life: The adaptive functions of assimilative persistence and accommodative flexibility. In J. Heckhausen & C. S. Dweck (Eds.), *Motivation and self-regulation across the life span.* New York: Cambridge University Press.

Burhans, K., & Dweck, C. S. (1995). Helplessness in early childhood: The role of contingent worth. *Child Development, 66,* 1719–1738.

Cain, K. M., & Dweck, C. S. (1995). The development of children's achievement motivation patterns and conceptions of intelligence. *Merrill-Palmer Quarterly, 41,* 25–52.

Cantor, N., & Sanderson, C. A. (1998). The functional regulation of adolescent dating relationships and sexual behavior: An interaction of goals, strategies, and situations. In J. Heckhausen & C. S. Dweck (Eds.), *Motivation and self-regulation across the life span.* New York: Cambridge University Press.

Diener, C. I., & Dweck, C. S. (1978). An analysis of learned helplessness: Continuous changes in performance, strategy, and achievement cognitions following failure. *Journal of Personality and Social Psychology, 36,* 451–462.

    (1980). An analysis of learned helplessness. II: The processing of success. *Journal of Personality and Social Psychology, 39,* 940–952.

Dweck, C. S. (1975). The role of expectations and attributions in the alleviation of learned helplessness. Journal of Personality and Social Psychology, 36, 451–462.

    (1991). Self-theories and goals: Their role in motivation, personality, and development. In R. Dienstbier (Ed.), *Nebraska symposium on motivation* (pp. 199–235). Lincoln: University of Nebraska Press.

Dweck, C. S., & Elliott, E. S. (1983). Achievement motivation. In P. Mussen & E. M. Hetherington (Eds.), *Handbook of child psychology.* New York: Wiley.

Dweck, C. S., & Leggett, E. L. (1988). A social-cognitive approach to motivation and personality. *Psychological Review, 95,* 256–273.

Dweck, C. S., & Reppucci, N. D. (1973). Learned helplessness and reinforcement responsibility in children. *Journal of Personality and Social Psychology, 25,* 109–116.

Elliott, E. S., & Dweck, C. S. (1988). Goals: An approach to motivation and achievement. *Journal of Personality and Social Psychology, 54,* 5–12.

Erikson, E. H. (1950). *Childhood and society.* New York: Norton.

Hebert, C., & Dweck, C. S. (1985). The mediators of persistence in preschoolers. Unpublished manuscript, Harvard University.

Heckhausen, J., & Schulz, R. (1998). Developmental regulation in adulthood: Selection and compensation via primary and secondary control. In J. Heckhausen & C. S. Dweck (Eds.), *Motivation and self-regulation across the life span.* New York: Cambridge University Press.

Henderson, V., & Dweck, C. S. (1990). Motivation and achievement. In S. S. Feldman & G. R. Elliott (Eds.), *At the threshold: The developing adolescent.* Cambridge MA: Harvard University Press.

Heyman, G. (1995). Children's thinking about traits: Implications for judgments of self and others. Unpublished doctoral dissertation, University of Illinois.

Heyman, G., Dweck, C. S., & Cain, K. (1992). Young children's vulnerability to self-blame and helplessness: Relationship to beliefs about goodness. *Child Development, 63,* 401–415.

Higgins, T., & Loeb, I. (1998). Development of regulatory focus: Promotion and prevention as ways of living. In J. Heckhausen & C. S. Dweck (Eds.), *Motivation and self-regulation across the life span*. New York: Cambridge University Press.

Hoffman, M. L. (1988). Moral development. In M. H. Bornstein & M. E. Lamb (Eds.), *Developmental psychology: An advanced textbook* (2d ed.). Hillsdale, NJ: Erlbaum.

Kamins, M., & Dweck, C. S. (1996). *The effects of adults' feedback on children's coping*. Unpublished manuscript, Columbia University.

Kuhl, J., & Fuhrmann, A. (1998). Decomposing self-regulation and self-control: The Volitional Components Inventory. In J. Heckhausen & C. S. Dweck (Eds.), *Motivation and self-regulation across the life span*. New York: Cambridge University Press.

Lewis, M., Alessandri, S. M., & Sullivan, M. W. (1992). Differences in shame and pride as a function of children's gender and task difficulty. *Child Development, 63*, 630–638.

Licht, B. G., & Dweck, C. S. (1984). Determinants of academic achievement: The interaction of children's achievement orientation with skill area. *Developmental Psychology, 20*, 628–636.

Little, T. D. (1998). Sociocultural influences on the development of children's action-control beliefs. In J. Heckhausen & C. S. Dweck (Eds.), *Motivation and self-regulation across the life span*. New York: Cambridge University Press.

Miller, A. T. (1985). A developmental study of the cognitive basis of performance impairment after failure. *Journal of Personality and Social Psychology, 49*, 529–538.

Mueller, C., & Dweck, C. S. (in press). Intelligence praise can undermine children's motivation and performance. *Journal of Personality and Social Psychology*.

Nicholls, J. G. (1978a). Development of causal attributions and evaluative responses to success and failure. *Developmental Psychology, 14*, 687–688.

(1978b). The development of the concepts of effort and ability, perceptions of academic attainment, and the understanding that difficult tasks require more ability. *Child Development, 49*, 800–814.

(1984). Achievement motivation: Conceptions of ability, subjective experience, task choice, and performance. *Psychological Review, 91*, 328–346.

Nolen-Hoeksema, S. (1998). Ruminative coping with depression. In J. Heckhausen & C. S. Dweck (Eds.), *Motivation and self-regulation across the life span*. New York: Cambridge University Press.

Rholes, W. S., Blackwell, J., Jordan, C., & Walters, C. (1980). A developmental study of learned helplessness. *Developmental Psychology, 16*, 616–624.

Pomerantz, E., & Ruble, D. (1998). The multidimensional nature of control: Implications for the development of sex differences in self-evaluation. In J. Heckhausen & C. S. Dweck (Eds.), *Motivation and self-regulation across the life span*. New York: Cambridge University Press.

Ryan, R. M. (1998). Human psychological needs and the issues of volition, control, and outcome focus. In J. Heckhausen & C. S. Dweck (Eds.), *Motivation and self-regulation across the life span.* New York: Cambridge University Press.

Smiley, P., & Dweck, C. S. (1994). Individual differences in achievement goals among young children. *Child Development, 65,* 1723–1743.

Stipek, D. J. (1984). Young children's performance expectations: Logical analysis or wishful thinking? In J. G. Nicholls (Ed.), *Advances in motivation and achievement* (Vol. 3). Greenwich, CT: JAI.

Stipek, D. J., Recchia, S., & McClintic, S. (1992). Self-evaluation in young children. *Monographs of the Society for Research in Child Development, 57.*

Yussen, S., & Kane, P. (1985). Children's conceptions of intelligence. In S. R. Yussen (Ed.), *The growth of reflection in children* (pp. 207–241). New York: Academic Press.

Zhao, W., & Dweck, C. S. (1994). *Implicit theories and vulnerability to depression-like responses.* Unpublished manuscript, Columbia University.

11 Sociocultural Influences on the Development of Children's Action-Control Beliefs

Todd D. Little

Abstract

This chapter focuses on children's action-control beliefs and how various facets of the action-control system are shaped and affected by sociocultural contexts. From an action theory viewpoint, the action-control system comprises at least three interconnected belief types. Each belief dimension reflects a link between the three constituents of human action: the agent, various means, and the ends (outcome). Children's perceptions of the action relations among these constituents form three primary belief systems: agency beliefs, means–ends (or causality) beliefs, and control expectancy. Recent comparative investigations using this tripartite action-control framework indicate that some aspects of the relations between children's beliefs and their performance can vary considerably across different sociocultural settings. In the school domain, consistent cross-sample differences have emerged in children's beliefs about their personal access (agency beliefs) to school performance–relevant means (e.g., effort, ability, teachers) and the extent to which they believe they can personally control school performance outcomes (control expectancy). The magnitude of correspondence between these beliefs and actual school performance (school grades) has shown sizable cross-sample differences as well. In contrast to these variable outcomes, important sociocultural commonalities exist in the basic structure of children's belief systems and in their everyday conceptions of what determines school performance (means–ends beliefs). In interpreting such outcomes, I discuss ways in which three general influences (cognitive, motivational, and sociocontextual), as proximal aspects of children's sociocultural environments, can affect the development and expression of children's action-control systems.

Introduction

Action-control beliefs are a powerful set of psychological constructs (Skinner, 1995). Their effects can be seen at every phase of an action sequence –

281

from intention, to initiation, action, interpretation, and subsequent intention – and at every step along the life course from infancy to old age (M. M. Baltes & P. B. Baltes, 1986; Berry & West, 1993; Brandtstädter, in press; Brandtstädter, Rothermund, & Schmitz, Chapter 14, this volume). Action-control beliefs account not only for group and *interindividual* differences in performance but also for *intraindividual* differences in actions and behaviors (Schmitz & Skinner, 1993). Particularly for children, as they begin to discover who they are and what they are capable of, evolving competence systems lay developmental foundations that they use repeatedly as they negotiate various developmental tasks and challenges (Cantor, 1994; Cantor & Sanderson, Chapter 7, this volume; Heckhausen & Schulz, 1993; 1995, and Chapter 2, this volume; Skinner, 1995; Weisz, 1983). In facing these challenges, children can be adaptive or maladaptive. A person with a developmentally adaptive profile has high aspirations, perseveres in the face of obstacles, sees more and varied options, learns from failures, and has a greater sense of personal empowerment and well-being – in short, this is a person with high personal agency and control expectancy. A person with a maladaptive profile, on the other hand, has limited personal resources: low aspirations, poor problem-solving skills, and feelings of helplessness and disempowerment – in short, this is a person with low personal agency and control expectancy (see Dweck, 1991, and Chapter 10, this volume; Graham, 1994, and Chapter 5, this volume; Skinner, 1995; Weisz, 1990).

As with most important psychological constructs, the range of individual differences between these extreme profiles is wide and many factors can influence the nature of the action-control system. In this chapter I review findings from an ongoing research project in which my collaborators and I conducted a series of cross-cultural studies examining children's action-control beliefs and the degree of contextual variability in their competence systems.[1] The chapter is organized into three main sections. In the first section, I present our action-control model of psychological control and highlight some of its similarities to and differences from related models. In the second section, I outline some of the strengths and weaknesses of cross-cultural investigations in this area as well as some of the methodological and interpretational problems that can arise. In the third section, I discuss some salient outcomes and life-span implications of our cross-national comparisons.

An Action Theory View on the Psychology of Control

Even when different instruments and models of psychological control are used, the importance of various psychological control perceptions has been repeatedly documented, particularly in the school domain (Dweck, Chapter 10, this volume; Graham, Chapter 5, this volume, Multon, Brown, & Lent, 1991; Stipek & Weisz, 1981; Skinner, 1995). This research shows, for example, that children's beliefs about the general causes of school outcomes and about their own role in producing such outcomes consistently and systematically relate to their actual school achievement. One important characteristic of many recent psychological control theories is that they differentiate between various belief types that children may hold. These belief types include: agency and means–ends beliefs, competence and contingency beliefs, strategy and capacity beliefs, self-efficacy and outcome expectations (M. M. Baltes & P. B. Baltes, 1986; Bandura, 1995; Connell, 1985; Dweck & Elliott, 1983; Flammer, 1995; Graham, 1994; Skinner, 1995; Weisz, 1986).

An action theory perspective explicitly differentiates the possible belief relations among the primary constituents of an action sequence (Chapman, Skinner, & Baltes, 1990; Little, Oettingen, Stetsenko, et al., 1995; Oettingen, Little, Lindenberger, et al., 1994; Skinner & Chapman, 1987; Skinner, Chapman, & Baltes, 1988a, 1988b). The three constituents of an action sequence are the actor, the goal, and the various means by which the goal (or end) can be obtained. Agentic action reflects an agent's general awareness of goals and the means to the goals, taking personal responsibility in pursuing a chosen goal, and being able to select and utilize potential means (Chapman & Skinner, 1985; see also Cantor & Fleeson, 1994). Action-control beliefs reflect three general belief types about the relations among the three constituents of an action sequence. Control expectancy reflects the link between an actor and the goal, personal agency beliefs reflect the links between an actor and the various means, and general means–ends beliefs reflect the links between the various relevant means and the goal or ends (Chapman, Skinner, & Baltes, 1990; Little, Oettingen, Stetsenko, et al., 1995; Oettingen, Little, Lindenberger, et al., 1994; Skinner, Chapman, & Baltes, 1988a, 1988b; see Table 11.1 for detailed definitions). These belief types are operationalized in the Control, Agency, and Means–Ends Interview (CAMI) (Little, Oettingen, Stetsenko, et al., 1995; Skinner, Chapman, & Baltes, 1988a, 1988b).

Means–Ends Beliefs

The CAMI has been quite useful for cross-cultural comparisons because of the nature of means–ends beliefs (see Skinner, 1995). As reflected in the CAMI, means–ends beliefs represent children's general conceptions of the importance of a given means (e.g., effort, luck) for obtaining an outcome

Table 11.1. *Summary of the action-control beliefs represented in the control, agency, and means–ends interview (CAMI)*

Definition	Belief dimensions	Symbolic belief relations
Means–ends or causality beliefs (**M** -> **E**) The child's general expectations about the utility or causal power of specific causes or means (**M**) for a given domain-specific outcome (**E**) such as achieving good or avoiding bad school performance.	Effort Ability Luck Teachers' role Unknown causes	Means **M** causes end **E**
Agency beliefs (**A** -> **M** :: **E**) The child's belief that he or she (**A**) (has access to / can use / can implement) a specific means (**M**) that is relevant (::) for outcome (**E**).	Effort Ability Luck Teachers' role	Agent **A** has means **M** to achieve end **E**
Control expectancy (**A** -> **E**) The child's personal expectation that he or she (**A**) can achieve a given outcome (**E**) without reference to any specific means.	Unspecified	Agent **A** can achieve end **E**

Note. Boldface denotes one of the constituents of intentional action: **A** symbolizes the agent, **M** symbolizes a given outcome-relevant means, and **E** symbolizes the desired outcome. Outcome **E**, such as school performance, implies either the desire to succeed by accomplishing a positive outcome (i.e., getting a good grade) or to succeed by avoiding a negative outcome (i.e., not getting a bad grade).

(see Table 11.1). These causality-related beliefs reflect perceptions of the reasons children generally succeed or fail in attaining their goals. Means–ends beliefs are not personal attributions of performance successes and failures, but instead indicate children's general notions of causality. Such causality conceptions are shaped through the interplay of reasoning skills and the naturally occurring contingencies embedded in a sociocultural context. In this regard, means–ends beliefs reflect children's naive theories of the causes of success and failure in a given domain (Little & Lopez, 1997).

Similar models of psychological control operationalize the means-to-ends connection as first-person or personal strategy beliefs (as opposed to third-person or general causality beliefs; see Skinner, 1995). Although first-person (self-focused) operationalizations are quite useful for many purposes, means–ends beliefs (other-focused and causality-related; or contingency beliefs, Flammer, 1995; Weisz, 1990) can be used as points of reference to determine the degree of commonality in children's views of the causal contingencies in their school-related worlds (see Oettingen, Little, Lindenberger, et al., 1994; Stetsenko, Little, Oettingen, et al., 1995).

The CAMI measures children's beliefs about the causal importance of five means: effort, ability, luck, teachers, and unknowns. Effort and ability are means that emanate from within the child, whereas luck, teachers, and unknowns emanate from outside the child (Little & Lopez, 1997). Children's perceptions of the causal importance of the self-oriented effort and ability dimensions (as well as the distinction between them) can be influenced by such factors as cognitive maturation (Nicholls, 1978; Nicholls & Miller, 1983), adaptive self-regulation and self-perceptions of performance feedback (Dweck, 1991; Graham, 1991; H. Heckhausen, 1984; Karoly, 1993), and common goal structures across modern schooling environments (e.g., teaching the merits of effort and ability in becoming a productive adult in a given society; Elliott & Dweck, 1988; Stetsenko, Little, Oettingen, et al., 1995). In contrast, the non-self-oriented dimensions (luck, teachers, and unknowns) primarily involve culturally determined value characteristics (e.g., the degree and type of authority a teacher may have). In addition to cognitive and motivational influences, children's perceptions of the non-self-oriented means may be shaped by factors such as sociocultural variations in the academic socialization practices of parents and teachers (Deci & Ryan, 1987; Dweck, 1986) and sociocultural variations in teachers' interpersonal styles and practices (Ames, 1992; Ames & Archer, 1988; Boggiano & Katz, 1991).

Self-Related Agency Beliefs and Control Expectancy

Agency beliefs are personal perceptions of whether one possesses or can use a given outcome-relevant means such as effort, luck, or ability (e.g., "When it comes to school, I'm pretty smart"; for sample items, see Oettingen, Little, Lindenberger, et al., 1994, and see Table 11.1). As self-related perceptions of one's personal action resources (e.g., behavioral and cognitive capacity), learning history, and domain-related experiences, these beliefs can vary across individuals and across sociocultural contexts. In terms of other theories of psychological control, agency beliefs are similar to self-efficacy (Bandura, 1995), competence beliefs (Flammer, 1995; Weisz, 1990), and capacity beliefs (Skinner, 1995).

In our action theory model, agency beliefs reflect a child's personal sense of empowerment for each specific means that is relevant to obtaining a goal. Control expectancy, on the other hand, reflects a child's general likelihood assessment of obtaining the desired outcome. In contrast to the agency beliefs, control expectancy reflects a child's global sense of whether he or she can produce or avoid a given outcome without referring to any specific means. Control expectancy is a means-unspecified agency conception of whether a child can personally affect a desired outcome (e.g., "If I want to do well in school, I can"). With such an operationalization, one could view the control-expectancy dimension as superfluous to the relevant agency dimensions. However, control expectancy reflects a broad self-related perception that is more susceptible to evaluative biases such as personal optimism or pessimism and self-protective buffering than are agency beliefs. In addition, control-expectancy judgments appear to be more affected by immediate (on-line) environmental influences than are agency beliefs (Lopez & Little, 1996).

Other models of psychological control such as locus of control theory (Rotter, 1966) and attribution theory (e.g., Graham, 1991, 1994; Weiner, 1986) are also highly related to the action theory framework. Two differences are the temporal direction (past, present, future) of the control judgments, and the first-person (self-focused) versus third-person (other-focused) distinction. For example, attributions are self-related judgments of the reasons for one's prior successes and failures. As such, they are most closely related to personal strategy beliefs (Skinner, 1995) and only moderately related to general means–ends beliefs. Again, the distinction is that means–ends beliefs are general causality-related conceptions (third-person, other-focused), and attributions or strategy beliefs are personal beliefs of what personally works for a child (first-person, self-focused).

The utility of these distinctions can be seen in many empirical patterns found for these action-control beliefs. For example, the role of luck functions differently when defined as a self-related agency belief as opposed to a causality-related means–ends belief. As an agency conception, luck behaves like a personal, self-oriented factor: Children who believe they have access to effort and ability also believe they have access to (i.e., can influence) their personal luck (Little, Oettingen, Stetsenko, et al., 1995; Oettingen, Little, Lindenberger, et al., 1994). In contrast, as a causality-related means–ends conception, luck behaves like a non-self-oriented dimension. Children who believe that external-related means such as teachers and unknown causes are responsible for school outcomes also view luck as a similar influence. At an individual-differences level, luck, teachers, and unknown causes correlate positively with each other but are independent of the self-oriented effort and ability dimensions (see Little & Lopez, 1997). Moreover, the predictive power of action-control beliefs is quite distinct. In the school domain, self-related agency beliefs predict school performance to a far greater degree (i.e., r generally greater than 0.40, and as high as 0.9; see, e.g., Oettingen & Little, 1993) than do causality-related means–ends beliefs (i.e., typically less than 10 percent overlap). The personal control expectancy is in the middle ground, but always positive.

The Utility of the Comparative Approach

Sociocultural settings provide a quasi-experimental manipulation of many features that can shape children's beliefs about their world and their perceptions of their own competence. Moreover, cross-cultural research designs enhance generalizability because they vary the contexts in which such developmental processes occur (Baltes, Reese, & Nesselroade, 1977; Grob, Little, Wanner, et al., 1996; Little, 1997; Van de Vijver & Poortinga, 1992). A potential benefit of such designs is that they can highlight mechanisms that may shape and form children's beliefs. Surprisingly, however, few studies have examined cross-cultural similarities and differences in children's competence systems, even though examining the development of these beliefs cross-culturally can highlight which facets of the competence system are independent of sociocultural variations and which are not. One reason for the lack of cross-cultural studies may be related to the inherent difficulties in establishing the validity of comparison.

Some Methodological Concerns

Because of the potential for translation errors and other sources of bias (Poortinga, 1989), a number of empirical preconditions must be met in order to examine similarities and differences in comparative investigations (Little, 1997). In our comparative analyses, we delineate two general levels of data analysis: measurement and construct. The measurement level focuses on the psychometric issues surrounding the reliability and validity of comparison as well as possible qualitative differences in the fundamental nature of what the items have actually measured. The construct level focuses on the substantive interpretation or meaning of the examined psychological dimensions (Little, 1997).

From a psychometric viewpoint, absence of structural correspondence (e.g., differing loadings; Little, 1997) reflects noncomparable constructs. Such constructs can arise from translation errors and/or cultural bias in the measurement instrument (Poortinga, 1989). In our own work, for example, we found that one CAMI dimension (agency beliefs for luck) lacked structural correspondence in a sample of Japanese children (Karasawa, Little, Miyashita, et al., 1997). This outcome, which likely reflects a fundamental qualitative cultural difference in the luck concept, is an important and informative sociocultural outcome; however, meaningful quantitative comparisons cannot be made for such a construct.

Measurement equivalence (e.g., mathematical equivalence of all reliable item-to-construct parameters; see Little, 1997) reflects quantitatively comparable constructs. When tenable, it indicates that the constructs' measurement structure is the same in each sociocultural setting. It is significant that measurement equivalence does not necessarily imply that the constructs' psychological meaning is identical (this information is contained in the relations among the constructs). Instead, measurement equivalence indicates that the constructs' psychometric properties are similar enough to assert that the construct labeled "X" in one sociocultural setting is also a form of "X" in another sociocultural setting (e.g., *X*, x, or **X**) and not some other undeterminable construct (e.g., *Z*, y, or **Q**).

Measurement equivalence is an important basis for any cross-cultural study because it shows that items have been comparably translated and responded to with minimal or no bias (e.g., no response sets, or ceiling and floor effects). Such constructs can be equivalently defined and their psychological meaning can be quantitatively compared across different sociocultural contexts (Little, 1997; Poortinga, 1989; Van de Vijver & Poortinga, 1992). Measurement equivalence is therefore a critical and necessary condition for valid cross-cultural comparisons. In our own work, we have shown that measurement equivalence is a tenable feature of our comparisons.

In contrast to the measurement level, the psychological level focuses on the *constructs'* underlying meaning. Assuming measurement equivalence of the manifest variables, the interpretable substantive information is contained in the constructs' mean levels, correlations, predictive relations, and so on. Even though measurement equivalence is a necessary precondition to compare constructs, many substantive outcomes can occur. *Specificity* reflects constructs that have mostly different mean levels, correlational structures, and predictive relations. *Functional similarity* reflects constructs that have moderately similar patterns across sociocultural contexts. Finally, *generality* reflects constructs that have mostly similar mean levels, correlational structures, and predictive relations.

As detailed below, children's causality-related means–ends beliefs show considerable sociocultural generality (or at least functional similarity), whereas children's personal agency and control-expectancy beliefs show more sociocultural specificity.

An Interpretive Framework

The structural-cognitive, motivational, and sociocontextual perspectives are three basic views that can be utilized to interpret the cross-cultural similarities and differences in children's psychological control (Little, Oettingen,

Stetsenko, et al., 1995; Little & Lopez, 1997; Oettingen, Little, Lindenberger, et al., 1994). These perspectives are not mutually exclusive, nor do they provide competing hypotheses about the similarities or dissimilarities that should emerge. Instead, these foci, as a group, provide a framework for organizing some of the influences that can contribute to sociocultural similarities and differences in children's action-control beliefs.

From a structural-cognitive perspective, certain developmental patterns might emerge as a function of cognitive maturity. For example, aspects of children's causality conceptions have been linked to cognitive advances (Nicholls & Miller, 1983; Little & Lopez, 1997; Stipek, 1992). Similar developmental patterns such as correlational differentiation (systematic decreases in the correlations) among two or more action-control beliefs may be shaped by cognitive maturity.

From a motivational perspective, certain developmental patterns may be related to adaptive and maladaptive self-regulatory processes. For example, children who focus on causes such as effort and ability in their performance-related attributions generally use more effective adaptation and adjustment strategies in school settings than do those children who focus on non-self-oriented causes such as luck and teachers (Boggiano & Katz, 1991; Dweck, 1991; Dweck & Elliott, 1983; Graham, 1991; Stipek, 1992). From this viewpoint, similar developmental patterns such as mean-level increases in the importance of effort may be indicative of common motivational processes.

Finally, certain developmental patterns may emerge as a result of the constraints, values, and naturally occurring contingencies embedded in a given sociocultural context. Because school-related contexts and their associated organizational features are generally embedded in the overarching sociocultural fabric of a given society, they generally serve as proximal carriers of the more distal sociocultural influences (Hofstede, 1991; Oettingen, 1995). Therefore, although many factors that shape and regulate children's action-control beliefs are similar, others can vary, such as parents' values about academic performance, types of performance feedback, teaching styles, types of learning experiences, and so on (Bandura, 1995; Bandura & Jourden, 1991; Butler, 1992; Dweck, Chapter 10, this volume; Dweck & Elliott, 1983; Graham, 1994, and Chapter 5, this volume; Karoly, 1993; Little, Oettingen, Stetsenko, et al., 1995; Mac Iver, 1987; Oettingen, Little, Lindenberger, et al., 1994; Stipek, 1992). In general, cognitive, motivational, context-common, and context-specific factors converge to provide the setting in which children acquire their self- and causality-related understandings of school performance.

Substantive Outcomes

Two general questions have guided our studies of children's action-control beliefs across various sociocultural settings.[3] First, what is the basic structure of children's action-control beliefs? Second, how do the various components of action-control function? Because we have couched both these questions within the context of our broader comparative approach, we therefore address their generality: What is the generality of the structure and function of action-control beliefs?

The Structure of Children's Action-Control Beliefs

One question in our cross-cultural explorations has been whether the structure of the action-control system is the same in non-Western sociocultural settings as it is in Western contexts. Assuming that active goal-directed behavior is a general human process, the basic structure of the CAMI should be equivalent across sociocultural settings. This question is particularly relevant because not only have most studies on children's psychological control been based on Western samples (particularly U.S. samples), but also some researchers have suggested that self-efficacious individuals emerge only in the context of the indigenous individualistic values of Western societies (see Karasawa, Little, Miyashita, et al., 1997; Stetsenko, Little, Oettingen, et al., 1995). For example, personal responsibility for performance is assumed to be a basic normative goal in Western countries (Grob, Little, Wanner, et al., 1996; Stetsenko, Little, Oettingen, et al., 1995).

At the most fundamental level, our cross-national comparisons have demonstrated that the measurement structure of children's action-control beliefs is quite uniform across the sociocultural contexts examined, with only one notable exception. We found that Japanese children's agency beliefs concerning luck did not follow the Western-based findings (Karasawa, Little, Miyashita, et al., 1997). Specifically, the luck concept in Japanese society appears to preclude individuals from having agentic beliefs in their own personal control of it. This outcome is significant for at least two reasons. First, it highlights the fact that our analysis system (MACS models; Jöreskog & Sörborn, 1989; Little, 1997) is sensitive to sociocultural differences in the measurement structure of the beliefs assessed by the CAMI. Second, it highlights the fact that some Western-based theorizing about psychological control does not generalize to all sociocultural settings.

Other than this one exception, our studies have demonstrated that nearly all the action-control dimensions are generalizable to many and varied sociocultural settings, and the measurement equivalence of the CAMI indicates that our comparisons at the psychological (construct) level are veridical. In addition to the measurement structure, the general internal correlational relations among the CAMI constructs showed considerable similarity across these different sociocultural settings. In particular, as detailed in the following paragraphs, at least three general features of the correlational structure are socioculturally consistent.

A first general consistency is that the correlations among the self-related agency and control-expectancy constructs form a moderately strong and positive correlational manifold (around 50 to 60 percent of the reliable variances are shared) (see Karasawa, Little, Miyashita, et al., 1997; Little, Oettingen, Stetsenko, et al., 1995). Such a pattern suggests that children who report that they have access to effort, for example, also report that they have access to both ability and luck and that they generally believe they can attain performance outcomes (i.e., control expectancy). On one hand, these correlational patterns suggest that a pervasive influence governs the self-related aspects of children's competence systems. This influence would also be of adaptive significance in that a child would have many different dimensions of his or her personal resources to call upon when faced with a challenge. On the other hand, the lack of perfect correlation indicates that each dimension contains unique and reliable variance. Such correlational patterns also indicate that differential predictive relations could emerge across sociocultural contexts.

Second, the cross-domain correlations between children's causality-related means–ends beliefs and the self-related agency and control-expectancy dimensions also show socioculturally consistent patterns. First, "Means–ends: Effort" correlated consistently and positively with each personal agency and control-expectancy dimension (r generally in the 0.20s). Such a pattern is consistent with an adaptive motivational profile (see also Dweck, Chapter 10, this volume). Specifically, those children who endorse the role of effort as an important means to acquire good grades (Means–ends: Effort) also report that they can exert effort (Agency: Effort), express their ability (Agency: Ability), influence their luck (Agency: Luck), solicit their teacher's support (Agency: Teacher), and generally achieve good grades (Control Expectancy). Second, the children's endorsements of the three non-self-oriented dimensions indicate an opposite, negative correlational pattern (r generally in the –0.20s). Such a pattern is consistent with a maladaptive motivational profile. Namely, those children who believe that factors such as luck, teachers, and unknown factors are important for obtaining school outcomes have lower self-related efficacy beliefs than do children who generally downplay the causal importance of these non-self-oriented causes. Finally, in contrast to these socioculturally consistent patterns, the other self-oriented causal dimension, ability, showed a more varied pattern. Only in the two Berlin samples was the correlational link to the self-related beliefs positive (*r* generally in the 0.20s). In the other samples this link was negative or essentially zero (see Karasawa, Little, Miyashita, et al., 1997; Little & Lopez, 1997). Thus, the motivational implications of children's conceptions of ability as a cause of school performance appear to be tied to their specific sociocultural contexts (Dweck, Chapter 10, this volume; Graham, Chapter 5, this volume).

The third general consistency is that the correlations among causality-related beliefs also indicate that these profiles are relatively independent. Specifically, although luck, teachers, and unknowns were moderately correlated with each other, as were effort and ability, children's ratings of the importance of effort were mostly uncorrelated with the non-self-oriented dimensions, and ability showed moderate overlap with luck, teachers, and unknowns (Little & Lopez, 1997). The mixed pattern of individual-differences relations for ability suggests that children's conceptions of the importance of ability in school performance are relatively complex (see Dweck, Chapter 10, this volume). That is, their ability perceptions contain unique self-oriented features (i.e., ability correlates with effort perceptions after controlling for the non-self-oriented dimensions) and unique non-self-oriented features (i.e., ability correlates with luck, teachers, and unknowns, after controlling for effort).

The link between the children's self-related beliefs in their personal access to teachers and their beliefs in the causal influence of teachers was also consistent across sociocultural contexts. Specifically, children who believed more in the role of teachers as a causal influence in their academic outcomes also believed they had less access to their teachers' help and support. This general negative relationship between the teacher-related means–ends and agency beliefs suggests that the social dynamic between students and teachers is one in which the more powerful a teacher is perceived to be, the less accessible or more distanced she or he appears to be. The motivational implications of such a relationship may ultimately be maladaptive. That is, although teachers generally are helpful (and gaining access to them would be beneficial), if they are perceived as very important then the benefits of access to them are diminished (cf. Boggiano & Katz, 1991).

In summary, both the measurement structure and the implied psychological structure (i.e., the pattern of internal correlations among the ten CAMI dimensions) have shown striking patterns of intercultural similarity.

These outcomes provide strong support for the action-related components of children's competence systems assessed by such instruments as the CAMI (Little, Oettingen, & Baltes, 1995; Little & Wanner, 1996; Skinner, 1995). In addition, these outcomes support the idea that cross-cultural investigations can provide useful and comparable domains of psychological inquiry.

The Generality of Functional Aspects of Children's Action-Control Beliefs

The Causality-Related Means–Ends Beliefs. Regarding the functional aspects of children's action-control beliefs, another goal that has arisen in our work has been to determine the degree to which children of different sociocultural settings share similar views of the causes of school outcomes. How similar are the children's causality-related means–ends beliefs? As summarized elsewhere (e.g., Little, Oettingen, Stetsenko, Little, Oettingen, et al., 1995; Little & Lopez, 1997; Oettingen, Little, Lindenberger, et al., 1994; Stetsenko, Little, Oettingen, et al., 1995), children's everyday conceptions about the causes of good and bad school performance (means–ends beliefs) and their correlation with school performance is likely to be similar within sociocultural settings because, in addition to shared cognitive-developmental and motivational influences, these beliefs are shaped and constrained by core similarities across modern schooling environments. Formal schooling contexts in industrialized nations share generally similar goals, basic procedures, uniform settings, and common activities (see Stetsenko, Little, Oettingen, et al., 1995). As such, school contexts have many fundamental characteristics that are uniform influences across modern sociocultural settings (Little, Oettingen, Stetsenko, et al., 1995; Stetsenko, Little, Oettingen, et al., 1995).

Given the basic school-related commonalities in these sociocultural settings (Stetsenko, Little, Oettingen, et al., 1995), we found that in each sociocultural setting children's beliefs about the utility of various school-relevant means were generally congeneric. In other words, children generally agree on the basic importance of causal influences such as effort and ability in producing school performance (see Figure 11.1A). Against the backdrop of basic similarities in these mean-level profiles, only three differences are evident in Figure 11.1A (Little, Oettingen, Stetsenko, et al., 1995). The Los Angeles children endorsed effort more highly than did the children in the other sociocultural settings, the children from the East and West Berlin samples endorsed ability more highly than Moscow and Los

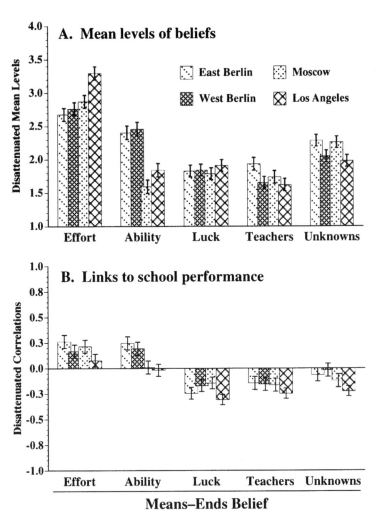

Figure 11.1. Sociocultural similarities in the correlations between the causality-related means–ends beliefs and actual school performance. (A) Disattenuated mean levels of the means–ends beliefs. (B) Disattenuated correlation between the means–ends beliefs and the teacher-assigned school grades. Note the cultural generality of the adaptive relations between effort and school performance and the maladaptive relations of the non-self-oriented dimensions: Luck, Teachers, and Unknowns (*Source:* Data from Little, Oettingen, Stetsenko, et al., 1995.)

Angeles children, and the children from the two formerly Communist contexts (East Berlin and Moscow) endorsed unknown factors more highly than did the children in the Western contexts. Notably, the differences in the ability ratings relative to the effort ratings suggest that in both German samples, effort and ability are nearly equally emphasized as contingent ways in which one can achieve school outcomes.

Similar to the mean-level patterns, striking sociocultural generality in the causality beliefs' correlational profiles with academic performance has emerged (see Figure 11.1B). Although the strength of the relations is generally quite small (as expected), these profiles are consistent with a number of motivational assumptions (Dweck & Elliott, 1983; Graham, Chapter 5, this volume). First, the adaptive significance of the self-oriented dimensions can be seen in their generally positive correlations with school performance; second, the maladaptive impact of the non-self-oriented dimensions can be seen in their generally negative performance correlations. In particular, the adaptive importance of effort is consistent across these sociocultural settings. The more children believe that effort is an important causal constituent of school outcomes, the higher is their actual school performance. This pattern is also consistent with the internal structure of the beliefs. Recall that children with higher agency beliefs and control expectancy also had higher beliefs in the causal importance of effort in each sociocultural setting. Moreover, these two profiles are independent from one another (i.e., the self-oriented dimensions are uncorrelated with the non-self-oriented dimensions) (see, e.g., Little & Lopez, 1997). Such relations indicate that both profiles consistently emerge across these diverse sociocultural settings.

The relations for ability, on the other hand, were not as consistent across these sociocultural settings. In both the Moscow and Los Angeles samples, the individual-differences links showed complete correlational independence. The East and West Berlin samples, on the other hand, showed positive correlations with school performance, suggesting that ability, as a means to good school performance, is a strongly emphasized contingency in these sociocultural settings (Little, Oettingen, Stetsenko, et al., 1995; Oettingen, Little, Lindenberger, et al., 1994; see also Figure 11.1A). Regarding the non-self-oriented causes of school performance (luck, teachers, and unknowns), the maladaptive relationships were nearly universal in both direction and magnitude: The more that children endorsed luck, teachers, or unknown factors as important causal processes in school performance, the less well they did (accounting for about 8 percent of the reliable variance).

In addition to the motivational influences reflected in our cross-cultural data sets, general cognitive-developmental processes can be seen. Nicholls and others have suggested that effort and ability are undifferentiated concepts in younger children (see Chapman & Skinner, 1989; Nicholls, 1978; Nicholls & Miller, 1983). Because young children are less cognitively mature, they are unable to grasp the idea that if two children of the same ability experience different outcomes then differential effort can produce the differences. If cognitive maturity is a general influence on children's conceptual understanding that effort and ability are distinct causes of school performance, then the individual-difference relations between effort and ability should show general and systematic correlational differentiation (Little & Lopez, 1997). That is, the correlations should decrease with age. As shown in Figure 11.2A, this pattern is precisely what has emerged. In addition to the general influence of cognitive maturity, the consistent difference between the East and West Berlin settings and the other four sociocultural contexts (i.e., Los Angeles, Moscow, Prague, and Tokyo) indicates that sociocontextual influences also have an impact on the overall magnitudes of the correlations. For example, in the two Berlin settings, both effort and ability are strongly emphasized as the contingent processes by which good school performance can be achieved (Little & Lopez, 1997). This emphasis on both dimensions is consistent with the generally higher magnitudes of correlation in each age cohort.

Another notable similarity in the means–ends dimensions that is related to cognitive-developmental influences, motivational influences, and sociocontextual influences is the pattern of mean-level differentiation among the causality-related conceptions. In Figure 11.2B, these developmental patterns are generally uniform in their age-related dispersion. Relative to the ratings of the older children, in second grade the five causal dimensions are closer together in their rated importance; only effort was distinguished in this youngest age cohort. However, in the sixth grade, the causal dimensions show greater separation. These older children rated effort as the primary cause of school outcomes, followed by ability, unknowns, teachers, and, finally, luck. The increased importance of effort and the decreased importance of the non-self-oriented dimensions indicates that the adaptive utility of effort, as a central component in achievement, becomes more clearly understood and differentiated with each successive age cohort (see Heckhausen, 1984; Little & Lopez, 1997). Second, Figure 11.2B shows that teachers were viewed as quite important in the second and sixth grades; however, the trajectories across the sociocultural settings follow a quadratic path, reaching a low point in the fourth grade. This U-shaped quadratic trend for the role of teachers may be related to cognitive changes during this age range (Little & Lopez, 1997). In this regard, the omnipotent powerful other

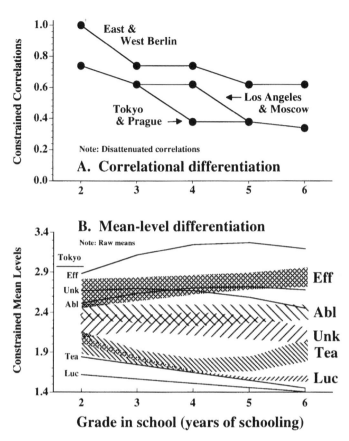

Figure 11.2. Sociocultural similarities in the development of the causality-related means–ends beliefs. (A) The correlational differentiation between children's ratings of the importance of effort and ability for school outcomes. (B) The range of the developmental trends in mean-level differentiation among the five causality-related beliefs in East Berlin, Los Angeles, Moscow, Prague, and West Berlin. (Note: Because of the relatively unique trajectories in the Tokyo sample, their developmental trends are superimposed on the ranges, or bandwidths, for the other sociocultural settings. Unless otherwise noted in text, the basic shape of the trajectory for each sociocultural context within a bandwidth was generally the same. The differences in slopes and locations are significant: $p < 0.01$). (*Source:* Data from Little & Lopez, 1997.)

in the early years may lose his or her status as children realize that teachers are people too (i.e., as children develop greater social understanding). However, the more subtle power that teachers actually do possess, as the controllers and guides of the classroom environment, may be recognized in the later years (i.e., understanding a teacher's position may require well-developed perspective-taking skills). Relatedly, teachers' behaviors may change during the elementary school years. Early on, teachers may institute highly structured social-play activities. As children become more familiar with the general rules of interaction, less structured social activities emerge. Gradually, however, an increased focus on highly structured educational activities comes to the foreground in the latter elementary school years. In either case, the factors influencing the children's high ratings of the teacher's importance in the early elementary years may be different from those in the later elementary years, and both may be dependent upon children's cognitive-maturational advances as well as the behavior of teachers.

Children's discriminations among the outcome-relevant causes of school performance may reflect adaptive self-regulatory acquisitions. For example, research on the motivational consequences of children's performance-related attributions indicates that a child's reliance on the self-oriented causal dimensions of effort and ability leads to better adaptation and adjustment in school settings (Graham, 1991, and Chapter 5, this volume). Moreover, evidence suggests that the distinction between the self-oriented (effort and ability) and non-self-oriented causes (luck, teachers, and unknowns) enhances performance (Boggiano & Katz, 1991) because it allows children to develop accurate, consistent, and self-enhanced views of themselves and their performance outcomes.

Both the mean-level and correlational patterns for effort and ability relative to luck, teachers, and unknowns are consistent with this view (see Little & Lopez, 1997, for more details). For example, the correlational differentiation between effort and ability is consistent with the proposition that such a distinction contributes to the emergence of achievement motivation (Dweck & Elliott, 1983; Heckhausen, 1984). Moreover, effort increases in importance and ability remains at least stable during this middle childhood era in each sociocultural setting, while the non-self-oriented dimensions generally decrease with age (except for the importance of teachers during the fifth and sixth grades; see Figure 11.2B). These mean-level trajectories may reflect the adaptive benefits of the self-oriented causal processes relative to the non-self-oriented processes (Boggiano & Katz, 1991).

The motivational implications of the patterns of relations in these causality-related beliefs presupposes sociocultural uniformity for the motivational basis of these developmental trends. Such an assumption, however, may not always be tenable. For example, in contrast to the other sociocultural settings, the development of intrinsic motivation in school contexts may occur sooner in Japanese children (Azuma, 1996; Hess & Azuma, 1991; Holloway, 1988). Given that the non-self-oriented dimensions showed distinct, stable, and highly differentiated patterns in the Tokyo sample, some motivationally based mechanisms may already be in place when the Japanese children begin their formal schooling (Little & Lopez, 1997). Ample evidence indicates that Japanese parents emphasize preschool experiences to prepare their children for formal schooling (Azuma, 1996). These early experiences may indeed prepare Japanese children to cope adaptively with the demands of education upon entrance into the formal setting. In contrast, evidence suggests that, at least for schoolchildren in the United States, these motivationally based processes appear to be acquired later, perhaps through learning experiences during the elementary school years (Boggiano & Katz, 1991).

The relations for ability also showed distinctive mean-level and correlational patterns that suggest that the motivational influence of ability perceptions may be tied to the values and contingencies embedded in the children's sociocultural contexts. In the Berlin samples, for instance, the emphasis on ability as a constituent of school performance showed up as higher mean levels relative to the other sociocultural contexts and as moderately positive correlations with both actual performance and the children's self-related beliefs about performance. In the other sociocultural settings, these correlations were essentially zero or slightly negative (see Dweck, Chapter 10, this volume).

In summary, the causality-related means–ends beliefs showed many sociocultural similarities. The general mean-level profiles for these dimensions were mostly similar in each sociocultural setting. The ability profile was distinctive in the East and West Berlin samples, and the non-self-oriented dimensions were distinctive in the Tokyo sample. The general correlation profiles for these dimensions were also quite similar across the sociocultural contexts. The two Berlin samples again showed distinctive patterns on the ability dimension. In contrast to the general similarities for the means–ends dimensions, the children's personal beliefs in their access to these school-relevant means have shown sizable cross-cultural variability, in terms of both the mean levels and the correlations with actual school performance.

Self-Related Agency Beliefs and Control Expectancy. A basic expectation in our research has been that the children's self-related beliefs (the agency dimensions and control expectancy) would show sizable mean-level differences and striking magnitude differences in the correlational link between these beliefs and actual school performance. Children's agency and control-expectancy beliefs, being self-related conceptions, should be readily influenced by unique contextual features such as differences in feedback practices and instructional formats. As mentioned, school contexts and their associated organizational features are embedded in the overarching sociocultural fabric of a given society. In addition to their unique influence, school contexts serve as carriers of the distal sociocultural features (Hofstede, 1991; Oettingen, 1995; Stetsenko, Little, Oettingen, et al., 1995) and therefore provide the proximal context in which children's self-perceptions of their academic competence are formed. Accordingly, our interpretations have focused on variable school-related features of sociocultural settings instead of on general distal characteristics such as societal values. Two such school-related attributes, which admittedly are a posteriori classifications, are degree of curriculum dimensionality and manner of performance feedback (Little, Oettingen, Stetsenko, et al., 1995; Oettingen, Little, Lindenberger, et al., 1994; Stetsenko, Little, Oettingen, et al., 1995).

Degree of dimensionality refers to the general distinction between uni- and multidimensional teaching structures (Mac Iver, 1987, 1988; Rosenholtz & Rosenholtz, 1981). Unidimensional curricula involve standardized and uniformly applied daily activities for all children in a classroom, whereas multidimensional formats involve generally individualized and often nonstandard daily activities that are geared to the specific learning needs of individuals or small groups within the larger classroom. Manner of feedback refers to varying aspects of feedback such as social transparency (public versus private feedback) (Oettingen, Little, Lindenberger, et al., 1994) and directness (critical and realistic feedback versus esteem-protective and supportive feedback) (see Ames, 1992; Ames & Archer, 1988; Boggiano & Katz, 1991; Deci & Ryan, 1987; Dweck, 1986; Stipek, 1992).

Figure 11.3 depicts the sizable variability across the various sociocultural settings in the degree to which school-related factors such as these may have contributed to the mean levels of children's self-related agency and control-expectancy beliefs and the degree of correspondence between these beliefs and actual school performance. The top line reflects the percentage of the highest possible score in terms of the children's self-related agency and control-expectancy beliefs. Higher scores reflect greater personal empowerment; in this regard, children in East Berlin and in Los Angeles reflect opposite ends of this distribution. The bottom line in Figure 11.3 reflects the correspondence between these self-beliefs and the teacher-assigned school

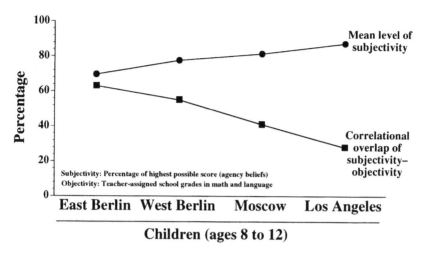

Figure 11.3. Cultural differences in subjectivity–objectivity: Action-control beliefs about one's own performance potential (subjectivity) versus actual school performance (objectivity). (*Source:* Adapted from Little, Oettingen, Stetsenko, et al., 1995.)

grades. Again, East Berlin and Los Angeles children represent opposite ends of this distribution.

The publicly communicated and highly critical feedback typical in East Berlin classrooms, coupled with a highly unidimensional teaching format, appear to have lowered the East Berlin children's subjective self-beliefs. These influences are consistent with the high correspondence between the action-control beliefs and actual school performance of the children from East Berlin (i.e., 63 percent) (Little, Oettingen, Stetsenko, et al., 1995; Oettingen, Little, Lindenberger, et al., 1994). For the Los Angeles children, the privately communicated and esteem-protective feedback they typically receive, coupled with a generally multidimensional teaching format, appear to have led to a level of subjective self-beliefs that is the highest of the sociocultural contexts that we have examined. These influences are also consistent with the very low beliefs–performance correspondence (i.e., 28 percent) (Little, Oettingen, Stetsenko, et al., 1995; Oettingen, Little, Lindenberger, 1994).

Compared to other sociocultural contexts, the Los Angeles setting reflects a culturally specific constellation of teaching factors that may have affected the children's action-control beliefs (Little, Oettingen, Stetsenko, et al., 1995): relatively more individualized and mastery-focused classroom training and relatively more private and generally esteem-protective feedback. In terms of psychological mechanisms that may be involved, type of feedback (e.g., critical versus esteem-protective) is an important influence on the formation and regulation of self-beliefs (Bandura, 1995; Bandura & Jourden, 1991; Karoly, 1993). The effects of such self-regulatory mechanisms can be found in both the mean-levels of the agency and control-expectancy beliefs as well as the strength of the beliefs–performance correlations. For example, highly supportive (esteem-protective; e.g., the Los Angeles setting) feedback likely enhances children's assessment of their own performance potential but attenuates the correspondence (correlation) with actual performance (Little, Oettingen, Stetsenko, et al., 1995; Oettingen, 1995; Stipek, 1988). In contrast, teachers' critical performance-based feedback (e.g., East Berlin) likely lowers children's personal sense of agency and control expectancy as well as strengthens the generally positive relations between these self-related action resources and actual performance (Ames, 1992; Dweck, 1986; Little, Oettingen, Stetsenko, et al., 1995; Oettingen, Little, Lindenberger, et al., 1994).

Uni- and multidimensional teaching formats also can influence children's agency and control-expectancy conceptions and their correspondence with school grades (Little, Oettingen, Stetsenko, et al., 1995; Oettingen, Little, Lindenberger, et al., 1994). These schooling formats differ in the extent to which they allow for social-comparison opportunities and self-mastery experiences (Bandura, 1995; Butler, 1992; Dweck, Chapter 10, this volume; Frey & Ruble, 1990; Little, Oettingen, Stetsenko, et al., 1995; Oettingen, Little, Lindenberger, et al., 1994; Ruble, 1983; Stipek, 1988). For instance, multidimensional systems limit comparisons between children because no or few other children participate in the same task at the same time. Multidimensional formats also provide children with comparatively more performance-relevant mastery experiences because teachers attempt to define skill-appropriate tasks at which each child can succeed. When combined with supportive and esteem-protective feedback, multidimensional systems would contribute to higher levels of children's agency and control expectancy, and to a lower beliefs–performance correlations. Unidimensional teaching formats, on the other hand, provide children with ample daily opportunities to compare their like-task performances with those of others. In addition, unidimensional formats tend to apply the same performance-based goals to all children (Dweck, 1986, 1991; Rosenholtz & Rosenholtz, 1981). Such unidimensional systems would contribute to lower mean levels of agency and control expectancy and higher beliefs–performance correlations.

Although these two extremes are remarkable, each comparison within

Figure 11.3 offers important insights into the nature of the sociocultural influences on the development of children's action-control beliefs. For example, when we initially compared the East and West Berlin children, we found that these two contexts also produced two opposing mean-level and correlational profiles (Oettingen, Little, Lindenberger, et al., 1994), although the differences are not as large when they are compared to the profiles of children from Moscow or Los Angeles. For the East Berlin children, the critical and public feedback as well as the unidimensional classroom format produced individual-difference relations between the children's beliefs about themselves and their actual performance that were higher than those of their West Berlin peers. In addition, the mean levels of the East Berlin children's beliefs were much lower than those of the West Berlin children (see Oettingen, Little, Lindenberger, et al., 1994; and Figure 11.3). Because these two samples share a generally common historical-cultural background, the East Berlin–West Berlin comparison demonstrates the powerful influence that differential features of educational environments can have when basic cultural features are similar. That is, in comparison to the other sociocultural contexts, these two settings share a common cultural heritage and a common socioeducational history. For example, both systems traditionally employed generally unidimensional teaching practices and critical feedback, although these features of the educational practices in the former East Berlin were accentuated in comparison to those of their West Berlin neighbors (Oettingen, Little, Lindenberger, et al., 1994). The accentuation of such practices was in accordance with the educational goal of former Communist regimes, to enhance realistic and accurate self-appraisal (see Oettingen, Little, Lindenberger, et al., 1994, for details).

Moreover, the basic goals of the educational systems in both East and West Berlin are also similar (Oettingen, Little, Lindenberger, et al., 1994). For example, near the end of the sixth year of elementary education in West Berlin, parents and children choose the next level of secondary education (e.g., Gymnasium, Realschule, and Hauptschule). This educational choice is available for some children in West Berlin even after the fourth year of elementary education. In conjunction with the general emphasis on realistic and accurate self-appraisal in the East Berlin system, a similar choice is made at the end of the eighth year of schooling. These educational streams are generally tied to the children's performance capabilities, and the parent–teacher–child triad actively discuss a child's personal capabilities in the process of choosing the most appropriate educational stream. Given the differentiated educational streams, teachers' evaluations are likely to carry important decision-making weight. As presented above, such structural similarities between the educational systems in East and West Berlin are consistent with the children's high evaluations of ability as a causal constituent of school outcomes, its positive correlations with actual school performance and self-related beliefs (agency beliefs and control expectancy), and its high levels of correlation with "Means–ends: Effort."

Notably, the developmental trends for agency and control-expectancy beliefs have not shown age-related differences (e.g., Oettingen, Little, Lindenberger, et al., 1994; Little, Oettingen, Stetsenko, et al., 1995; Skinner & Chapman, 1987; Skinner & Connell, 1986; Stetsenko, Little, Oettingen, et al., 1995), indicating that the overall outcomes (Figure 11.3) are not due to moderating developmental patterns. That is, the differences in the sociocultural contexts are evident as early as the second grade and remain stable at least during middle childhood. In addition, agency and control-expectancy beliefs have consistently exhibited a high positive manifold that is generally invariant across these ages.

A final point of comparison shown in Figure 11.3 is the location of the Moscow children within these patterns. Moscow children shared a political system and educational policy similar to those of children in East Berlin, but differed in their cultural heritage and socioeducational history (Oettingen, 1995). Because Moscow schools were predominantly collective-oriented (as compared to the individual-oriented teaching practices of Western schools), teachers would typically emphasize the interests of the collective rather than the individual, teaching students in the context of a group with a curriculum and pace anchored to the overall group (i.e., moderately unidimensional). Therefore, although educational reforms toward more cooperative educational formats were afoot in Moscow schools, individual needs were generally taken into account to a lesser extent than in Western schooling contexts but more so than in East Berlin (see Stetsenko, Little, Oettingen, et al., 1995). Moreover, the Moscow system did not employ differentiated educational streams. Although certain schools were considered better than others, these schools were not integrated into the educational practices such that all children would progress through them; instead, these schools were often available only to the children of favored political party members. Such features of the educational context in Moscow are consistent with the outcomes for those children: They had higher mean levels of subjective self-beliefs and lower beliefs–performance correlations than did the children in the Berlin settings.

Potential Moderator Effects. In a further comparison of East and West Berlin children (Oettingen & Little, 1993), we addressed the role that in-

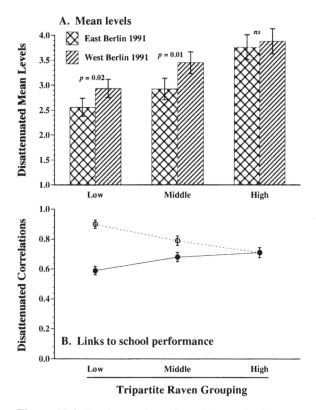

Figure 11.4. The interactive effect of Raven intelligence as a potential moderator of sociocultural influences on children's psychological control. (A) Disattenuated mean levels of the children's agency beliefs. (Note: Effort, ability, and luck are aggregated into a single construct.) (B) Disattenuated correlations between the agency beliefs and the teacher-assigned school grades. (*Source:* Data from Oettingen & Little, 1993.)

telligence might play in moderating the East–West Berlin differences (Figure 11.3; Oettingen, Little, Lindenberger, et al., 1994; see also Oettingen, 1995). Specifically, when we examined these relations by level of Raven intelligence, a powerful interactive effect emerged: The mean-level differences were centered primarily in the low- and moderate-Raven children and nonexistent in the high-Raven children (see Figure 11.4A). The correlational patterns followed a similar pattern (see Figure 11.4B). The low-Raven children in East Berlin had a very high correlation between their self-beliefs and actual performance while their low-Raven compatriots in West

Berlin had a quite low correlation between beliefs and performance. The two middle-Raven groups were closer to one another, but still different, and the high-Raven groups showed an identical beliefs–performance correlation.

Such strong interactive effects with level of Raven intelligence are consistent with the differences in the educational practices within these two settings. East Berlin had a stronger emphasis on accurate self-appraisal and, accordingly, teachers provided appropriate feedback to their pupils. Such practices, in addition to learning conferences wherein teachers candidly discussed each child's performance capabilities in front of the other children, had their greatest impact on the low-Raven group. These children showed nearly a 90 percent overlap between their self-related beliefs and their actual performance, and reported the lowest levels of personal empowerment.

How Our Findings Compare with the Literature on U.S. Children. The patterns of similarity found in the children's causality-related beliefs indicate that many basic commonalities exist across educational settings in the United States and Europe. In addition to cognitive-developmental influences and basic motivational assumptions, core aspects of the formal educational environment appear to be general influences across sociocultural settings. However, because the outcomes for the Los Angeles sample are clearly within the patterns found in previous research on samples from the United States (Findley & Cooper, 1983; Multon, Brown, & Lent, 1991; Stipek & Weisz, 1981), the variable sociocultural patterns suggest that the majority of work on the self-related beliefs about school performance among children in the United States is restricted to U.S. settings (Little, Oettingen, Stetsenko, et al., 1995).

Given that these general patterns were replicated in our Los Angeles sample, two conclusions can be drawn. First, the sizable cross-cultural variability in the nature of these action-control beliefs and their connection to school performance are not an artifact of our theoretical and measurement framework, nor of our analytic system. Instead, these comparative outcomes reflect comparable constructs that are now solidly linked to the plethora of studies based in the United States (e.g., Multon, Brown, & Lent, 1991). Second, the U.S. pattern represents one extreme of the distributional profiles found among these sociocultural contexts. The Los Angeles children evinced the highest mean levels of agency and control-expectancy beliefs and the lowest correlations between these beliefs and actual school grades. The opposite extreme is found in the East Berlin children, who displayed the lowest sense of personal agency and control expectancy and the highest degree of beliefs–performance correspondence. These differences in the beliefs–performance correlations are sizable in terms of the variance explained (63 percent in East Berlin, 28 percent in Los Angeles; see Figure 11.3).

Future Directions and Life-Span Implications

Because the explanatory possibilities that we have used in our work are a posteriori, they must be explored more thoroughly; however, independent of how accurate our explanations are, the diversity of the outcomes raises several new research challenges. That is, not only are the mean levels of the children's self-related agency and control-expectancy beliefs affected by sociocultural differences, but so too are the correlations between these beliefs and actual school performance. As a result, these comparative findings may serve as a catalyst for gaining better insights into the sizable plasticity of children's action-control systems and the ways in which action-control beliefs optimally relate to both immediate performance and long-term development.

Although discussion has emerged concerning the most functional levels of beliefs (Baumeister, 1989; Taylor & Brown, 1988), surprisingly few studies have addressed how children's competence systems optimally contribute to future development gains and produce agentic and successful individuals within adult society (see Little, Oettingen, Stetsenko, et al., 1995). Given that these complex relations likely differ across sociocultural, individual, and domain contexts, the answer to such questions may center on gains and losses (P. B. Baltes, 1987). The gains associated with present functioning may yield losses in future capacities, and vice versa; the gains in one domain may yield losses in another domain, and vice versa; or the gains in the mean levels of children's self-beliefs may yield losses in their beliefs–performance correspondence, and vice versa. Perhaps, by focusing on the gains and losses between the level of personal agency and its correspondence to actual performance, future research may be able to determine the optimal balances that lead to maximum performance gains and contribute to enhanced self-evaluations at each phase along the life span.

Whether the profile differences presented here reflect benefits or detriments to children's future (life-span) performance gains is difficult to address (Little, Oettingen, Stetsenko, et al., 1995). On the one hand, some outcomes could be viewed as developmental risk factors for these children. For example, the self-related agency and control-expectancy beliefs of children in East Berlin may be too low and too rigidly tied to actual performance to enable them to maximize their life-span developmental potential. Such a pattern may inhibit these children from engaging in new challenges and may contribute to general feelings of ill-being and unempowerment that hamper motivation and goal pursuit throughout the life span. Conversely, the children in the United States may be too agentic and reflect dysfunctionally low levels of beliefs–performance correspondence. Such a pattern may contribute to unrealistic expectations that, if brought in line with the reality of one's performance capabilities, could lead to feelings of disappointment and apathetic attitudes toward education, perhaps even contributing to behaviors such as dropping out of school (see e.g., Lerner, in press) and to a continuing life-span cycle of low aspirations and personal failures.

One could also evaluate the outcomes for these children as protective factors. For example, the East Berlin children's self-related agency and control-expectancy beliefs may indeed be realistic and accurately tied to their actual performance capabilities. Such a pattern may facilitate these children's choices of realistic and achievable goals and contribute to greater feelings of self-worth and well-being, thereby providing realistic action-control resources that may be called upon throughout development. Conversely, the Los Angeles children's belief profile may provide a self-belief buffer that protects their feelings of personal agency. Such a pattern may allow them to persist in the face of challenges and disappointments or to choose seemingly unattainable goals that, because of the additional personal resources of their self-beliefs, are indeed attainable (see, e.g., Seligman, 1991).

The optimal profile that provides the greatest opportunity for future growth and development may lie somewhere between these extremes or involve combinations such as the high mean levels of the Los Angeles sample coupled with the high beliefs–performance correspondence of the East Berlin sample. However, what is optimal and adaptive in one sociocultural context or a given developmental phase may not be for another. Is there developmental continuity in how and which of one's personal action-control resources best serve to facilitate successful adaptation to developmental challenges (Brandtstädter, in press; J. Heckhausen, 1998)? Do these developmental processes generalize to other sociocultural contexts? More research is necessary in order to determine what is most adaptive for immediate performance and long-term developmental gains.

More specifically, one goal of future research might be to understand the mechanisms that have produced the high mean levels of agency and control-expectancy beliefs and the low correlations with actual performance among children in the United States – especially in light of the generally higher beliefs–performance correlations and lower mean levels found in other sociocultural settings. To gain such understanding, researchers would need to include many school settings within a given sociocultural context and also explicit measures of the processes that likely contribute to the formation of these action-control beliefs. Conceptualizing relatively amorphous cultural differences as a set of individual-difference variables would allow researchers to examine the nature of these influences in terms of both within-culture and between-culture variability (Little & Lopez, 1997) as well as to examine whether the sources of cultural variability have differential influences at different phases of the life span.

A second goal of future research might be to determine the long-term symbiosis between action-control beliefs and performance attainments as well as how they function in other life contexts. Here, following particular cohorts longitudinally, it would be necessary to detail the antecedent conditions that optimally lead to performance gains and successful development (M. M. Baltes & P. B. Baltes, 1987). To attain this goal, researchers need to incorporate additional and more broad-based outcome measures (e.g., affective, behavioral, and cognitive) to obtain more information about the developmental consequences of actions and their interpretations and to examine broader age ranges across the life span. Moreover, research such as this must begin to move beyond the relatively circumscribed domain of school performance to more ill-defined yet commonly encountered domains of functioning such as friendships, work, family, and community (see, e.g., Diewald, Huinink, & Heckhausen, 1996; J. Heckhausen, 1998; J. Heckhausen & Hundertmark, 1995; Lopez & Little, 1996).

Notes

1. The data reviewed were collected as part of a collaborative cross-cultural project that examined children's action-control beliefs about school performance, between the Action Control and Child Development Project, codirected by Todd D. Little, Gabriele Oettingen, and Paul B. Baltes at the Max Planck Institute for Human Development and Education, and the Performance Beliefs Project, codirected by Hiroshi Azuma, Takahiro Miyashita, Mayumi Karasawa, and Mari Mashima at Shirayuri College. Other cooperating members include Anna Stetsenko, now at the University of Berne, and the late J. Kotaskova from the University of Prague.
2. The CAMI and related instruments (e.g., Multi-CAM) are available upon request.
3. Although many comparisons and analyses are yet to be performed, only those findings from analyses that have been conducted are presented. As an overview, however, the samples to which I refer – and which were

successively collected after the initial comparison between children from East Berlin and children from West Berlin (Oettingen et al., 1994) – are as follows: East Berlin, spring 1990 (N = 313), East Berlin, spring 1991 (N = 297); East Berlin, spring 1992 (N = 422); West Berlin, spring 1991 (N = 517); West Berlin, spring 1992 (N = 452); West Berlin, spring 1993 (N = 516); Los Angeles, spring 1992 (N = 657); Moscow, fall 1990 (N = 551); Prague, spring 1991 (N = 768); Tokyo, winter 1993 (N = 817).

References

Ames, C. (1992). Classrooms: Goals, structures, and student motivation. *Journal of Educational Psychology, 84,* 261–271.

Ames, C., & Archer, J. (1988). Achievement goals in the classroom: Students' learning strategies and motivation processes. *Journal of Educational Psychology, 80,* 260–267.

Azuma, H. (1996). Two modes of cognitive socialization in Japan and the United States. In P. Greenfield & R. Cocking (Eds.), *Cross-cultural roots of minority child development* (pp. 275–284). Hillsdale, NJ: Erlbaum.

Baltes, M. M., & Baltes, P. B. (Eds.) (1986). *The psychology of control and aging.* Hillsdale, NJ: Erlbaum.

Baltes, P. B. (1987). Theoretical propositions of life-span developmental psychology: On the dynamics between growth and decline. *Developmental Psychology, 23,* 611–626.

Baltes, P. B., Reese, H., & Nesselroade, J. R. (1977). *Life-span developmental psychology: Introduction to research methods.* Hillsdale, NJ: Erlbaum.

Bandura, A. (1995). *Self-efficacy: The exercise of control.* New York: Freeman.

Bandura, A., & Jourden, F. J. (1991). Self-regulatory mechanisms governing the impact of social comparison on complex decision making. *Journal of Personality and Social Psychology, 60,* 941–951.

Baumeister, R. F. (1989). The optimal margin of illusion. *Journal of Social and Clinical Psychology, 8,* 176–189.

Berry, J. M., & West, R. L. (1993). Cognitive self-efficacy in relation to personal mastery and goal setting across the life span. *International Journal of Behavioral Development, 16,* 351–379.

Boggiano, A. K., & Katz, P. (1991). Maladaptive achievement patterns in students: The role of teachers' controlling strategies. *Journal of Social Issues, 47,* 35–51.

Brandtstädter, J. (in press). Action perspectives on human development. In W. Damon (Ed.), *Handbook of Child Psychology.*

Brandtstädter, J., Rothermund, K., & Schmitz, U. (1998). Maintaining self-integrity and efficacy through adulthood and later life: The adaptive functions of assimilative persistence and accommodative flexibility. In J. Heckhausen & C. S. Dweck (Eds.), *Motivation and self-regulation across the life span.* New York: Cambridge University Press.

Butler, R. (1992). What young people want to know when: Effects of mastery and ability goals on interest in different kinds of social comparisons. *Journal of Personality and Social Psychology, 62,* 934–943.

Cantor, N. (1994). Life task problem solving: Situational affordances and personal needs. *Personality and Social Psychology Bulletin, 20,* 235–243.

Cantor, N., & Fleeson, W. (1994). Social intelligence and intelligent goal pursuit: A cognitive slice of motivation. In W. D. Spaulding (Ed.), *Nebraska Symposium on Motivation* (Vol. 41, pp. 125–179), Lincoln: University of Nebraska Press.

Cantor, N., & Sanderson, C. A. (1998). The functional regulation of adolescent dating relationships and sexual behavior: An interaction of goals, strategies, and situations. In J. Heckhausen & C. S. Dweck (Eds.), *Motivation and self-regulation across the life span.* New York: Cambridge University Press.

Chapman, M., & Skinner, E. A. (1985). Action in development/development in action. In M. Frese & J. Sabini (Eds.), *Goal-directed behavior: The concept of action in psychology* (pp. 199–213). Hillsdale, NJ: Erlbaum.

(1989). Children's agency beliefs, cognitive performance, and conceptions of effort and ability: Individual and developmental differences. *Child Development, 60,* 1229–1238.

Chapman, M., Skinner, E. A., & Baltes, P. B. (1990). Interpreting correlations between children's perceived control and cognitive performance: Control, agency, or means-ends beliefs? *Developmental Psychology, 26,* 246–253.

Connell, J. P. (1985). A new multidimensional measure of children's perceptions of control. *Child Development, 56,* 1018–1041.

Deci, E. L., & Ryan, R. M. (1987). The support of autonomy and the control of behavior. *Journal of Personality and Social Psychology, 53,* 1024–1037.

Diewald, M., Huinink, J., & Heckhausen, J. (1996). Lebensverläufe und Persönlichkeitsentwicklung im gesellschaftlichen Umbruch: Kohortenschicksale und Kontrollverhalten in Ostdeutschland nach der Wende [Life histories and developmental control in times of macrosocial rupture: The case of different birth cohorts in the East German transformation process]. *Kölner Zeitschrift für Soziologie und Sozialpsychologie, 48,* 219–248.

Dweck, C. S. (1986). Motivational processes affecting learning. *American Psychologist, 41,* 1040–1048.

(1991). Self-theories and goals: Their role in motivation, personality, and development. In R. Dienstbier (Ed.), *Nebraska Symposium on Motivation* (Vol. 38, pp. 199–235). Lincoln: University of Nebraska Press.

(1998). The development of early self-conceptions: Their relevance for motivational processes. In J. Heckhausen & C. S. Dweck (Eds.), *Motivation and self-regulation across the life span.* New York: Cambridge University Press.

Dweck, C. S., & Elliott, E. S. (1983). Achievement motivation. In P. Mussen & E. M. Hetherington (Eds.), *Handbook of child psychology* (Vol. 4, pp. 643–692). New York: Wiley.

Elliott, E. S., & Dweck, C. S. (1988). Goals: An approach to motivation and achievement. *Journal of Personality and Social Psychology, 54,* 5–12.

Findley, M. J., & Cooper, H. M. (1983). Locus of control and academic achievement: A literature review. *Journal of Personality and Social Psychology, 44,* 419–427.

Flammer, A. (1995). Developmental analysis of control beliefs. In A. Bandura (Ed.), *Self-efficacy in a changing society.* New York: Cambridge University Press.

Frey, K. S., & Ruble, D. N. (1990). Strategies for comparative evaluation: Maintaining a sense of competence across the life span. In R. J. Sternberg & J. Kolligian, Jr. (Eds.), *Competence considered* (pp. 167–189). New Haven, CT: Yale University Press.

Graham, S. (1991). A review of attribution theory in achievement contexts. *Educational Psychology Review, 3,* 5–39.

(1994). Motivation in African Americans. *Review of Educational Research, 64,* 55–117.

(1998). Social motivation and perceived responsibility: Attributions and behavior of African American boys labeled as aggressive. In J. Heckhausen & C. S. Dweck (Eds.), *Motivation and self-regulation across the life span.* New York: Cambridge University Press.

Grob, A., Little, T. D., Wanner, B., Wearing, A. J., & EURONET. (1996). Adolescents' well-being and perceived control across fourteen sociocultural contexts. *Journal of Personality and Social Psychology, 71,* 785–795.

Heckhausen, H. (1984). Emergent achievement behavior: Some early developments. In J. Nicholls (Ed.), *Advances in achievement motivation* (pp. 1–32). Greenwich, CT: JAI.

Heckhausen, J. (1998). *Developmental regulation in adulthood.* Cambridge, MA: Cambridge University Press.

Heckhausen, J., & Hundertmark, J. (1995). *Action-related beliefs in adulthood. Measurement of perceived agency, means-ends relations, and personal control in three adult life domains.* Manuscript under review.

Heckhausen, J., & Schulz, R. (1993). Optimisation by selection and compensation: Balancing primary and secondary control in life-span development. *International Journal of Behavioral Development, 16,* 287–303.

(1995). A life-span theory of control. *Psychological Review, 102,* 284–304.

(1998). Developmental regulation in adulthood: Selection and compensation via primary and secondary control. In J. Heckhausen & C. S. Dweck (Eds.), *Motivation and self-regulation across the life span.* New York: Cambridge University Press.

Hess, R. D., & Azuma, H. (1991). Cultural support for schooling: Contrasts between Japan and the United States. *Educational Researcher, 20,* 2–8, 12.

Hofstede, G. (1991). *Culture and organizations.* London: McGraw-Hill.

Holloway, S. D. (1988). Concepts of ability and effort in Japan and the United States. *Review of Educational Research, 58,* 327–345.

Jöreskog, K. G., & Sörborn, D. (1989). *LISREL 7: A guide to the program and applications.* Chicago: Scientific Software International.

Karasawa, M., Little, T. D., Miyashita, T., Mashima, M., & Azuma, H. (1997). Japanese children's action-control beliefs about school performance. *International Journal of Behavioral Development, 20,* 405–423.

Karoly, P. (1993). Mechanisms of self-regulation: A systems view. *Annual Review of Psychology, 44,* 23–52.

Lerner, R. M. (in press). *America's children and adolescents in crisis: Challenges and options for programs and policies.* Thousand Oaks, CA: Sage.

Little, T. D., & Wanner, B. (1996). *Multi-CAM: A multidimensional instrument to assess children's action-control beliefs* (ACCD Tech. Rep. No. 2). Berlin: Max Planck Institute.

Little, T. D. (1997). Mean and covariance structures (MACS) analyses of cross-cultural data: Practical and theoretical issues. *Multivariate Behavioral Research, 32,* 53–76.

Little, T. D., & Lopez, D. F. (1997). Regularities in the development of children's causality beliefs of school performance across six sociocultural contexts. *Developmental Psychology, 33,* 165–175.

Little, T. D., Oettingen, G., & Baltes, P. B. (1995). *The revised control, agency, and means-ends interview (CAMI): A multicultural validity assessment using mean and covariance (MACS) analyses* (Materialen aus der Bildungsforschung, No. 49). Berlin: Max Planck Institute.

Little, T. D., Oettingen, G., Stetsenko, A., & Baltes, P. B. (1995). Children's action-control beliefs and school performance: How do American children compare to German and Russian children? *Journal of Personality and Social Psychology, 69,* 686–700.

Lopez, D. F., & Little, T. D. (1996). Children's action-control beliefs and emotional adjustment in the social domain. *Developmental Psychology, 32,* 299–312.

Mac Iver, D. (1987). Classroom factors and student characteristics predicting students' use of achievement standards during self-assessment. *Child Development, 58,* 1258–1271.

——— (1988). Classroom environments and the stratification of pupils' ability perceptions. *Journal of Educational Psychology, 80,* 495–505.

Multon, K. D., Brown, S. D., & Lent, R. W. (1991). Relation of self-efficacy beliefs to academic outcomes: A meta-analytic investigation. *Journal of Counseling Psychology, 38,* 30–38.

Nicholls, J. G. (1978). The development of the concepts of effort and ability, perception of academic attainment, and the understanding that difficult tasks require more ability. *Child Development, 49,* 800–814.

Nicholls, J. G., & Miller, A. T. (1983). The differentiation of the concepts of luck and skill. *Developmental Psychology, 21,* 76–82.

Oettingen, G. (1995). Cross-cultural perspectives on self-efficacy. In A. Bandura

(Ed.), *Self-efficacy in changing societies* (pp. 149–176). New York: Cambridge University Press.

Oettingen, G., & Little, T. D. (1993). Intelligenz und Selbstwirksamkeitsurteile bei Ost- und Westberliner Schulkindern [Intelligence and performance-related self-efficacy beliefs in East and West Berlin children]. *Zeitschrift für Sozialpsychologie, 24,* 186–197.

Oettingen, G., Little, T. D., Lindenberger, U., & Baltes, P. B. (1994). Causality, agency, and control beliefs in East versus West Berlin children: A natural experiment on the role of context. *Journal of Personality and Social Psychology, 66,* 579–595.

Poortinga, Y. H. (1989). Equivalence of cross-cultural data: An overview of basic issues. *International Journal of Psychology, 24,* 737–756.

Rosenholtz, S. J., & Rosenholtz, S. H. (1981). Classroom organization and the perception of ability. *Sociology of Education, 54,* 132–140.

Rotter, J. B. (1966). Generalized expectancies for internal versus external control of reinforcement. *Psychological Monographs* (No. 80).

Ruble, D. (1983). The development of social-comparison processes and their role in achievement-related self-socialization. In E. T. Higgins, D. Ruble, & W. W. Hartup (Eds.), *Social cognition and social development* (pp. 134–157). New York: Cambridge University Press.

Schmitz, B., & Skinner, E. (1993). Perceived control, effort, and academic performance: Interindividual, intraindividual, and multivariate time-series analyses. *Journal of Personality and Social Psychology, 64,* 1010–1028.

Seligman, M. E. P. (1991). *Learned optimism.* New York: Alfred Knopf.

Skinner, E. A. (1995). *Perceived control, motivation, and coping.* Thousand Oaks, CA: Sage.

Skinner, E. A., & Chapman, M. (1987). Resolution of a developmental paradox: How can perceived internality increase, decrease, and remain the same across middle childhood? *Developmental Psychology, 23,* 44–48.

Skinner, E. A., Chapman, M., & Baltes, P. B. (1988a). Children's beliefs about control, means-ends, and agency: Developmental differences during middle childhood. *International Journal of Behavioral Development, 11,* 369–388.

 (1988b). Control, means-ends, and agency beliefs: A new conceptualization and its measurement during childhood. *Journal of Personality and Social Psychology, 54,* 117–133.

Skinner, E. A., & Connell, J. P. (1986). Control understanding: Suggestions for a developmental framework. In M. M. Baltes & P. B. Baltes (Eds.), *The psychology of aging and Control* (pp. 35–69). Hillsdale, NJ: Erlbaum.

Stetsenko, A., Little, T. D., Oettingen, G., & Baltes, P. B. (1995). Agency, control and means-ends beliefs in Moscow children: How similar are they to their Western peers? *Developmental Psychology, 31,* 285–299.

Stipek, D. J. (1988). *Motivation to learn: From theory to practice.* Englewood Cliffs, NJ: Prentice Hall.

(1992). The child at school. In M. H. Bornstein & M. E. Lamb (Eds.), *Developmental psychology: An advanced textbook* (pp. 579–625). Hillsdale, NJ: Erlbaum.

Stipek, D. J., & Weisz, J. R. (1981). Perceived personal control and academic achievement. *Review of Educational Research, 51,* 101–137.

Taylor, S. E., & Brown, J. D. (1988). Illusion and well-being: A social psychological perspective on mental health. *Psychological Bulletin, 103,* 193–210.

Van de Vijver, F. J. R., & Poortinga, Y. H. (1992). Testing in culturally heterogeneous populations: When are cultural loadings undesirable? *European Journal of Psychological Assessment, 8,* 17–24.

Weiner, B. (1986). *An attributional theory of motivation and emotion.* New York: Springer-Verlag.

Weisz, J. R. (1983). Can I control it? The pursuit of veridical answers across the life span. In P. B. Baltes & O. G. Brim, Jr. (Eds.), *Life-span development and behavior* (Vol. 3, pp. 233–300). New York: Academic Press.

(1986). Understanding the developing understanding of control. In M. Perlmutter (Ed.), *Cognitive perspectives on children's social and behavioral development: The Minnesota symposia on child psychology* (Vol. 18, pp. 219–278). Hillsdale, NJ: Erlbaum.

(1990). Development of control-related beliefs, goals, and styles in childhood and adolescence: A clinical perspective. In J. Rodin, C. Schooler, & W. Schaie (Eds.), *Self-directedness: Cause and effects throughout the life course* (pp. 19–49). Hillsdale, NJ: Erlbaum.

12   Commentary: Self-Regulation, Motivation, and Developmental Psychopathology

John R. Weisz

Abstract

The research and theory described in this volume carries considerable potential for enriching and informing the emerging field known as developmental psychopathology. This chapter offers several illustrations of how such an "informing" function might operate. Research on motivation and self-regulation in a developmental context, as reflected in chapters of this book, is discussed in the light of three central themes of developmental psychopathology: efforts to link basic developmental issues, theory, and research to psychopathology; the use of insights from atypical populations or psychological states to enrich understanding of normal developmental processes; and application of developmental theory and findings to the construction of interventions for dysfunction. Through a focus on these three themes, research on motivation and self-regulation may enrich the study of clinical phenomena and provide strong tests of its own basic precepts.

Introduction

I was trained in both developmental and clinical psychology, and my research spans the two areas. Thus, my reaction to the chapters in this volume may differ from that of most contributors. From my perspective, one of the most puzzling facts about the exciting work described in this book is the limited extent to which it has been used to inform research on developmental psychopathology. Therefore, in this chapter I offer several illustrations of how this "informing" function might operate. I review some of the recurrent themes of developmental psychopathology and suggest how development of these themes might be enriched by research on motivation and self-regulation within a life-span developmental context. I use examples from the work described in this volume.

316

Highlighting Three Contributions

Before turning to the general theme of developmental psychopathology, I will focus in particular on three chapters, the contributions I was asked to address as discussant for the conference that generated this volume. Each chapter raises important questions warranting discussion in their own right.

Dweck on Helplessness and Early Self-Conceptions

Carol Dweck's systematic, theory-driven work, described in Chapter 10 of this volume, is legendary in the field of motivation and development. Beginning with her research as a graduate student and continuing to the present time, Dweck has assembled a logically coherent account of how children develop learned helplessness. Her early work on causal factors was made especially credible by her dissertation, which shows that the Dweck model can be used to alleviate helplessness (Dweck, 1975). In later work, she and her students (e.g., Diener & Dweck, 1978, 1980) provided insight into how helplessness and mastery orientation relate to children's thought processes as they experience failure and success (e.g., Diener & Dweck, 1978, 1980) and to children's own theories of intelligence – for example, whether intelligence is viewed as a fixed entity–like attribute or as an organic, incremental process (see, e.g., Dweck & Elliott, 1983) – and other personal attributes.

For a time, many in the field associated this work with the notion that young children, who appear to subscribe to incremental theories, are rather invulnerable in the face of adverse experiences that lead to helplessness in older children. This notion always seemed implausible, given the fact that research with even infrahuman species (e.g., blue jays) has shown clear evidence of learned helplessness. Now, in her most recent work, Dweck (Chapter 10, this volume) has shown that even preschoolers are susceptible to the helplessness syndrome when the experimental conditions are structured appropriately – for example, when children are questioned in the presence of a visible reminder of previous failure. Her work also shows that signs of helplessness may be generated not only by actual failure but also by criticism alone. Particularly worrisome are the findings by Dweck and her colleagues that young children who do respond in helpless ways to failure or criticism may be especially likely to see deficient performance as indicating that they are bad children, and that they deserve punishment.

Dweck's findings have important implications for our understanding of the child's developing cognitions about self, and the interplay of these cognitions with daily events to produce self-evaluations. Although the work is clearly linked to research on development and motivation, it also may have considerable clinical significance. Psychologists have only recently discovered not only that young children can experience helplessness, but also that they can experience depression. Investigators are still trying to learn what may differentiate child, adolescent, and adult depression, and whether different treatment methods may be needed for the condition at different ages. Some clinical researchers harbor the suspicion that the nature of depression is influenced by the cognitive patterns of those who experience it, and that this almost certainly means that the experience of depression differs with cognitive developmental level. Dweck's studies suggest an example of how this might work.

Given that helplessness and depression have frequently been linked in the theoretical and empirical literature, it is possible that Dweck's findings on helplessness in childhood have relevance for childhood depression. It may be true that the kinds of global self-related cognitions that lead some young children to experience helplessness and to consider themselves "bad" as a result of failure or criticism are seen in children with depression, and that negative outcomes combined with criticism contribute to globally negative self-evaluation in vulnerable children. Thus, globality of negative self-perception may be particularly characteristic of depression in young childhood.

Dweck's work also suggests interesting ideas about intervention strategies for depression in young children. For example, researchers who are testing cognitive-behavioral interventions for child depression may want to consider the kinds of candidates for "therapeutic self-talk" suggested by the work Dweck and Kamin (cited in Dweck, Chapter 10, this volume) are doing – for example, replacing "That's not what I call doing it the right way" with "Think of another way to do it."

Little on Development of Action-Control Beliefs in Sociocultural Context

Todd Little and his colleagues at the Max Planck Institute have produced a rich body of work on the development of control-related beliefs in theoretically important sociocultural settings (see Little, Chapter 11, this volume). Working within an action theory perspective on control that links agents, means, and ends, and using assessment methods built on that perspective, Little and his prolific team at Max Planck have generated data on action-control beliefs in such diverse settings as East and West Berlin, Moscow, Tokyo, and Los Angeles. What emerges from this work is a picture of intriguing differences, and similarities, in the patterning and correlates of these control-related beliefs across the various settings.

Interpreting these differences and similarities is a challenge, as most of us who have done cross-cultural research can testify. Different regions and different cultures differ along so many dimensions that it is always difficult to be confident of causal explanations of regional differences on our psychological measures. Little and his colleagues certainly recognize the complexity of the task; indeed, the section entitled "The Utility of the Comparative Approach" in Chapter 11 of this volume is a particularly thoughtful and sophisticated statement of the problem and the steps that can be taken to address it. As Little suggests, cross-setting differences in the responses people give to our measures may often reflect cross-setting differences in the structure or meaning of the measures; this possibility certainly needs to be addressed, as best we can, before we embark on substantive interpretations of the manifest differences. Moreover, when we do detect differences at the measurement level or the construct level, those differences may convey important information about a culture or region in its own right, as suggested by Little's example of the *luck* concept in Japan.

Our own experience with research in Thailand and the United States (reviewed in Weisz, McCarty, Eastman, et al., 1997) suggests, however, that even rather sophisticated tests for cross-setting differences at the measurement level and the construct level may not detect subtle differences that may be quite influential. One example comes from our studies of children's behavioral and emotional problems in the two countries. Although we have used a number of different measurement approaches, several of our studies have used parent reports on a standardized checklist of child problems. On the checklist measure, we were surprised to find (in Weisz, Suwanlert, Chaiyasit, et al., 1987) that Thai children were rated significantly higher than age- and gender-matched children in the United States on the problem "unusually loud." By contrast, most people from the United States who visit Thailand would no doubt report that Thai children are "unusually quiet." My suspicion is that large setting differences may exist in what people consider "usual," and that these differences have a significant impact on whether people report that a particular child's behavior is "unusual."

This is one of many examples I could cite from our findings, all of which raise a key question about the appropriate goal for comparisons across settings or cultures. In such comparisons, should we aim for precise factual equivalence (e.g., comparing, say, decibel levels for children from Thailand

and the United States) or "setting-adjusted" equivalence? Advocates of the latter might well argue that whether a child exceeds what is considered usual in that child's setting is precisely what we want to know, independent of actual decibel levels. The optimum approach to cross-setting comparisons may well depend on the precise question one seeks to answer, and there may be value in developing a capacity for the kind of measurement equivalence Little describes as well as some degree of setting-linked variability that allows concepts to be used in ways that make sense within the sociocultural milieus of interest.

Beyond the theoretical-methodological dimension, important substantive issues are suggested by Little's fascinating findings. One of the most intriguing issues concerns the relation between self-related cognitions (e.g., about control) and self-related behavior. As Chapter 11 suggests, children in different settings may differ markedly in the veridicality of their self-perceptions. Children from East Berlin showed the closest correspondence between subjective expectations of control in the school setting and actual control as measured by school performance; children from Los Angeles showed the highest level of subjective expectation and the lowest level of correspondence between perception and reality. An important question for developmentalists is: In what way do these differences matter? Is it important (as the East German perspective evidently held) for children to be accurate in their self-appraisal? Or is it more developmentally useful for children to retain positive illusions about themselves? What are the relative benefits and risks of accuracy versus aggrandizement in self-perception, and how do the trade-offs shift with developmental level, culture, and the interplay of development and culture? One of the valuable contributions of cross-setting comparison is that it generates such significant questions for further study. We return to this particular question later in the chapter.

Little's discussion of his findings prompts a return to the issue of causal explanation in cross-setting comparisons. Little suggests that the pattern of findings in Los Angeles may reflect "the privately communicated and esteem-protective feedback [the Los Angeles children] received, coupled with a generally multidimensional teaching format" (see Little, Chapter 11, this volume). This explanation may be correct, but as a relatively recent arrival in the sometimes puzzling culture of Los Angeles, I can think of several alternative causal hypotheses. One example involves culturally mediated styles of self-presentation. In our research with schoolchildren in Los Angeles, we sometimes use a questionnaire that asks about indicators of depression (e.g., sleep problems, low self-esteem). We have learned that many children in this city are uncomfortable acknowledging sad feelings. One child wrote a marginal note beside her answers on the questionnaire, telling us, "This doesn't mean I'm depressed or anything." A cultural ideal, at least in some Los Angeles communities and schools, appears to be that children should report that they are happy and highly competent in all spheres that matter to them. This seems to be the socially acceptable way to present oneself as a child.

I could offer other causal explanations, but perhaps the self-presentation hypothesis is sufficient to make the general point that Los Angeles, Moscow, East Berlin, and West Berlin differ(ed) in so many ways that it may simply not be possible to determine which of the differences had causal force. Generally speaking, cross-setting research and cross-cultural research are inherently correlational enterprises, and cross-setting differences are inevitably overdetermined. The comparisons involve children who were – fortunately – not randomly assigned to setting, and the settings compared will differ along an infinite array of dimensions. Consequently, definitive causal interpretation is likely to remain elusive in research that compares children from markedly different environments.

What then is to be gained from cross-setting comparison? Quite a lot, it seems to me. This question can be considered in the light of the distinction between the "context of discovery" and the "context of confirmation," as proposed by philosophers of science (e.g., Popper, 1961) and applied to psychology by developmental theorists (e.g., Achenbach, 1982). In the context of discovery, ideas are generated (e.g., via intuition, naturalistic observation); in the context of confirmation, these ideas are subjected to systematic test. In my view, cross-setting comparison is best construed as part of the context of discovery. Such research generates, for instance, hypotheses regarding causal processes – hypotheses that can later be tested more rigorously, but perhaps through those experimental means that are not feasible within a cross-setting or cross-cultural design.

Nolen-Hoeksema on Styles of Coping with Depression

Susan Nolen-Hoeksema (Chapter 9, this volume) has generated an already influential body of work on the effects of a ruminative cognitive style on mood. This research suggests that the ways people respond to initial symptoms of depression may affect the later course of those symptoms. People who display a ruminative style (passively and repetitively focusing on their symptoms, possible causes, possible consequences) tend to show increased intensity and duration of depressive symptoms, compared to people who show more active, less ruminative styles.

This finding is reminiscent of what Diener and Dweck (1978) found with regard to children's styles of responding to failure; in that study, helplessness was associated with a style of responding that Nolen-Hoeksema might well consider "ruminative." Performance deterioration following failure among helpless children was associated with a tendency to engage in high levels of self-talk about the causes and possible consequences of failure. By contrast, children who did not show performance deterioration also tended not to spend much time thinking about their failure or examining its possible causes. Thus, research with children doing problem-solving tasks and with adults confronting depression suggests that a ruminative style may be bad for intellectual performance and bad for mental health, at least for some groups in some situations.

The research described in Chapter 9 has important clinical implications, some of which I will consider later in this chapter; it also raises intriguing challenges for further study. One such challenge is to disaggregate – that is, to determine whether all or only some aspects of the "ruminative cluster" are responsible for the negative effects identified in the research. Nolen-Hoeksema describes the ruminative style as the tendency to focus passively and repeatedly on one's depressive symptoms and on the possible causes and consequences of those symptoms, without acting to relieve them. In principle, it seems possible that passivity, in the form of a failure to take action to relieve symptoms, might be associated with more severe and prolonged depression than would an active style, regardless of what cognitions the people involved engage in.

Perhaps the cognitions Nolen-Hoeksema describes exert an independent effect, over and above the influence of passivity. If that is the case, it would be useful to know which kinds of ruminations (e.g., about symptoms versus causes versus consequences versus other) are particularly harmful, and whether some forms of cognition may be beneficial. Certainly, some of the most popular forms of psychotherapy for treating depression involve *encouraging* cognitive activity, including cognitions about symptoms, causes, and consequences. This suggests the possibility that such cognitions may not be harmful in and of themselves, but rather that whether they have harmful or beneficial effects may depend on how they are used, or on subtle aspects of their content, or on other factors yet to be discovered. In order to examine this issue, one useful step may be to identify individuals whose style is apparently ruminative but whose sad feelings do *not* tend to spiral into depression. Learning how the ruminative patterns of these individuals differ from the patterns of those whose ruminations are associated with increased depression may contribute to the disaggregation I am suggesting.

Another challenge is to assess how the phenomena Nolen-Hoeksema describes relate to biological risk, which appears to be a component in a large subset of serious cases of depression, and which is often associated with the need for antidepressant medication. It is possible that the data on ruminative styles may be relevant only to psychologists' understanding of, and possible interventions for, depressions that have a primarily situational and cognitive genesis. It also seems possible, however, that the Nolen-Hoeksema analysis may apply to cases involving biologically prepotent depression. The possibility is suggested indirectly by longitudinal research in which Nolen-Hoeksema, Parker, and Larson (1994) found that ruminative style is associated with longer periods of depressed mood even when severity of mood was statistically controlled. Perhaps even those episodes of depression that are initiated by biological forces can be influenced – in the subsequent severity and duration of their course – by the coping style with which the individual responds. If this is the case, then the Nolen-Hoeksema analysis may enrich psychologists' understanding of, and efforts to intervene with, a particularly broad range of depressions.

Using Research on Motivation and Self-Regulation to Enrich the Study of Developmental Psychopathology

In addition to their distinctive contributions, the bodies of work described by Dweck, Little, Nolen-Hoeksema and other contributors to this volume share a general relevance to certain recurrent themes of developmental psychopathology. It is to these themes that I now turn.

Although definitions of developmental psychopathology would certainly differ across theorists and researchers, three broad themes appear to characterize many of the efforts in the field (for extended discussion, and illustrations, see Luthar, Burack, Cicchetti, et al., in press): efforts to link basic developmental issues, theory, and research to psychopathology; the use of insights from atypical populations or psychological states to enrich understanding of normal developmental processes; and application of developmental theory and findings to the construction of interventions for dysfunction. In what follows, I will try to illustrate how the kinds of work described in this volume might relate to these three themes and thus enliven their pursuit.

Linking Basic Developmental Issues, Theory, and Research to Psychopathology: Development of "The Self"

I focus in particular on one of the most enduring issues in developmental psychology: The developing construction of the self. Although diverse perspectives have been brought to bear on the question of how individuals construct a sense of self, and what consequences accrue (see Harter, 1983), considerable research and theory has focused on feelings of trust and attachment very early in development, the decline of cognitive egocentrism and the increasing capacity to distinguish between self and others in early and middle childhood, and the development of identity in adolescence. The lines of research described in the present volume could be applied to this core developmental issue in ways that might broaden the picture of the emerging self and of the implications for dysfunction.

Self as a Causal Force. I first consider the work described by Little, in Chapter 11 of this volume. One potential contribution of this work is that it broadens the understanding of how children's experiences in interaction with the world provide information about self as a causal force. Through such information, children form judgments about means–ends relationships ("causality" in Little's work, "contingency" in my own; e.g., Weisz, 1986; Weisz & Stipek, 1982), about whether they themselves have access to specific means that are relevant to outcomes of interest ("agency" in Little's work, "competence" in mine), and about whether they can achieve particular outcomes ("control expectancy" in Little's work, "perceived control" in mine). Moreover, the ways children move from their experience in the real world to more general judgments about these self-relevant concepts seems to differ markedly as a function of culture, with some cultural settings fostering relatively veridical judgments – say, about personal agency – and other settings associated with what appear to be self-serving, beneffectant judgments.

The work of Little and his colleagues could enrich the literature on the self in a number of ways. First, the work could broaden the conceptualization, underscoring the relevance of perceived causal agency to an integrated concept of self. Second, the work highlights the significant role of culture, adding significantly to previous conceptual work on self and culture (e.g., Weisz, Rothbaum, & Blackburn, 1984a, 1984b). And third, particularly relevant to developmental psychopathology, the work suggests intriguing questions about the adaptive consequences of various control-related belief patterns.

An example of the third point is the relative adaptiveness of veridical versus beneffectant beliefs about self as a causal agent. Research with adults has shown that a positive bias in both perceptions of personal competence (e.g., Lewinsohn, Mischel, Chaplin, et al., 1980) and perceptions of contingency between one's actions and outcomes (e.g., Alloy & Abramson,

1979) is negatively correlated with depression, and similar findings have been obtained with other measures of mental health (see Taylor, 1989). Research with children and adolescents has shown that both kinds of positive bias are common in childhood but tend to decline with age, from early childhood to adolescence (see Weisz, 1986, 1990); however, little is known about the consequences of such bias for affect or psychopathology. The work of Little and his colleagues offers new ways to assess control-related cognitions, and beneffectant bias, during the school years, and thus may help psychologists examine the degree to which such bias is associated with adjustment or dysfunction.

It is possible that sociocultural context determines whether self-serving bias is adaptive or not. In research to date, there has been little opportunity to examine this possibility, because most of the relevant research has been conducted with North American samples. However, recent work by Markus and colleagues (see Markus & Kitayama, 1991) suggests that the positive correlation between illusory self-perceptions and various measures of mental health, found in multiple American studies, is not replicated in Japanese samples. A particular strength of the work by Little and colleagues is that it offers methods that can be, and already have been, applied to the study of children from quite diverse cultural settings. What needs to be added to connect this work to developmental psychopathology are appropriate measures of child adaptation and mental health.

Self in Relation to Learned Helplessness. The work described by Dweck (Chapter 10, this volume) offers a perspective on children's constructions of self as they relate to motivational deficits – particularly the pattern known as learned helplessness. The Dweck research suggests that children as young as preschoolers may experience the classical helplessness pattern, including risk aversion and impaired performance, in the face of difficulty or negative feedback, just as do older children. However, the dimensions of self-perception that are involved may be quite different for older versus younger children. For older children, the development of helplessness appears to involve conceptions of their intelligence (entity models as opposed to incremental models). For younger children, the processes appear to involve an altogether different dimension of self – not intelligence, but goodness versus badness.

This finding carries significant implications for the study of developmental psychopathology in relation to children's self-conceptions. It suggests that patterns of child dysfunction that may look virtually identical in their outward manifestations (e.g., behavior and performance deficits associated with helplessness) across developmental levels may differ markedly in the pattern of underlying cognitions related to the self. Those who do research on other forms of child dysfunction – for example, such formal psychiatric diagnoses as depressive disorders or conduct disorders – might well take heed.

Potentially Deleterious Effects of Attentional Focus on Self. Yet another kind of connection between the self and developmental psychopathology is illustrated by Nolen-Hoeksema's findings (Chapter 9, this volume). Those findings suggest that excessive attentional focus on concerns related to the self – for example, "How sad do I feel?" "What caused me to feel this way?" "What will happen to me next?" – may cause sad feelings to spiral down- ward into full-fledged depression. Viewed another way, the work suggests that dysfunctional consequences may result not only from particular ways of construing or thinking about the self, but also from the very tendency to focus persistently on the self. This conclusion is consistent with that reached by influential researchers outside the Nolen-Hoeksema group who study depression (e.g., Pyszczynski & Greenberg, 1987) and other clinical disor- ders (e.g., Ingram, 1990).

Using Insights from Atypical or Infrequently Studied Populations (or Psychological States) to Study Normal Developmental Processes

A second general theme of developmental psychopathology is that useful inferences about normal developmental processes may be derived from re- search with atypical or rarely studied groups. Several examples appear in the chapters of this volume.

Studying the Development of Personal and Social Motivation and Per- ceived Responsibility by Focusing on Aggressive African American Boys. Sandra Graham (Chapter 5, this volume) reviews her research on at- tributional processes and personal and social motivation among African American boys labeled as aggressive. The focus on this particular popula- tion is important for a number of theoretical and practical reasons. For the purposes of the present chapter, the focus on unusually aggressive youth provides an excellent means of studying the linkage among attributions (e.g., of responsibility), emotions (e.g., anger), and behavior (e.g., aggres- sion), precisely because the behavior of interest is particularly salient and because its base rate in this group is higher than average. The high base rates and enhanced variability make it feasible, and productive, for Graham and her colleagues to study such correlates of the attribution-emotion-action sequence as maternal behavior, and to investigate the impact of interventions. As a result, Graham's work provides a good deal of information, not only about aggressive African American boys, but also about the general development of perceived responsibility and how it operates in concert with emotions and overt behavior.

Studying the Development of Regulatory Focus by Studying Atypical Emotional States. E. Tory Higgins and Israela Loeb (Chapter 3, this volume) present a theory of the development of regulatory processes. They distinguish between two regulatory foci: *promotion,* involving an emphasis on generating accomplishment; and *prevention,* involving an emphasis on maintaining safety. They suggest that the former is fostered by nurturance-oriented parenting, the latter by security-oriented parenting. Higgins and Loeb also propose a stagewise developmental account of the emergence of these two broad orientations, integrating their ideas with those of earlier developmentalists such as Mead, Piaget, and Bruner.

Of particular interest here is the notion that a promotion focus is associated with self-regulation via *ideal* self-guides (i.e., hopes, wishes, aspirations), whereas a prevention focus is associated with self-regulation via *ought* self-guides (i.e., perceived duties, obligations, responsibilities). When regulation involving a promotion focus breaks down, as when an individual chronically falls short of valued ideals, the theoretical model predicts that one result will be dejection or a depression-like syndrome. By contrast, when regulation involving a prevention focus breaks down, as when an individual repeatedly fails to live up to perceived obligations, the theory predicts that one result will be agitation or an anxiety-like syndrome. This aspect of the model is based in the realm of developmental psychopathology; again, it is evident that psychologists need to study atypical groups (i.e., depressed and anxious), or – as in the work Higgins and Loeb cite – normal groups in atypical psychological states, in order to test central tenets of a general developmental theory.

Other Examples, Briefly Noted. Although space limitations prevent a detailed account here, I will briefly note a few other illustrations of this second general theme of developmental psychopathology. Julius Kuhl and Arno Fuhrmann (Chapter 1, this volume) present a model of human volition involving two different modes – that is, self-control and self-regulation – and they describe a number of relevant findings with a questionnaire designed to tap key elements of their model. To test certain principles of the model, they invoke a comparison between a control group and other groups diagnosed with alcoholism versus anxiety disorders versus overeating; in this way they illustrate how tests of a general theory about normal development may rely on comparisons across rather abnormal groups.

Eva Pomerantz and Diane Ruble (Chapter 6, this volume) present a multidimensional model of control as employed in parental socialization of children, with some intriguing implications regarding possible outcomes for boys and girls. One of the most intriguing ideas – supported by some of their data – is that parents may use control processes differently with sons versus daughters, and that the difference may foster gender differences in certain self-evaluative antecedents of depression. Drawing on normal range samples, Pomerantz and Ruble present interesting findings bearing on this notion. I suspect, however, they would agree that some of their ideas about the developmental processes involved could be particularly well-tested with samples that include depressed youngsters.

Other chapters in this volume illustrate the value of research with atypical and rarely studied groups in understanding normal development. In the work described by Nolen-Hoeksema (Chapter 9, this volume), research on depressed individuals and depressive states is used to explain why the very normal experience of disappointment may be surmounted by some but prove crippling and debilitating to others. In the work described by Little (Chapter 11, this volume), children from the rarely studied setting of East Germany were compared to groups from other countries to generate hypotheses about sociocultural influences on the normal development of control beliefs, and the correlates thereof.

Applying Developmental Theory and Findings to the Construction of Interventions for Dysfunction

A third general theme of developmental psychopathology is that general developmental theory and findings may be used to construct interventions for psychological dysfunction. The chapters of this book offer both explicit and implicit illustrations of this notion.

Interventions for Internalizing Distress and Disorder: Depression and Anxiety. Perhaps most abundant in the book are ideas that could be used to construct interventions for internalizing forms of distress and disorder. Nolen-Hoeksema's (Chapter 9, this volume) work suggests that teaching people ways to distract themselves from, rather than ruminate on, their sad mood and its causes may help prevent the downward spiral of sad feelings into full-blown depression. The work by Pomerantz and Ruble (Chapter 6, this volume) suggests the intriguing possibility that parents might play a role in preventing the development of depression in their children, particularly their daughters; one element of this role might be adjustments in parental style to foster increased autonomy-granting. This notion nicely complements Higgins and Loeb's (Chapter 3, this volume) analysis of how nurturance-oriented and security-oriented parental styles may engender risk for offspring depression and anxiety, respectively. To the extent that social regulation in the family influences children's affect self-regulation, it should be possible to identify in the family potential targets for intervention that could reduce risk of later affective distress and disorder.

In addition to suggesting new approaches to intervention with internalizing problems and disorders, the contributions to this volume may generate important questions about current practices. For example, the most popular current treatments for depression are cognitive-behavioral and psychodynamic therapies (including "interpersonal therapy"). In both, clients are encouraged to examine closely their depressed state and its causes and consequences, and to assess their current mood and thoughts repeatedly. Viewed in the light of Nolen-Hoeksema's work, these components of treatment could be seen as essentially training clients to ruminate about their depressive feelings, a practice that Nolen-Hoeksema's findings suggest is likely to have deleterious effects. Yet there is evidence that these current treatments produce significant beneficial effects, in both children and adolescents (see Weisz, Rudolph, Granger, et al., 1992; Weisz, Weiss, Han, et al., 1995) and adults (see Robin, Berman, & Neimeyer, 1990).

How can such "ruminative" interventions have curative effects in treatment but harmful effects in Nolen-Hoeksema's research? As discussed earlier, perhaps rumination per se is not responsible for the negative effects in Nolen-Hoeksema's research, but instead passive behavior, or particular – and perhaps subtle – *ways* of ruminating. The elements that generate the adverse effects may be absent from current treatments. Alternatively, perhaps the ruminative aspects of these popular current treatments are not actually the treatment components that produce the positive effects, and the interventions are successful *in spite of,* rather than because of, their ruminative elements. If this is the case, it is possible that existing treatments can be made more effective by replacing their prorumination components with, for example, training focused on distraction from depressive feelings.

Interventions for Externalizing Problems and Disorders: Aggression. Turning now to externalizing problems and disorders, I consider the treatment implications of Graham's (Chapter 5, this volume) careful analysis of attribution-emotion-action sequences in aggressive youth. Graham's descriptive studies alone suggest that modifying the attributions that tend to precede aggressive acts might reduce the likelihood of aggression. A study by Hudley and Graham (1993) provides direct support for this notion. Aggressive boys trained to alter their biased attributions of negative intent on the part of others, compared to aggressive boys not thus trained, subsequently showed less perceived malicious intent, less endorsement of hostile behavior, lower teacher ratings of aggression, and less verbal aggression toward a peer in a laboratory task in which the peer appeared to cause the loss of a prize. Graham proposes that this effective intervention targeting youngsters might be broadened to include parent training, as well. Clearly, this developmental research is generating findings that could significantly enrich the intervention literature.

Interventions for Motivational Deficits. Finally, I consider the possibility of interventions aimed not at classical clinical disorders but at persistent motivational deficits. One set of ideas comes from the Dweck laboratory (Chapter 10, this volume), which has already demonstrated that attribution retraining can be successful in alleviating learned helplessness in school-aged children (see Dweck, 1975). With younger children, Dweck's work suggests that intervention may need to take a slightly different form. Because young children who link negative performance feedback to global self-judgments may fall prey to helplessness, Dweck and her colleagues propose that person-oriented feedback (e.g., "I'm very disappointed in you") may incline young children toward helpless responses. By contrast, they suggest, strategy-oriented feedback (e.g., "Maybe you could think of another way to do it") may enhance young children's mastery orientation. Early evidence from Dweck and Kamins (see Dweck, Chapter 10, this volume) supports this view.

Moving along the age spectrum to adulthood and the aging population, psychologists must recognize that motivational deficits may arise from the loss of capacity for particular types of primary control, as described by Jutta Heckhausen and Richard Schulz (1995; and Chapter 2, this volume). Evidence presented by these investigators suggests that older adults tend to use increased levels of *compensatory secondary control,* as evidenced by high endorsement of satisfaction with their current life. Although such compensatory patterns may be normative, they are not universal among older persons, and they might help point the way to useful interventions for older persons for whom reductions in primary control access produce significant motivational deficits. The somewhat related work by Laura Carstensen (Chapter 13, this volume), growing out of her socioemotional selectivity theory, focuses attention on social goals and motives, in particular. It suggests that adjustment to advancing age may involve reorganization of objectives and priorities within the social sphere, with increasing emphasis placed on the affective potential of social interaction. To the extent that declines in overall psychological adjustment relate to losses and frustrations experienced by adults in the social domain, the patterns identified by Carstensen and her colleagues may inform the development of helpful interventions at the adult end of the life span.

Persistent Problems in Developmental Psychopathology That Research on Self-Regulation and Motivation May Help Address

In this concluding section, I suggest a few of the recurrent problems faced by researchers in developmental psychopathology that are addressed by the work described in this book.

"One Size Fits All" Diagnostic Categories May Be Unrealistic

The most recent version of the *Diagnostic and Statistical Manual of Mental Disorders* (American Psychiatric Association, 1994) contains more than 500 pages of disorders, most of which may be applied to adults, adolescents, and children. Most of the categories involve either identical or virtually identical lists of symptoms and features for individuals at all ages. There must be more important age-related differences in the character and content of many disorders than are currently reflected in this diagnostic system. Surely, for example, the marked cognitive differences associated with development must influence the thinking patterns that accompany depression and anxiety: For example, Dweck (Chapter 10) has found that young children, unlike older ones, link failure to global goodness–badness judgments. To understand the nature of developmental differences as they impinge on psychological disorders, clinical researchers may need to collaborate much more actively with the kinds of developmental investigators represented in this book.

Similar Trauma Leads to Different Outcomes in Different Individuals

A second problem confronted in developmental psychopathology is that forms of trauma and threat that seem quite similar may lead to quite different responses and outcomes in different individuals. To make sense of these differences, developmental psychopathologists may need to draw from research on individual differences in the specificity of vulnerability. Work as diverse as that of Kuhl and Furhmann (Chapter 1), Higgins and Loeb (Chapter 3), Graham (Chapter 5), Pomerantz and Ruble (Chapter 6), Dweck (Chapter 10), and Carstensen (Chapter 13) is all relevant to this task.

Explanations Are Needed for Gender Differences in Problem Prevalence and Their Developmental Changes

Another key task of developmental psychopathologists has been to understand why gender differences exist in the prevalence of various problems and disorders, and why the nature and even the direction of the differences may shift with development. For example, most evidence suggests that depression is either equally prevalent in girls and boys, or more prevalent in boys, prior to adolescence, but that in adolescence and adulthood, depression is considerably more prevalent in males than in females. The chapters by Ruble and Pomerantz and Nolen-Hoeksema (Chapters 6 and 9, respectively) offer very specific ideas about why this pattern may arise. These ideas, and the supporting research, illustrate the potential explanatory power of a linkage between developmental psychopathology and developmental research on self-regulation and motivation.

Most Interventions for Children and Adolescents Are Potentially Inappropriate

Most evidence suggests that the current array of psychotherapies for children and adolescents does produce significant positive effects (see Weisz & Weiss, 1993; Weisz, Weiss, Han, et al., 1995). However, mean effect sizes found in various meta-analyses range from only about 0.5 (i.e., about half the standard deviation of the average outcome measure used) to about 0.8. It seems likely that these effects could be improved, and researchers certainly do not yet know what the upper limit of benefit may be. One reason to suspect that there is considerable room for improvement is this: The procedures used in many psychotherapies for children and adolescents are junior versions of treatments originally developed for adults. In general, child and adolescent therapies do not incorporate much of what research has discovered about children, adolescents, or development.

As a case in point, I return briefly to cognitive-behavioral therapy (CBT), arguably the hottest form of treatment in the current child and adolescent outcome research literature. CBT involves, in part, teaching clients to identify their own cognitions (e.g., about self, others, stressful events), examine them critically, test them for veridicality, and replace the dysfunctional cognitions with accurate, adaptive ones. Such methods appear to work well with adults, and with many adolescents, but developmentalists might be forgiven for questioning whether such "thinking about thinking" falls within the cognitive capacities of most children at or below elementary school age levels. Such questions are reinforced by the findings of a recent meta-analysis of CBT outcome studies with young people, conducted by Durlak, Fuhrman, and Lampman (1991). Durlak and colleagues found that the mean effect size for adolescents (0.92) was almost twice as large as the mean effect size for children aged 5 to 7 and for children aged 7 to 11. This finding suggests that at least some aspects of the treatment may not fit the characteristics or capacities of children as well as those of adolescents. Perhaps what is needed is a more active collaboration between proponents of CBT and those who study development, cognitive and otherwise. Perhaps such a collaboration would be healthy for proponents of many other forms of child and adolescent psychotherapy.

One way to construe this problem is that those who are developing treatments for young people may fall prey to developmental uniformity assumptions. They may also be making unwarranted uniformity assumptions about young people at similar developmental levels. Such assumptions are implicit in a number of child and adolescent treatment programs in which every child receives the same program, guided by the same manual. Ignoring individual differences – say, in patterns of self-regulation, motivation, or cognition – among youth of the same age may generate a risk of quite nonuniform therapeutic benefit. Conversely, recognizing individual differences, and responding to them with appropriate variations in treatment approach, may make treatment beneficial to a broader range of young people.

This general notion can be illustrated by reference to chapters in this book. It seems possible, for example, that different approaches to treatment might be needed for emotionally disturbed children who subscribe to entity versus incremental theories of intellect, ability, or personality (see Dweck, Chapter 10, this volume), for aggressive children who attribute others' actions to harmful intent versus those whose aggression grows out of modeling peer behavior (see Graham, Chapter 5, this volume), or for underachieving children who show strong means–ends beliefs versus those who believe that nothing kids do matters very much (Little, Chapter 11, this volume). In other words, psychologists may be able to use dimensions of cognition, motivation, and self-regulation such as those discussed in this volume in order to tailor interventions to child characteristics in ways that are more precise than current treatment technology permits. One objective of such work would be to learn how individual differences in what children bring to therapy may influence the impact of particular intervention procedures.

Finally, basic science can profit from applications such as those I am suggesting. Testing interventions that are based on notions about causes and maintaining factors can help psychologists assess the validity of these notions. Dweck's (1975) research on the alleviation of helplessness via attribution retraining not only is important clinically, but also provides a persuasive test of the validity of her ideas about the role of attributions. Similarly, Hudley and Graham's (1993) intervention research not only shows that these investigators can modify aggressive tendencies, but also supports the validity of their attribution-emotion-action causal model. My friend Urie Bronfenbrenner is fond of quoting a teacher who once told him, "If you want to understand something, try to change it." Following this advice, it seems to me, could be beneficial for clinical researchers and basic developmentalists alike.

References

Achenbach, T. M. (1982). *Developmental psychopathology* (2d ed.). New York: Wiley.

Alloy, L. B., & Abramson, L. Y. (1979). Judgment of contingency in depressed and nondepressed college students: Sadder but wiser. *Journal of Experimental Psychology: General, 108,* 441–485.

American Psychiatric Association (1994). *Diagnostic and statistical manual of mental disorders* (4th ed.). Washington, DC: American Psychiatric Association.

Carstensen, L. L. (1998). A life-span approach to social motivation. In J. Heckhausen & C. S. Dweck (Eds.), *Motivation and self-regulation across the life span.* New York: Cambridge University Press.

Diener, C. I., & Dweck, C. S. (1978). An analysis of learned helplessness: I. Continuous changes in performance, strategy, and achievement cognitions following failure. *Journal of Personality and Social Psychology, 36,* 451–462.

(1980). An analysis of learned helplessness. Vol. II: The processing of success. *Journal of Personality and Social Psychology, 39,* 940–952.

Durlack, J. A., Fuhrman, T., & Lampman, C. (1991). Effectiveness of cognitive-behavior therapy for maladapting children: A meta-analysis. *Psychological Bulletin, 110,* 204–214.

Dweck, C. S. (1998). The development of early self-conceptions: Their relevance for motivational processes. In J. Heckhausen & C. S. Dweck (Eds.), *Motivation and self-regulation across the life span.* New York: Cambridge University Press.

(1975). The role of expectations and attributions in the alleviation of learned helplessness. *Journal of Personality and Social Psychology, 36,* 451–462.

Dweck, C. S., & Elliott, E. S. (1983). Achievement motivation. In P. Mussen & E. M. Hetherington (Eds.), *Handbook of child psychology.* New York: Wiley.

Graham, S. (1998). Social motivation and perceived responsibility: Attributions and behavior of African American boys labeled as aggressive. In J. Heckhausen & C. S. Dweck (Eds.), *Motivation and self-regulation across the life span.* New York: Cambridge University Press.

Harter, S. (1983). Developmental perspectives on the self-system. In P. H. Mussen (Ed.), *Handbook of child psychology* (Vol. 4, pp. 275–385). New York: Wiley.

Heckhausen, J., & Schulz, R. (1995). A life-span theory of control. *Psychological Review, 102,* 284–304.

(1998). Developmental regulation in adulthood: Selection and compensation via primary and secondary control. In J. Heckhausen & C. S. Dweck (Eds.), *Motivation and self-regulation across the life span.* New York: Cambridge University Press.

Higgins, T., & Loeb, I. (1998). Development of regulatory focus: Promotion and prevention as ways of living. In J. Heckhausen & C. S. Dweck (Eds.), *Motivation and self-regulation across the life span.* New York: Cambridge University Press.

Hudley, C., & Graham, S. (1993). An attributional intervention to reduce peer-directed aggression among African American boys. *Child Development, 64,* 124–138.

Ingram, R. (1990). Self-focused attention in clinical disorders: Review and a conceptual model. *Psychological Bulletin, 107,* 156–176.

Kuhl, J., & Fuhrmann, A. (1998). Decomposing self-regulation and self-control: The Volitional Components Inventory. In J. Heckhausen & C. S. Dweck (Eds.), *Motivation and self-regulation across the life span.* New York: Cambridge University Press.

Lewinsohn, P., Mischel, W., Chaplin, W., & Barton, R. (1980). Social competence and depression: The role of illusory self-perceptions. *Journal of Abnormal Psychology, 89,* 203–212.

Little, T. D. (1998). Sociocultural influences on the development of children's action-control beliefs. In J. Heckhausen & C. S. Dweck (Eds.), *Motivation and self-regulation across the life span.* New York: Cambridge University Press.

Luthar, S. S., Burack, J., Cicchetti, D., & Weisz, J. R. (Eds.) (in press). *Developmental psychopathology: Perspectives on adjustment, risk, and disorder.* New York: Cambridge University Press.

Markus, H. R., & Kitayama, S. (1991). Culture and the self: Implications for cognition, emotion, and motivation. *Psychological Review, 98,* 224–253.

Nolen-Hoeksema, S. (1998). Ruminative coping with depression. In J. Heckhausen & C. S. Dweck (Eds.), *Motivation and self-regulation across the life span.* New York: Cambridge University Press.

Nolen-Hoeksema, S., Parker, L., & Larson, J. (1994). Ruminative coping with depressed mood following loss. *Journal of Personality and Social Psychology, 67,* 92–104.

Pomerantz, E., & Ruble, D. (1998). The multidimensional nature of control: Implications for the development of sex differences in self-evaluation. In J. Heckhausen & C. S. Dweck (Eds.), *Motivation and self-regulation across the life span.* New York: Cambridge University Press.

Popper, K. R. (1961). *The logic of scientific discovery.* New York: Science Editions.

Pyszczynski, T., & Greenberg, M. (1987). Self-regulatory perseveration and the depressive self-focusing style: A self-awareness theory of reactive depression. *Psychological Bulletin, 102,* 122–138.

Robin, L. A., Berman, J. S., & Neimeyer, R. A. (1990). Psychotherapy for the treatment of depression: A comprehensive review of controlled outcome research. *Psychological Bulletin, 108,* 30–49.

Taylor, S. E. (1989). *Positive illusions: Creative self-deception and the healthy mind.* New York: Basic Books.

Weisz, J. R. (1986). Understanding the developing understanding of control. In M. Perlmutter (Ed.), *Social cognition: Minnesota symposia on child psychology* (Vol. 18, pp. 219–278). Hillsdale, NJ: Erlbaum.

(1990). Development of control-related beliefs, goals, and styles in childhood and adolescence: A clinical perspective. In J. Rodin, C. Schooler, & K. W. Schaie (Eds.), *Self-directedness: Causes and effects throughout the life course* (pp. 103–145). Hillsdale, NJ: Erlbaum.

Weisz, J. R., McCarty, C. A., Eastman, K. L., Chaiyasit, W., & Suwanlert, S. (1997). *Developmental psychopathology and culture: Ten lessons from Thailand.* In S. S. Luthar, J. Burack, D. Cicchetti, & J. R. Weisz (Eds.), *Developmental psychopathology and culture: Perspectives on adjustment, risk, and disorder.* (pp. 568–592) New York: Cambridge University Press.

Weisz, J. R., Rothbaum, F. M., & Blackburn, T. F. (1984a). Standing out and standing in: The psychology of control in America and Japan. *American Psychologist, 39,* 955–969.

(1984b). Swapping recipes for control. *American Psychologist, 39,* 974–975.

Weisz, J. R., Rudolph, K. D., Granger, D. A., & Sweeney, L. (1992). Cognition, competence, and coping in child and adolescent depression: Research findings, developmental concerns, therapeutic implications. *Development and Psychopathology, 4,* 627–653.

Weisz, J. R., & Stipek, D. J. (1982). Competence, contingency, and the development of perceived control. *Human Development, 25,* 250–281.

Weisz, J. R., Suwanlert, S., Chaiyasit, W., Weiss, B., Achenbach, T. M., & Walter, B. (1987). Epidemiology of behavioral and emotional problems among Thai and American children: Parent reports for ages 6–11. *Journal of the American Academy of Child and Adolescent Psychiatry, 26,* 890–897.

Weisz, J. R., & Weiss, B. (1993). *Effects of psychotherapy with children and ado-lescents.* Newbury Park, CA: Sage.

Weisz, J. R., Weiss, B., Han, S., Granger, D. A., & Morton, T. (1995). Effects of psychotherapy with children and adolescents revisited: A meta-analysis of treatment outcome studies. *Psychological Bulletin, 117,* 450–468.

PART FOUR

Developmental Goals in Adulthood

13   A Life-Span Approach to Social Motivation

Laura L. Carstensen

Abstract

Social contact declines across adulthood. Socioemotional selectivity theory claims that such reductions are, in large part, volitional and result from changes in the salience of specific social goals. Information acquisition and the regulation of emotion are two principal classes of goals that are achieved through social contact. The essential premise of the theory is that the relative importance of these goals changes as a function of perceived time. When time is perceived as largely open-ended, future-oriented goals such as information acquisition are of paramount importance; however, when time is perceived as limited, present-oriented goals – namely emotional goals – are most important. Place in the life cycle and associated normative events serve as gentle and not so gentle reminders of the passage of time. Subsequently, age is associated with preferences for certain types of social contact (e.g., emotionally satisfying contact) over others (e.g., information-rich contact). This chapter is an overview of empirical evidence for the theory, highlighting aspects that pertain to life-span issues of motivation and control. The adaptiveness of the phenomenon, individual differences, and self-regulation are discussed.

Introduction

Human volition, intention, will, and desire have fascinated psychologists since the field of psychology began (Bandura, 1987; H. Heckhausen, 1991; James, 1890; Maslow, 1968; White, 1959). Each of these important constructs addresses what is arguably the most intriguing question about human behavior: What moves human beings to act?

Very early theory and research attempted to describe an essential set of human motives. It was only during the past two decades that researchers began systematically to address the dynamic interplay of emotions and cognitions with particular environmental conditions that leads to the subsequent pursuit of particular goals. Empirical research on motivation currently encompasses a broad range of topics, from the strategies that people use to obtain conscious goals (Cantor & Sanderson, Chapter 7, this volume; Fleeson & Cantor, 1995) to the automatized ways that goal relevance contributes to the processing of new information (Bargh, 1982). Even superordinate goal intentions that remain largely out of consciousness are being isolated and primed such that the pursuit of specific goals is reliably activated (Gollwitzer & Kirchhoff, Chapter 15, this volume; Gollwitzer, 1986).

At the very heart of theory and research on human motivation is the presumption that there is an intrinsic need for social relatedness (Deci & Ryan, 1991; Ryan, 1991, 1993a, and Chapter 4, this volume). Social connections are so integral to survival that mechanisms predisposing humans to attend to and affiliate with other humans probably have evolved over the millennia. Infants show an uncanny readiness to understand, seek out, and bond with other people (Tronick, 1989). Young children acquire identity beliefs in part by incorporating the beliefs and values of adults around them (Harter, 1993). Adults continue to seek confirmatory evidence from others throughout life, not only to learn about the world, but also to develop and sustain their views of themselves.

Of course, in order to adapt effectively to a complex world, affiliative goals must be balanced with other basic needs, such as autonomy and agency, which at times oppose or at least diminish the need for relatedness (Ryan, 1993b). In fact, the constellation of motives that underlies human action is regularly reorganized as goals interact and compete with one another. Whereas under certain conditions people may be motivated to seek confirmatory evidence of their self-views, under other conditions, the same people may be motivated to disconfirm self-relevant ideas. Moreover, even though emotional self-regulation clearly motivates much behavior (Higgins, 1987; Higgins & Loeb, Chapter 3, this volume), in many cases, emotional gratification is sacrificed in the service of self-verification (Swann, 1990) or information-seeking (Carstensen, 1993). Indeed, social partners are sometimes selected precisely because they elicit aversive emotions that will motivate achievement in some other domain (Norem & Cantor, 1986).

In short, the past two decades have witnessed considerable gains in the understanding of the working dynamics of motivation. Relatedness and affiliation appear to be core social motives. It is also clear that specific motives are raised and lowered in importance depending on the demands of particular social contexts. The core argument put forth in this chapter is that a set of conditions associated with, but not limited to, position in the life cycle influences which social motives are most important, the selection of social partners, and the nature of ensuing social interactions.

Human Development and Motivation

Consideration of developmental aspects of motivation has generally focused on the early years, specifically on the ways in which cognitive maturation influences comprehension and subsequent responses to childhood events (see Dweck, Chapter 10, this volume). Far less attention has been paid to potential changes in motivation across the entire life span, especially in adulthood and old age. In part, this is due to the presumption that there is continuity in basic human needs for competence, relatedness, and autonomy across the life course. For example, there is every reason to expect that regardless of age, people seek to control their worlds. J. Heckhausen and Schulz (Chapter 2, this volume), for example, argue that as people age and the potential to realize primary control (e.g., instrumental activities) diminishes, an increase in the use of secondary control strategies (e.g., cognitive reconstruals) serves to protect the motivational system. Thus, motivation may increasingly target mental activities. Brandtstädter, Rothermund, and Schmitz (Chapter 14, this volume) contend that lowering goal standards allows people to adjust psychologically to reduced competence in old age. Both of these models point to ways that motivation may change when instrumental competencies are reduced.

Other life-span developmental theories point to ways that goals and goal attainment may change throughout the life course (P. B. Baltes & M. M. Baltes, 1990; Carstensen, 1993; Carstensen, Hanson, & Freund, 1995; Hess, 1994; Labouvie-Vief & Blanchard-Fields, 1982; Labouvie-Vief & DeVoe, 1991). In fact, virtually all the fundamental tenets of life-span theory (see P. B. Baltes, 1987) are pertinent to the consideration of developmental aspects of motivation. For example, life-span theory holds that development is never fully adaptive because adaptation to one set of circumstances inevitably reduces flexibility to adapt to another. In this way, development always entails gains and losses. Subsequently, life-span theory obviates the presumption that antecedent losses are the only or even the primary reasons for motivational changes that occur with age (Carstensen & Freund, 1994).

Perhaps most relevant to motivation are two principal stays of life-span theory: First, adaptation is always bound by time and space; second, development demands selection. The first principle means that behavioral adjustment must occur within a particular environmental and social niche. In the life-cycle context, what is adaptive in infancy and early childhood may not be adaptive in adolescence and adulthood. For example, stranger anxiety may serve a highly adaptive function in infancy because it motivates dependent creatures to stay in close proximity to caregivers. It may also facilitate attachment to primary adult figures, a key developmental task of early life. However, stranger anxiety among adults is clearly maladaptive. Similarly, it can be argued that pursuing multiple prospective mates is adaptive in adolescence and early adulthood as people "practice" intimate relationships. However, it is less so in middle and old age, at which point emotional investment in a select few may hold greater gains than the continual exploration of all possible mates.[1]

The second stay of life-span theory, which speaks directly to social motivation, is that development inevitably demands selection (P. B. Baltes & M. M. Baltes, 1990). In order for specialized (i.e., effective) adaptation to occur within a particular social, historical, and physical niche, active and passive selections must be made. Specialization involves the acquisition of expertise about the social and physical world. Much specialization occurs via social contact. For example, the intergenerational transmission of language, values, and culturally shared mental representations is accomplished largely through social means (D'Andrade, 1981; Shweder & Sullivan, 1990).

Undoubtedly, one essential human motive is to seek information from and about other people. The fact that children learn the awesome amount that they do about the social world within a few short years of life suggests that there is a readiness at birth for social learning that involves the motivation to seek contact with other people. Throughout the early years of life, when the premium placed on acquiring information is extremely high, virtually all social contact satisfies the desire for information. So much of the world is novel that even the discovery that a particular person is unlikable is rich with information. However, as knowledge structures develop, information-seeking demands greater selection of social partners. That is, the set of people who can potentially contribute to an individual's store of knowledge narrows as the individual himself or herself becomes increasingly specialized or expert. For example, at 5 years of age, a young girl interested in math may be able to ask most any adult for answers to her questions. However, as a high school student of advanced calculus she needs to be highly selective about the people to whom she directs her inquiries. Thus, knowledge structures influence whether or not and to whom information-seeking behavior is directed. The basic motivation to seek information may remain constant throughout life, but it will instigate more specialized social contact as individuals develop expertise.

Although, to the best of my knowledge, there have been no empirical tests of these contentions, some support can be extrapolated from existing research findings. In a highly creative line of research designed to test self-completion theory, for example, Gollwitzer and colleagues have shown that when subjects are given feedback that is inconsistent with an important identity striving, subjects engage in self-symbolizing behavior. That is, when the self is undermined in one way, people attempt to reassert aspects of the self in other, often symbolic, ways. For example, an athlete who is told that a personality inventory has shown that she is unlike most other athletes may be more likely to write down positive self-descriptions directly relevant to her athletic prowess on a subsequent experimental task. Significantly, these researchers find that competence is inversely related to self-symbolizing in public settings (Wicklund & Gollwitzer, 1981). In other words, expertise reduces the need for symbolic social gestures that serve self-confirmatory functions. They note that people who are most secure in their self-views are least likely to engage in symbolic representations of these views. Subsequently, one can presume an age effect. Self-symbolizing behavior, for example, should be highly apparent in a sample of medical students, but far less so among a group of established surgeons. Indeed, accomplished surgeons – informed that they are dissimilar to most surgeons – may wear this information as a badge of honor. Absent its negative predictive value, such information may not serve to undermine a sense of self at all, but may serve to affirm the distinctiveness of self.

I propose that there are two broad classes of social motives that follow different developmental trajectories. One class is characterized by attempts to acquire knowledge about the self and the social world. The knowledge trajectory is future-oriented and stimulates social contact most when knowledge is limited. It includes information-seeking, social comparison, identity strivings, and achievement motivation. Developmentally, this trajectory starts high during the early years of life and declines gradually over the life course as knowledge accrues and the future for which it is banked grows shorter. The second class of social motives stems from needs for emotional gratification. Included under this general rubric are motives to feel good, derive emotional meaning from life, establish intimacy, and verify the self. Although such needs are clearly important throughout life, their relative importance among the constellation of social motives is highest during infancy and early childhood when emotional trust and relatedness is initially established and rises again in old age when future-oriented strivings are less relevant. From late adolescence to middle adulthood, however, knowledge strivings are so important that they are pursued relentlessly even at the cost of emotional satisfaction.

In conclusion, many questions remain about developmental shifts in motivation during adulthood and old age. I have argued above that from a life-span perspective, the equivalence of goal hierarchies across life is unlikely. Rather, different goals will come to the fore as a function of the particular life contexts within which individuals function and the developmental tasks they face (see also J. Heckhausen, 1995).

Socioemotional Selectivity Theory

Socioemotional selectivity theory (Carstensen, 1991, 1993, 1995) is based on the life-span framework elaborated above. According to the theory, social interaction is motivated by basic human needs or goals that range from instrumental assistance (e.g., physical protection) to psychological needs that include the regulation of emotional experience and the seeking of information about ones' culture and social surroundings. Socioemotional selectivity theory claims that although the same essential set of social goals operates throughout life, with age, the constellation of goals is reorganized such that social interaction is increasingly likely to be motivated by attempts to regulate emotion and increasingly less likely to be motivated by relatively future-oriented social goals, such as the acquisition of novel information. As a result, the type of social partners that people choose, as well as the dynamics of social interaction itself, changes in fundamental ways. Social partners are chosen for their emotional value and social interactions are regulated such that emotional outcomes are optimized.

A fundamental tenet of socioemotional selectivity theory is that perception of time is the underlying mechanism that triggers reorganization of goals. The presumption is that people regularly take account – both consciously and subconsciously – of the time that they have left in their lives. When the conclusion of this appraisal process is that time is limited, social goals change, shifting increasingly from those that are future-oriented to those that are present-oriented. This type of cognitive appraisal assists people in balancing long- and short-term goals in order to adapt effectively to their particular niche in the life cycle. Early in life it is highly adaptive to select goals with long-term payoffs; later in life, given the inevitable constraints of mortality, the pursuit of long-term goals is less adaptive. Thus, the first half of adulthood is characterized by the knowledge trajectory and the second half of adulthood is characterized by the emotion trajectory.

According to the theory, social partner choice is affected by the salience of particular social goals. When knowledge goals are accentuated, novel social partners are most appealing, because their unfamiliarity increases the likelihood that an individual will learn something new. When emotional goals are salient, familiar social partners are preferred because they are more likely to provide support and feelings of social embeddedness than are relative strangers. Moreover, because many people fall into the novel (or acquaintance) category and a relative few in the familiar (or intimate) category, a goal shift that favors emotional pursuits is likely to entail fewer social contacts.

Below, I elaborate the age-related phenomenon – namely, a decline in social contact – that socioemotional selectivity theory was initially developed to address. Then I provide evidence that social changes observed in old age are, in part, motivated and adaptive. I demonstrate that position in the life cycle, which serves as a proxy for construals of the future, is associated with people's mental representations of prospective social partners, their preferences for contact with certain types of social partners, and qualitative aspects of social interchanges. In each of these domains, constraints on the future are associated with the heightened salience of emotion.

Age-Related Declines in Social Contact

Older people engage in social interaction less often than do younger people. This age-related decline in social contact is arguably the most reliable phenomenon in social gerontology. Cross-sectional (Cumming & Henry, 1961; Gordon & Gaitz, 1976; Harvey & Singleton, 1989; Lang & Carstensen, 1994; Lawton, Moss, & Fulcomer, 1987) and longitudinal studies (Lee & Markides, 1990; Palmore, 1981) have shown that contact with others grows increasingly limited with age. Figure 13.1 illustrates the prototypical slope of declining social contacts from early to late old age (Lang & Carstensen, 1994).

For many years the widespread reaction to this age-related change was one of concern. Quite a number of gerontologists argued that barriers to social contact, rooted in an insidious ageism in Western societies and coupled with deaths of friends and loved ones and poor health, led to the impoverishment of available social opportunity structures. What came to be known as *activity theory* held that if people are to age successfully they need to make efforts to remain socially active and involved (Havighurst & Albrecht, 1953; Maddox, 1963).

An alternative interpretation of declining rates of interaction was offered by disengagement theory (Cumming & Henry, 1961). According to disengagement theory, the reduction in contact observed in old age represents a diminished desire for social connectedness in anticipation of impending

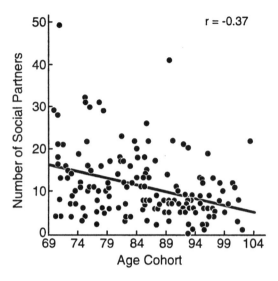

Figure 13.1. Social network size as a function of age in the Berlin Aging Study. (*Source:* Reprinted with permission from Lang and Carstensen, 1994.)

death. The theory states that social contact is diminished as a result of a mutual withdrawal between the older person and society. The theory suggests that the preconscious awareness of the imminence of death on the part of the individual instigates increased self-awareness and social withdrawal. Emotional quiescence and pensive self-reflection are the manifestations of disengagement. Recognition by the social world that the older individual will soon die leads to concurrent societal detachment from the individual. In the disengagement view, social inactivity represents a normal adaptive process.

Albeit tacit, these two contrasting gerontological theories actually pose very interesting questions about aging and motivation. The former suggests that older people want to interact with others but are obstructed from doing so; the latter suggests that there is diminished motivation to interact as a result of the recognition of the imminence of death. However, over three decades after these models were introduced, findings from empirical investigations pose serious challenges to both. For one, the picture of the status of the elderly has changed dramatically. Older people are fairing far better than previously thought. Barring serious illness, older people are happier and less lonely than their younger counterparts and are quite satisfied with their social worlds. Therefore, although one cannot deny that there are some distressed older people, a characterization of old age as a time of desolation

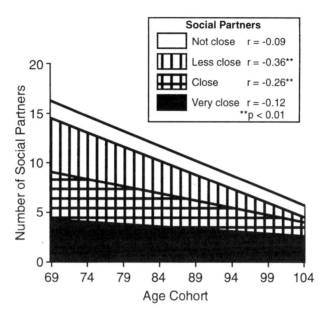

Figure 13.2. Selective reductions in types of social partners as a function of age in the Berlin Aging Study. (*Source*: Reprinted with permission from Lang and Carstensen, 1994.)

is clearly unwarranted (M. M. Baltes & Carstensen, 1996a; M. M. Baltes & Carstensen, 1996b). Subsequently, the reliable reductions in social contact do not appear to be associated with psychological distress as activity theory predicts. Indeed, one could take such evidence as support for disengagement theory. However, neither have contentions about emotional disengagement in late life been supported. In fact, as I will demonstrate below, there is growing evidence to the contrary. Moreover, compelling evidence has accrued that contact with social confidants is important for older people, predicting morbidity and even mortality (Antonucci & Jackson, 1987; Berkman & Syme, 1979; Blazer, 1982).

Recent investigations of social networks and interaction patterns have also allowed for a refinement of the phenomenon itself. It appears that older people may interact less overall, but the reduction in contact is selective. There are remarkably few changes in the number of long-time friends and loved ones older people include in their social networks (Lang & Carstensen, 1994). Even in very old age, people maintain contact with emotionally close social partners. Moreover, because the overall number of contacts declines, the proportion of emotionally close social partners in the

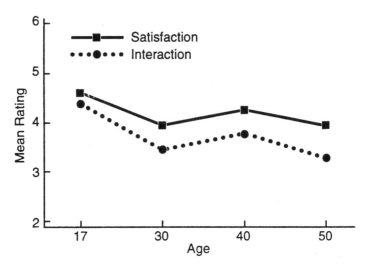

Figure 13.3. Longitudinal change in contact with acquaintances from 17 to 50 years of age. (*Source:* Reprinted with permission from Carstensen, 1992.)

network actually increases. Figure 13.2 shows the proportional distribution of social network members according to the degree of emotional closeness. Note that the drop in social contact occurs primarily among more peripheral social partners.

Finally, a longitudinal analysis of adults from early to middle adulthood provides evidence for a selective narrowing of the social world long before old age (Carstensen, 1992). A study investigating the frequency of contact and satisfaction with six different types of relationships also reveals a selective narrowing of social contacts. Figures 13.3 and 13.4 illustrate patterns of contact with acquaintances and spouses, respectively, from the age of 18 to 50 years. Note that the significant drop in contact observed with acquaintances is not observed in spousal relationships, nor is it observed in other close relationships. Thus, the selective narrowing of the social world is evidenced across adulthood, far too early for events unique to old age to account for it.

In summary, social contact declines with age. Early theoretical models attributed this decline to events specific to old age, either obstructed access to social partners or approaching death. Empirical evidence, however, shows not only that older people are satisfied with their relationships (Ryff, 1982; 1989) and in relatively good mental health (Weissman et al., 1991) de-

SPOUSES

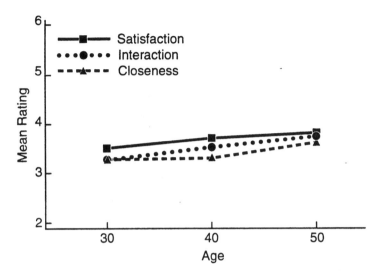

Figure 13.4. Longitudinal change in contact with spouses from 30 to 50 years of age. (*Source:* Reprinted with permission from Carstensen, 1992.)

spite reductions in social contact, but also that even very old people retain social contact with emotionally close social partners (Field & Minkler, 1988) and that the decline in this contact starts relatively early in life (Carstensen, 1992). Older people interact less with certain types of social partners but continue to interact and feel close to family and longtime friends.

There is no doubt that external and/or undesirable events contribute to the reduction in contact in old age. However, findings about social structural changes in social networks are consistent with the age-related changes in the prioritizing of social goals suggested by socioemotional selectivity theory (Lawton, Moss, & Fulcomer, 1987; Lee & Markides, 1990; Palmore, 1981). In the remainder of the chapter, I present evidence that reductions in social contact are, in part, volitional and that they are instigated by the heightened salience of emotional goals and the subsequent preference for emotionally close social partners.

Motivated Changes in Social Behavior Across Adulthood

Motivation is an illusive concept, and accessing specific motivations for social contact is a difficult task. Simply asking people why and with whom they interact is problematic. The potential influence of social desirability is enormous but, even more pertinent, conscious access to motives is questionable. Although certainly there are times when people know why they interact, the superordinate goals that motivate social contact are often outside of human awareness. The approach that my colleagues and I have taken is to search for converging evidence across domains of human functioning. We reasoned that if emotional goals assume greater importance in social interactions as people age or approach social endings, there is likely to be evidence of this in the way that people think about prospective social partners and in the prominence of emotion in their memories about social interactions. We also expected that preferences for particular types of social partners would be more likely at certain ages – specifically, that older people would prefer familiar social partners over unfamiliar partners because these social partners would be more likely to fulfill emotional goals. Further, we reasoned that if emotion is indeed more salient for older people relative to their younger counterparts, qualitative aspects of social interaction would reveal age-related differences. We predicted that compared with younger people, older people would talk about emotion more and display attempts to regulate the emotional climate of emotionally charged discussions.

Cognitive Conceptualizations of Social Partners

One of the first studies we conducted was designed to examine the ways that younger and older people mentally represent social partners (Fredrickson & Carstensen, 1990). We developed an experimental paradigm that was based on similarity judgments. Subjects were presented with a set of eighteen cards, each of which described a potential social partner. Examples include: a sibling, a new neighbor, a close friend, a person you know but dislike, an attractive person you do not know, the author of a book you just read, and so on. Subjects were asked to group the cards according to how similarly they would feel interacting with the people described on the cards. This approach allowed us to avoid asking subjects directly about their relative likes and dislikes, which we suspected would be influenced by demand characteristics, and explore the basis for their cognitive categorizations.

Using multidimensional scaling techniques, we identified three primary dimensions that accounted for most of the variance (77 percent) in subjects' card sorts. They were: affective potential (i.e., a likable/dislikable dimension), information potential (i.e., people from whom new information would be available versus people who were already well-known), and future possibilities (i.e., people who may become better known versus people who may not). The first two of the dimensions corresponded directly to the two principal motivational trajectories discussed above. The third – future possibilities – suggested an awareness of time in people's cognitive representations of social partners.

The subjects in this first study included adolescents, middle-aged people, and two age-matched subsamples of older people, which included healthy older people living in the community and infirm older people living in nursing homes. Multidimensional scaling techniques allowed us to calculate dimension weights for each subsample, indicating the prominence that each particular dimension played in the conceptualizations of social partners. As we hypothesized, age was related to the relative weight that the affective dimension played among subsamples. Whereas adolescents placed greatest weight on future possibilities, middle-aged subjects placed more emphasis on affect. Older subjects sorted even more exclusively along the affective dimension. As predicted, the two subsamples of older people also differed from one another. Even though comparably aged, infirm subjects showed an exaggerated tendency to consider social partners in affective terms, sorting virtually exclusively according to the affective valence of the social partners described. We were particularly excited by the difference between the two older subsamples. Infirm nursing home residents are surely closer to the end of their lives than healthy elderly people living in the community. Thus, life expectancy, not simply chronological age, influenced the salience of affect.

In a second project using the same experimental paradigm and analytic techniques, we replicated the effect in a larger, more diverse sample (Carstensen & Fredrickson, in press) that included 240 people, ranging in age from 18 to 88, representing both blue- and white-collar workers. One-third of the sample was African American, and the remainder was white. Multidimensional scaling does not allow for calculation of significance levels, but the relationship of age to the prominence of affect generalized across the socioeconomic and ethnic groups represented in the sample.

In a third project using identical methods, we investigated cognitive representations of social partners in a very different sample (Carstensen & Fredrickson, in press). This time we recruited a sample of gay men whose average age was 37. Of the 120 men who participated in the study, 40 were HIV-negative, 40 were HIV-positive and without symptoms of AIDS, and 40 were HIV-positive and with symptoms of AIDS. Thus, although this was a relatively young sample, participants differed notably in their life expectancies. We predicted that the weight placed on affect in categorizing social partners would covary with life expectancy. Our hypothesis was supported. In fact, the profile of results was highly similar to the cross-sectional age samples in our earlier studies.

The profile of findings suggests that the affective potential of social interaction assumes increasing importance as people approach the ends of their lives. Although chronological age is naturally correlated with life expectancy, when the two factors are separated it becomes clear that approaching the end of life is a more powerful predictor of affective salience than chronological age.

In another project, we employed an incidental memory paradigm to explore the cognitive processing of emotional material (Carstensen & Turk-Charles, 1994). We reasoned that if emotion is more salient to older adults, they are likely to process emotional information more deeply than nonemotional information and consequently remember it better. We recruited a sample of subjects ranging in age from 20 to 83 and asked them to read a two-page selection from a popular novel.[2] The selection described a social interaction and contained comparable amounts of neutral and emotionally relevant information. At the end of the experimental hour, during which subjects completed other unrelated questionnaires, they were asked to recall all that they could about the story. Responses were transcribed and classified as emotional or nonemotional. We then calculated the proportion of emotional to nonemotional information recalled, and we examined its relationship to age. Figure 13.5 illustrates the results. The proportional increase was not due to an increase in the absolute amount of emotional material recalled; it was more directly the result of a decrease in the amount of neutral information recalled. Thus, memory for emotional information may be relatively well-preserved with age.

Findings reported thus far suggest that people think about social partners and even process information differently according to their place in the life cycle. People who are approaching the final stage of life appear to be particularly attuned to emotion. They think about social partners in affective terms, and they remember emotionally charged information better than neutral information.

Time Perspective and Social Preferences

A fundamental premise of socioemotional selectivity theory is that the construal of limited time activates a reorganization of social motives in which emotional goals are prioritized. Because familiar social partners are typically better resources for satisfying emotional goals than are novel social partners, we also expected that people would favor familiar social partners

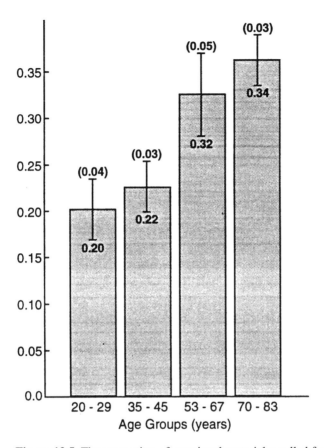

Figure 13.5. The proportion of emotional material recalled from a story narrative as a function of age. (*Source:* Reprinted with permission from Carstensen and Turk-Charles, 1994.)

under conditions that limited time. We postulated that because old age itself imposes a social ending, older people would prefer familiar over novel social partners. However, we also postulated that under conditions that constrain time, younger people would also prefer familiar social partners. In order to test the hypotheses that age and time perspective are related to social partner choices, we recruited a sample of 380 people ranging in age from 11 to 92 years and queried them about their preferred social partners under two conditions (Fredrickson & Carstensen, 1990). In the first condition, subjects were asked to imagine that they had thirty minutes free, with no pressing commitments, and that they wanted to spend some time with another person. They were asked to choose among three prospective social partners, each of whom represented one of the dimensions uncovered in our previous work: a member of your immediate family (affect), a recent acquaintance with whom you seem to have much in common (future possibilities), and the author of a book you just read (information seeking). In the second condition, the instructions were changed slightly in order to prime social endings. Subjects were asked to imagine that they were in the same situation described in the first condition, with one important exception: They were also to imagine that in a few weeks they would be moving across the country, unaccompanied by family or friends. The same three social partner options were presented, and subjects were asked to choose among them.

As predicted, we found that under both open-ended and time-constrained conditions, older people favored familiar over novel social partners. Under unspecified conditions, younger peoples' social choices were distributed remarkably similarly across the three options; that is, no age-differential pattern of preferences was apparent for younger subjects. However, when younger people were asked to anticipate a social ending, their choices were strikingly similar to those of older people. They too demonstrated strong preferences for familiar social partners. By priming a social ending, we caused younger people's social choices to become very similar to the choices older people made.

We recently replicated the basic age-related preference for familiar social partners in another experiment. In this subsequent experiment, however, we modified the second experimental condition in order to see if removing the implicit constraint that age places on time would change older peoples' social partner preferences (Fung, Carstensen, & Lutz, 1998). The experimental paradigm was identical to the social partner choice study described above, with one exception. In the second condition, rather than imposing a time constraint we asked subjects to imagine an expanded future. Subjects were asked to imagine that they had just been informed by their physician that there had been a new medical advance that would allow them to live about twenty years longer than they had expected, in relatively good health.

Both conditions were presented to 170 subjects ranging in age from 8 to 93. Results from the first condition replicated our original findings: Older people preferred familiar social partners, whereas younger people showed no decided preferences. In the second condition, however, older subjects' preferences – but not those of younger subjects – shifted such that the favoring of familiar social partners disappeared. In the second condition, older people equally likely to choose either a novel social partner or a familiar social partner.

These two studies allowed us to examine social partner preferences in old and young adults. Whether time is implicitly constrained by age, or endings are primed through a simple experimental instruction, social endings are associated with preferences for familiar social partners.

The Centrality and the Regulation of Emotion in Social Interactional Contexts

The third line of research that we have undertaken concerns social interactional dynamics. If emotion and emotional regulation grow increasingly important with age, this increasing importance is likely to be evident in the qualitative aspects of social interaction. I describe here two observational studies that targeted the social exchanges of younger and older people (Carstensen, Gottman, & Levenson, 1995; Levenson, Carstensen & Gottman, 1993; 1994; Pasupathi & Carstensen, 1994). In one, we observed young and old women telling stories to a young child (Pasupathi & Carstensen, 1994). In the other, we observed middle-aged and older married couples discussing a conflict in their relationship. In both we were interested in the ways that older and younger people use emotion in social interactions. The telling of stories to children is a familiar task for women. It is also a task that can take many forms. Stories can be told in great detail, filled with action and drama, or they can be simplified and told around moral or emotional themes. Given our thinking about the relationship of age to emotional salience, we hypothesized that older storytellers would accentuate emotions and internal states of characters, whereas younger storytellers would place greater emphasis on action (Pasupathi & Carstensen, 1994).

Subjects came to the laboratory and were provided with a book entitled *Frog, Where Are You?* Because the book contains pictures but no text, it affords both control over the story topic and considerable flexibility in how the story can be told. After subjects were allowed to review the book alone and prepare a story, they were introduced to a young child. The child was actually an experiment confederate.[3] Interactions were videotaped, dialogue was transcribed and parsed into simple idea units. Raters, who were blind to subject age and experimental hypotheses, coded the units, then calculated the proportions of the story content that comprised action, description, beliefs, and emotion statements. Analysis revealed that only the proportion of emotion statements significantly differentiated the two groups: Older storytellers were more likely than young storytellers to include talk about emotion.

Relatively little research has addressed the developmental course of emotion regulation, and virtually none has examined life-span developmental aspects of the social regulation of emotion. Indubitably, social relationships provide a context both for the elicitation and the quelling of emotion. If, as we predict, emotional experience is more salient for older than for younger people, older people are likely to be more motivated to manage social exchanges such that negative emotions are tempered.

In a study of long-term marriages, my colleagues and I examined age differences in emotional interchanges between middle-aged and older husbands and wives (Carstensen, Gottman, & Levenson, 1995; Levenson, Carstensen & Gottman, 1993; Levenson, Carstensen, & Gottman, 1994). The experimental paradigm was identical to that used previously by Levenson and Gottman (1983) in a study of younger couples. Couples came to the laboratory after eight hours of separation. Independently, they completed a conflict questionnaire on which they rated the severity of various conflicts. Then, with an interviewer's assistance, the couple identified a mutually agreed upon conflict and engaged in a videotaped discussion about it.

We found two interesting age differences pertinent to the present discussion. First, ratings of problem severity were lower for older couples than for younger couples (Levenson, Carstensen, & Gottman, 1993) even though both happy and unhappy couples were included in the sample. Middle-aged couples disagreed more than older couples about children, money, religion, and recreation. None of the topics was more conflictual for older couples than middle-aged couples. Moreover, older couples derived more pleasure than middle-aged couples from four sources: talking about children and grandchildren, doing things together, dreams, and vacations. It appears that older couples experience less conflict and more pleasure in their marriages. Second, even after controlling statistically for problem severity, compared to middle-aged couples older couples expressed lower levels of anger, disgust, belligerence, and whining and a higher level of one important emotion: affection. Significantly, these findings are based on the discussion of highly charged emotional issues. Older couples were no different from middle-aged couples in their expression of tension, domination, or contempt – they were clearly involved in the task. However, relative to middle-aged couples, older couples managed to keep the negative emotional experience more in check, by interweaving expressions of affection along with the negative emotions they were expressing to their spouses.

We interpret these findings as evidence for a positive age-related trend in the social management of emotion. Interestingly, our findings are consistent with Guilford and Bengtson's (1979) longitudinal findings about marriage. Over time, the couples they studied reported that they experienced more positivity and less negativity in their marriages.

Thus, to date, we have observed emotional expression in two very different types of dyadic exchanges: adults telling stories to young children and married couples discussing a conflict in their relationship. In both social contexts, older adults are distinguished from younger adults in terms of emotion expression. Older adults use more emotional content in storytelling, and older married couples, attempting to resolve an emotionally charged conflict, interweave affection along with negative emotions. We take findings from both studies as support for an increase in the salience of emotion in older peoples' lives.

Summary and Conclusion

This chapter considers human motivation from a life-span perspective. The organizing theoretical framework is socioemotional selectivity theory. The theory is premised on the contention that social motives compete with one another, increasing and decreasing in salience as a function of social contextual factors. Socioemotional selectivity theory claims that there is a systematic reorganization of social motives across adulthood that is associated with the implicit and inevitable constraints that place in the life cycle imposes on the future. Early in adulthood, when time is perceived as largely open-ended, future-oriented goals such as information-seeking and self-development are prioritized over short-term goals. In later adulthood, goals such as self-verification and affect regulation assume higher priority because social contact services these goals immediately.

Significantly, the primary triggering mechanism in goal reorganization is the perception of time. Social endings focus attention on emotional aspects of life. Because the construal of time is associated with place in the life cycle, the relative strength of particular social motives varies predictably across the life course.

Specific social motives also influence the selection of social partners because certain types of social partners are most likely to satisfy particular goal strivings. When novel information is sought, unfamiliar social partners are likely to fulfill social goals. When emotional gratification motivates contact, however, familiar social partners are favored. Subsequently, as people age they become increasingly less willing to invest in superficial relationships. Instead, they invest in emotionally meaningful, affectively rich relationships and engage in social regulatory strategies that optimize the emotional climate of these relationships.

Socioemotional selectivity theory presumes that adaptation is not a general phenomenon. Nor does complex social behavior change simply as a result of experience or the passage of time. Rather, adaptation targets specific social and physical niches and follows from a network of interactions representing a person's past, present, and future percepts, as well as opportunities afforded in the environment to satisfy fundamental human needs.

Notes

1. Of course, age is only a correlate of life cycle demands. At 70 years of age, a new widow may reengage in exploration of multiple prospective mates.
2. Subjects were randomly assigned to read one of two selections. One was taken from Agatha Christie's (1972) *Elephants Can Remember* and the second from Rosamunde Pilcher's (1987) *The Shell Seekers*. Results did not differ by selection.
3. We used a confederate child in order to restrict the influence that the child's input had on the story subjects told. Confederates were instructed to speak only when subjects asked questions of them. These children were excellent research assistants.

References

Antonucci, T. C., & Jackson, J. S. (1987). Social support, interpersonal efficacy, and health. *Handbook of clinical gerontology* (pp. 291–311). New York: Pergamon Press.

Baltes, M. M., & Carstensen, L. L. (1996a). Gutes Leben im Alter. Überlegungen zu einem proze.orienrrosten Metamodel gelingenden, erfolgreichen Alters. *Psychologische Rundschau, 47,* 199–215.

(1996b). The process of successful aging. *Ageing and Society, 16,* 397–422.

Baltes, P. B. (1987). Theoretical propositions of life-span developmental psychology: On the dynamics between growth and decline. *Developmental Psychology, 23,* 611–626.

Baltes, P. B., & Baltes, M. M. (1990). Psychological perspectives on successful aging: The model of selective optimization with compensation. In P. B. Baltes & M. M. Baltes (Eds.), *Successful aging: Perspectives from the behavioral sciences* (pp. 1–34). New York: Cambridge University Press.

Bandura, A. (1987). Self-regulation of motivation and action through goal systems. In V. Hamilton, G. H. Bower; & N. H. Frijda (Eds.), *Cognitive perspectives on emotion and motivation* (pp. 37–61). Dordrecht: Kluwer Academic Publishers.

Bargh, J. A. (1982). Attention and automaticity in the processing of self-relevant information. *Journal of Personality and Social Psychology, 43,* 425–436.

Berkman, L., & Syme, S. L. (1979). Social networks, host resistance and mortality: A nine year follow-up study of Alameda County residents. *American Journal of Epidemiology, 109,* 186–204.

Blazer, D. (1982). Social support and mortality in an elderly community population. *American Journal of Epidemiology, 115,* 684–694.

Brandtstädter, J., Rothermund, K., & Schmitz, U. (1998). Maintaining self-integrity and efficacy through adulthood and later life: The adaptive functions of assimilative persistence and accommodative flexibility. In J. Heckhausen & C. S. Dweck (Eds.), *Motivation and self-regulation across the life span.* New York: Cambridge University Press.

Cantor, N., & Sanderson, C. A. (1998). The functional regulation of adolescent dating relationships and sexual behavior: An interaction of goals, strategies, and situations. In J. Heckhausen & C. S. Dweck (Eds.), *Motivation and self-regulation across the life span.* New York: Cambridge University Press.

Carstensen, L. L. (1991). Selectivity theory: Social activity in life-span context. In K. W. Schaie (Ed.), *Annual Review of Gerontology and Geriatrics* (Vol. 11, pp. 195–217). New York: Springer.

  (1992). Social and emotional patterns in adulthood: Support for socioemotional selectivity theory. *Psychology and Aging, 7,* 331–338.

  (1993). Motivation for social contact across the life span: A theory of socioemotional selectivity. *Nebraska Symposium on Motivation, 40,* 209–254.

  (1995). Evidence for a life-span theory of socioemotional selectivity. *Current Directions in Psychological Science, 4,* 151–156.

Carstensen, L. L., & Fredrickson, B. F. (in press). Socioemotional selectivity in healthy older people and younger people living with HIV: The centrality of emotion when the future is constrained. *Health Psychology.*

Carstensen, L. L., & Freund, A. (1994). The resilience of the aging self. *Developmental Review, 14,* 81–92.

Carstensen, L. L., Gottman, J. M., & Levenson, R. W. (1995). Emotional behavior in long-term marriage, *Psychology and Aging, 10,* 140–149.

Carstensen, L. L., Hanson, K., & Freund, A. (1995). Selection and compensation in adulthood. In R. A. Dixon & L. Backman (Eds.) *Psychological compensation: Managing losses and promoting gains* (pp. 106–126). Hillsdale, NJ: Erlbaum.

Carstensen, L. L., & Turk-Charles, S. (1994). The salience of emotion across the adult life course. *Psychology and Aging, 9,* 259–264.

Christie, A. (1972). *Elephants can remember* (pp. 60–63). New York: Dell.

Cumming, E., & Henry, W. E. (1961). *Growing old: The process of disengagement.* New York: Basic Books.

D'Andrade, R. G. (1981). The cultural part of cognition. *Cognitive Science, 5,* 179–195.

Deci, E. L., & Ryan, R. M. (1991). A motivational approach to self: Integration in personality. *Nebraska Symposium on Motivation, 38,* 237–288.

Dweck, C. S. (1998). The development of early self-conceptions: Their relevance for motivational processes. In J. Heckhausen & C. S. Dweck (Eds.), *Motivation and self-regulation across the life span.* New York: Cambridge University Press.

Field, D., & Minkler, M. (1988). Continuity and change in social support between young-old, old-old, and very-old adults. *Journal of Gerontology, 43,* P100–P106.

Fleeson, W., & Cantor, N. (1995). Goal relevance and the affective experience of daily life: Ruling out situational explanations. *Motivation and Emotion, 19,* 25–57.

Fredrickson, B. L., & Carstensen, L. L. (1990). Choosing social partners: How old age and anticipated endings make us more selective. *Psychology and Aging, 5,* 335–347.

Fung, H., Carstensen, L. L., & Lutz, A. (1998). The role of time perspective in age differences in social preferences. Manuscript under review.

Gollwitzer, P. M. (1986). The implementation of identity intentions: A motivational-volitional perspective on symbolic self-completion. In F. Halisch & J. Kuhl (Eds.), *Motivation, intentions and volition* (pp. 349–369). Heidelberg: Springer-Verlag.

Gollwitzer, P. M., & Kirchhoff, P. M. (1998). The willful pursuit of identity. In J. Heckhausen & C. S. Dweck (Eds.), *Motivation and self-regulation across the life span.* New York: Cambridge University Press.

Gordon, C., & Gaitz, C. (1976). Leisure and lives. In R. Binstock & E. Shanas (Eds.), *Handbook of aging and the social sciences* (Vol. 1, pp. 310–341). New York: Van Nostrand.

Guilford, R., & Bengtson, V. (1979). Measuring marital satisfaction in three generations: Positive and negative dimensions. *Journal of Marriage and the Family, 39,* 387–398.

Harter, S. (1993). Visions of self: Beyond the me in the mirror. *Nebraska Symposium on Motivation, 40,* 99–144.

Harvey, A. S., & Singleton, J. F. (1989). Canadian activity patterns across the life span: A time budget perspective. *Canadian Journal on Aging, 8,* 268–285.

Havighurst, R. J., & Albrecht, R. (1953). *Older people.* New York: Longmans.

Heckhausen, H. (1991). *Motivation and action.* Berlin: Springer.

Heckhausen, J. (1995). *Developmental regulation in adulthood: Age-normative and sociostructural constraints as adaptive challenges.* Habilitation monograph, submitted to the Free University of Berlin.

Heckhausen, J., & Schulz, R. (1998). Developmental regulation in adulthood: Selection and compensation via primary and secondary control. In J. Heckhausen & C. S. Dweck (Eds.), *Motivation and self-regulation across the life span.* New York: Cambridge University Press.

Hess, T. M. (1994). Social cognition in adulthood: Aging-related changes in knowledge and processing mechanisms. *Developmental Review, 14,* 373–412.

Higgins, E. T. (1987). Self-discrepancy: A theory relating self and affect. *Psychological Review, 94,* 319–340.

Higgins, T., & Loeb, I. (1998). Development of regulatory focus: Promotion and prevention as ways of living. In J. Heckhausen & C. S. Dweck (Eds.), *Moti-

vation and self-regulation across the life span. New York: Cambridge University Press.

James, W. (1890). *The principles of psychology* (Vols. 1 and 2). New York: Holt.

Labouvie-Vief, G., & Blanchard-Fields, F. (1982). Cognitive aging and psychological growth. *Aging and Society, 2,* 183–209.

Labouvie-Vief, G., & DeVoe, M. (1991). Emotional regulation in adulthood and later life: A developmental view. *Annual Review of Gerontology and Geriatrics, 11,* 172–194. New York: Springer.

Lang, F. R., & Carstensen, L. L. (1994). Close emotional relationships in late life: Further support for proactive aging in the social domain. *Psychology and Aging, 9,* 315–324.

Lawton, M. P., Moss, M., & Fulcomer, M. (1987). Objective and subjective uses of time by older people. *International Journal of Aging and Human Development, 24,* 171–188.

Lee, D. J. & Markides, K. S. (1990). Activity and mortality among aged persons over an eight-year period. *The Journals of Gerontology: Social Sciences, 45,* S39–S42.

Levenson, R. W., Carstensen, L. L. & Gottman, J. M. (1993). Long-term marriage: Age, gender and satisfaction. *Psychology and Aging, 8,* 301–313.

   (1994). Marital interaction in old and middle-aged long-term marriages: Physiology, affect, and their interrelations. *Journal of Personality and Social Psychology, 67,* 56–68.

Levenson, R. W., & Gottman, J. M. (1983). Marital interaction: Physiological linkage and affective exchange. *Journal of Personality and Social Psychology, 45,* 587–597.

Maddox, G. L. (1963). Activity and morale: A longitudinal study of selected elderly subjects. *Social Forces, 42,* 195–204.

Maslow, A. H. (1968). *Toward a psychology of being* (2nd ed.) New York: Van Nostrand.

Norem, J., & Cantor, N. (1986). Defensive pessimism: "Harnessing" anxiety as motivation. *Journal of Personality and Social Psychology, 51,* 1208–1217.

Palmore, E. (1981). *Social patterns in normal aging: Findings from the Duke Longitudinal Study.* Durham, NC: Duke University Press.

Pasupathi, M., & Carstensen, L. L. (1994, July). Storytelling to children from a life-span perspective. Invited paper presented at the meetings of the International Society for the Study of Behavioral Development, Amsterdam, The Netherlands.

Pilcher, R. (1987). *The shell seekers* (pp. 13–15), London: Coronet Books.

Ryan, R. M. (1991). The nature of the self in autonomy and relatedness. In J. Strauss & G. R. Goethals (Eds.), *The self: Interdisciplinary approaches* (pp. 208–238). New York: Springer-Verlag.

   (1993a). Agency and organization: Intrinsic motivation, autonomy, and the self in psychological development. *Nebraska Symposium on Motivation, 40,* 1–58.

(1993b). Commentary on the fortieth Nebraska Symposium on Motivation, *Nebraska Symposium on Motivation, 40,* 255–268.

Ryff, C. D. (1982). Successful aging: A developmental approach. *Gerontologist, 22,* 209–214.

(1989). In the eye of the beholder: Views of psychological well-being among middle-aged and older adults. *Psychology and Aging, 4,* 195–210.

(1998). Human psychological needs and the issues of volition, control, and outcome focus. In J. Heckhausen & C. S. Dweck (Eds.), *Motivation and self-regulation across the life span.* New York: Cambridge University Press.

Shweder, R. A., & Sullivan, M. A. (1990). The semiotic subject of cultural psychology. In L. A. Pervin (Ed.), *Handbook of personality: Theory and research* (pp. 399–418). New York: Guilford Press.

Swann, W. B. (1990). To be adored or to be known?: The interplay of self-enhancement and self-verification. In E. T. Higgins & R. M. Sorrentino (Eds.), *Handbook of motivation and cognition: Foundations of social behavior* (Vol. 2, pp. 408–448). New York: Guilford Press.

Tronick, E. Z. (1989). Emotions and emotional communications in infants. *American Psychologist, 44,* 112–119.

Weissman, M. M., Bruce, M. L., Leaf, P. J., Florio, L. P., Holzer, C., III (1991). Affective disorders. In L. N. Robins & D. A. Regier (Eds.), *Psychiatric disorders in America: The Epidemiological Catchment Area Study* (pp. 53–80). New York: Free Press.

White, R. W. (1959). Motivation reconsidered: The concept of competence. *Psychological Review, 66,* 297–333.

Wicklund, R. A., & Gollwitzer, P. M. (1981). Symbolic self-completion, attempted influence and self-deprecation. *Basic and Applied Social Psychology, 2,* 89–114.

14 Maintaining Self-Integrity and Efficacy Through Adulthood and Later Life: The Adaptive Functions of Assimilative Persistence and Accommodative Flexibility

Jochen Brandtstädter, Klaus Rothermund, and Ulrich Schmitz

Abstract

Some widespread assumptions concerning the concept of control are in need of a critical revision. First, it is increasingly recognized that self-percepts of control and efficacy may have untoward side effects; relationships between variables of control and well-being are subject to various moderating effects. Second, there is ample evidence that, despite irreversible losses in functional resources, a sense of control and efficacy does not generally wane in later life. Findings from two large-scale research projects combining cross-sectional and longitudinal observations form the basis for a theoretical model that integrates these lines of evidence. It is argued that the maintenance of control and self-esteem through adulthood involves the interplay of strategic and automatic processes. In particular, the model stresses the functional role of readjusting goals and priorities.

Introduction

The transition to old age poses serious adaptive strain on the aging self. In many physiological parameters, losses in adaptive reserves become manifest as early as middle adulthood; as age advances, such changes increasingly take their toll on health and physical fitness. The developmental convoy of persons who have accompanied the aging person through the life cycle is increasingly reduced; role losses further contribute to an increasing social marginalization of the aged person. Not least, there is the problem of narrowing future perspectives. We gain meaning in life essentially from plans and goals that extend into the future; with the fading of time yet to be lived, individuals also lose leeway for resolving goal conflicts through a sequential arrangement of priorities in time. Recognizing that personally valued goals cannot

This research was supported by the German Research Foundation.

365

be achieved in the remaining lifetime is a common experience of old age (Brandtstädter & Wentura, 1994; Breytspraak, 1984). Though such constraints may afflict elderly persons to different degrees, they are generally experienced as aversive, and to some extent unavoidable, accompaniments of age and tend to threaten individual self-definitions that have been established and consolidated during early and middle adulthood.

In fact, when people in middle and old age are questioned about their developmental past and future, the dominant aspect is one of increasing deficits in personally valued areas of life and functioning (Brandtstädter, Wentura, & Greve, 1993). Although such responses may be influenced partly by implicit naive theories of aging (McFarland, Ross, & Giltrow, 1992), they often refer to very concrete experiences of loss. The aging individual, as a purposeful actor, strives to avoid aversive losses and debilitating impairments (Brandtstädter, 1984); consequently, it is not surprising that the changes in later life that are experienced as negative are also mostly perceived as being outside of personal control (Heckhausen & Baltes, 1991). In sum, it appears that the notion of successful aging cannot simply be conceived of in terms of an absence of losses and restraints; rather, it must be understood in terms of the activities and processes that serve to maintain personal continuity and self-esteem despite the partly aversive and uncontrollable changes that accompany the processes of aging.

Subjective Quality of Life in Later Adulthood: Some Empirical Puzzles

A closer consideration of such self-protective processes is necessitated by some puzzling observations about subjective life quality in later adulthood. There is no consistent evidence for a general or dramatic decrease in subjective life quality in the elderly. For example, there is no clear evidence that depressive problems appear more strongly or frequently among older persons (for overviews, see, e.g., Blazer, 1989; Häfner, 1992), except in terminal phases of life that often are overshadowed by problems of bereavement and serious illness (Lawton, 1991). Large-scale epidemiological studies have even reported a reduced risk for depressive disorders in older samples (e.g., Myers, Weissman, Tischler, et al., 1984). Although we would not suggest that depression in old age is a "myth" (Feinson, 1985), the view that elderly persons are more vulnerable to depression than younger groups apparently must be abandoned.

It is of course tempting to search for possible artifacts here. Most studies on late-life depression have followed a cross-sectional approach and thus are subject to the notorious shortcomings of this type of design. Furthermore, simple linear correlations may conceal possible curvilinear relationships (Kessler, Foster, Webster, et al., 1992). One might also point to the fact that depressive states in the elderly often appear in the guise of somatic complaints (e.g., Weiss, Nagel, & Aronson, 1986). This latter argument, however, may prove to be a boomerang; as Newmann, Engel, and Jensen (1990) have cogently argued, one must be careful not to conflate depressive reactions with symptoms of physical depletion. In old age, such symptoms are likely to occur also in nondepressive persons; this is why more recently designed scales for assessing depression in samples of older people have excluded such items (e.g., Yesavage, Brink, Rose, et al., 1983). Many traditional depression scales, however, comprise somatic items; the implication obviously is that epidemiological studies using such scales may have overestimated, rather than underestimated, the risk of depression in older populations.

In brief, though the objections mentioned above partly raise valid points, they do not appear strong enough to explain away the phenomenal resiliency of the aging self. This argument is further supported by convergent evidence from research on life satisfaction in older people. According to meta-analytic studies (e.g., Mayring, 1987; Stock, Okun, Haring, et al., 1983), the bulk of reported correlations of life satisfaction with age in adult samples is distributed around a central value near, or perhaps even slightly above, zero. Using measures of life satisfaction as indicators of positive aging is not without problems, of course. For example, implicit social rules prescribe when and under what conditions one should, as an older person, be satisfied with one's life, and individual responses presumably are affected by such rules. Nevertheless, the lack of any general or strong drop in life satisfaction with age is intriguing. We are familiar with the so-called paradoxes of satisfaction, i.e., with the fact that many people who live under depressing circumstances apparently refuse to become depressive (see, e.g., Schwarz & Strack, 1991). William James (1890) once defined satisfaction as the ratio of success to pretensions. According to the logic of this formula, lowering ambitions may be as effective as increasing personal achievements for maintaining satisfaction.[1] This is a point of some theoretical interest, to which we return later in this chapter.

Research on perceived control in later life lends further support to the argument advanced so far. The construct of control is of particular interest to the study of successful aging (e.g., M. M. Baltes & P. B. Baltes, 1986); a broad spectrum of findings indicates that a sense of control and personal efficacy is of crucial importance to maintaining a positive view of self and personal future. Persons with self-confident efficacy beliefs are less threat-ened by aversive developmental prospects, more persistent in their efforts to cope with adversity, and less vulnerable to feelings of despondency and depression (e.g., Bandura, 1986). In longitudinal assessments, for example, decreases in perceived control are generally accompanied by shifts toward a more negative and pessimistic evaluation of past and future personal de-velopment (Brandtstädter, 1992). Generally, only goals and self-ideals that are considered to be within one's span of control can provide motivating and meaningful perspectives for personal development. With regard to later life, many researchers have held the view that the gradual shrinking of physical, social, and temporal resources, as well as the exposure of older people to negative stereotypes of aging, are likely to undermine a sense of control (e.g., Rodin & Langer, 1980; Seligman & Elder, 1986). Surprisingly, re-search in this area has not substantiated this plausible assumption. Statisti-cal associations between age and measures of perceived control tend to be low, even when domain-specific facets of control are considered (e.g., Lach-man, 1986; Rodin, Timko, & Harris, 1985).

Some observations from our own research may illustrate this point. In our projects, we have assessed the degree of perceived control over personal de-velopment in the following way (cf. Brandtstädter & Baltes-Götz, 1990). We presented the participants with a list of developmental goals that covered dif-ferent desirable aspects of personal, physical, or mental development.[2] Par-ticipants were asked to rate to what extent they considered attainment of the goals as depending on their own effort. By aggregating these ratings, we de-rived a global index of personal control over development. The data were obtained from a core sample of 878 participants (441 women; 437 men) in the initial age range from 54 to 78 years, grouped into three age cohorts. The assessments were repeated after a longitudinal interval of four years (age ranges for cohorts at second measurement, 1995 – cohort 1: 58 to 65 years; cohort 2: 66 to 73 years; cohort 3: 74 to 82 years).[3] Figure 14.1 shows the cross-sequential findings. Neither the cross-sectional nor the longitudinal comparisons show clear indications for age-related losses in perceived con-trol; despite the sample size, the corresponding ANOVA main effects for co-hort and measurement remain insignificant. Interaction effects with gender hint that longitudinal stability in perceived control is somewhat higher for men than for women, particularly in the oldest group; these effects, how-ever, are only slight ($F[1,872] = 5.02$, $p < 0.05$; $F[2,872] = 3.40$, $p < 0.05$). The findings indicate that perceived control over personal development is considerably stable even in late phases of life; in particular, simple cohort-based explanations of this phenomenon are not supported by these data.

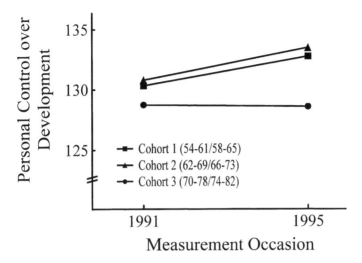

Figure 14.1. Personal control over development: Cross-sectional comparisons and four-year longitudinal change.

It has to be reiterated at this point that chronological age as such does not affect anything; age effects are always mediated by variables that correlate with the age variable, and that also may vary within age-homogeneous groups. Considering possible mediated effects, it is particularly puzzling that age differences do not map to variables of subjective life quality, although they are known to affect negatively resource variables that tend to be related positively to subjective life quality (e.g., subjective and objective health, role status, social integration). Though the transition to old age involves losses and constraints in personally valued domains, it apparently does not generally undermine a sense of control and a positive outlook on self- and personal development.

A classical line of argument in this regard has been to emphasize potential positive aspects of later life, viewing them as a kind of compensation for naturally occurring losses. As early a writer as Cicero applied this formula: Among the compensations of old age that he particularly praised was the waning of sensuous passions and of related troubles such as "drunkenness, indigestion, and uneasy sleep" (cited in Faltner, 1988, p. 57). In the eighteenth century, the French philosopher Buffon wrote a multivolume natural philosophy centering around the principle of compensation. He argued that this principle also does justice to older persons, in that "gains in the moral sphere more than make up for losses in the physical sphere" (Buffon, 1777; cited in Svagelski, 1981). The ancient ideals of equanimity and abstinence are no longer a part of present-day conceptions of successful aging; however, in the recent literature the general theme recurs that in old age, gains emerge that compensate losses (e.g., P. B. Baltes, 1987; Uttal & Perlmutter, 1989). In interview studies with elderly people that we carried out in combination with experimental studies and questionnaire assessments (Dillmann, Felser, & Brandtstädter, 1992), our elderly subjects mentioned as compensations of later life, e.g., greater calmness and self-security, more time for oneself, more freedom to arrange daily routines, relief from occupational and family responsibilities, the opportunity of passing on one's life experiences, or (to cite from the protocols) the freedom to "leisurely let things run their course and not believe that you can change the world."

Whether a developmental change is experienced as a gain or loss, however, primarily depends on how it relates to personal goals and values, and how the individual construes this relation (cf. Cantor & Fleeson, 1991; Cantor & Sanderson, Chapter 7, this volume; Carstensen, Chapter 13, this volume). Accordingly, we hold the view that claims about the presumed "bads and boons" of old age must be replaced, on the theoretical level, by a set of more precise questions: How do individuals maintain a favorable balance of gains and losses in later life? What kind of strategic and automatic processes contribute to mitigate or neutralize experiences of loss? What are the mechanisms that the aging self engages in order to secure personal continuity and integrity?

Adjusting to Age-Related Change: Assimilative and Accommodative Processes

We have approached these questions from a theoretical position that views the self as a dynamic, self-perpetuating, and self-protective system (Brandtstädter & Greve, 1994). It has become customary in self-concept research to discern three different modes or facets of self-representations (cf. Higgins, Klein, & Strauman, 1985; Kihlstrom & Cantor, 1984; Markus & Wurf, 1987): the *actual self,* which is the perceptual and conceptual representation of actual states of personal behavior and development; the *desired self,* which comprises representations of what one would like to be or become, and which is expressed in the person's developmental goals and identity projects (for the sake of simplicity, we also include here personal representations of how, according to socially shared behavioral norms or developmental tasks, one ought to be or become); and the *potential self,* that is, representations of what one possibly could be or become. Generally, developmental losses and identity deficits can be described in terms of discrepancies between actual and desired self-states. Whether perceived or anticipated discrepancies are experienced as aversive, however, also depends on the extent to which the individual feels capable of reducing them; here, the potential or "possible" self (Markus & Nurius, 1986) becomes relevant. This system apparently has many degrees of freedom of alleviating or neutralizing goal discrepancies. To account for the resiliency of the aging self, apparently it is necessary to focus on processes and mechanisms that serve to coadjust representations of the actual, desired, and potential self in such ways that states of frustration, helplessness, and depression are avoided.

The model of assimilative and accommodative coping that has guided our research (Brandtstädter, 1989; Brandtstädter & Renner, 1990, 1992) distinguishes two classes of interrelated processes through which perceived developmental losses or self-discrepancies can be prevented or neutralized. In the assimilative mode, the individual actively tries to change the actual situation so that it better fits personal goals and standards. In the accommodative mode, aversive goal discrepancies, as well as the negative emotional states associated with them, are neutralized by adjusting personal goals and ambitions to situational circumstances. The concepts of assimilation and accommodation, as they are used here, refer to two distinct and mutually inhibiting, but also complementary, ways of achieving congruence between actual (perceived) and desired states or courses of personal development. The theoretical conception has emerged from an application of action-theoretical notions to development and aging (Brandtstädter, 1984); it also addresses mechanisms that operate on nonintentional or subpersonal levels.

Maintaining Goals Under Diminishing Resources: Assimilative Activities

Assimilative efforts that aim at achieving or maintaining desired developmental outcomes, or at preventing deviations from desired courses of personal development, are an essential aspect of the individual's life activity. Assimilative activities are related to the self in a double sense: First, such activities are directed back on the *subjects themselves;* second, they are guided and regulated by the individual's *self,* that is, they are related to representations of actual, desired, and potential selves.

Generally, any domain of behavior or development that is open to intentional modification can become the target of assimilative action. In later life, preserving personally valued competencies and maintaining desired levels of performance become a dominant concern of assimilative activities. Depending on personal means–ends beliefs, such preventive or corrective intentions may involve a broad diversity of assimilative behaviors. For example, to maintain a youthful appearance or to stay physically and mentally in shape, individuals may change nutritional behaviors, daily routines, and patterns of social interaction; they may also employ a variety of proxies or compensatory means that science and technology in any culture offer for such purposes. Such self-corrective efforts will be intensified to the extent that experiences of functional losses loom larger, at least as long as individuals see a chance to maintain desired levels of functioning. The strength and persistence of assimilative efforts depend on the personal valence of the functional domain in question and on the degree of perceived control over that domain (cf. Brandtstädter, 1989). Assimilative activities will preferably center on those domains of behavior or development that are relevant to the person's identity goals or personal ambitions.

A key characteristic of assimilative actions as defined above is the tenacious adherence to personal goals and self-evaluative standards. Efforts to alleviate developmental loss through assimilative activity can of course fail or become increasingly demanding. Assimilative efforts operate on limited physical, material, and temporal resources. The psychological problems of later life result not only from the experience of losses and diminishing resources in personally valued domains, but also from the fact that attempts to counteract such losses become increasingly difficult (otherwise, there would presumably be no losses at all).

In order to maintain goals and ambitions under narrowing action reserves, individuals may for a while try to optimize or boost their reserves by selective and compensatory efforts (P. B. Baltes & M. M. Baltes, 1990; Salthouse, 1987; see also Heckhausen & Schulz, Chapter 2, this volume). In terms of the present model, such efforts mark a late or final phase of assimilative effort. Unfortunately, a principle of diminishing returns sets limits to such efforts. To borrow terms from economics: As systems approach their production limits, further production increases will demand disproportionately high investments in terms of time, energy, or money (see also Samuelson & Nordhaus, 1985). This principle also applies to compensatory efforts. Thus, with decreasing action reserves, the resulting costs of maintaining a given standard or goal will eventually outweigh the prospective benefits (Brandtstädter & Wentura, 1995). This sets the stage for accommodative changes in the personal system of goals and standards.

When Goals Become Unfeasible: Accommodative Processes

When goals or standards drift outside the feasible range that is delimited by personal control potentials and subjectively accessible resources of action, reactions tend to shift from assimilative to accommodative modes. Accommodative reactions, as we define them, comprise a family of processes. A prototypical facet of accommodation is the downgrading of, or disengagement from, blocked goals and the rescaling of aspiration levels. When a goal or ambition is blocked, individuals initially may increase their assimilative efforts and mobilize resources in a reactant effort to overcome the obstacle; in this phase (which still belongs to the assimilative mode), goals may even gain attractive valence (Wright & Brehm, 1989). Repeated unsuccessful attempts to overcome the goal, however, undermine the action-outcome expectations that motivate further assimilative effort; the goal loses attractive valence, and the individual eventually disengages from it (an adaptive function of this process may be to avoid the wasting of action resources; see also Klinger, 1975). Accommodative processes may also be backed by a cognitive deconstruction of those meanings and implications that make the blocked goal attractive, by a corresponding positive reappraisal of alternative goals and standards, or by tendencies to reappraise experiences of loss by attaching positive meanings to them. In contrast to assimilative processes, which involve a maintenance of goals and ambitions, the defining feature of accommodative processes is the flexible adjustment of preference structures to situational constraints. Some selected examples from interview studies with elderly people may provide a more vivid impression of how accommodative flexibility is manifested in the thought of older persons (cf. Brandtstädter, Rothermund, & Schmitz, 1997):

> It's strange, like a lot of other things in life: You get used to it after a while. You regret the fact you're getting old, that your body's getting old, that you, well, don't look very attractive in a bikini anymore. But somehow, after a certain amount of time, you come to terms with it, because other things are always happening that are nice and have little to do with your appearance. (57 years, female)

> You have to accept . . . now that doesn't mean that for instance you should give yourself over to fate, rather I'm trying to say you have to be humble enough to say, "You aren't 40 anymore! Taking a break is normal! It's normal that you get more tired on some days." (63 years, male)

> When you're younger, you try to perfect your natural talents and abilities. I think that is both healthy and proper. But that feeling goes away bit by bit. You don't want to, maybe because you can't, but maybe too because it doesn't seem to make all that much sense anymore. (62 years, female)

> Nowadays I say, "You're old now, you've got to write that off." And that's why I don't see anything negative about it. It just comes with age. I have to act accordingly. (76 years, female)

> Things that I can't change – I don't worry about them that much. Because if I moped about, the wrinkles would get worse (laughs). And when I don't think about it, then it just follows its natural course, but I don't do anything to worsen it. (73 years, female)

> Lots of things have lost their significance in old age, things that once were very important. Earlier you wanted to look good, to be recognized, to be accepted, you wanted to play a certain role. These things now have become rather secondary. (75 years, male)

Adjusting personal preferences and ambitions to situational limitations has often been associated in the psychological literature with notions of helplessness and depression. This position is seriously misleading and has to some extent also biased contemporary notions of successful aging toward a strong preference for active-offensive modes of coping. In the model of assimilative and accommodative coping, feelings of depression and resignation, on the contrary, reflect difficulties in shifting to accommodative modes. Ruminative thinking about the blocked goals that often accompanies such difficulties indicates that the goals retain attractive valence and continue to bind attentional resources (cf. Kuhl & Helle, 1986; Martin & Tesser, 1989).

These considerations add an important perspective to current theorizing about the etiology of depression. According to prevailing views, the perceived inability to reach blocked goals is a central risk factor for reactions of helplessness and depression. From the point of view taken here, a second and perhaps equally important risk factor – one that particularly control-theoretical accounts of depression (e.g., Bandura, 1989; Ingram, 1990; Peterson & Seligman, 1987) have tended to neglect – is the inability to let go of goals and downgrade ambitions that are outside the person's span of control (see also Brandtstädter & Baltes-Götz, 1990; Carver & Scheier, 1990). Paradoxically, the downscaling of goals that are, or have become, unfeasible may even serve to maintain a sense of personal control. We will come back to this point.

Individuals cannot adjust preferences or disengage from goals merely because it seems advantageous to do so. Accommodative processes need not be, and often cannot be, intentionally enacted (see also Gilbert, 1993; Kunda, 1990). Often the accommodation of preference systems is a very gradual process that does not involve a particular decision. Though this process can eventually manifest itself in particular intentions and decisions, it appears that accommodative processes have already done their work when such intentions are formed. The changing self does not require an intentional homunculus who changes it. This point is of considerable theoretical importance, because it brings to attention the constraints and automatisms that may promote accommodation.

The readiness and capability to accommodate goals depends on a diversity of situational and personal conditions. As mentioned above, self-percepts of control and efficacy tend to instigate further assimilative effort, and, by the same token, will inhibit accommodation. The stronger the individual's self-beliefs of control, the more resistant they are against disconfirming feedback arising from repeated unsuccessful assimilative attempts; but the more they should also inhibit or retard the shift toward accommodation of goals and preferences. Accordingly, people harboring self-percepts of high efficacy may possibly be put at a disadvantage when confronted with factually irreversible losses. Such dysfunctional side effects of high subjective control have recently gained increasing attention, and they may partly account for the inconsistencies of findings that have related perceived control to measures of well-being and coping efficiency (cf. Coyne & Gotlib, 1983).

Further important constraints on the processes of assimilation and accommodation relate to the structure of the individual's system of goals and beliefs. Generally, people find it most difficult to disengage from goals that are central to their identity and for which substitutes are not easily available. High "self-complexity" (Linville, 1987) – that is, a diversified and multifocal structure of personal projects and identity goals – may thus enhance accommodative processes.

The extent to which cognitions that can serve to deconstruct the attractiveness of blocked ambitions are personally accessible is another constraint that is likely to affect accommodative flexibility. The cognitive and heuristic processes that operate on the personal system of beliefs must be sufficiently potent to generate such new and palliative meanings, and the belief system must be sufficiently open or malleable to accept them. From a contextualist point of view, as individuals move along the life cycle, they also enter different symbolic and informational contexts in which different self-evaluative standards or standards of social comparison may become salient (e.g., Frey & Ruble, 1990). Such contextual conditions, which also change in historical time, may impede or enhance accommodative (and assimilative) processes. It becomes evident at this point that negative stereotypes of aging, apart from their alleged disabling functions that have been stressed in the literature, may also have positive side effects, in that they provide a context for positive self-evaluation. In fact, it has been observed that the majority of elderly people think that they are better off than most of their peers (cf. Hagestad & Neugarten, 1985; Heckhausen & Krueger, 1993).

Among the automatisms that support accommodative processes, mechanisms of attention regulation seem to be of particular importance. Attention generally focuses on situational aspects that are relevant to an ongoing course of action. This general principle suggests that attention tends to be withdrawn from problems that have turned out to be uncontrollable (Brandtstädter & Renner, 1992). We may even speculate further that when attentional capacity is reduced (which may be the case in older individuals), the shifting of attention away from difficult or unsolvable problems may be accelerated. As mentioned above, particular types of problems may continue to bind attention even after repeated unsuccessful attempts to solve them; this is likely to be particularly true of problems that are so basic or central to the person's design of life and identity that assimilative efforts continue to have high subjective utility even when perceived chances of success are dim. Problem-centered thought may under such conditions degenerate into ruminative thinking that continues to cycle around a blocked goal. In our view, rumination may also generate cognitions that enhance deconstruction of the positive valences of blocked goals, and thus eventually may enhance the relinquishing of barren commitments. Because of their ability to neutralize aversive emotional states, palliative cognitions are more likely to become integrated into the individual's system of beliefs, so that they eventually can override a tendency to generate mood-congruent thought (cf. Blaney, 1986; Brandtstädter & Renner, 1992; Kunda, 1990).

The mentioned constraints and moderating conditions tend to affect assimilative and accommodative processes in opposed ways, reflecting the antagonistic nature of these modes. However, there is a specific class of processes that tends to dampen both assimilative and accommodative modes. Elsewhere, the concept of immunization has been suggested to refer to such processes (see Brandtstädter & Greve, 1994; Greve, 1990). Immunization denotes the notorious tendency to interpret self-related evidence in ways that are consistent with established self-descriptions and to twist situational evidence in self-enhancing ways. For example, elderly persons with hearing difficulties may attribute such problems externally by assuming that others speak too low or indistinctly, difficulties in remembering items from a shopping list may be attributed to noisy surroundings in the mall rather than to impaired memory capacities, and so on. In the literature, constructs such as "self-serving bias," "positive illusion," or "denial" denote such well-documented effects (e.g., Taylor & Brown, 1988). We are reluctant to use such concepts here because even within the limits of rationality, there is often room to negotiate evidence in ways that preserve self-consistency and self-esteem (Snyder, 1989). In later life, immunizing processes may reduce the salience or accessibility of deficits, and thus are likely to inhibit both assimilative and accommodative processes. Immunization may also be a last line of self-defense on which the individual falls back when both assimilative efforts and accommodative processes fail to reduce identity problems.

Generally, self-discrepant feedback has to become strong and consistent enough to override the inherent tendency of the self-system to preserve firmly established self-definitions. Akin to the ways in which scientific theories are defended against discrepant evidence, parts of the individual's system of self-related beliefs may have to be adjusted to preserve stability in other, more central domains. It has been observed that in depressive states, self-serving negotiation of evidence seems inhibited (e.g., Alloy and Abramson, 1988); in terms of the present model, this inhibition may enhance accommodative readjustments in the self-schema and thus help to break through the feedback cycles that maintain states of hopelessness and depression.

Empirical Illustrations

In ongoing research projects, we have used a specifically designed questionnaire to assess dispositional differences in assimilative and accommodative tendencies. This instrument comprises two scales, denoted here as *assimilative persistence* and *accommodative flexibility* (see Brandtstädter & Renner, 1990).[4] Both scales represent statistically independent facets of coping competence; moreover, both scales substantially correlate with measures of subjective life quality such as optimism, life satisfaction, and (low) depression. Despite such similarities in correlational patterns, both scales show opposed regressions on the age variable; in particular, accommodative flexibility becomes increasingly dominant in later life (Brandtstädter, 1992; for converging observations, see also Heckhausen & Schulz, Chapter 2, this volume). Apparently, this shift toward accommodative flexibility is a functional response, given the cumulation of uncontrollable and irreversible losses and the gradual fading of action resources in later life. It should also be noted that one's past life history is inherently not amenable to active-assimilative modes of coping. The task of coming to terms with one's own biography, which constitutes a central concern in later life (cf. Coleman, 1986; Sherman, 1991; Wong & Watt, 1991), is likely to involve primarily accommodative modes of coping. In contexts of biographical reminiscence, accommodative processes are likely to enhance the positive interpretation and reconstruction of one's personal history.

A broad array of findings attests to the specific adaptive significance of accommodative flexibility in later life. For example, persons scoring high in accommodative flexibility tend to adjust their desired self more stringently to their actual self (Greve & Brandtstädter, 1994), they tend to generate palliative thoughts more readily when confronted with threatening scenarios (Wentura, 1995; Wentura, Rothermund, & Brandtstädter, 1995), and they are more likely to enrich their personal concept of "being old" with positive meanings (Rothermund, Wentura, & Brandtstädter, 1995). Using moderated regression techniques, we have found that accommodative flexibility buffers the negative impact of health problems (physical impairments, chronic pain) on psychological well-being (e.g., Brandtstädter, Wentura, & Greve, 1993; Schmitz, Saile, & Nilges, 1996) and helps to maintain a positive outlook in spite of narrowing future perspectives (Brandtstädter & Wentura, 1994). Moderating effects for assimilative persistence were generally weaker or even tended in an opposite direction.

In the following sections we discuss findings that illustrate the ways in which accommodative processes may help the older person to maintain a sense of efficacy and to neutralize experiences of loss.

Stabilizing Perceived Control by Shifts in Goal Importance

Our first example takes issue with the stability of control beliefs in later life, to which we have already referred. This phenomenon still awaits a satisfying theoretical explanation. The theory of assimilative and accommodative coping affords an explanatory account along the following lines. We assume that the extent to which losses in control in specific goal domains affect the person's general sense of control critically depends on the personal importance of that domain. Obviously, the concepts of control and efficacy conceptually imply the subjective ability to reach personally important goals. Accordingly, downscaling the personal importance of goals over which control is reduced is likely to serve to maintain a global sense of control, although it should not be considered as a means or "strategy" that is deliberately chosen for that purpose (Brandtstädter & Wentura, 1994).

We have assessed in our research general and domain-specific perceptions of control. With respect to a list of 23 developmental goals, participants rated the extent of personal control over the particular goal, as well as the personal importance of the goal. These ratings were repeatedly taken over a longitudinal interval of four years on a core sample of 878 participants ranging in age from 58 to 82 (last measurement, 1995). Global control beliefs were estimated by aggregating domain-specific ratings. Moderated regression analyses were used to test whether and how the relationship

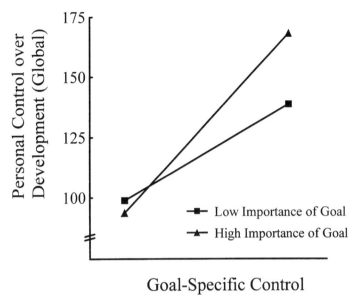

Figure 14.2. Moderating effect of goal importance on the relation between goal-specific and general perceptions of control (sample case: goal 16, "Satisfying friendship").

between domain-linked and global self-percepts is influenced by the personal importance of the respective goals. The obtained moderation effects clearly conform with the theoretical predictions. First, the impact of domain-linked percepts of control on the global measure of control was found to depend in the predicted way on the personal importance of the goal. Figure 14.2 exemplifies the effect for a sample case (goal 16, "Satisfying friendship"), giving the conditional regressions for high ($+2z$) and low ($-2z$) levels of goal importance. With decreasing importance of the goal, perceived deficits in the particular goal domain have a less negative impact on the individual's global sense of control (the interaction effect is significant with $t[854] = 5.27$, $p < 0.001$). Similar significant interaction effects were found for twenty-one out of the twenty-three goal domains.

Even stronger support for our theoretical assumptions comes from the observation that the same type of interaction effect emerges when longitudinal change scores in goal importance and in control ratings are taken as the basis for moderated regression. Here, the overall pattern of effects shows that decreases in perceived control over the longitudinal interval are less predictive of corresponding changes in the global measure of control when the importance of the given goal is downscaled in the same interval. This effect emerged in nineteen out of the twenty-three goal domains considered (in the four discrepant cases, effects did not reach significance). These results replicate and extend similar findings that have been obtained by Brandtstädter and Rothermund (1994) for a younger sample (age range 30 to 59 years).

Negotiating Developmental Gains and Losses

We have posited that the experience of developmental gains and losses depends on the relation of developmental changes to personal goals and on how this relation is individually construed. In the above-mentioned longitudinal project with older participants, we assessed developmental gains and losses in terms of changes in perceived goal distance. According to our theoretical model, there should be a tendency to neutralize loss by downgrading the importance of goal dimensions in which perceived distances increase over the longitudinal interval.

This predicted tendency in fact emerges in our longitudinal data; as expected, increases in goal distances are accompanied by decreases in rated importance for the corresponding goal (for the whole sample, correlations between residualized change scores in distance and importance ratings range between –0.03 for goal 1, "Health," and –0.35 for goal 21, "Being indispensable to other people"; the average correlation is –0.22). To illustrate how these accommodative shifts affect the personal balance of developmental gains and losses, we have weighted longitudinal changes in goal distances using the goal importance ratings obtained prior to the change, at the first measurement point ("preaccommodative" gain/loss), and the importance ratings obtained after the change, at the second measurement point ("postaccommodative" gain/loss). On average, preaccommodative losses are larger than postaccommodative losses ($F[1,701] = 38.56$, $p < 0.001$), whereas the obverse holds for gains ($F[1,701] = 4.58$, $p < 0.05$); the interaction effect is significant ($F[1,701] = 43.50$, $p < 0.001$). Interestingly, the tendency to boost gains (which was not specifically predicted) appears somewhat slighter than the tendency to dampen losses; this finding is consistent with the assumption that accommodative processes are primarily triggered by experiences of loss.

Concluding Remarks

In recent years, evidence has accumulated attesting to an intriguing stability and resilience of older people against the constraints and losses experi-

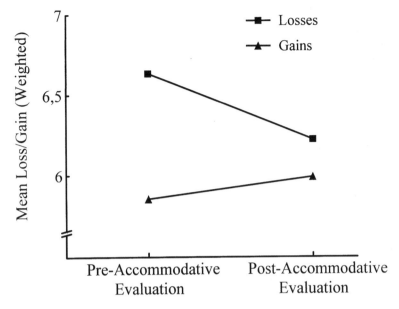

Figure 14.3. Gain and loss in developmental goal domains, weighted by prechange (preaccommodative) and postchange (postaccommodative) ratings of goal importance (aggregated measures).

enced in later life. Although the aging self is certainly not invulnerable, there apparently are potent self-mechanisms that tend to preserve self-integrity and personal continuity. Investigation of these mechanisms holds much promise for the study of successful aging (see also Heckhausen & Schulz, 1995, and Chapter 2, this volume; Staudinger, Marsiske, & Baltes, 1995). The model of assimilative and accommodative coping basically suggests that adaptation to later life depends on the interplay between both active-offensive modes of fighting losses and on the flexible adjustment of personal goals and ambitions to situational constraints. Basically, the model applies to the entire life span: By specifying differential and contextual conditions affecting the basic processes, it provides a basis for explaining age-related change as well as situational and individual differences in coping with developmental crises and losses.

Although the processes of assimilation and accommodation are functionally antagonistic, they should be considered not as mutually exclusive, but rather as complementary modes of maintaining self-continuity and self-esteem. First, situations of crisis and loss (e.g., health problems, physical impairment, or situations of bereavement) often involve a multifaceted complex of problems, the management of which may require assimilative persistence in some respects, and accommodative flexibility in others. Second, there is a permanent interplay of assimilative and accommodative processes over the life span; accommodation by no means terminates any assimilative effort, but often sets new reference points for further instrumental activities (Brandtstädter & Wentura, 1995; Rothermund & Brandtstädter, 1997). Over the entire life span, individuals actively adjust their personal development to their desired and possible selves, but these selves also change over the life course, and they do so partly as a result of difficulties experienced in the pursuit of developmental ambitions (Brandtstädter, 1998; Brim, 1992; Carstensen, Chapter 13, this volume).

With regard to the management of aging, the theoretical considerations presented put into question a lopsided emphasis on active-offensive modes of coping that to some extent characterizes contemporary notions of successful aging. As theories of control and efficacy have rightly stressed, a premature acceptance of limitations involves the risk of not fully exploiting developmental reserves (e.g., Bandura, 1981). A comprehensive theoretical view, however, must also account for the fact that to maintain a sense of efficacy and self-esteem, personal goals and self-evaluative standards have to be continually revised and adjusted to the changes that characterize the processes of physical, psychological, and social aging.

Notes

1. It might be noted that James's formula was anticipated by ancient Stoic and Epicurean philosophers. For example, Seneca argued that "No man can have what he will, but he may choose whether he will desire what he has not" (*"Quicquid vult habere nemo potest, illud potest nolle quod non habet"*).
2. The list of goals comprised the following domains: Health, physical well-being; Emotional stability; Wisdom, mature understanding of life; Self-esteem; Social recognition; Occupational efficiency; Assertiveness, self-assurance; Harmonious partnership; Empathy; Personal independence; Family security; Prosperity, comfortable standard of living; Intellectual efficiency; Self-development; Physical fitness; Satisfying friendship; Commitment to ideals; Contentment in daily work; Accepting the finiteness of one's life; Mastering the process of growing old; Being indispensable to other people; Shaping one's life in accordance with one's own plans and wishes; Finding meaning in life.
3. Dropout effects (including mortality; through the longitudinal interval of four years: 28.6 percent of the initial sample) were found to be unrelated to initial measures of control.

4. Previously, the scales were denoted as *tenacious goal pursuit* and *flexible goal adjustment*.

References

Alloy, L. B., & Abramson, L. Y. (1988). Depressive realism: Four theoretical perspectives. In L. B. Alloy (Ed.), *Cognitive processes in depression* (pp. 223–265). New York: Guilford Press.

Baltes, M. M., & Baltes, P. B. (Eds.). (1986). *The psychology of aging and control.* Hillsdale, NJ: Erlbaum.

Baltes, P. B. (1987). Theoretical propositions of life-span developmental psychology: On the dynamics between growth and decline. *Developmental Psychology, 23,* 611–626.

Baltes, P. B., & Baltes, M. M. (1990). Psychological perspectives on successful aging: The model of selective optimization with compensation. In P. B. Baltes & M. M. Baltes (Eds.), *Successful aging: Perspectives from the behavioral sciences* (pp. 1–34). New York: Cambridge University Press.

Bandura, A. (1981). Self-referent thought: A developmental analysis of self-efficacy. In J. H. Flavell & L. Ross (Eds.), *Social cognitive development. Frontiers and possible futures* (pp. 200–239). Cambridge: Cambridge University Press.

—— (1986). *Social foundations of thought and action: A social cognitive theory.* Englewood Cliffs, NJ: Prentice Hall.

—— (1989). Perceived self-efficacy in the exercise of personal agency. *The Psychologist: Bulletin of the British Psychological Society, 10,* 411–424.

Blaney, P. H. (1986). Affect and memory. *Psychological Bulletin, 99,* 299–246.

Blazer, D. (1989). Depression in late life: An update. *Annual Review of Gerontology and Geriatrics, 9,* 197–215.

Brandtstädter, J. (1984). Personal and social control over development: Some implications of an action perspective in life-span developmental psychology. In P. B. Baltes & O. G. Brim Jr. (Eds.), *Life-span development and behavior* (Vol. 6, pp. 1–32). New York: Academic Press.

—— (1989). Personal self-regulation of development: Cross-sequential analyses of development-related control beliefs and emotions. *Developmental Psychology, 25,* 96–108.

—— (1992). Personal control over development: Some developmental implications of self-efficacy. In R. Schwarzer (Ed.), *Self-efficacy: Thought control of action* (pp. 127–145). New York: Hemisphere.

—— (1998). Action perspectives on human development. In R. M. Lerner (Ed.), *Theoretical models of human development (Handbook of child psychology)* (Vol. 1, 5th ed. pp. 807–863). New York: Wiley.

Brandtstädter, J., & Baltes-Götz, B. (1990). Personal control over development and quality of life perspectives in adulthood. In P. B. Baltes & M. M. Baltes (Eds.),

Successful aging. Perspectives from the behavioral sciences (pp. 197–224). New York: Cambridge University Press.

Brandtstädter, J., & Greve, W. (1994). The aging self: Stabilizing and protective processes. *Developmental Review, 14,* 52–80.

Brandtstädter, J., & Renner, G. (1990). Tenacious goal pursuit and flexible goal adjustment: Explication and age-related analysis of assimilative and accommodative strategies of coping. *Psychology and Aging, 5,* 58–67.

(1992). Coping with discrepancies between aspirations and achievements in adult development: A dual-process model. In L. Montada, S.-H. Filipp, & R. M. Lerner (Eds.), *Life crises and experiences of loss in adulthood* (pp. 301–319). Hillsdale, NJ: Erlbaum.

Brandtstädter, J., & Rothermund, K. (1994). Self-percepts of control in middle and later adulthood: Buffering losses by rescaling goals. *Psychology and Aging, 9,* 265–273.

Brandtstädter, J., & Rothermund, K., & Schmitz, U. (1997). Coping resources in later life. *European Review of Applied Psychology, 47,* 107–114.

Brandtstädter, J., & Wentura, D. (1994). Veränderungen der Zeit- und Zukunftsperspektive im Übergang zum höheren Erwachsenenalter: entwicklungspsychologische und differentielle Aspekte. *Zeitschrift für Entwicklungspsychologie und Pädagogische Psychologie, 26,* 2–21.

(1995). Adjustment to shifting possibility frontiers in later life: Complementary adaptive modes. In R. Dixon & L. Bäckman (Eds.), *Compensating for psychological deficits and declines: Managing losses and promoting gains* (pp. 83–106). Hillsdale, NJ: Erlbaum.

Brandtstädter, J., Wentura, D., & Greve, W. (1993). Adaptive resources of the aging self: Outlines of an emergent perspective. *International Journal of Behavioral Development, 16,* 232–349.

Breytspraak, L. M. (1984). *The development of self in later life.* Boston: Little, Brown.

Brim, G. (1992). *Ambition. How we manage success and failure throughout our lives.* New York: Basic Books.

Cantor, N., & Fleeson, W. (1991). Life tasks and self-regulatory processes. In M. L. Maehr & P. R. Pintrich (Eds.), *Advances in motivation and achievement* (Vol. 7, pp. 327–369). Greenwich, CT: JAI.

Cantor, N., & Sanderson, C. A. (1998). The functional regulation of adolescent dating relationships and sexual behavior: An interaction of goals, strategies, and situations. In J. Heckhausen & C. S. Dweck (Eds.), *Motivation and self-regulation across the life span.* New York: Cambridge University Press.

Carstensen, L. L. (1998). A life-span approach to social motivation. In J. Heckhausen & C. S. Dweck (Eds.), *Motivation and self-regulation across the life span.* New York: Cambridge University Press.

Carver, C. S., & Scheier, M. F. (1990). Origins and functions of positive and negative affect: A control-process view. *Psychological Review, 97,* 19–35.

Coleman, J. C. (1986). *Aging and reminiscence processes: Social and clinical implications*. New York: Wiley.

Coyne, J. C., & Gotlib, I. H. (1983). The role of cognition in depression: A critical appraisal. *Psychological Bulletin, 94*, 472–505.

Dillmann, U., Felser, G., & Brandtstädter, J. (1992). *Veränderung von Bewältigungsprozessen und subjektive Lebensqualität im höheren Alter (VBL-Projekt): Konzeption der Interviewstudie* (Berichte aus der Arbeitsgruppe "Entwicklung und Handeln" Nr. 44). Trier: Universität.

Faltner, M. (Hrsg.). (1988). *Marcus Tullius Cicero. Cato der Ältere über das Alter– Laelius über die Freundschaft.* München: Artemis.

Feinson, M. C. (1985). Aging and mental health: Distinguishing myth from reality. *Research on Aging, 7*, 155–174.

Frey, K. S., & Ruble, D. N. (1990). Strategies for comparative evaluation: Maintaining a sense of competence across the life span. In R. J. Sternberg & J. Kolligian, Jr. (Eds.), *Competence considered* (pp. 167–189). New Haven, CT: Yale University Press.

Gilbert, D. T. (1993). The assent of man: Mental representation and the control of belief. In D. M. Wegner & J. W. Pennebaker (Eds.), *Handbook of mental control* (pp. 57–87). Englewood Cliffs, NJ: Prentice Hall.

Greve, W. (1990). Stabilisierung und Modifikation des Selbstkonzeptes im Erwachsenenalter: Strategien der Immunisierung. *Sprache & Kognition, 9*, 218–230.

Greve, W., & Brandtstädter, J. (1994). *Selbstbild und Selbstbewertung im Erwachsenenalter: stabilisierende Dynamiken.* (Berichte aus der Arbeitsgruppe "Entwicklung und Handeln" Nr. 49). Trier: Universität.

Häfner, H. (1992). *Psychiatrie des höheren Lebensalters.* In P. B. Baltes & J. Mittelstraß (Hrsg.), Zukunft des Alterns und gesellschaftliche Entwicklung (S. 151–179). Berlin: DeGruyter.

Hagestad, G. O., & Neugarten, B. L. (1985). Age and the life course. In R. H. Binstock & E. Shanas (Eds.), *Handbook of aging and the social sciences* (pp. 35–61). New York: Van Nostrand Reinhold.

Heckhausen, J., & Baltes, P. B. (1991). Perceived controllability of expected psychological change across adulthood and old age. *Journal of Gerontology: Psychological Sciences, 46*, 165–173.

Heckhausen, J., & Krueger, J. (1993). Developmental expectations for the self and "most other people": Age-grading in three functions of social comparison. *Developmental Psychology, 29*, 539–548.

Heckhausen, J., & Schulz, R. (1995). A life-span theory of control. *Psychological Review, 102*, 284–304.

(1998). Developmental regulation in adulthood: Selection and compensation via primary and secondary control. In J. Heckhausen & C. S. Dweck (Eds.), *Motivation and self-regulation across the life span.* New York: Cambridge University Press.

Higgins, E. T., Klein, R., & Strauman, T. (1985). Self-concept discrepancy theory:

A psychological model for distinguishing among different aspects of depression and anxiety. *Social Cognition, 3,* 51–76.

Ingram, R. E. (Ed.). (1990). *Contemporary psychological approaches to depression.* New York: Plenum Press.

James, W. (1890). *The principles of psychology.* New York: Holt.

Kessler, R. C., Foster, C., Webster, P. S., & House, J. S. (1992). The relationship between age and depressive symptoms in two national surveys. *Psychology and Aging, 7,* 119–126.

Kihlstrom, J. F., & Cantor, N. (1984). Mental representations of the self. In L. Berkowitz (Ed.), *Advances in experimental social psychology* (Vol. 17, pp. 1–47). New York: Academic Press.

Klinger, E. (1975). Consequences of commitment to and disengagement from incentives. *Psychological Review, 82,* 1–25.

Kuhl, J., & Helle, P. (1986). Motivational and volitional determinants of depression: The degenerated-intention hypothesis. *Journal of Abnormal Psychology, 95,* 247–251.

Kunda, Z. (1990). The case for motivated reasoning. *Psychological Bulletin, 108,* 480–498.

Lachman, M. E. (1986). Locus of control in aging research: A case for multidimensional and domain-specific assessment. *Psychology and Aging, 1,* 34–40.

Lawton, M. P. (1991). A multidimensional view of quality of life in frail elders. In J. E. Birren, J. E. Lubben, J. C. Rowe, & D. E. Deutchman (Eds.), *The concept and measurement of quality of life in the frail elderly* (pp. 3–27). San Diego, CA: Academic Press.

Linville, P. W. (1987). Self-complexity as a cognitive buffer against stress-related illness and depression. *Journal of Personality and Social Psychology, 52,* 663–676.

Markus, H., & Nurius, P. (1986). Possible selves. *American Psychologist, 41,* 954–969.

Markus, H., & Wurf, E. (1987). The dynamic self-concept: A social psychological perspective. *Annual Review of Psychology, 38,* 299–337.

Martin, L. L., & Tesser, A. (1989). Toward a motivational and structural theory of ruminative thought. In J. S. Uleman & J. A. Bargh (Eds.), *Unintended thought* (pp. 306–326). New York: Guilford Press.

Mayring, P. (1987). Subjektives Wohlbefinden im Alter. Stand der Forschung und theoretische Weiterentwicklung. *Zeitschrift für Gerontologie, 20,* 367–376.

McFarland, C., Ross, M., & Giltrow, M. (1992). Biased recollections in older adults: The role of implicit theories of aging. *Journal of Personality and Social Psychology, 62,* 837–850.

Myers, J. K., Weissman, M. M., Tischler, G. L., Holzer, L. E., Leaf, A. J., Orvaschel, H., Anthony, J. L., Boyd, J. H., Burke, J. D., Kramer, M., & Stoltzman, R. (1984). Six-month-prevalence of psychiatric disorders in three communities: 1980 to 1982. *Archives of General Psychiatry, 41,* 959–967.

Newmann, J. P., Engel, R. J., & Jensen, J. (1990). Depressive symptom patterns among older women. *Psychology and Aging, 5,* 101–118.

Peterson, C., & Seligman, M. E. P. (1987). Explanatory style and illness. *Journal of Personality, 55,* 237–265.

Rodin, J., & Langer, E. (1980). Aging labels: The decline of control and the fall of self-esteem. *Journal of Social Issues, 36,* 12–29.

Rodin, J., Timko, C., & Harris, S. (1985). The construct of control: Biological and psychosocial correlates. *Annual Review of Gerontology and Geriatrics, 5,* 3–55.

Rothermund, K., & Brandtstädter, J. (1997). Entwicklung und Bewältigung: Festhalten und Preisgeben von Zielen als Formen der Bewältigung von Entwicklungsproblemen. In C. Tesch-Römer, C. Salewski, & G. Schwarz (Eds.), *Psychologie der Bewältigung* (pp. 120–133). Weinheim: Psychologie Verlags Union.

Rothermund, K., Wentura, D., & Brandtstädter, J. (1995). Selbstwertschützende Verschiebungen in der Semantik des Begriffs "alt" im höheren Erwachsenenalter. *Sprache und Kognition, 14,* 52–63.

Salthouse, T. A. (1987). Age, experience, and compensation. In K. Schooler & K. W. Schaie (Eds.), *Cognitive functioning and social structure over the life course* (pp. 142–150). Norwood, NJ: Ablex.

Samuelson, P. A., & Nordhaus, W. D. (1985). *Economics* (12th ed.). New York: Mc-Graw-Hill.

Schmitz, U., Saile, H., & Nilges, P. (1996). Coping with chronic pain: Flexible goal adjustment as an interactive buffer against pain-related distress. *Pain, 67,* 41–51.

Schwarz, N., & Strack, F. (1991). Evaluating one's life: A judgment model of subjective well-being. In F. Strack, M. Argyle, & N. Schwarz (Eds.), *Subjective well-being. An interdisciplinary perspective* (pp. 27–47). Oxford: Pergamon Press.

Seligman, M. E. P., & Elder, G. (1986). Learned helplessness and life-span development. In A. B. Sorensen, F. W. Weinert, & L. Sherrod (Eds.), *Human development and the life course: Multidisciplinary perspectives* (pp. 377–428). Hillsdale, NJ: Erlbaum.

Sherman, E. (1991). *Reminiscence and the self in old age.* New York: Springer.

Snyder, C. R. (1989). Reality negotiation: From excuses to hope and beyond. *Journal of Social and Clinical Psychology, 8,* 130–157.

Staudinger, U. M., Marsiske, M., & Baltes, P. B. (1995). Resilience and reserve capacity in later adulthood: Potentials and limits of development across the life span. In D. Cicchetti & D. J. Cohen (Eds.), *Developmental psychopathology. Vol. 2: Risk, disorder, and adaptation* (pp. 801–847). New York: Wiley.

Stock, W. A., Okun, M. A., Haring, M. J., & Witter, R. A. (1983). Age and subjective well-being: A meta-analysis. In R. J. Light (Ed.), *Evaluation studies: Review annual* (Vol. 8, pp. 279–302). Beverly Hills, CA: Sage.

Svagelski (1981). *L'idée de compensation en France, 1750–1850.* Lyon: Editions l'Hermès.

Taylor, S., & Brown, J. D. (1988). Illusion and well-being: A social psychological perspective on mental health. Psychological *Bulletin, 103,* 193–210.

Uttal, D. H., & Permutter, M. (1989). Toward a broader conceptualization of development: The role of gains and losses across the life span. *Developmental Review, 9,* 101–132.

Weiss, I. K., Nagel, C. L., & Aronson, M. K. (1986). Applicability of depression scales to the old person. *Journal of the American Geriatrics Society, 34,* 215–218.

Wentura, D. (1995). *Verfügbarkeit entlastender Kognitionen: Zur Verarbeitung negativer Lebenssituationen.* Weinheim: Psychologie Verlags Union.

Wentura, D., Rothermund, K., & Brandtstädter, J. (1995). Experimentelle Analysen zur Verarbeitung belastender Informationen: differential- und alternspsychologische Aspekte. *Zeitschrift für Experimentelle Psychologie, 42,* 152–175.

Wong, P. T. P., & Watt, L. M. (1991). What types of reminiscence are associated with successful aging? *Psychology and Aging, 6,* 272–279.

Wright, R. A., & Brehm, J. W. (1989). Energization and goal attractiveness. In L. A. Pervin (Ed.), *Goal concepts in personality and social psychology* (pp. 169–210). Hillsdale, NJ: Erlbaum.

Yesavage, J. A., Brink, T. L., Rose, T. L., Lum, O., Huang, V., Adey, M., & Leirer, V. O. (1983). Development and validation of a geriatric depression scale. *Journal of Psychiatric Research, 17,* 31–49.

15   The Willful Pursuit of Identity

Peter M. Gollwitzer and Oliver Kirchhof

Abstract

The achievement of an identity is commonly construed as a choice between options, for instance, between becoming a physician or a chemist, a housewife or a professional. This approach, however, ignores the fact that identity choices, even when based on cumbersome deliberation, need to be followed up by implementational efforts. The present chapter focuses on this willful construction of a chosen identity (i.e., the implementation of identity goals) and attempts to delineate those features that distinguish it from other forms of goal-striving. More specifically, it is suggested that the pursuit of identity goals is enduring over time, as such goals cannot actually be completed and are not easily halted by failure. In fact, failure experiences invigorate identity goal pursuits, as suggested by various experiments demonstrating that identity-related failures affect subsequent identity-relevant performances positively. Moreover, it has been shown that identity-related social recognition hampers goal-directed efforts instead of facilitating them. Apparently, identity goals entail the mere claim to be, for example, a physician in the eyes of others (i.e., are represented on the level of social reality). The chapter also addresses issues of whether the willful pursuit of identities is moderated by people's framing of the identity goal in question (i.e., as a mastery goal as opposed to a learning goal, with a positive-outcome as opposed to a negative-outcome focus), and it discusses how the processes involved with choosing an identity differ from processes associated with the implementation of the chosen identity. Finally, the present approach is related to classic notions of life-span development (i.e., the model of selective optimization with compensation, the distinction between primary and secondary forms of control), and it is suggested that people of old age and very old age are likely to remain able to maintain their identity claims, an ability that is facilitated by their tendency to reduce their social contacts to a few intimates.

389

Introduction

The psychology of the self (Suls & Greenwald, 1983; Suls, 1993) and the sociology of identity (Yardley & Honess, 1987; Stryker & Statham, 1985) focus on the following question: How does a person conceive of his or her self? In this sense, the term *self* (or *identity*) refers to a cognitive structure that incorporates all the ways in which a person characteristically answers the question "Who am I?" Following James's (1890/1950) lead, researchers consider the answers given to this question as falling into a number of different categories (Gordon, 1968; Rosenberg, 1979). One group of answers relates to physical attributes (e.g., "I am tall"); another relates to the broader categories of social identities, which include the various informal and formal, chosen or assigned social roles an individual occupies (e.g., "I am a youngster," "I am a daughter," "I am a student," "I am a butcher,"). Some answers may refer to perceived traits and dispositions (e.g., "I am tolerant"), to skills and aptitudes (e.g., "I am a math whiz-kid"), or to values and interests (e.g., "I love to travel").

The answers that researchers studying the self or identity give to the question of how a person conceives of her or his self depend on the theoretical background and the self-aspects (i.e., physical, social, or personal aspects) that are focused on. For instance, Bem's self-perception theory (1972) claims that people make inferences about the self-aspects they possess by observing their own behaviors, feelings, and thoughts. More sociologically inclined approaches postulate that people infer the contents of their identity by observing the behavior of other people toward them (based on Cooley, 1902) or by analyzing the role that people play in the social community to which they belong (based on Mead, 1934). Socioecological approaches (e.g., Hormuth, 1986) point out that people also use the material objects that surround them and the opportunity structures in which they feel embedded to make inferences about the self.

Social-psychological approaches to the self assert that a person searching for self-knowledge actively creates his or her social environments. Such an approach is exemplified by Swann (1983), who hypothesizes in his self-verification theory that people verify self-related beliefs by choosing interaction partners who are known to support their preferred self-conceptions. Social-interactionist approaches (e.g., Stryker's 1985 identity salience theory; see Stryker & Statham, 1985) assign a similar active role to the individual in the context of acquiring self-knowledge.

The various approaches listed so far assert that self or identity is construed as something the individual needs to cognize. It is not surprising, then, that researchers in this tradition prefer to speak of the self or identity in terms of the self-concept. The emphasis is on how the individual conceives the self. This is also true for the intriguing extension of this work, which deals with people's conceptions of what they hope or fear to become (for the concept of possible selves, see Markus & Nurius, 1986). Controversies in self-concept research surround issues of whether the self is construed as a coherent entity or is composed of many partial selves (Greenwald, 1982), whether the self-concept is stable or malleable (Gergen, 1982), and whether the self-concept is accurate or illusionary (Brown, 1991).

Another important branch of research focuses on how people evaluate the self (Greenwald, 1980; Stahlberg, Osnabrügge, & Frey, 1985). This affective response is discussed in its most global form as a person's self-esteem. It is commonly assumed that people have a pervasive need for high self-esteem, so discussion focuses on where this need comes from and how it is served. Greenberg, Pyszczynski, and Solomon (1986) point to the terror associated with the fear of death as the critical source of the need for self-esteem; Baumeister and Tice (1990) refer to the terror of social exclusion. Various ideas have also been offered about how positive self-evaluations come about. Some researchers see a link between structural qualities of the self-concept and positive self-evaluations (clarity of self-concept, Campbell, 1990; complexity of self-concept, Linville, 1987). Others (Higgins, 1987) point out that a person's affective responses toward the self are associated with the discrepancies that people experience between so-called self-guides (i.e., the ideal or ought self) and the actual self. Finally, research on the psychology of the self has also analyzed how relating to others affects a person's self-evaluations. Tesser (1988), in his self-evaluation maintenance theory, focuses on social comparison processes and basking in the reflected glory of others. Baumeister (1982), on the other hand, points to strategic self-presentations as a means to boosting one's self-evaluation.

Research on positive self-evaluation processes and self-esteem construes the self as something that is (to be) evaluated by the individual. This adds an affective and motivational dimension to the self-concept research that traditionally looked at the self as something to be cognized. What research on positive self-evaluations does not yet capture, however, is how the desired self is achieved behaviorally. The self or identity (or aspects of it) may be construed as goals the individual attempts to attain. This goal perspective on the self has been exemplified in Wicklund and Gollwitzer's (1982) theory of symbolic self-completion, which focuses on how self-defining goals are implemented by the individual. Heckhausen (1989) and Gollwitzer (1990; Heckhausen & Gollwitzer, 1987) have distinguished between motivational and volitional processes of wish fulfillment. Whereas motivational processes guide a person's choice between goals, volitional processes are assumed to determine a person's implementation of the chosen goals. The former relate to issues of the feasibility and desirability of potential goals (i.e., wishes and desires), whereas the latter relate to a person's commitment to the chosen goal, holding on to the goal in the face of difficulties, and successful goal pursuit. From the perspective of a distinction between motivation and volition, research on the self has traditionally been concerned with motivational issues of the feasibility and desirability of the various aspects of the self (i.e., self-concept research and self-evaluation research, respectively). Self-completion theory, on the other hand, is concerned with the volitional issue of implementing identity-related (self-defining) goals.

Self-Completion Theory

Historical Roots

Self-completion theory (Wicklund & Gollwitzer, 1982) is based on Lewin's (1926) ideas on goal-directed action. According to Lewin, quasi-needs originate when people set themselves goals. A quasi-need is associated with a tension state that persists until the goal is attained. The tension state is linked to the person's commitment to reach the goal. Accordingly, this tension is said to persist when a person's goal-directed activities are disrupted and thus do not lead to goal attainment (as demonstrated by Lewin's colleagues Lissner, 1933; Mahler, 1933; Ovsiankina, 1928; Zeigarnik, 1927). However – and this is particularly important for self-completion processes – Lissner and Mahler demonstrated early on that the persevering tension state can be reduced by performing alternative goal-directed activities when disruption of an original goal-directed action has occurred. This implies that tension reduction stems not only from completion of an ongoing goal-directed action but also from successfully performing substitute actions.

In the experimental studies analyzing this principle, Lewin's colleagues employed simple tasks such as building a tower out of wooden blocks, translating a French piece of prose into German, solving mathematical problems with pencil and paper, and creating small sculptures from modeling clay. Shortly after beginning the task, subjects were interrupted and asked to solve a substitute task. They were then allowed to return to the interrupted original task. Of interest was whether subjects would take advantage of this opportunity to *complete the original task*. Mahler (1933) postulated that whenever subjects experience a correspondence between the quality of the goal served by solving the *substitute* task and the quality of the goal served by the *original* task, they are no longer inclined to return to the original task because substitute completion had occurred. Accordingly, in the event that solving a substitute task reduces the frequency of resumption of the original task, it can be inferred that the goal of the original task entails qualities that are served by the substitute task performed. Mahler reasoned that the substitution paradigm not only tests Lewin's quasi-need theory but also unveils the individual goal conceptions or inner goals people have when approaching a task. One simply has to analyze which activities can substitute for the original goal-striving.

Mahler observed that for people who were asked to build a house of wooden blocks but were interrupted, drawing a picture of that house qualified as a powerful substitute. More interestingly, when people were asked to perform more intellectual tasks (e.g., solving a mathematical problem), other quite different intellectual tasks (e.g., solving a puzzle) served as substitutes. Apparently, although the experimenter instructed subjects to perform a particular mathematical problem (i.e., the original task), subjects did not subscribe to the external goal assigned by the experimenter but tried to meet the self-set goal of showing creativity, intelligence, and ambition. Henle (1944) and Hoppe (1930) demonstrated that the subjects' inner goals may already touch such higher spheres of the ego when rather simple and concrete tasks are at stake (e.g., creating a sculpture out of modeling clay or solving simple mathematical problems).

Mahler also discovered that inner goals that involve such self-related issues as creativity and intelligence are conceived of by the individual *on the plane of social reality.* She argued that whenever solving a certain task was interpreted by the individual as a test of intelligence, creativity, or of any other self-related attribute, it was necessary that others take notice of the completion of the substitute task. No sense of having reached a self-related goal would occur as long as relevant task solutions did not become a social fact by being noticed by others. To demonstrate this, for the original task Mahler gave her subjects mathematical problems or asked them to construct creative sentences from lists of words. The substitute tasks required that subjects solve some other intellectual problems either through silent deliberation or through speaking aloud. Speaking aloud proved to be more effective with respect to suppressing the resumption of the original task. Apparently, subjects not only sought to find solutions to the mathematical or creative problems posed as the original task, but also wanted others (in this case, the experimenter) to recognize that they were smart or creative. Only solving the substitute tasks aloud provided the subjects with a sense of having attained the self-related goals of being smart or creative to which they had aspired while working on the original tasks.

The Concept of Self-defining Goals

The theory of self-completion describes the dynamics of striving for self-defining goals. The distinction between self-defining goals and non-self-defining goals (Gollwitzer & Wicklund, 1985b) is illustrated in the following example. Two students undertake their first major task in the laboratory of an experimental psychology class. The assigned objective is clear and distinct: Train a pigeon to execute a peculiar behavior with high reliability. Suppose that one student (a work-study student) is solely interested in training the pigeon to behave in the way demanded; the other student's interest is only peripherally on the external goal (the advisor's) and more centrally on the goal of becoming an experimental psychologist.

Both students fail to achieve the task set by the advisor. Given that the first student's goal orientation in the situation is defined by the non-self-defining goal of simply meeting the set task, one might expect that student to feel frustrated and perhaps to try alternative means to train the bird to perform the peculiar behavior. The reaction of the second student who aspires to become an experimental psychologist may well be much different. Assuming that an accomplished feat of animal training is nothing more than one possible indicator of being a psychologist, the student can readily resort to alternative routes of completing his self-definition, such as attempting to put his name on publications, becoming associated with recognized psychologists, acquiring a collection of psychology books and journals, or taking a temporary job as a psychology instructor.

Self-completion theory applies the term *self-defining goals* to refer to people's ideal conceptions of themselves as possessing a readiness or potential to enact certain content-specific classes of behavior. If the self-defining goal is, for instance, to be a jogger, then the related activities involve running, wearing the appropriate clothes, associating with runners, and so on. With the concept of goal, the theory points to the individual's commitment to reach the ideal condition that embodies all the qualities pertaining to the aspired self-definition.

Indicators of Completeness and Social Reality

To acquire self-defining goals means accumulating relevant indicators or symbols. Self-completion theory assumes that each particular self-defining goal is composed of a whole set of various symbols. Accordingly, indicating the possession of the aspired self-definition (the theory speaks of self-symbolizing) may take different forms. It is possible, for instance, to self-symbolize through the exercise of identity-related social influence (e.g., an academic psychologist may engage in teaching psychology), by displaying material symbols (e.g., a pious person may wear a golden cross), through the fulfillment of the daily duties and performances associated with a particular identity (e.g., a baker bakes bread), by simply making a verbal claim to possession of a particular identity (e.g., "I am a psychologist"), or through the acquisition of the skills and tools associated with a specific identity (e.g., a musician acquires an education in music theory and a fine-quality instrument).

These various forms of self-symbolizing obviously differ in terms of their accessibility. For instance, showing off relevant symbols one already possesses as well as making self-descriptions that state a claim to possession of the intended identity are readily accessible and easily achievable approaches. This is less true for the actual acquisition of relevant symbols, such as attaining advanced education. From the perspective of self-completion theory, however, accessibility of self-symbolizing is not a crucial variable. Not only the forms of self-symbolizing that are easily attainable, but also those that are difficult to perform, potentially indicate to others one's claim to possess the intended self-definition.

What matters more is whether the chosen form of self-symbolizing effectively indicates one's claim to others. Self-completion theory asserts that the possession of relevant symbols in and of itself is not sufficient to create a sense of identity-related completeness. These indicators must serve their indicative function and therefore must become a social fact. This occurs when the social community recognizes the indicators as a claim to the possession of particular self-definitions. It is this recognition by others that strengthens a person's sense of identity-related completeness.

Research Stimulated by Self-Completion Theory

Self-completion theory has stimulated many empirical studies on people's pursuits of all kinds of self-defining goals: being a good mother, religious person, feminist, athlete, business manager, or a physician. The studies can be grouped with respect to the central hypotheses tested.

The Compensation Hypothesis. Self-completion theory postulates that whenever people who strive for a self-defining goal experience the lack of a relevant symbol, a sense of incompleteness arises. This incompleteness may come about because comparing oneself to others makes salient that one is falling short of certain indicators (e.g., when colleagues repeatedly recount their recent successes). However, incompleteness also originates when people receive negative feedback (e.g., through teachers) about identity-relevant performances or when their attempts to acquire relevant symbols fail. Self-completion theory assumes that experiences of incompleteness are not accepted passively but that people attempt to strive for the desired identity goal via alternative routes – similar to the manner in which Mahler's subjects embraced the substitute task when the original task had been interrupted. As identity goals commonly imply a whole array of symbols, the individual does not have to focus her or his compensatory efforts on the experienced shortcoming or incompleteness. Compensatory efforts can be expressed in any of the many alternative routes of self-symbolizing.

This compensation hypothesis has been supported in a series of experiments that used the following paradigm. Subjects were selected on the basis of being committed to one or another self-defining goal (e.g., musician, physician, mother, religious person). Half the subjects (incomplete subjects) were made to feel incomplete by pointing out to them that they lacked a relevant indicator. The other half of the subjects (complete subjects) were made to feel that they possessed this indicator. Finally, in a different situational context (i.e., a different experimenter in a presumably unrelated second experiment) subjects had a chance to acquire an alternative symbol or at least point to its possession. The extent to which subjects made use of this chance to self-symbolize was measured.

A typical example of such an experiment is a study with young business managers who returned to the business school of the University of Texas to attend summer school courses (Gollwitzer, 1983). The study was conducted by two experimenters. The first experimenter introduced himself as a personality psychologist and asked subjects to fill out a semantic differential type of questionnaire that presented several pairs of adjectives (e.g., weak–strong, warm–cold, active–passive). Subjects were informed that they were to fill out the questionnaire so that the personality psychologist could determine whether young business managers possessed the ideal personality profile observed in successful businesspeople. Once subjects had completed the questionnaire, the second experimenter introduced himself as an industrial psychologist and explained that he would conduct a study in which the subjects would take part in a staged executive committee meeting. Subjects could choose from among six roles to play, ranging from chair of the board to secretary and keeper of the minutes. Shortly before subjects were asked to make their choices, the first experimenter (the personality psychologist) disrupted the proceedings of the study of the industrial psychologist and handed his feedback to the subjects. Half the subjects were told that their personality profile differed greatly from the ideal profile of a successful businessperson; the other half were told that their personality profile closely matched the ideal profile.

This feedback was intended to create feelings of either incompleteness or completeness. As expected, subjects with negative personality feedback chose the chair position significantly more often than did the subjects with positive personality feedback. Self-completion theory interprets this finding by holding that the lack of one symbol of an intended identity (i.e., lacking the proper personality attributes) is substituted with self-symbolizing efforts focusing on an alternative symbol (i.e., laying claim to a relevant position of high status).

Compensatory self-symbolizing has been demonstrated in numerous other studies, in which other types of self-symbolizing were offered. Incomplete subjects showed a greater readiness to teach others in the domain relevant for their identity (Wicklund & Gollwitzer, 1981). They also invented more positive self-descriptions and refused to admit to failures (Gollwitzer, Wicklund, & Hilton, 1982). Further, they distanced themselves from unsuccessful people (Wagner, Wicklund, & Shaigan, 1990), displayed material symbols (e.g., articles symbolic of religious beliefs such as a cross or a star of David; Wicklund & Gollwitzer, 1982, chap. 9), or used prestigious tools (Braun & Wicklund, 1989). All of self-symbolizing, of course, was observed in the field of interest pertaining to subjects' identity goals.

For the induction of the experience of incompleteness, the negative personality feedback procedure was not the only paradigm used. In some studies, subjects were asked to write about their worst teacher in their field of interest (see Wicklund & Gollwitzer, 1981), or subjects were induced to come up with positive self-descriptions, which were then disrupted (see Gollwitzer, Wicklund, & Hilton, 1982). Finally, subjects were asked to list accomplishments relevant to their identity that, by all means, they could not yet have achieved (e.g., psychology undergraduates were asked to list their major publications; Wagner et al. 1990). In all these compensation studies, subjects were convinced that the so-called first experiment in which the incompleteness experience occurred was not related to the second study. In addition, the second experimenter was not aware of subjects' feelings of incompleteness.

The Social Reality Hypothesis. Based on Mahler's (1933) observation that self-defining goals are located on the level of social reality, self-completion theory postulates that self-symbolizing that becomes a social fact is likely to be particularly effective in reducing a sense of incompleteness. This hypothesis has been confirmed by two types of experimental studies (Gollwitzer, 1986a, studies 1 to 4). In the first experimental paradigm (see studies 1 and 2), subjects are first given the opportunity to engage in a self-symbolizing activity. In order to vary whether these efforts become a social fact, subjects are placed in a situation where self-symbolizing either is noticed by others or remains unnoticed. Given that identity goals are located on the level of social reality, striving for an identity in front of an audience is expected to provide a stronger sense of possessing the intended identity than striving in the absence of an audience. To determine whether this is the case, subjects are brought to a new situational context where they are provided a further opportunity to strive for the intended identity. If self-symbolizing noticed by others provides a stronger sense of completeness than does self-symbolizing that remains unnoticed, comparatively less self-symbolizing is likely to be observed in subjects whose original self-symbolizing is noticed by others.

Following this logic, Gollwitzer (1986a, study 1) asked female college students with the identity goal of raising a family to write down personal skills relevant to succeeding as a mother. Subjects were told either that these self-descriptions would be carefully studied by a partner subject or that their descriptions would not become known to others. Thereafter, all subjects were given the opportunity to engage in further self-symbolizing by completing a personality profile questionnaire. This questionnaire carried a sample profile that was said to represent the ideal personality of a mother. The subjects who were told that their initial self-symbolizing would not be made known to the partner subject felt compelled to engage in further self-symbolizing by drawing their own profile close to the ideal mother profile provided. Subjects who were told that their initial self-descriptions would be noticed by a partner subject, however, ascribed attributes to themselves that were at variance with the ideal mother profile.

In a second study following the same logic (Gollwitzer, 1986a, study 2), subjects were medical students committed to becoming physicians. All subjects were induced to work on a stack of simple medical problems in a paper and pencil format. After the third problem had been completed, subjects' work was turned into a social fact (i.e., a confederate either took notice of task performance or ignored it). It was then observed how long subjects persisted working on the rest of the stack. Subjects whose prior performance was taken notice of by another person persisted comparatively less. This finding demonstrates that identity performances noticed by others make further identity-striving less necessary, thus supporting the self-completion theory notion of social reality. Apparently, a stronger sense of completeness arises when indications of the possession of an intended identity are socially realized.

The hypothesis that self-symbolizing that becomes a social fact is particularly effective has also been tested via a different approach. This approach is based on the idea that individuals who are oriented toward achieving a particular identity but feel incomplete are likely to be especially concerned with finding an audience for their identity-related strivings. Accordingly, one has to manipulate people's readiness to engage in identity-related goal-striving (by making some subjects incomplete and others complete), and then observe subjects' self-initiative in making self-symbolizing noticed by others. Two experiments reported by Gollwitzer (1986a, studies 3 and 4) followed this logic. In study 3, medical students with the expressed intention of becoming physicians were made either complete or incomplete by being given positive or negative personality feedback with respect to their prospects as physicians. In a subsequent, presumably independent, experiment subjects were provided with the opportunity to engage in self-symbolizing through finding solutions to a series of simple medical problems (i.e., a stack of fifteen problems stated on index cards was placed in front of subjects, who were to write their solutions on these cards). The subjects were told that they could submit completed sections of the assignment to the experimenter whenever desired (i.e., before having completed the entire stack of fifteen tasks). More than 50 percent of the incomplete subjects attempted to bring their completed tasks to the experimenter's notice before finishing the entire stack of tasks; for the complete subjects this percentage was drastically lower (i.e., only 8 percent).

Self-initiative to make one's self-symbolizing efforts known to others was also observed among female undergraduates who pursued the identity goal of dancer. Subjects who wrote a lengthy essay on their worst dancing instructor (incomplete subjects) wanted to be scheduled for a public dancing session about two weeks earlier than subjects who had to write about their best dancing instructor (complete subjects). Apparently, subjects whose readiness to engage in self-symbolizing had been stimulated (i.e., incomplete subjects) selected comparatively earlier dates for the public performance of a dance routine. Assuming that performing this dance routine qualifies as an indicator of the identity of dancer, these results suggest that people are more anxious for self-symbolizing efforts to be noticed by others when they are in a state of incompleteness.

The Social Insensitivity Hypothesis. Knowing that self-symbolizing individuals turn to others in an effort to strengthen their sense of possessing an intended identity, the next question is "How do self-symbolizing individuals relate to their audiences?" Self-completion theory suggests that this type of relating to others is best described as a pseudosocial interaction. Self-symbolizing individuals do not conceive of their audiences as partners for mutual exchange. Rather, these individuals regard the audience as serving the sole function of taking notice of their claim to possess the aspired identity. Attributes of the audience that go beyond this purpose (e.g., the audience's own feelings and interests) are largely neglected.

This hypothesis of social insensitivity was tested in experiments with the following paradigm. As in classic self-presentation studies (Baumeister, 1982), subjects were first told about the personal wishes and desires of the audience. These wishes and desires were posed in a way that either contradicted subjects' self-symbolizing efforts or were in line with them. Finally, it was observed how incomplete and complete subjects followed the audience's wishes and desires.

Gollwitzer and Wicklund (1985a) conducted two experiments that demonstrate that individuals who strive to self-symbolize neglect the thoughts and feelings of the audiences to which their efforts are directed. In the first study, female undergraduates with the identity goal of being a career woman were made either complete or incomplete by feedback that their personality attributes either did or did not predestine them to professional success. In a presumably different second experiment, complete and incomplete subjects were then grouped into pairs and told to cooperate with each other. They were instructed to create positive self-descriptions related either to the intended identity or to an identity that they did not care to possess. When the self-descriptions to be created were related to the identity of career woman, incomplete subjects dominated the interaction by producing more positive self-descriptive statements than did their complete partner subjects. Even though incomplete subjects knew that the partner subject was also trying to create many positive self-descriptions, the orientation toward self-symbolizing provoked by the negative personality feedback suppressed such interpersonal concerns.

In the second study, male undergraduates committed to various sports (e.g., swimming, tennis, track) were first made to feel either incomplete or complete and then asked to participate in a supposed second study on first impressions. The target person to be encountered was described as an attractive female undergraduate who had expressed a preference for getting to know either modest or proud people. Before subjects were asked to introduce themselves to the target person via a written self-description of their strengths and weaknesses in their self-definitional area (i.e., swimming, tennis, track), they rated their feelings of attraction to the target person. When we analyzed subjects' self-descriptions in terms of their positivity, incomplete subjects produced more self-aggrandizing descriptions than did complete subjects, regardless of the target person's preference for meeting individuals with modest as opposed to proud self-descriptions. Moreover, self-symbolizing individuals ignored even their own interpersonal interests. Whereas complete subjects followed the target person's self-presentational cue to the degree to which they felt attracted to her, incomplete subjects' self-descriptions were totally unaffected by their feelings of attraction.

In summary, self-symbolizing individuals do not seem to care much about their audiences' interests. They focus on making their self-definitional strengths known to others. This is true whether the audience is present in person or not and whether the audience explicitly expresses its interests or not.

Self-Completion Processes: Controversial Issues and Open Questions

Mutual Exchangeability of Symbols

Consistent with the theoretical position guiding self-completion research, Wurf and Markus (1991) have claimed that in the domain of identity strivings, "failure of particular routes to achievement will often lead to enhanced rather than decreased striving, . . . and the person will flexibly and creatively try multiple pathways to achievement" (p. 58). However, Wurf and Markus also argued that symbolic validation of the self (e.g., claiming the possession of a self-definition via positive self-descriptions) might be less satisfying than actual achievements (e.g., mastering performances implied by the self-definition). In contrast, from the standpoint of self-completion theory, positive self-descriptions are likely to be as effective in generating a sense of self-definitional completeness as self-defining task performances when the given self-description is recognized by others, thereby becoming a social reality (Gollwitzer, 1986b).

We have addressed this issue directly in two recent experiments (Brunstein & Gollwitzer, 1996), both of which employed an experimental paradigm commonly used in research on learned helplessness. Subjects were asked to work on a first task (so-called training task), and they were given failure feedback or no performance feedback. Subsequently subjects worked on a second task (so-called test task), and their level of performance was assessed. In our first experiment, medical students who intended to become physicians were instructed to solve simple interpersonal problems presented

Identity-relevant Training Task

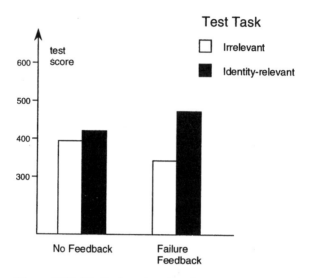

Figure 15.1. Medical students' performance on a mental concentration test (test task) described as either irrelevant or relevant to the identity of physician. Prior to test performance, subjects had received either no performance feedback or failure feedback on a task (training task) either irrelevant or relevant to being a physician (*Source:* Adapted with permission from Brunstein & Gollwitzer, 1996, study 1).

on index cards. The problems were related either to interpersonal conflicts that physicians commonly experience in their profession or to interpersonal problems that anyone might experience in everyday life. Subsequently, subjects were asked to perform a mental concentration test (d2 test; Brickenkamp, 1981) that was described as measuring a skill either relevant or irrelevant to being a physician. Performance on this test task peaked when subjects had been given failure feedback on solving the physician-related interpersonal problems and when the test task was said to measure a physician-related skill. Test performance dropped when subjects with failure feedback on the physician-related interpersonal problems worked on the concentration test described as measuring skills unrelated to being a physician (see Figure 15.1). For the rest of the conditions, test results on the d2 test were in between these two groups and did not differ from each other.

These results nicely demonstrate that identity-relevant performances are

Irrelevant Training Task

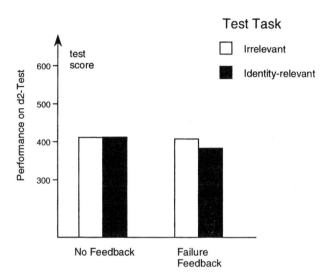

Figure 15.1. (*cont.*)

powerful indicators that an individual possesses the respective identity. When such indicators are absent, individuals feel highly incomplete, which causes them to strive intensively for alternative indicators. When these indicators are not available, individuals become so absorbed with their incompleteness that non-identity-related performances are hampered.

Having demonstrated this, in a second study we investigated whether an incompleteness experience stemming from a weak identity-related performance can also be effectively reduced through self-symbolizing based on positive self-descriptions. In that case, further self-symbolizing in the form of a strong alternative identity-related performance is no longer likely to be necessary. Brunstein and Gollwitzer (1996, study 2) asked students of the computer sciences to perform a concept formation test (Brunstein & Olbrich, 1985) that was said to assess a number of mental skills (e.g., logical reasoning) commonly found in successful computer scientists. Subjects received failure or no feedback on their performance in this training task before they were asked to perform the test task. The d2 test was again used, this time described as measuring a skill either that is irrelevant to a computer scientist (i.e., vigilance in road traffic situations) or relevant (i.e., precision in performing mental tasks). Failure-feedback subjects performed

Identity-relevant Training Task

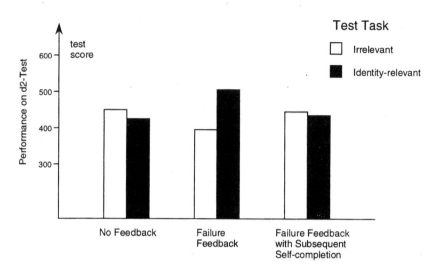

Figure 15.2. Computer science students' performance on a mental concentration test (test task) described as either irrelevant or relevant to the identity of computer scientist. Prior to test performance, subjects had received either no performance feedback or failure feedback on a training task described as relevant to the identity of computer scientist (*Source:* Adapted with permission from Brunstein & Gollwitzer, 1996, study 2).

better on the d2 test than did no-feedback subjects when the test was described as identity-relevant; a comparatively worse performance was observed when the d2 test was described as irrelevant (see Figure 15.2). This finding is consistent with the observations made in study 1.

After having received feedback on the concept formation test (training task), half of the negative feedback subjects were allowed to describe their personality on a semantic differential type of questionnaire. Before these subjects started to work on the d2 test (test task), they received feedback from a second experimenter who told them that they possessed personality attributes observed in successful computer scientists. This intervention completely wiped out the performance effects of the failure feedback (see Figure 15.2). Whereas no-intervention subjects reduced the experienced incompleteness by stepping up their performance on the d2 test, incomplete subjects who demonstrated the possession of identity personality attributes

to the second experimenter no longer needed to do so. Their feelings of incompleteness were already reduced, so that self-symbolizing in the form of
identity-related performances was no longer necessary. This finding implies
that performance-related indicators of an identity are mutually exchange-
able with indicators that are easily accessible, such as publicly recognized
positive self-descriptions. This interpretation is further supported by the observation that the interference effect of incompleteness on the d2 test (i.e.,
a weakened performance when the test was described as irrelevant) was also
alleviated when incomplete subjects learned that they possessed personality attributes conducive to being a successful computer scientist (see Figure
15.2).

From Incompleteness to Completeness: A Process Account

What do people feel when they experience self-definitional incompleteness? How is this state of incompleteness translated into compensatory efforts that reestablish completeness? In recent studies by Brunstein and Gollwitzer (1996), subjects were asked about their feelings immediately after
experiencing failure on the training task and prior to performing the test
task. Failure on an identity-relevant training task made subjects feel more
worried, pessimistic, dissatisfied, and blocked than failure on an identity-
irrelevant training task. However, this frustration and ruminative self-
concern over a poor identity-relevant performance transforms into feeling
energetic and vigorous when subjects are given a second chance (i.e., a second identity-relevant task is presented as the test task). Whereas incomplete
subjects to whom the second task (test task) was described as identity-
irrelevant continued to worry and to feel frustrated, this was not true when
the second task was described as identity-relevant.

It appears then that incompleteness experiences are highly frustrating
and a severe burden to an individual's striving for identity goals. These feelings of being burdened, however, are immediately converted into feeling
energized when an opportunity for compensation arises. Obviously, self-
symbolizing is an action-oriented state in which no thought is directed at
the experienced self-definitional shortcoming. Attention rests solely on successful compensation.

This switch from self-reflection about failure to involvement with self-
symbolizing activities is nicely demonstrated in a study by Gollwitzer,
Stevenson, and Wicklund (reported in Wicklund & Gollwitzer, 1983). Subjects striving for identity goals were made to feel incomplete and then were
offered an opportunity to self-symbolize – either in front of a mirror or not.

The incompleteness experience led to less self-symbolizing when these efforts had to be executed in front of a mirror. Based on the assumption that mirrors induce self-awareness and self-reflection, these data suggest that self-reflective thoughts hamper self-symbolizing, which appears to be an impulsive activity.

The impulsiveness of self-symbolizers was analyzed in a study by Flüge and Gollwitzer (1986). Incomplete and complete subjects were given an opportunity to compensate immediately or at a later point in time. The catch was that the immediately accessible audience was highly critical of subjects' identity-related potentials, whereas the delayed audience was more accepting. Incomplete subjects preferred to self-symbolize in front of the immediately accessible audience, whereas complete subjects preferred to wait.

Are All Identity Goals Alike?

Are there features of identity goals that force self-completion theory to make qualifications? In other words, are self-completion processes more of an issue for some identity goals than for others? According to Dweck (1996, and Chapter 10, this volume), goals can be differentiated as learning goals and performance goals. If a person has an implicit theory that the amount of ability is fixed and cannot easily be changed (i.e., an entity theorist), he or she will prefer to set him- or herself performance goals. Such goals focus on finding out how capable one is. In contrast, an incremental theorist believes that the amount of ability can be improved by learning. Incremental theorists set themselves learning goals that allow them to find out where and why they are making mistakes. These distinct types of goals have important behavioral consequences particularly in the context of coping with failure. For individuals with performance goals, negative outcomes signal a lack of ability and result in helpless reactions (e.g., low persistence). People with learning goals, on the other hand, view setbacks as cues to focus on new behavioral strategies. When people set themselves identity or self-definitional goals, some are likely to conceive of these goals in terms of performance goals, and others are likely to conceive of them as learning goals. What does that imply for people's self-symbolizing efforts when they experience incompleteness? One may speculate that entity theorists prefer different types of self-symbolizing than do learning theorists. An entity theorist with the identity goal of musician, for example, may point to symbols he has acquired in the past (e.g., past recitals, high-quality instruments), whereas a learning theorist may engage in forms of self-symbolizing that are focused on acquiring new skills (e.g., extending her repertoire). Also, whereas entity theorists may be more sensitive to incompleteness experiences that relate to their aptitude (e.g., not being able to play by ear), learning theorists are particularly sensitive to incompleteness experiences that relate to their efforts (e.g., not having practiced enough).

Similarly, whether people construe their self-defining goals in terms of a negative or positive outcome focus is also likely to affect self-symbolizing (Higgins, 1996; Higgins & Loeb, Chapter 3, this volume). People with negative-outcome-focus goals are said to be responsive to security needs and have a predilection for avoidance strategies. People with positive-outcome-focus goals are said to be responsive to nurturance needs and show a predilection for approach strategies. People who are driven by their duties are likely to form negative-outcome-focus goals. This should also hold true when they set themselves identity goals. Given the identity goal of musician, such a duty-driven individual would be likely to symbolize himself as unlike a nonmusician. A person driven by her ideals, on the other hand, would be likely to form positive-outcome-focus identity goals. Such a person would focus on symbolizing herself as a musician.

Negative-outcome framing puts the person in a particular bind. In this case, many routes to self-symbolizing are available that have nothing to do with acquiring indicators of an intended identity (e.g., showing that one does not have the symbols of any profession other than musician). Accordingly, the person fails to collect indicators of being a musician. As a result, the person's possession of relevant indicators remains limited and, consequently, incompleteness experiences become even more likely. In addition, for the person with a negative-outcome-focus identity goal, any evidence that she or he possesses indicators of identities that are inconsistent with the intended identity may elicit feelings of incompleteness with respect to her or his identity goal. In summary, then, people with negative-outcome-focus identity goals are prone to experience a sense of incompleteness rather frequently, to which they respond in a way that perpetuates the experience of incompleteness. In contrast, the person with positive-outcome-focus identity goals responds to incompleteness differently: Self-symbolizing is aimed at acquiring indicators of the intended identity goal, thus stimulating the active construction of the intended identity.

Self-definitional goals may also differ in terms of how strongly they serve a person's need for self-esteem (e.g., being a good mother may serve a particular person's self-esteem needs more than being a good skier). In a model of self-affirmation processes, Steele (Liu & Steele, 1986; Steele, 1988) argued that people's responses to events that threaten self-esteem are not confined to the domain in which the self-threat occurred. Rather, according to

Steele, people strive toward a global sense of self-integrity or self-esteem. This superordinate goal or motive enables individuals to engage in a variety of highly flexible compensation processes while they try to cope with self-threatening information. Furthermore, incompleteness experiences with respect to identity goals that are strongly linked to the superordinate goal of self-esteem protection and maintenance may be reduced not only by achieving indicators relevant to the threatened self-definition, but also by self-esteem pampering maneuvers (e.g., putting oneself in a good mood by partying).

Even when a self-definition is strongly linked to self-esteem, however, the range of substitutability may be limited to (using Lewin's terms) the goal region of the self-definition only and may not encompass the goal region of protecting and maintaining self-esteem. Whether one or the other is the case is likely to be moderated by a person's feelings of commitment to the self-definitional goal in question. If the individual is highly committed to the self-definitional goal, effective substitution must involve self-symbolizing in the form of acquiring or pointing to indicators of the aspired self-definition. If the individual feels less committed to the self-definitional goal, however, one may only observe compensatory efforts directed at affirming one's self-esteem.

That commitment is a powerful moderator of self-symbolizing has been demonstrated in the many self-completion studies reported in Wicklund and Gollwitzer (1982). In most of the studies, subjects who were only weakly committed to the analyzed self-definitions responded to incompleteness manipulations with retreat. Whereas incomplete committed individuals showed more self-symbolizing than did their complete counterparts, incomplete noncommitted individuals tended to show less self-symbolizing. Apparently, the latter subjects took the lack of self-definitional indicators to mean that they were not suited for the identity in question and therefore felt less compelled to engage in identity-relevant activities than those non-committed individuals who received positive feedback.

How commitment can be assessed most effectively remains an open question. Research on self-completion theory, however, suggests various ways to measure commitment to an identity goal. When people have just begun to pursue a new identity goal (e.g., undergraduates who intend to become professional musicians, athletes, mathematicians), it seems wise to monitor their daily routines. People who have not recently (e.g., within the last two weeks) pursued activities related to the respective identity are not likely to feel strongly committed to the identity in question. More direct measurement approaches are also possible. The researcher might ask subjects if they continue to entertain ideas on how to promote their self-definition. Subjects could be asked how frustrated and disappointed they would be if, for one reason or another, they had to give up striving for their self-definitions. All these different ways of assessing commitment have been successfully used in self-completion research. Clearly, however, this list is not exhaustive.

The Choice of Identity Goals

In a historical analysis of human identity, Baumeister (1986) maintains that society no longer assigns identity to its members but instead forces individuals to create their own identities. In Baumeister's view, identity achievement has become a struggle for self that necessitates the making of choices and the execution of effort. For instance, becoming an athlete, a physician, or a religious person requires the making of a decision and the willful implementation of that decision.

The willful pursuit of identity as described by self-completion theory focuses only on the second of these two tasks, even though it is recognized that the making of identity choices is a prerequisite for the effortful pursuit of this task. A complete account of the willful pursuit of identity definitely must also address how people arrive at such identity choices (i.e., commit themselves to certain identities). Developmental psychologists, following the lead of Erikson's (1956) ideas on identity development, have addressed this issue. It is assumed (Marcia, 1966, 1967, 1980) that identity formation originates with the experience of an identity crisis, which is conceived of as a state of vigorous deliberation. The individual is torn between possible options and therefore continues weighing alternatives until definite identity commitments are formed. Marcia's theory of ego-identity development proposes various stages that range from identity confusion to identity achievement; it also allows for leaving options open (moratorium status) and for taking an easy way out (foreclosure status; e.g., a student simply follows the lead or explicit suggestions of others).

With respect to self-completion theory, most interesting about this work are the psychological differences between individuals searching for an identity and self-symbolizing individuals (Gollwitzer, 1986a). Individuals who are searching for an identity (i.e., experiencing an identity crisis) display an open-mindedness with respect to processing information. Keniston (1965) reports intensive contemplation on the meaning and implications of one's actions, and Newman and Newman (1973) observed a critical examination of one's personal values. Slugowski, Marcia, and Koopman (1984) report a heightened integrative cognitive complexity in subjects who are in the midst of an identity crisis. These subjects are very receptive to various kinds of incoming information – except that which comes from authority figures (Podd, Marcia, & Rubin, 1970; Toder & Marcia, 1973).

This cognitive orientation of open-mindedness is diametrically opposed to the self-symbolizing individuals' closed-minded action orientation (see Brunstein & Gollwitzer, 1996). Self-symbolizing individuals seem to be immunized against questioning their identity choices. Identity failures lead to incompleteness experiences associated with ruminative thoughts; however, when an opportunity to self-symbolize arises, these thoughts are immediately put aside and a sole focus on the execution of self-symbolizing actions occurs. In this sense, the cognitive orientation of self-symbolizing individuals is comparable to an implemental mindset (Gollwitzer, 1990), which is observed in individuals who plan the execution of goal-directed actions: Information on the execution of goal-directed action is processed more readily and effectively than information on the expected value of these actions. In contrast, the cognitive orientation of individuals undergoing an identity crisis is comparable to the deliberative mindset that is observed in individuals who are asked to make choices between goals: Information on the feasibility and desirability of the goals is preferably processed, whereas information on how to implement these goals is secondary (Gollwitzer, Heckhausen, & Steller, 1990; Taylor & Gollwitzer, 1995, study 3).

Life-Span Psychology

The Endurance of Self-Definitional Goal Pursuit

The mental representation of an identity goal is probably best described as a claim to possess the respective identity, which is indicated by the possession of relevant symbols. These indicators range from possessing relevant tools to owning status symbols, and from being able to execute relevant actions to pointing to past performances. Realizing an identity goal thus implies a continued accumulation of relevant indicators. Goal pursuit is not finished simply because a powerful indicator has been acquired. As soon as the lack of other alternative indicators becomes salient, an incompleteness occurs and self-symbolizing becomes necessary. This is true even when a person holds extremely powerful symbols, such as many years of experience in a given field. As demonstrated in many self-completion experiments, even people with many years of experience can easily be made to feel incomplete by classic incompleteness manipulations (see Wicklund & Gollwitzer, 1982).

Many factors prevent people from achieving their identity goals permanently. When a person progresses with respect to the pursuit of an identity goal, he or she does not relent in the pursuit of that goal. When a person gains increased competence in a given field, new horizons with a host of new, more sophisticated indicators come into sight. In addition, most career identities include different arrays of symbols associated with different sections of the life course. With professional identity goals, for instance, different social and physical surroundings unfold while the person climbs upward. For example, the identity of a physician is defined differently during the phases of university training, hospital rotation, and, running a private practice. Each step of this career implies, more or less, a new start with respect to indicating the physician identity.

Most interestingly, the social community – formally or informally – defines the indicators for a certain identity and thus guides individuals in their goal pursuit. It also revises such definitions from time to time. For example, twenty years ago a person could easily indicate the identity of experimental psychologist without having to refer to a laboratory filled with computers. Today, this hardly seems possible. In this way, the social community induces a constant striving for new indicators to reach identity goals.

Finally, even the performance deficits that are associated with old or very old age (P. B. Baltes & M. M. Baltes, 1990) are not likely to end a person's identity-striving. For example, Brunstein and Gollwitzer (1996) point out that self-symbolizing that is easily accessible (e.g., positive self-descriptions) is as valuable as self-symbolizing that is based on effortful and skillful performances. This implies that old and very old people who can no longer acquire performance-related indicators may remain in the field and are not forced to give up their claim to possess an intended identity. They can focus on self-symbolizing that does not demand much effort and skill (e.g., by pointing to performances achieved in the past via positive self-descriptions).

But people do give up on identity goals. How can this phenomenon be explained? Raynor and Entin (1982) have suggested the concept of the contingent action path, which is defined as "a series of steps to a goal in which success in a more immediate step is necessary to earn the opportunity to move on to the next step of the path" (pp. 19–20). Raynor (1982, pp. 287–288) points out that self-relevant failure in a contingent path not only means a negative identity achievement but also rules out a host of future opportunities to strive for the respective identity goal (e.g., when a law or medical student fails to earn his or her diploma and therefore cannot move along the path of striving for the respective professional career). Thus, failure in contingent paths not only makes feel people incomplete, it also reduces their options to acquire further indicators of the respective identity. Under such circumstances, failure might prompt a reappraisal of identity goals and instigate disengagement.

Similarly, a person may experience reduced possibilities to self-symbolize when his or her social surroundings do not support his or her self-symbolizing as a claim to possessing the respective identity. For example, when a young lawyer who comes from a family of artists arrives home for a family event in his three-piece-suit, the relatives may fail to recognize its symbolic character and focus instead on the aesthetic quality of the fabric. In this case, self-symbolizing will not become a social fact and, consequently, will not be very effective. However, the symbolic world of most self-definitions (e.g., lawyer, physician) is culturally shared knowledge, so that self-symbolizers can be certain that their self-symbolizing does register on others. Accordingly, failures to attain social reality are more likely to occur when self-definitions are shared within certain narrowly defined subcultures (e.g., techno music fans).

The most powerful force for disengagement processes seems to be the conflict between identity goals, such as the conflict that women experience when they are torn between the roles of mother and professional (Barnett & Baruch, 1985; McBride, 1990). Identity goals conflict when they compete for one and the same opportunity to acquire relevant symbols. For example, a free Saturday afternoon is highly conducive not only to finishing work on a scientific manuscript but also to playing with one's children. If a female professional continues to choose to play with her children instead of working on her scientific manuscript, she is likely to begin to disengage from her identity goal of professional. In the long run, this female professional is also likely to fail to use other relevant opportunities to promote her self-definition of being a professional.

It appears, then, that experienced and expected shortcomings and the associated feelings of incompleteness are not responsible for people's disengagement from identity goals. Instead, a lack of access to or a refusal to make use of opportunities to acquire relevant symbols is responsible. Committed individuals are oriented toward symbolizing the possession of the intended identity; therefore, in the face of failure, they are not much concerned with outcome expectations and feasibilities. Rather, they focus on effectively acquiring and pointing to alternative indicators of completeness. In the many cases of individuals who need to be discouraged in their pursuit of self-definitions (e.g., a businessperson who continues to self-symbolize in the face of diminishing returns or a child with no musical talent who is bent on becoming a soloist), it is necessary to point them away from self-symbolizing. One such strategy has recently been suggested by Oettingen (1996). People do begin to consider negative-outcome expectations and weak self-efficacy when they are made to contrast their idealistic views of the future with reflections on aspects of the present reality that stand in the way of reaching this positive future.

Many Forms of Compensation

Life-span psychology uses various models that describe how people compensate for the physical and mental deficits associated with old and very old age (Bäckman & Dixon, 1992). The starting point of these models is a skill–demand mismatch. The most prominent model is the "selective optimization with compensation" notion proposed by Baltes and Baltes (1990; Marsiske, Lang, Baltes, & Baltes, 1995). The model posits that compensation for age-related declines in the mechanics of intelligence is a prototypical feature of the adult aging process. Within this perspective, life-span development is portrayed as a dynamic interaction between gains and losses. When the skill–demand mismatch exceeds a certain threshold, the aging person may begin to select and thereby narrow the range of domains or goals for continued development. Second, the person may try to optimize his or her performances within this narrow domain. Optimization is directed at efficacious and desirable functioning and thus implies training, practice, and motivational enhancement. Finally, as a last resort, compensation strategies aim to minimize age-related losses and limits by relying on alternative internal or external resources.

To summarize, people utilize various strategies to respond to age-related skill–demand mismatches, with compensation being a last resort. For instance, when a scientist suffers age-related losses of memory, she may first try to ameliorate the skill–demand mismatch by limiting her research to certain themes that are very familiar. Second, she may try to acquire and maximize mnemonic skills that are particularly conducive to the chosen field of interest. Finally, she may even actively compensate for the age-related memory deficits by employing all kinds of substitutes, such as a sophisticated index system or a skilled research assistant.

The important implications of this model to self-completion processes extend to the notion of gains and losses. Self-completion theory has so far not addressed the losses of compensation. These losses become immediately apparent when considering, for example, the person who focuses primarily on self-symbolizing that is easily accessible (e.g., positive self-descriptions). This person fails to develop his or her identity-related performance potential. On the other hand, self-completion theory has implications for understanding the compensation notion that is prevalent in life-span psychology. According to the tradition of Lewin and his collaborators, self-completion theory stresses the necessity of distinguishing between the inner goal of the individual and the external or outer goal considered by researchers (or experimenters). This distinction is important. If one considers the inner goal of a self-symbolizing individual, it does not matter whether this person employs self-descriptions or self-definitional performances. In both cases the individual advances equally well with respect to the inner goal of indicating the possession of an identity to others. From the perspective of a life-span psychologist who considers the outer goal of attaining an identity, however, the self-symbolizer who employs only self-descriptions and no actual achievements does not advance at all.

More important, self-completion theory allows one to recognize that there is more than one type of compensation relevant to a person's life-span development. Whereas Baltes and Baltes (1990; see also Bäckman & Dixon, 1992) consider compensational efforts elicited by skill–demand mismatches (which we would call *functional compensation*), self-completion theory focuses on compensating self-definitional incompletenesses by pointing out alternative indicators of the intended identity. However, still other forms of compensation are important to life-span development. One of them is self-esteem compensation (Adler, 1912; Steele, 1988; Tesser, Martin, & Cornell, 1996), in which lowered self-esteem produced by a personal shortcoming is said to lead to compensation achieved by pointing to a personal strength in any area that relates to a person's self-worth. Another form is life-plan compensation, as described by Jung (1939). Jung assumes that a life plan that is too narrowly constructed (e.g., being only a scientist with only scientist friends) creates feelings of incompleteness that lead to compensation focused on enriching one's life by adding goals that use dormant capacities.

Primary and Secondary Control

Recently, Heckhausen and Schulz (1995, and Chapter 2, this volume) have applied Rothbaum, Weisz, and Snyder's (1982) distinction between primary and secondary control to life-span psychology. *Primary control* refers to attempts to influence the external environment in order to make it fit the needs and desires of the individual. *Secondary control* refers to attempts to accommodate existing realities and is targeted at a person's internal states and processes, such as expectations, wishes, goals, attitudes, and attributions.

Secondary control aims to help the person cope with failure by channeling motivational resources toward selected action goals throughout the person's life course. Heckhausen and Schulz (1995, and Chapter 2, this volume) hold that secondary control serves to minimize losses in, maintain, and expand existing levels of primary control. In this sense, primary control has functional primacy over secondary control.

A primary versus secondary control perspective on self-completion theory must differentiate two forms of self-symbolizing. Self-symbolizing related to pointing at already acquired symbols in the form of positive self-descriptions would qualify as secondary self-symbolizing because there is no influencing of existing realities. Self-symbolizing in the form of identity-related performances would qualify as primary self-symbolizing, as it is targeted at changing existing realities.

Does primary self-symbolizing have functional primacy over secondary self-symbolizing? The results of Brunstein and Gollwitzer's (1996) study contradict the view that secondary self-symbolizing puts a person in a better position to engage in primary self-symbolizing. We observed that subjects who were induced to engage in secondary self-symbolizing (in terms of positive self-descriptions) showed less subsequent primary self-symbolizing (in terms of solving identity-related problems), not more. How does one resolve this puzzle? Above, we distinguished between two goal perspectives: the inner goal of the individual and the outer goal assumed by the life-span psychologist. For the individual, it does not matter how possession of an identity is indicated; once it is symbolized via primary or secondary means, further self-symbolizing (primary or secondary) becomes less necessary. In other words, in the individual's striving for an identity, all forms of self-symbolizing are primary because they indicate to others the possession of the identity in question.

For the life-span psychologist focusing on the development of people's potentials, however, secondary self-symbolizing may be seen as functional for later primary self-symbolizing. After all, as described above, striving for an identity – in particular for a professional identity – implies that there is a long way to go. If primary forms of self-symbolizing are not available because certain skills have not yet been acquired, secondary self-symbolizing allows the individual to stay in the field until such skills or resources have developed.

Social Contact Across the Life Span

In her theory of socioemotional selectivity, Carstensen (1992, and Chapter 13, this volume) suggests that people's reasons for social contact change across the life span. Social contact in the service of learning more about the self (in the sense of "Who am I?") or the world and other people is infrequent in early age, peaks in adolescence and middle age, and then declines again with old age. Social contact for the purpose of emotional experiences and regulation is strong in infancy, weakened in adolescence and middle age, and strong again in old age. These different reasons for contact with others have implications with respect to what kind of people one relates to. As it turns out, emotional regulation is more easily achieved if one is surrounded by a few intimates. Accordingly, Carstensen postulates and observes that older people prefer to engage in social contacts with a few intimates and stay away from getting to know new people, as the former are more emotionally satisfying than the latter.

Self-completion theory also speaks to the social contacts of the self-symbolizer. It could be demonstrated that self-symbolizers' relating to others serves the sole purpose of socially registering the possession of the intended identity. This has implications with respect to what types of social encounters are most conducive to successful self-symbolizing. What kinds of people or audiences are willing to tolerate such pseudosocial encounters? Social psychologists have observed that people generally refrain from conveying to others negative feedback (Blumberg, 1972; Tesser & Rosen, 1975). As Goffman (1959) stated, only the socially disgruntled will question the realness of what is presented. It can be assumed, therefore, that strangers will give a person's self-symbolizing efforts the benefit of the doubt. However, strangers tend to challenge an individual's sense of self-definitional completeness out of ignorance or carelessness and are thus a constant source of incompleteness experiences.

This is not likely to be true for a person's intimates. They know the self-definitions to which the person aspires and thus will refrain from behaviors that raise questions about his or her possessing a particular self-definition. In addition, they know about the person's life history and thus about the self-definitional indicators the individual has acquired in the past. This allows the older self-symbolizer to refer readily to these achievements in positive self-descriptions if incompleteness experiences should arise – which is very fortunate given that age-related declines in skills and resources hamper identity-related performances.

It appears, then, that intimates provide a narrow and stable social reality that makes it easy to self-symbolize effectively. For individuals who have a relatively low sense of completeness with respect to their aspired identity and thus opt for effective self-symbolizing, the tendency focus on a narrow and stable social reality is likely to be particularly pronounced. Indeed, when Havighurst (1980) asked scientists who were approximately at retirement age about the main sources of their professional recognition, subjects who had a weak publication record referred significantly more often to approval by the family, the local community, and local colleagues than did subjects with a strong publication record. In summary, older people may focus their social contacts on a few intimates not only for the enjoyment and more effective regulation of their emotions (Carstensen, 1992, and Chapter 13, this volume) but also because it allows older people to feel in possession of the identities to which they have aspired throughout their lives – and this despite age-related declines in relevant skills and resources.

Summary and Conclusion

In the present chapter we suggested that people willfully pursue chosen identities (e.g., being a good mother, athlete, physician, lawyer). Based on self-completion theory, this process is described as a persistent pursuit of self-defining goals that demands the continuous accumulation of relevant symbols or indicators (e.g., verbal claims, relevant performances, possession of relevant tools and status symbols) pointing to the possession of the intended identity. We presented research stimulated by self-completion theory to delineate the basic principles that govern this goal pursuit. According to the substitution principle, the various identity symbols effectively substitute for each other in the sense that incompleteness experiences stemming from a noticed lack of one type of symbol are readily reduced by acquiring alternative symbols (i.e., through various forms of self-symbolizing efforts). According to the social reality principle, self-symbolizing that is noticed by others is particularly effective in reducing incompleteness experiences. We have speculated how different types of goal contents (e.g., performance goals versus mastery goals, positive-outcome focus versus negative-outcome focus) modify people's pursuit of self-defining goals, and have pointed out that the choice of identity, or self-defining, goals is governed by rules that are quite different from those that govern the pursuit of these goals.

In the final sections of this chapter we discussed various implications of self-completion theory and research for life-span psychology. Most important, the substitution principle of self-defining goal pursuit suggests that old and very old people may not have to give up on their identity claims. This is because easily accessible forms of self-symbolizing (e.g., positive self-descriptions pointing to relevant successes in the past) are as effective in reducing incompleteness experiences as less accessible forms (e.g., demonstrating identity-relevant skills). Moreover, the social reality principle suggests that the tendency of old and very old people to reduce their social contacts to a few intimates is beneficial to their identity pursuits. Intimates provide a narrow and stable social reality that makes it easy to self-symbolize effectively and thus to maintain one's claim of possessing the intended identity.

References

Adler, A. (1912). *Über den nervösen Charakter: Grundzüge einer vergleichenden Individual-Psychologie.* Wiesbaden: Bergmann.

Bäckman, L., & Dixon, R. A. (1992). Psychological compensation: A theoretical framework. *Psychological Bulletin, 112,* 259–283.

Baltes, P. B., & Baltes, M. M. (1990). Psychological perspectives on successful aging: The model of selective optimization with compensation. In P. B. Baltes & M. M. Baltes (Eds.), *Successful aging: Perspectives from the behavioral sciences* (pp. 1–34). New York: Cambridge University Press.

Barnett, R. C., & Baruch, G. K. (1985). Women's involvement in multiple roles and psychological distress. *Journal of Personality and Social Psychology, 49,* 135–145.

Baumeister, R. F. (1982). A self-presentational view of social phenomena. *Psychological Bulletin, 91,* 3–26.

   (1986). *Identity: Cultural change and the struggle for self.* New York: Oxford University Press.

Baumeister, R. F., & Tice, D. M. (1990). Anxiety and social exclusion. *Journal of Social and Clinical Psychology, 9,* 165–195.

Bem, D. J. (1972). Self-perception theory. In L. Berkowitz (Ed.), *Advances in experimental social psychology* (Vol. 6, pp. 1–62). New York: Academic Press.

Blumberg, H. H. (1972). Communication of interpersonal evaluations. *Journal of Personality and Social Psychology, 23,* 157–162.

Braun, O. L., & Wicklund, R. A. (1989). Psychological antecedents of conspicuous consumption. *Journal of Economic Psychology, 10,* 161–187.

Brickenkamp, R. (1981). *Test d2* (4th ed.). Göttingen, Germany: Hogrefe.

Brown, J. D. (1991). Accuracy and bias in self-knowledge. In C. R. Snyder & D. R. Forsyth (Eds.), *Handbook of social and clinical psychology* (pp. 158–178). New York: Pergamon Press.

Brunstein, J. C., & Gollwitzer, P. M. (1996). Effects of failure on subsequent performance: The importance of self-defining goals. *Journal of Personality and Social Psychology, 70,* 395–407.

Brunstein, J. C., & Olbrich, E. (1985). Personal helplessness and action control: Analysis of achievement-related cognitions, self-assessments, and performance. *Journal of Personality and Social Psychology, 48,* 1540–1551.

Campbell, J. D. (1990). Self-esteem and the clarity of the self-concept. *Journal of Personality and Social Psychology, 59,* 538–549.

Carstensen, L. L. (1992). Social and emotional patterns in adulthood: Support for socioemotional selectivity theory. *Psychology and Aging, 7,* 331–338.

———(1998). A life-span approach to social motivation. In J. Heckhausen & C. S. Dweck (Eds.), *Motivation and self-regulation across the life span.* New York: Cambridge University Press.

Cooley, C. H. (1902). *Human nature and the social order.* New York: Scribner.

Dweck, C. S. (1996). Implicit theories as organizers of goals and behavior. In P. M. Gollwitzer & J. A. Bargh (Eds.), *The psychology of action: Linking cognition and motivation to behavior* (pp. 69–90). New York: Guilford Press.

———(1998). The development of early self-conceptions: Their relevance for motivational processes. In J. Heckhausen & C. S. Dweck (Eds.), *Motivation and self-regulation across the life span.* New York: Cambridge University Press.

Erikson, E. H. (1956). The problem of ego-identity. *Journal of the American Psychoanalytic Association, 4,* 56–121.

Flüge, R., & Gollwitzer, P. M. (1986, April). *Volitionale Aspekte der Selbstergänzung.* Vortrag auf dem 3. Workshop der Fachgruppe Sozialpsychologie, Erlangen, FRG.

Gergen, K. J. (1982). From self to science: What is there to know? In J. Suls (Ed.), *Psychological perspectives on the self* (Vol. 1, pp. 129–149). Hillsdale, NJ: Erlbaum.

Goffman, E. (1959). *The presentation of self in everyday life.* Garden City, NJ: Doubleday.

Gollwitzer, P. M. (1983, July). *Audience anxiety and symbolic self-completion.* Paper presented at the International Conference on Anxiety and Self-Related Cognitions. Berlin.

———(1986a). Striving for specific identities: The social reality of self-symbolizing. In R. A. Baumeister (Ed.), *Public self and private self* (pp. 143–159). New York: Springer.

———(1986b). The implementation of identity intentions: A motivational-volitional perspective on symbolic self-completion. In F. Halisch & J. Kuhl (Eds.), *Motivation, intention, and volition* (pp. 349–382). Heidelberg: Springer.

———(1990). Action phases and mind-sets. In E. T. Higgins & R. M. Sorrentino (Eds.), *Handbook of motivation and cognition: Foundations of social behavior* (Vol. 2, pp. 53–92). New York: Guilford Press.

Gollwitzer, P. M., Heckhausen, H., & Steller, B. (1990). Deliberative versus implemental mindsets: Cognitive tuning toward congruous thoughts and information. *Journal of Personality and Social Psychology, 59,* 1119–1127.

Gollwitzer, P. M., & Wicklund, R. A. (1985a). Self-symbolizing and the neglect of others perspectives. *Journal of Personality and Social Psychology, 48,* 702–715.

———(1985b). The pursuit of self-defining goals. In J. Kuhl & J. Beckmann (Eds.), *Action control: From cognition to behavior* (pp. 61–85). Heidelberg: Springer.

Gollwitzer, P. M., Wicklund, R. A., & Hilton, J. L. (1982). Admission of failure and symbolic self-completion: Extending Lewinian theory. *Journal of Personality and Social Psychology, 43,* 358–371.

Gordon, C. (1968). Self-conceptions: Configurations of content. In C. Gordon & K. J. Gergen (Eds.), *The self in social interaction* (pp. 115–136). New York: Wiley.

Greenberg, J., Pyszczynski, T., & Solomon, S. (1986). The causes and consequences of a need for self-esteem: A terror management theory. In R. F. Baumeister (Ed.), *Public self and private self* (pp. 189–212). New York: Springer.

Greenwald, A. G. (1980). The totalitarian ego: Fabrication and revision of personal history. *American Psychologist, 35,* 603–618.

(1982). Is anyone in charge? Personalysis versus the principle of personal unity. In J. Suls (Ed.), *Psychological perspectives on the self* (Vol. 1, pp. 151–181). Hillsdale, NJ: Erlbaum.

Havighurst, R. J. (1980). The life course of college professors and administrators. In K. W. Back (Ed.), *Life course: Integrative theories and exemplary populations* (pp. 79–96). Boulder, CO: Westview Press.

Heckhausen, H. (1989). *Motivation and Handeln: Lehrbuch der Motivationspsychologie* (2. Aufl.). Berlin: Springer.

Heckhausen, H., & Gollwitzer, P. M. (1987). Thought contents and cognitive functioning in motivational versus volitional states of mind. *Motivation and Emotion, 11,* 101–120.

Heckhausen, J., & Schulz, R. (1995). A life-span theory of control. *Psychological Review, 102,* 284–304.

(1998). Developmental regulation in adulthood: Selection and compensation via primary and secondary control. In J. Heckhausen & C. S. Dweck (Eds.), *Motivation and self-regulation across the life span.* New York: Cambridge University Press.

Henle, M. (1944). The influence of valence on substitution. *The Journal of Psychology, 17,* 11–19.

Higgins, E. T. (1987). Self-discrepancy: A theory relating self and affect. *Psychological Review, 94,* 319–340.

(1996). Ideals, oughts, and regulatory outcome focus: Relating affect and motivation to distinct pains and pleasures. In P. M. Gollwitzer & J. A. Bargh (Eds.), *The psychology of action: Linking cognition and motivation to behavior* (pp. 91–114). New York: Guilford Press.

Higgins, T., & Loeb, I. (1998). Development of regulatory focus: Promotion and prevention as ways of living. In J. Heckhausen & C. S. Dweck (Eds.), *Motivation and self-regulation across the life span.* New York: Cambridge University Press.

Hoppe, F. (1930). Erfolg und Mißerfolg. *Psychologische Forschung, 14,* 1–63.

Hormuth, S. E. (1990). *The ecology of the self.* Cambridge: Cambridge University Press.

James, W. (1890/1950). *The principles of psychology* (2 vols.). New York: Dover.

Jung, C. G. (1939). *The integration of the personality.* New York: Farrar & Rinehart.

Keniston, K. (1965). *The uncommitted: Alienated youth in American society.* New York: Harcourt, Brace, & World.

Lewin, K. (1926). Vorsatz, Wille and Bedürfnis. *Psychologische Forschung, 7,* 330–385.

Linville, P. W. (1987). Self-complexity and affective extremity: Don't put all of your eggs in one basket. *Social Cognition, 3,* 94–120.

Lissner, K. (1933). Die Entspannung von Bedürfnissen durch Ersatzhandlungen. *Psychologische Forschung, 18,* 218–250.

Liu, T. J., & Steele, C. M. (1986). Attributional analysis as self-affirmation. *Journal of Personality and Social Psychology, 51,* 531–540.

Mahler, W. (1933). Ersatzhandlungen verschiedenen Realitätsgrades. *Psychologische Forschung, 18,* 27–89.

Marcia, J. E. (1966). Development and validation of ego-identity status. *Journal of Personality and Social Psychology, 3,* 551–558.

(1967). Ego-identity status: Relationship to change in self-esteem, general adjustment, and authoritarianism. *Journal of Personality, 35,* 118–133.

(1980). Identity in adolescence. In J. Adelson (Ed.), *Handbook of adolescent psychology* (pp. 159–187). New York, Springer.

Markus, H., & Nurius, P. (1986). Possible selves. *American Psychologist, 41,* 954–969.

Marsiske, M., Lang, F. R., Baltes, P. B., & Baltes, M. M. (1995). Selective optimization with compensation: Life-span perspectives on successful human development. In R. A. Dixon & L. Bäckman (Eds.), *Compensating for psychological deficits and decline: Managing losses and promoting gains* (pp. 35–79). Hillsdale, NJ: Erlbaum.

McBride, A. B. (1990). Mental health effects of women's multiple roles. *American Psychologist, 45,* 381–384.

Mead, G. H. (1934). *Mind, self, and society.* Chicago: University of Chicago Press.

Newman, B. M., & Newman, P. R. (1973). The concept of identity: Research and theory. *Adolescence, 13,* 157–166.

Oettingen, G. (1996). Positive fantasy and motivation. In P. M. Gollwitzer & J. A. Bargh (Eds.), *The psychology of action: Linking cognition and motivation to behavior* (pp. 236–259). New York: Guilford Press.

Ovsiankina, M. (1928). Die Wiederaufnahme unterbrochener Handlungen. *Psychologische Forschung, 11,* 302–379.

Podd, M. H., Marcia, J. E., & Rubin, B. M. (1970). The effects of ego identity and partner perception on a prisoner's dilemma game. *Journal of Social Psychology, 82,* 117–126.

Raynor, J. O. (1982). A theory of personality functioning and change. In J. O. Raynor & E. E. Entin (Eds.), *Motivation, career striving, and aging* (pp. 249–302). Washington, DC: Hemisphere.

Raynor, J. O., & Entin, E. E. (1982). Theory and research on future orientation and achievement motivation. In J. O. Raynor & E. E. Entin (Eds.), *Motivation, career striving, and aging* (pp. 13–82). Washington, DC: Hemisphere.

Rosenberg, M. (1979). *Conceiving the self.* New York: Basic Books.

Rothbaum, F., Weisz, J. R., & Snyder, S. S. (1982). Changing the world and changing the self: A two-process model of perceived control. *Journal of Personality and Social Psychology, 42,* 5–37.

Slugowski, B. R., Marcia, J. E., & Koopman, R. F. (1984). Cognitive and social interactional characteristics of ego-identity statuses in college males. *Journal of Personality and Social Psychology, 47,* 646–661.

Stahlberg, D., Osnabrügge, G., & Frey, D. (1985). Die Theorie des Selbstwertschutzes and der Selbstwerterhöhung. In D. Frey & M. Irle (Hrsg.), *Theorien der Sozialpsychologie* (Bd.3, pp. 79–124). Bern: Huber.

Steele, C. M. (1988). The psychology of self-affirmation: Sustaining the integrity of the self. In L. Berkowitz (Ed.), *Advances in experimental social psychology* (Vol. 21, pp. 261–302). San Diego, CA: Academic Press.

Stryker, S., & Statham, A. (1985). Symbolic interaction and role theory. In G. Lindzay & E. Aronson (Eds.), *Handbook of social psychology* (Vol. 1, pp. 311–378). New York: Random House.

Suls, J. (Ed.). (1993). *Psychological perspectives on the self* (Vol. 4). Hillsdale, NJ: Erlbaum.

Suls, J., & Greenwald, A. G. (Eds.). (1983). *Psychological perspectives on the self* (Vol. 2). Hillsdale, NJ: Erlbaum.

Swann, W. B., Jr. (1983). Self-verification: Bringing social reality into harmony with the self. In J. Suls & A. G. Greenwald (Eds.), *Psychological perspectives on the self* (Vol. 2, pp. 33–66). Hillsdale, NJ: Erlbaum.

Taylor, S. E., & Gollwitzer, P. M. (1995). Effects of mindset on positive illusions. *Journal of Personality and Social Psychology, 69,* 213–226.

Tesser, A. (1988). Toward a self-evaluation maintenance model of social behavior. In L. Berkowitz (Ed.), *Advances in experimental social psychology* (Vol. 21, pp. 181–227). New York: Academic Press.

Tesser, A., Martin, L., Cornell, D. (1996). On the substitutability of self-protective mechanisms. In P. M. Gollwitzer & J. A. Bargh (Eds.), *The psychology of action: Linking cognition and motivation to behavior* (pp. 48–68). New York: Guilford Press.

Tesser, A., & Rosen, S. (1975). The reluctance to transmit bad news. In L. Berkowitz (Ed.), *Advances in experimental social psychology* (Vol. 8, pp. 194–232). New York: Academic Press.

Toder, N. L., & Marcia, J. R. (1973). Ego identity status and response to conformity pressure in college women. *Journal of Personality and Social Psychology, 26,* 287–294.

Wagner, U., Wicklund, R. A., & Shaigan, S. (1990). Open devaluation and rejection of a fellow student: The impact of threat to a self-definition. *Basic and Applied Social Psychology, 11,* 61–76.

Wicklund, R. A., & Gollwitzer, P. M. (1981). Symbolic self-completion, attempted influence, and self-deprecation. *Basic and Applied Social Psychology, 2,* 89–114.

(1982). *Symbolic self-completion.* Hillsdale, NJ: Erlbaum.

(1983). A motivational factor in self-report validity. In J. Suls & A. G. Greenwald (Eds.), *Psychological perspectives on the self* (Vol. 2, pp. 67–92). Hillsdale, NJ: Erlbaum.

Wurf, E., & Markus, H. (1991). Possible selves and the psychology of personal growth. In R. Hogan (Series Ed.) & D. Ozer, J. M. Healy & A. Stewart (Vol. Eds.), *Perspectives in personality: Vol. 3A. Self and emotion* (pp. 39–62). London: Kingsley.

Yardley, K., & Honess, T. (Eds.). (1987). *Self and identity.* New York: Wiley.

Zeigarnik, B. (1927). Das Behalten erledigter and unerledigter Handlungen. *Psychologische Forschung, 9,* 1–85.

16 Commentary: Motivation and Self-Regulation in Adult Development

Richard Schulz

Abstract

How do orientations toward goals vary as a function of the individual's temporal location in the life course? This is the common theme underlying Chapters 13, 14, and 15, which are reviewed here, although each author takes a different approach to answering this question. Laura Carstensen (Chapter 13) focuses on how location in the life cycle influences which social motives are most important, while Brandtstädter, Rothermund, and Schmitz (Chapter 14) examine transitions to old age and how individuals maintain personal continuity and self-esteem despite the many aversive and uncontrollable declines associated with aging. Gollwitzer and Kirchhof (Chapter 15) address the complementary question: How and why do individuals construct their identities in early adulthood, and how do they respond to threats to their identities? In varying ways, these authors show how individuals are motivated to develop a sense of who they are and then maintain and elaborate that sense of self throughout the life course. In addition to identifying themes common to all three perspectives, each of the three theoretical positions is examined in detail with the aim of identifying strengths, weaknesses, and unanswered questions.

Introduction

Richard Ryan appropriately characterizes motivation as the "cornerstone in the science of human behavior" (see Ryan, Chapter 4, this volume). Assumptions or theories about motivation serve as the building blocks for vast literatures in social, personality, and developmental psychology (H. Heckhausen, 1991). Indeed, one could analyze virtually any area in personality or social psychology (e.g., aggression, altruism, intergroup behavior) in terms of a motivational perspective. Chapters 13 through 15 of this volume fall squarely within this tradition in that they explicitly articulate a motivational basis for a diverse set of observable behaviors.

The importance of motivation as an organizing psychological concept is in one sense remarkable given its status as a hypothetical construct that can be only indirectly inferred from observed behaviors. As such, it can take on many forms, and this is reflected in the wide variety of theories and taxonomies of motivation (H. Heckhausen, 1991; Gollwitzer & Brandstatter, 1995). A hypothetical construct is valid only if it proves useful in the interpretation of experiential and behavioral data. This volume, and the three chapters in Part IV in particular, serve as a strong testament to the importance of this construct; not only does it help psychologists understand existing data, but it also encourages them to ask new questions and collect data that expand their understanding of "What moves a person?" (Ryan, Chapter 4, this volume).

According to contemporary motivation theorists, "Motivation represents an orientation toward a particular goal, at a particular time, by a particular individual" (H. Heckhausen, 1991, p. 3). This widely accepted characterization of motivation as being dependent on the individual and context parallels the empirical literature on motivation, which tends to emphasize one or the other of the person–environment dichotomy, depending loosely on whether the researcher is a personality or social psychologist.

Although the person–environment interaction perspective is universally accepted among researchers, little attention has been paid to the element of time as part of that perspective. In experimental studies, time is inextricably intertwined with the environmental context created through experimental manipulations. As such, it is not treated as a unique feature of the situation. However, one can imagine time being construed in other ways. For example, a developmental psychologist might think of time in terms of a developmental stage or chronological age, just as a life-span psychologist might view time in terms of the individual's location in the life course or in terms of time left to live. What makes these perspectives unique is that time is treated as a critical conceptual variable. This is the perspective adopted by the authors of the three chapters reviewed here. They pose an interesting question: How do orientations toward goals vary as a function of the temporal location of the individual? Laura Carstensen (Chapter 13) asks how place in the life cycle influences which social motives are most important. Brandtstädter, Rothermund, and Schmitz (Chapter 14) focus specifically on the transitions to old age and how individuals maintain personal continuity and self-esteem despite the many aversive and uncontrollable declines associated with processes of aging. Gollwitzer and Kirchhof (Chapter 15) ask the complementary questions: How and why do individuals construct their identities in early adulthood, and how do they respond to threats to their identities, once formed? The common motivational theme in all three chapters is that individuals are motivated to develop a sense of who they are and then maintain and elaborate that sense of self throughout their life course.

Carstensen's Life-Span Approach to Social Motivation

In Chapter 13, Carstensen proposes two broad superordinate classes of social motives that follow different developmental trajectories: information-seeking and emotional. Information-seeking motives strive to acquire knowledge about the self and the social world. The second class of social motives, which derives from a need for emotional gratification, includes motives such as the desire to feel good, derive emotional meaning from life, establish intimacy, and verify the self. Emotional motives are at their peak both early and late in life, whereas information-seeking motives are dominant during adolescence and young adulthood. In keeping with her interest in aging, Carstensen has further articulated a socioemotional selectivity theory that postulates that in late life, social interaction is increasingly likely to be motivated by attempts to regulate emotion and increasingly less likely to be motivated by information-seeking goals. This motivation affects the type of social partners older people choose, as well as the types of social interaction they engage in. Carstensen presents an impressive array of evidence to support this proposition, including the facts that social contacts decline with age, older persons are more likely to prefer familiar social partners over those who are unfamiliar, and older persons are more likely to think about social partners in affective terms.

Like most researchers on motivation, Carstensen confronts the challenge of how to link a body of observable data to fundamentally unobservable hypothetical constructs. In her case, the task is more difficult because the critical data can take a lifetime to unfold. Alternatively, one can take a cross-sectional approach to generating relevant data, but this approach carries with it the problems inherent in using samples of subjects of widely varying ages. Nevertheless, Carstensen's research program has yielded an impressive body of convergent data by using innovative and creative paradigms. Moreover, she has delineated a rich agenda for future empirical work.

I think it would also be useful to examine the large epidemiologic literature on social support, social contacts, and well-being in older people. This is potentially a rich source of data to evaluate the nomothetic net Carstensen has cast. For example, this literature shows that while social contacts with friends and relatives decrease with age, they have little impact on psychological well-being (George, Blazer, Hughes, et al., 1989; Krause, 1987; Oxman, Berkman, Kasl, et al., 1992). The mere fact that older people reduce their interactions does not necessarily provide support for Carstensen's theory; indeed, researchers active in this area would posit that these changes are a reflection of declining individual resources needed to maintain interactions and structural constraints that impede access to social networks. The literature also shows that outcomes such as depression and life satisfaction appear to be determined by the perceived support available to older persons, particularly instrumental or tangible support (George, Blazer, Hughes, et al., 1989; Newsom & Schulz, 1996). These findings appear to be at odds with socioemotional selectivity theory. For example, in our recent analysis of determinants of well-being in a large cohort ($N = 5,201$) of older individuals, we found that instrumental support was far more predictive of depressive symptoms than appraisal (i.e., informational) or emotional support. These findings suggest that among older people, a sense of security and perhaps control associated with knowing that material assistance is available when needed, rather than informational assistance or emotional support, is the critical factor in maintaining a sense of well-being (Newsom & Schulz, 1996).

On the whole, the socioemotional selectivity framework that Carstensen proposes is both innovative and compelling. However, its value as a hypothesis-generating theory will depend on further clarification and development of key concepts. In particular, the central concept of her theoretical framework – emotion regulation – has a great deal of appeal as well as promise in terms of elaboration and clarification. The idea that older persons might be more concerned than younger persons with regulating emotional experiences rings true, but one could refine the question by asking older persons to specify which aspects of their emotional lives they are most interested in regulating. It seems to me that older persons are more concerned with avoiding negative interactions than they are with facilitating positive ones. This idea is consistent with some of the current theoretical thinking about affect and aging (Schulz, 1985; Schulz, O'Brien, & Tompkins, 1994) as well as with data on the relationship between social interaction and well-being in older people. Negative social interactions have a greater impact on well-being than do positive or supportive social interactions (Rook, 1994). These observations lead to a series of potentially fascinating questions concerning which aspects of emotion older persons are interested in regulating and why. For example, does emotion regulation mean that one wants to eliminate the peaks (good feelings) and valleys (bad feelings) of one's emotional life or does it mean that one wants to minimize the valleys and/or maximize the peaks? Much of the discussion in this area focuses on feeling good or bad, either explicitly or implicitly. What about other types of emotional experiences, such as fear, anger, disgust, surprise, and so on? Does emotion regulation include these states as well? Also, why is it assumed that social interaction is the primary vehicle for regulating one's emotional well-being? What other mechanisms are available for achieving these ends, and how might they vary with age?

In sum, Carstensen's socioemotional selectivity theory is both explanatory and generative. Her work raises some fascinating questions that deserve the avid attention of researchers in the future. When it is further elaborated, I am certain it will become a valuable tool for understanding adult development and aging.

Brandtstädter, Rothermund, and Schmitz on Maintaining Self-Integrity

The motivational engine underlying the conceptual framework proposed by Brandtstädter, Rothermund, and Schmitz is the threat to "self-definitions that have been established and consolidated during early and middle adulthood" (Chapter 14, this volume). These self-definitions are threatened by structural constraints and normative declines associated with aging. The fundamental empirical data this theory seeks to explain are in a sense nonfindings; that is, despite measurable objective declines associated with aging, there is no general or significant drop in life satisfaction with age. The model of assimilative and accommodative coping is proposed as an answer to this apparent paradox.

The model distinguishes two classes of interrelated processes that enable the individual to prevent or neutralize the losses or self-discrepancies experienced in late life. In the assimilative mode, the individual tries actively to change the situation so that it better fits personal goals and standards. In the accommodative mode, aversive goal discrepancies, as well as negative emotional states associated with them, are neutralized by adjusting personal goals and ambitions to situational circumstances. A third mechanism in this model, although it receives relatively little emphasis, is immunization, which "tends to dampen both assimilate and accommodative modes" and is characterized by the "tendency to interpret self-rated evidence in ways that are consistent with established self-descriptions, and to twist situational evidence in self-enhancing ways" (Brandtstädter, Rothermund, & Schmitz,

Chapter 14, this volume). Notwithstanding the assessment of others (e.g., Skinner, in press), these mechanisms bear a striking resemblance to the constructs of primary and secondary control as they have been elaborated by Heckhausen and Schulz (1995, and Chapter 2, this volume); assimilation is very similar to primary control, whereas accommodation is similar to secondary control, and immunization, according to our perspective, is simply a subclass or type of secondary control.

The model proposed by Brandtstädter and colleagues is both elegant and logically compelling. This theory makes a lot of sense for those who frequently think about, not to mention directly experience, the vicissitudes of aging. Moreover, Brandtstädter and colleagues have amassed large quantities of empirical data in support of some of their key propositions. In terms of significant advances in both theoretical and empirical work on psychosocial aspects of adult development and aging, this work is among the best available.

The specifics of this theoretical formulation have been discussed and evaluated elsewhere (e.g., Brandtstädter & Greve, 1994); my goal here is to examine some of the broad motivational issues that serve as a foundation for this enterprise. As noted above, the motivational engines driving assimilative and accommodative processes are threats to the individual's self-definitions or self-integrity. The authors note that self-definitions are established and consolidated during early and middle adulthood, and furthermore that normative aging processes threaten that self-integrity. Although reasonable at first glance, this assumption is perhaps not as straightforward as it might seem. In their summary of the relevant research in this area, Gollwitzer and Kirchhof note that "controversies in self-concept research surround issues of whether the self is construed as a coherent entity or is composed of many partial selves, of whether the self concept is stable or malleable, and of whether the self-concept is accurate or illusionary" (Chapter 15, this volume). Therefore, one might ask: What evidence is there that the self is "established and consolidated during early and middle adulthood," as claimed by Brandtstädter, Rothermund, and Schmitz? As noted by Gollwitzer and Kirchhof (Chapter 15, this volume), the self can have many constituent elements; some of these elements might remain relatively stable with age (e.g., personality) and others will surely change (e.g., physical appearance, roles, abilities). In other words, the sense of self may be much more dynamic than is assumed by Brandtstädter, Rothermund, and Schmitz. This dynamism raises the further question of what does and does not constitute a threat to the self. For example, when is a random negative event (e.g., falling down and breaking a hip) a threat to the self and when is it not?

It seems to me that invoking self-integrity as the motivating force in the conceptual system creates more problems than it solves. It requires that the self be clearly defined, that individuals know how it comes to be consolidated and when, and that individuals know a priori what constitutes a threat to the self. Furthermore, one might also raise tricky questions about experiences that threaten self-definition in the positive direction. For example, if I think of myself as shallow and thoughtless, yet people start telling me that I am wise and considerate, does this instigate accommodative and assimilative processes in the same way that they are energized with negative discrepancies?

The parsimonious solution to all these questions would be to drop the idea of self-discrepancy. Recall that this theoretical framework was designed to address the riddle of decline and subjective well-being in later life. Brandt-städter, Rothermund, and Schmitz point out that there is general consensus that many of the constraints and losses in later life are aversive, undesirable, and generally negative. If this is true, then the events themselves and the fact that they can generate negative affect serve as a motivational force, whether or not they are discrepant with an individual's sense of self.

The second major theme in Chapter 14 is the "phenomenal resilience of the aging self." Literatures on depression, subjective well-being, and perceived control are reviewed to make the point that on a variety of outcome measures such as these, there is little age-related variation despite the constraints and declines of later life. But is this really so? When considering the case of depression, Brandtstädter, Rothermund, and Schmitz are correct in pointing out that the diagnosis of major depression is relatively rare among older people, and is certainly less prevalent among older individuals than among younger individuals. A number of hypotheses have arisen to account for the low rates of depression, including methodologic or sampling errors as well cohort or period effects. Increasingly, psychiatric epidemiologists are reporting evidence that the rates of subsyndromal or minor depression – depressive symptoms not reaching the threshold of criteria for a DSM-IV diagnosis – are considerably higher among older people and are of great clinical significance. In a recent population study of over 1,300 individuals aged 65 years or older, Blazer (Blazer, Hughes, & George, 1987; Hocking, Koenig, & Blazer, 1995) found an overall rate of depressive disorder of 27 percent; for major depressive disorder the rate was 0.8 percent, mixed depression and anxiety syndrome 1.2 percent, dysthimia 2 percent, symptomatic depression 5 percent, and mild dysphoria 19 percent. These findings suggest that current methods of assessing depression leave many clinically depressed elders undiagnosed. "Older persons may suffer a syndrome of minor depression that is unique to late life and associated with physical illness and cognitive difficulties" (Hocking, Koenig, & Blazer, 1995, p. 442). Rates of subsyndromal depression are highest among women, individuals of low education, unmarried people, and socioeconomically deprived people.

These data do not necessarily call into question the decline–quality of life riddle that motivated the development of Brandtstädter, Rothermund, and Schmitz's theory, but they draw attention to the fact that older people may not be as resilient as portrayed in some theories. Furthermore, these data suggest that more attention be paid to how accommodative and assimilative processes break down in later life to account for the declines in quality of life observed in epidemiologic studies. In this arena, competing pathogenetic theories attempt to explain the causes of outcomes such as depression in older people. In the case of medical illness and depression in older people, the competing theories might include factors such as genetic diatheses or lifestyle choices. Alternatively, depression may cause or contribute to medical illness, whether by direct physiological routes (e.g., neuroendocrinological or psychoneuorimmunological alterations) or by behavioral correlates (e.g., tobacco use, noncompliance with medications). Finally, medical illnesses may cause or contribute to depression. The latter relation may occur through several routes: Medical illnesses might directly alter neurobiological functioning, leading to a depressive syndrome. Or medical illnesses may have effects at the psychological level – that is, the subjective experience of the illness may evoke depressive symptoms. Finally, medical illnesses may act as stressors – functional disability from a medical illness may lead to changes in role performance, which in turn may affect depression by altering factors such as social support or family dynamics (Lyness, Bruce, Koenig, et al., 1996). Some of these explanations (e.g., the last two) are consistent with the model proposed by Brandtstädter, Rothermund, and Schmitz, but others are not. The important point here is that if the goal is to explain a particular outcome, then it should be evaluated in the context of competing explanations for that outcome.

Finally, these theories must come to terms with broad and robust empirical findings. For example, it has been shown that older women, persons who are not married, persons with few economic resources, and persons with low educational attainment are more likely to become depressed. How would a theory based on self-integrity explain these individual differences? Do some individuals have goals and values that make them more susceptible to this outcome, or do they possess accommodative/assimilative strategies that are relatively ineffective in dealing with threats to the self? Exploring individual differences on key outcome variables may be a fruitful area for future research.

Gollwitzer and Kirchhof on the Willful Pursuit of Identity

Research on the psychology and sociology of the self is a well-established tradition in the social sciences dating back to at least the turn of the century. In Chapter 15 of this volume, Gollwitzer and Kirchhof's discussion of the willful pursuit of identity falls squarely within this tradition. Their work carves out its own particular niche and thereby makes a number of unique contributions to this literature. First, unlike much of the existing work on the self, which focuses on the self as a cognitive entity, their work shows how the self is achieved behaviorally. Second, they place their work in the broader context of the motivation-action system developed by H. Heckhausen (1991) and Gollwitzer (1990). They note that self-completion theory is concerned specifically with the volitional issue of implementing identity-related (self-defining) goals. Finally, an important strength of this particular chapter is that the authors attempt to relate their theoretical ideas to broad issues of life-course development (Baltes & Baltes, 1990) and to other theoretical frameworks such as control (J. Heckhausen & Schulz, 1995) and socioemotional selectivity (Carstensen, Chapter 13, this volume).

Self-completion theory describes how individuals strive for self-defining goals. Each goal has associated with it a set of symbols that indicate the possession of the aspired-to identity. Once individuals have chosen and committed themselves to a particular goal, they will tenaciously pursue the symbols associated with that goal. An important element of the theory is that possession of relevant symbols is not sufficient to create a sense of identity. These indicators must be socially acknowledged. For example, it is not sufficient for an individual to think of herself as being a great scientist; others must see her as such too. A large and innovative body of experimental research supports the main propositions of this theory.

Chapter 15 represents a notable extension of earlier work in this area in that it extends self-completion theory to questions of life-span development. In thinking about identity goal pursuit over the life course, one might ask if identity goals are ever completely reached. According to Gollwitzer and Kirchhof, the answer to this question is *no*. Goal pursuit does not end simply because a particular symbolic indicator has been achieved. Instead, as soon was one symbol is achieved, other alternative symbolic indicators become salient and the self-symbolizing process is set in motion again. Professional identities, in particular, have an externally defined gradient of symbols that the individual can pursue throughout the adult life course. For example, the gradient for a university professor might include obtaining a Ph.D., attaining a position as an assistant professor, becoming tenured, becoming a full professor, being elected to a prestigious scientific society, and so on.

This view of self-identify development is quite different from the perspective of Brandtstädter, Rothermund, and Schmitz, who assume that the self becomes consolidated and relatively stable during middle age. Despite the compelling empirical evidence reported by Gollwitzer and Kirchhof in support of their perspective on this issue, it is difficult to dismiss the notion that there must be some variability across the life course in terms of the intensity of self-symbolizing activity. For example, one might ask whether the established middle-aged professional in the midst of raising a family is less concerned about and involved in self-symbolizing behaviors than the young adult struggling with career choices and relational issues. Similar questions might be raised about the extent to which self-symbolizing processes characterize the behavior of individuals whose life-course trajectories include few externally defined gradients of symbols to strive for, as might be the case for a person stuck in a "dead-end" job.

Three types of questions emerge when these issues are considered. I have already alluded to the first question: Is there variability over the life course in terms of the intensity of self-symbolizing activity? Second: Does self-symbolizing vary according to individual structural characteristics such as social status? Inasmuch as socioeconomic status is related to the number of different roles that individuals occupy, does this necessarily require more self-symbolizing activity? The third question is related to both of the previous two questions and concerns the population prevalence of the phenomenon. The experimental research clearly establishes the existence of the phenomenon. How prevalent is self-symbolizing in the population at different ages, and to what extent does it make a difference in terms of goal-striving, self-esteem, quality of life, and so on?

The second life-span issue that Gollwitzer and Kirchhof address concerns how self-completion theory deals with the losses encountered in later life. They suggest that mechanisms such as self-esteem compensation and adding new goals are means of compensating for self-definitional incompleteness brought about by late-life losses. Their approach to gains and losses over the life course appears to suggest a kind of symmetry that requires further empirical testing. Aside from the fact that gains are good and losses are potentially bad, the process of acquiring identity symbols appears very different from the process of losing them. First, as a volitional process, the acquisition of identity symbols is preceded by motivational processes that guide a person's choices among alternative goals; losses, on the other hand, are relatively unpredictable events that afford little preparation. Second, self-symbols appear to be acquired incrementally, whereas losses in late life are often experienced in large doses that potentially undermine the superordinate constructs of the self. Third, acquiring identity symbols helps to promote the status of an individual as unique, whereas losses tend to have the opposite effect: They tend to group individuals into broad categories based on the type of loss experienced (e.g., cognitively impaired, physically disabled). My intent in raising these distinctions is not to cast doubt on self-completion theory, but rather to stimulate further application of these ideas to late-life phenomena. Gollwitzer and Kirchhof have shown that a great deal is known about the acquisition of self-identities; their work also has the potential to illuminate the process of relinquishing those identities.

Concluding Comments

Obviously, I bring to this review my own set of biases on how to think about motivational issues concerning adult development and aging. My views are heavily influenced by my own training as a psychologist and by some of the divergent roads I have followed since that training. Because I studied in a very traditional social psychology program in the 1970s, reading these chapters is in some ways a homecoming. I am reminded of Kurt Lewin's often repeated dictum, "There is nothing like a good theory." Chapters 13 through 15 of this volume serve as outstanding examples of theory-building at its best. They tackle very difficult questions and – just as important – the authors creatively generate a wide array of empirical findings to support their positions. In this sense, the work I have had the privilege of reviewing here brings back much of the excitement I experienced as a graduate student in late-night discussions with mentors such as Ned Jones, Jack Brehm, and David Aderman.

The second perspective I bring to this area is grounded in interests I have developed over the years in adult development and in applied explorations of what happens to individuals as they grow older. When confronted with a theory that addresses issues of adult development, I immediately ask myself how it is related to available descriptive data about aging. For example, just as epidemiologists ask about the population prevalence of a health-related state, I find myself asking about the population prevalence or incidence of psychological phenomena such as motivational processes and the extent to which those processes are linked to important policy-relevant outcomes. To varying degrees, I think this perspective is shared by the authors of the three chapters reviewed here. Carstensen and Brandtstädter and colleagues have already erected bridgeheads between theory and applied data, and Gollwitzer and colleagues are moving in that direction as well. From my perspective, this hybridization of abstract theory with applied settings and outcomes has potential for yielding significant advances in the understanding of adult development and aging. The contributors to this volume should be commended for being pioneers in this important effort.

References

Baltes, P. B., & Baltes, M. M. (1990). Psychological perspectives on successful aging: The model of selective optimization with compensation. In P. B. Baltes & M. M. Baltes (Eds.), *Successful aging: Perspectives from the behavioral sciences* (pp. 1–34). New York: Cambridge University Press.

Blazer, D. G., Hughes, D. C., & George, L. K. (1987). The epidemiology of depression in an elderly community population. *Gerontologist, 27,* 281–287.

Brandtstädter, J., & Greve, W. (1994). The aging self: Stabilizing and protective processes. *Developmental Review, 14,* 52–80.

Brandtstädter, J., Rothermund, K., & Schmitz, U. (1998). Maintaining self-integrity and efficacy through adulthood and later life: The adaptive functions of assimilative persistence and accommodative flexibility. In J. Heckhausen & C. S. Dweck (Eds.), *Motivation and self-regulation across the life span.* New York: Cambridge University Press.

Carstensen, L. L. (1998). A life-span approach to social motivation. In J. Heckhausen & C. S. Dweck (Eds.), *Motivation and self-regulation across the life span.* New York: Cambridge University Press.

George, L. K., Blazer, D. G., Hughes, D. C., & Fowler, N. (1989). Social support and the outcome of major depression. *British Journal of Psychiatry, 154,* 478–485.

Gollwitzer, P. M. (1990). Action phases and mind-sets. In E. T. Higgins & R. M. Sorrentino (Eds.), *Handbook of motivation and cognition: Foundations of social behavior* (Vol. 2, pp. 53–92). New York: Guilford Press.

Gollwitzer, P. M., & Brandstädter, M. (1995). Motivation. In A. S. R. Manstead and M. Hewstone (Eds.), *The Blackwell Encyclopedia of Social Psychology* (pp. 397–403). Oxford, U.K.: Blackwell Publishers.

Gollwitzer, P. M., & Kirchhoff, O. (1998). The willful pursuit of identity. In J. Heckhausen & C. S. Dweck (Eds.), *Motivation and self-regulation across the life span.* New York: Cambridge University Press.

Heckhausen, H. (1991). *Motivation and action.* Berlin: Springer-Verlag.

Heckhausen, J., & Schulz, R. (1995). A life-span theory of control. *Psychological Review, 102,* 284–304.

(1998). Developmental regulation in adulthood: Selection and compensation via primary and secondary control. In J. Heckhausen & C. S. Dweck (Eds.), *Motivation and self-regulation across the life span*. New York: Cambridge University Press.

Hocking, L. B., Koenig, H. G., & Blazer, D. G. (1995). Epidemiology and geriatric psychiatry. In M. T. Tsuang, M. Tohen, & G. E. P. Zahner (Eds.), *Textbook in psychiatric epidemiology* (pp. 437–452). New York: Wiley-Liss.

Krause, N. (1987). Chronic strain, locus of control, and distress in older adults. *Psychology and Aging, 2,* 349–356.

Lyness, J. M., Bruce, M. L. Koenig, J. G., Parmelee, P. A., Schulz, R., Lawton, M. P., & Reynolds, C. F. (1996). Depression and medical illness in late life. *Journal of the American Geriatric Association, 44,* 198–203.

Newsom, J. T., & Schulz, R. (1996). Social support as a mediator in the relation between functional status and quality of life in older adults. *Psychology and Aging, 11,* 34–44.

Oxman, T., E., Berkman, L. F., Kasl, S., Freeman, D. H., & Barrett, J. (1992). Social support and depressive symptoms in the elderly. *American Journal of Epidemiology, 135,* 356–368.

Rook, K. S. (1994). Assessing the health-related dimensions of older adults' social relationships. In M. P. Lawton & J. A. Teresi (Eds.), *Annual review of gerontology and geriatrics. Vol. 14: Focus on assessment techniques* (pp. 142–181). New York: Springer.

Ryan, R. (1998). Human psychological needs and the issues of volition, control and outcome focus: A commentary on the initial conference proceedings. New York: Cambridge University Press.

Schulz, R. (1985). Emotions and affect. In J. Birren and K. W. Schaie (Eds.), *Handbook of the psychology of aging* (2d ed.). New York: Van Nostrand.

Schulz, R., O'Brien, A. T., & Tompkins, C. A. (1994). The measurement of affect in older people. In M. P. Lawton & J. A. Teresi (Eds.), *Annual review of gerontology and geriatrics. Vol. 14: Focus on assessment techniques* (pp. 210–233). New York: Springer.

Skinner, E. (in press). A guide to constructs of control. *Journal of Personality and Social Psychology.*

Name Index

Subject Index

ability, 139; children's beliefs about, 261, 284–5, 286, 291, 292, 293–5, 296, 298, 299, 304; conceptions of, 4, 169, 170; fixed, 406; and goodness, 274–5; and motivational patterns, 258, 259
ability inferences, 83
academic competence: children's self-perceptions of, 300
academic socialization, 285
accessible categories, 79
accessibility: of self-regulated knowledge, 85
accommodation, 381–2, 429; constraints and automatisms promoting, 375
accommodative coping/processes, 55, 370–7, 382, 428, 429, 431
accommodative flexibility: adaptive functions of, 365–88; empirical illustrations, 377–81; in thought of older persons, 373–4
achievement: control beliefs and, 274
achievement failure, 137
achievement goals, 210, 258–9
achievement motivation, 125, 217, 298, 345; developmental changes and, 228
achievement motivation research/literature, 2, 272
achievement patterns, adaptive, 274
achievement tasks, 209–10
action control, 15
Action Control and Child Development Project, 309n1
action-control beliefs: development of, in sociocultural context, 318–21; generality of functional aspects of, 293–307; sociocultural influences on development of, 281–315; structure of, 290–3
action-control system, 281, 282; cognitive influences, 281, 295–6, 306; structure of, 290–3
action orientation, 28, 30, 31, 35, 44, 119, 260
action sequence: belief relations among constituents of, 283
action theory, 2–3, 281; applied to develop-

ment and aging, 371; view on psychology of control, 282–6
active avoidance, 28
activity theory, 347, 349
actor (action sequence), 283
actual self, 370–1, 378
adaptation, 121, 122, 360; bound by time and space, 343–4; changing goals in, 346; to later life, 381; social changes in old age, 347, 348; specialized, 344
adaptive consequences: of action-control beliefs, 324–5
adaptive functioning, 57, 58; origins of, 257
adaptive patterns, 6–7, 258
adaptive process, 289; age-relativity of, 6
adaptive profile, 282, 291
adaptive self-regulation, 285
adaptive significance: of accommodative flexibility, 377–8; of means–ends beliefs, 295, 296, 298
adolescence, 105, 106, 107, 185, 187–91, 208, 227, 229; gender differences in depression in, 246–8, 250; pursuit of social dating in, 191–202, 209
adolescent dating relationships/sexual behavior: functional regulation of, 185–215
adolescents, 84; goal orientation, 222; identity issues, 276; social dating, 220
adult development, 434–5; motivation and self-regulation in, 424–36
adulthood: developmental regulation at different ages in, 60–4; developmental regulation in, 50–77; maintaining self-integrity and efficacy through, 365–88; motivated changes in social behavior across, 351–9; subjective quality of life in later, 366–70
adults: social comparisons in, 67–8
affect, 3, 128; and aging, 427; cognition and, 4
affect-cognition modulation hypotheses, 28, 40; first, 18–19; second, 20, 37
affect regulation, 359; parents expectations and, 249–50

447